OMAHA BEACH

It was difficult to run in wet clothes, the rifle jolting awkwardly on his shoulder. But he had a job to do. He stopped and stood still for a second, every inch of his body expecting the horrible whack of a bullet; then he started to run up the beach. It was such ordinary sand, he thought. It was so like the sand on the beaches of Long Island where children built castles and ran and shouted. Things came into the little circle of his vision as he ran: a German obstacle, a mangled body in uniform, blood, wreckage, rifles, torn equipment. He ran over them and around them, and hardly knew they were there.

D DAY

The Sixth of June, 1944

DAVID HOWARTH

BANTAM BOOKS
TORONTO · NEW YORK · LONDON · SYDNEY

D DAY; THE SIXTH OF JUNE, 1944

*A Bantam Book/published by arrangement with
McGraw-Hill Inc.*

PRINTING HISTORY

*McGraw-Hill edition published 1957
A Selection of Books Abridged, Inc.,
and an Alternate Selection of History Book Club*

Bantam edition/October 1982

Illustrations by Greg Beecham and Tom Beecham.

We fought all day for this stretch of Omaha Beachhead. Its
benign green bluffs and valley entrance were a maze of crossfire
from enfiladed 88's, mortars and machine guns which raked the
beaches and pinned the infantry to the shingle before the
fiendish minefields. By mid-afternoon disabled landing craft
were clogging the few gaps in the beach obstacles, while under
a rain of short and long range artillery fire support waves
circled and jockeyed for an opening. Destroyers moved far into
shoal water to pump salvos of 5-inch shells into stubborn
emplacements and mobile targets of opportunity. The house in
the valley and the spire of Colleville-Sur-Mer on the hill were
landmarks of Fox Green. The spire was used as an artillery
control tower by the Germans. Its lovely renaissance-type
architecture crumbled into sad rubble when a shore fire-control
party called on the destroyer BMMONS to demolish it.

ISBN 0-553-22832-3

Published simultaneously in the United States and Canada

PRINTED IN THE UNITED STATES OF AMERICA

O   0 9 8 7 6 5 4 3 2 1

MALE MENOPAUSE

DEAR MEG: I'm 74 years old and I keep reading about the male menopause. What the heck is the male menopause? Did I miss something? — FIT AS A FIDDLE, Springfield, Mo.

DEAR FIT: You didn't miss a thing, sweetheart. The male menopause isn't really a physical change of life like a woman has when her hormones slow down, it's more of a psychological change, characterized by anxiety, depression, and moodiness. That's what you missed. So count your blessings!

FOREWORD

This is not a military textbook. Military histories of battles deal with military units, and the way their generals maneuvered them; they do not usually tell what individual soldiers saw or did, or what they thought or felt or feared. But this is the aspect of battles which interests me—not only the actions and opinions of the generals who planned them, but also those of the soldiers and junior officers who had to fight them.

There are already several technical military works about the invasion of Normandy, and several generals' memoirs. I have tried simply to give an impression of the experience of the men who landed in the night and dawn of D Day—an impression of what it was like to be dropped from the sky that morning, or pitched ashore from a landing craft on a hostile beach.

This is a simple intention, but it can only be carried out with limitations. Churchill himself said the invasion of Normandy was the most complicated and difficult operation that has ever taken place. Tens of thousands of men took part in even its earliest stages. One can only give an impression of such a vast sum of human activity by choosing the experiences of a few men as examples of the rest. However many one chose, they could be only a small proportion of the whole, and I think that to choose too many would make the story dull and repetitious. Therefore I have taken just over thirty; but I have chosen them carefully, to make the impression as balanced as I can.

One result of this method is that if readers who were there

look in this book for the names of their units, or descriptions of the exact parts of the action which they saw, the chances are they will not find them. But I hope they will understand why, and will be equally interested to learn what other people were doing there; for although I have left out so much for the sake of clarity, I have certainly been able to tell far more of what happened that morning than any single man knew when he landed.

To write a book like this, an author depends on the help of a great many people. The main characters in the book have taken endless trouble to tell me all they remember. I think they all know how grateful I am. For many facts about the town of Sainte-Mère-Église I am indebted not only to the conversation of M. Renaud, who is still the mayor, but also to his charming book *Sainte-Mère-Église: Première Tête de Pont Américaine en France*. In America, Britain, and Germany, I have met with equal kindness from officers of defense departments and veterans' organizations in my search for representative men. In America, Mr. David Legerman helped me enormously to find my way around.

In talking to all the people in the book, and many others, about the events of the morning of D Day, I have noticed how widely their impressions of what happened vary. Some of them disagree with official reports. Naturally, a battle looks quite different to an old soldier and to a young man who has never been in danger before. I have even met one American officer whose impression was that Omaha Beach was quiet. It is often impossible to give a purely objective account of events which were only observed by people in the stress of intense emotions.

My general outline of this battle is objective, and I believe it is accurate; the details are accurate too, but they are deliberately subjective. So, if any reader says of his own beach or his own dropping zone that it was not like this at all, I shall truthfully answer that this was how it looked to the men I have chosen to describe it.

CONTENTS

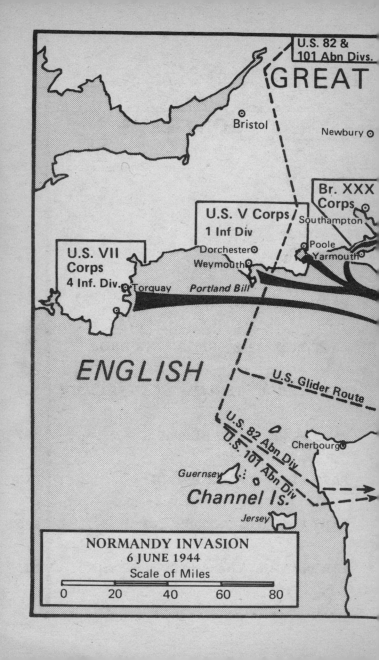

U.S. 82 &
101 Abn Divs.

GREAT

⊙
Bristol

Newbury ⊙

Br. XXX
Corps

U.S. V Corps
1 Inf Div

Southampton

Poole
Yarmouth

Dorchester⊙

U.S. VII
Corps
4 Inf. Div.

Weymouth⊙

⊙Torquay *Portland Bill*

ENGLISH

U.S. Glider Route

U.S. 82 Abn Div
U.S. 101 Abn Div

Cherbourg⊙

Guernsey

Channel Is.

Jersey

NORMANDY INVASION
6 JUNE 1944
Scale of Miles

0   20   40   60   80

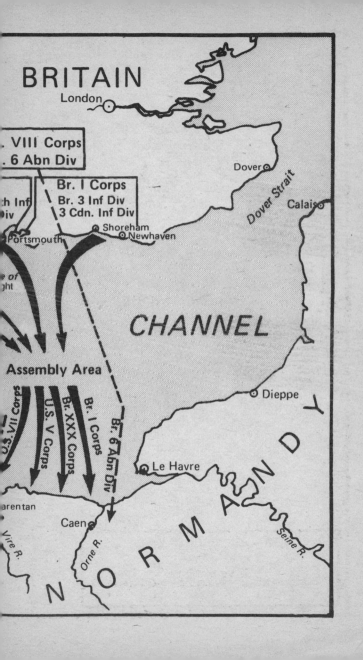

PART ONE
ENGLAND

All over the south of England, on the night of the fifth of June, people awoke, or else, if they were going late to bed, stopped what they were doing and went outside to listen. Those who had lived there for the past four years were used to noisy nights. The noise at nights had changed through the years, from the distinctive beat of German bombers and the din of air raids, to the sound of British bombers outward bound at dusk and homeward bound at dawn. But people who heard the noise on the fifth of June remember it as different from anything that had ever been heard before. Life in war had made them adept at guessing what was happening from what they could hear, and as they listened that night, with increasing excitement and pride, they knew that by far the greatest fleet of aircraft they had ever heard—and therefore the greatest fleet that anyone had ever heard—was passing overhead from north to south.

Nobody had much doubt of what the noise implied; even those who had nothing to do with military secrets had known it would happen soon. They simply said to themselves or to each other, "This is it"; and probably most of them heard the sound with such deep emotion that they did not try to put their feelings into words. It was the invasion, as everybody either knew or guessed; and the invasion, if it succeeded, was to be the redemption of the defeat of Dunkirk, and the justification of the British refusal to admit defeat when everyone else in the world believed they were finished. It would be a reward for the four years' grinding labor by which they had

1

dragged themselves up from the depths of 1940 to a state of national strength which made them an equal partner of the United States. And personally, to the British, it had a significance like a first gleam of sunshine after rain, or a first bud after winter; it would be a sign, if it succeeded, of hope that the worst was over, the first glimpse of the beginning of the end of the sorrow, boredom, pain, and frustration in which they had lived for so long.

That was to be its significance if it succeeded. What if it failed? People could not bring themselves to imagine what would happen if it failed; but they knew that failure would be a military disaster which at best would take years to retrieve, and in the back of their minds they doubted their own ability, exhausted by war as they were, to survive such a disappointment and start again, as they had at Dunkirk, and build everything up anew.

They went to sleep that night, if they slept any more, with a sense of great events impending, and of comradeship in a vast adventure, knowing the day would bring news of a battle which would influence all their lives forever more. On the whole, they were certainly thankful the time had come to put everything to the test; but of course they thought anxiously of the thousands of their own people who even then, in the night, were on their way to battle, and of the Americans, whom many of them had met for the first time in the past few months. And many of these people, perhaps most, thought with special anxiety of one man who they imagined, rightly or wrongly, was on his way to France by air or sea.

In the morning, the main news in the papers and on the radio was still of the fall of Rome, which had been announced on the day before, and nothing was said of events which were nearer home. But just after nine o'clock the bare announcement came: "Under the command of General Eisenhower, Allied naval forces supported by strong air forces began landing Allied armies this morning on the coast of France." Within a few minutes, this news, which the people of southern England had anticipated, was repeated all round the world.

The purpose of this book is to give an impression of what happened in the English Channel and on the coast of France that morning, roughly between the time when the aircraft were heard over England, and the time when the news was given. But to make the impression clear, one must start with a summary of eighteen months of concentrated thought and work which preceded the invasion, and of the reasoning which decided when and where it should be made, and the plans of what the high commanders intended to happen that morning.

The idea of an invasion of the continent from England could be said to have started at Dunkirk in 1940, when the more far-sighted British soldiers, struggling across the shore to escape from the German army, already knew that a British army would have to cross the shore of Europe in the opposite direction before the war was won. At that time, it seemed a very distant project; distant, but never impossible. In that same year, while most of Britain was preoccupied with improvising its own defense, the organization called Combined Operations had already been founded, and was studying the technique of landing on hostile coasts. Eighteen months later, when Capt. Lord Louis Mountbatten took over command of Combined Operations, Churchill told him "to plan for the offensive." When Russia and America joined Britain in the war, the prospect had become less distant; and in January 1943, Churchill and Roosevelt, meeting at Casablanca, agreed to appoint a joint staff to make a definite plan for the invasion. The head of this staff was Lt. Gen. F. E. Morgan, who was appointed Chief of Staff to the Supreme Allied Commander— COSSAC for short—although the Supreme Commander himself had not yet been chosen.

For six months in 1943, COSSAC studied the coasts of Europe, and the Allied and German forces which might be joined in the battle, and the complicated technical details of the project. It was in that period—a year before the invasion— that the question of where to land in Europe was decided; this decision had to remain an elaborately guarded secret till the very moment when the invasion fleet was sighted from the shore.

Many considerations were weighed and balanced in this decision: beaches suitable for landing, and country suitable for deploying an army behind the beaches; weather and tides; the distances from bases for short-range fighter aircraft, and from foreign ports which could be captured to help to support the army; and of course, the German defense. Of the whole of the coast of Europe from Norway to the Bay of Biscay, strict military logic narrowed the choice to two places: the district of Calais, or the coast of Normandy between Cherbourg

and Le Havre. In the choice between these, there was room
for opinion. Normandy is much farther than Calais from
English ports, but that made very little difference. The fleet
which was planned was so large that all the ports from the
Thames to the Bristol Channel would be needed to load it,
and so most of the ships would have a long crossing wherever
the landing was made. The Americans favored Calais, although
it was the most strongly defended part of the whole of the
coast, because it offered a more direct route to Germany. The
British rather more emphatically favored Normandy, because
its defenses were weaker and because it could be cut off from
the rest of Europe by bombing the bridges over the Seine
and Loire. In the end, the COSSAC staff agreed to recommend
Normandy, and their plan was approved by Churchill, Roosevelt
and the Combined Chiefs of Staff at the conference in Quebec
in August 1943. In Quebec it was also agreed that the
Supreme Commander should be American, and that his
deputy and his three commanders in chief should be British,
and May 1944 was fixed as the target date.

It was not till December, after some weeks of hesitation,
that Roosevelt appointed General Eisenhower, who was then
Supreme Commander in the Mediterranean, to take command
of the invasion of France; and in January the names of his
British subordinates were announced: Air Chief Marshal Tedder
as Deputy Supreme Commander, and Admiral Ramsay, General
Montgomery and Air Chief Marshal Leigh-Mallory to command
the navies, armies and air forces. Already, at the Teheran
conference at the end of November, Stalin had shown himself
very impatient for the opening of what was called a second
front, where the Americans and British could take a fairer
share of the burden of fighting from the Russians, and
Roosevelt and Churchill had promised him the invasion
would start in May; and so, when the commanders took up
their appointments in January, there were only four months
to go.

When Eisenhower and Montgomery saw the details of the
COSSAC plan for the first time, they both declared the area
of the landing was too narrow and the troops for the first
assault too few. General Morgan had thought so himself, but
as a chief of staff without a commander, he had had to plan
with the forces which the two governments had told him
could be used; and the size of the whole operation had been
limited by the number of landing craft which existed or could

be built in time. At Eisenhower's demand, landing craft were gathered in from all over the world; but still there were not enough for the extra forces he wanted. As a last resort, the landing was postponed till early June, so that another month's production of new craft would be available, although Churchill was worried by the thought of what Stalin would say when May was ended and the promise had not been fulfilled.

The exact date which was chosen in June was decided by the tides, the plan of attack, and the German defenses. Reconnaissance photographs of the coast of France were taken by aircraft every day that spring; and they showed Germans and French civilians hard at work building new gun emplacements and installing several kinds of obstacles on the beaches. The obstacles were wooden stakes and ramps, and steel barricades and spikes. Some of them were mined.

As the Germans intended, these obstacles offered a choice of evils. If a landing were made at high tide, when the obstacles were submerged and invisible, a large proportion of the landing craft might be lost by hitting them. If it were made at low tide, the troops would have to cross an open beach under German fire; and in Normandy the beaches slope gently and the range of tide is large, so that at low tide some beaches are three or four hundred yards wide.

Eisenhower and Montgomery chose to take the latter risk, and to minimize it by landing tanks ahead of the infantry, and by bombarding the defenses very heavily just before the landing. They decided to land just after low tide, and planned to demolish the obstacles at once, so that landing could continue as the tide rose.

The navy wanted to approach the coast under cover of night, but both navy and air force needed an hour of daylight for the bombardment of the defenses. These considerations fixed the time of the landing at an hour after dawn; and by combining this time with the state of the tide, the date of the landing was fixed. Low tide in Normandy was an hour after dawn on June 6th. On June 5th, and 7th, it was near enough to be acceptable. After that, of course, the tides were not right again for a fortnight, until about June 20th; but by then the moon would have waned, and the airborne forces preferred moonlight for the parachute and glider landings which were planned. Besides, by June 20th, fulfillment of the promise to Stalin would be another fortnight overdue. So June 5th was chosen as D Day, with the next two days as alternatives if the

weather was bad. H Hour, the moment of landing, was 6:30
A.M. at the western end of the area of the landing, which the
tide reached soonest, and 7:30 at the eastern end.*

Of course, the Germans knew an invasion was coming. At
that moment, the only front where America and Britain were
fighting Germany on land was in Italy, and there was nothing
like enough scope in Italy for the Allies to deploy their whole
strength. To try an invasion of northwest Europe was the only
way they could get to grips with Germany. Just before
Montgomery was appointed to command the invading army,
his old adversary of the desert war in Africa, Field Marshal
Rommel, was appointed to the defense of the coast of Europe.
For two years, German propagandists had talked of the
Atlantic Wall, which was supposed to be a chain of impregnable
defenses all along the coast. But Rommel found the Atlantic
Wall was very little more than propaganda. Its strength had
been exaggerated to discourage British or American raids and
to encourage the Germans. But in fact, the building of it had
been given a low priority, its materials had often been diverted
to other works which had seemed more urgent, and on many
parts of the coast its construction had been neglected by local
commanders who regarded an appointment to France as a
rest cure from the Russian front. But Rommel was a man, as
the British had reason to know, of tremendous energy, and
during the last few months, while preparations for the invasion
were being completed in Britain, he was working at top
speed to build fortifications to defeat it; it was his work which
reconnaissance showed in progress. But the work was still
made difficult by shortages of material, and even more difficult
by differences of opinion among the high command. Rommel
himself believed an invasion could only be halted at sea and
on the shore. His immediate senior, Field Marshal von
Rundstedt, thought that was impossible, and put his trust in

*D Day and H Hour are standard military expressions. In most
operations, preparations have to be made at specific intervals of time
before the operation begins, and they usually have to be planned and
discussed before the date of the operation is decided. It is convenient
then to refer to the date of the operation as D Day, so that the
preparations can be dated D—1, D—2 and so on. D Day has come
to mean the date of the invasion of France because that was the most
important operation in which the expression was ever used, and
because the general public thought of it as D Day for so long
beforehand.

Field Marshal Rommel

reserves which he proposed to keep intact till the exact
intentions of the invading forces could be seen. The whole of
the German high command, using the same logic which had
guided COSSAC, had decided on Normandy or Calais as the
most likely points of invasion, but they could not agree in the
choice between the two places. Von Rundstedt was convinced
the main landing would be in Calais, and so was the higher
command of the army in Germany. Rommel favored Normandy,
and so, it is said, did Hitler.

These disagreements were the result, at least in part, of
deliberate deception by the Allies. Having decided on
Normandy, they did everything they could to persuade the
Germans they had decided on Calais. While the armies and
fleets were assembling in the southwest of England, dummy
army camps and dummy fleets were assembled in the southeast.
All the radio activity of an army was simulated in Kent.
General Patton, whom the Germans knew well, was brought
back from the Mediterranean to England with ample publicity
to command this nonexistent army. More reconnaissance
flights and more preliminary bombing attacks were made in
Calais than in Normandy. At the last moment, while the
fleets were sailing to Normandy, dummy fleets of ships and
aircraft sailed to Calais, using devices which made them
appear on radar much larger than they were.

The British secret service was also at work to implant this
false belief in the minds of the German commanders. Its task
was probably simplified by disagreement between the German
secret service and the Nazi leaders. Admiral Canaris, the
head of the secret service, had recently been dismissed, and
most of his organization disbanded. A new all-Nazi service
had been started under Himmler; but its agents are said to
have been clumsy and amateurish, and easy game for the
practiced cunning of the British. After the war, in German
files, about 250 reports from Himmler's men were found to
predict the place and time of the invasion. All of them were
wrong except one. The wrong ones simply repeated the
rumors and false information which were circulated by British
agents; and nobody in Berlin had taken any action on the
single report which was right.

The deception was so successful that von Rundstedt, for
one, went on believing for several weeks after the invasion
that the landing in Normandy was a feint and that the main
attack was still to come in Calais, and he still kept his

reserves in the Calais area. In fact, it was much more successful than anyone expected at the time, and looking back at it now, it seems likely that some kind of deception more convincing than dummies or rumors was in use, and that the British had a direct method of giving false information to the German high command, and giving it with such authority that the Germans could not bring themselves to disbelieve it. Students of spy stories may imagine what the method might have been; but whatever it was, it is still kept secret and probably always will be.

During May, the troops who were to lead the attack had finished a long and arduous and often dangerous training. The seaborne forces had landed in exercises against live ammunition on beaches in Britain which resembled the beaches in Normandy, especially on Slapton Sands in Devon and at Burghead in the Moray Firth; and each unit had practiced assaults on replicas of the particular German defenses it was expected to attack. But none of them had yet been told where they would be going, or when. Most of the training had been as thorough as it possibly could have been; but the troops could not appreciate its thoroughness till they were told precisely what it was for, and in May, packed into great camps in the south of England with very little to do, men began to feel first bored and then apprehensive. The weather was perfect that month. There seemed to be no reason why they should not start and get it over. Waiting was enough to make anyone nervous.

Most of this feeling disappeared at the end of the month when briefing began. The briefing gave every man the feeling that he was being told exactly what he had to do, and that whoever was planning the thing was making a good job of it and not leaving anything to chance. Every man was shown maps and models of his own objective, and photographs of the shore which were taken from aircraft flying low above the sea, and were so good and clear that in some of them the individual German soldiers manning the defenses could be seen. Everyone was allowed to study these for as long as he liked, and officers explained in the greatest detail exactly what each unit was to do and what other units would be doing in the neighborhood. The only fault that could be found with this briefing, in retrospect, was that it was so good that it made some units overconfident.

Once the briefing had started, the whole vast process of

the invasion was irreversible; it had to go on, or else forever be abandoned. Its success depended entirely on surprise and secrecy. Even during the briefing, the maps had no real names on them, only code names, and nobody except individually selected officers\had yet been told what part of the coast they represented. Most men were not told this final secret till after they had actually embarked. But of course everybody could make his own guess; and in fact anybody who knew France well, or had an ordinary map for comparison, could easily have discovered that Poland meant Caen and that Sword Beach, for example, was at Ouistreham. And as for the time, anybody, not only the soldiers in the camps but anybody who lived near the coast, could tell that it was coming very soon.

The camps in which men were briefed were therefore cut off from the rest of the world. Men and materials were allowed in, but nobody was allowed out again except on the strictest compassionate grounds; the only way out was on a ship to France. The people of England, who had put up with so much already, had to submit to new sets of restrictions. Mail was stopped, and travel was restricted. A zone along the coast was sealed off. As a second line of defense against leakage, the few remaining ways out of the country were closed, and diplomats of neutral countries found they could not communicate with their governments, which was an unprecedented breach of international custom. Ireland was especially under suspicion, because the Germans still had a flourishing embassy in Dublin. But this state of readiness could not be kept up for long, and the longer it lasted the more chance there was that the secret, now shared in whole or in part by hundreds of thousands of people, would leak out of the country and somehow reach Germany.

The people responsible for security had a series of minor scares. There was an American major general sent home to America as a colonel for what was thought to be careless talk in Claridges; and on a hot morning in May, when a window was open in the War Office in London, all twelve copies of a top-secret communiqué that gave away the whole show blew out and fluttered down into the crowded street below. Distraught staff officers pounded down the stairs and found eleven copies, and spent the next two hours in an agonized search for the twelfth. It had been picked up by a passer-by, who gave it to the sentry on the Horse Guards Parade on the opposite side of Whitehall. Who was this person? Would he be likely to gossip? Nobody ever knew, and the only comfort was that the sentry said he had very thick glasses and seemed to find it difficult to read.

A railwayman who retired in 1957 announced then that in 1944, just before the invasion, he had found the plans of it in a briefcase in a train, and had given them to the station master at Exeter, who had kept them in his safe, watched by the Home Guard, till an officer came to claim them the next morning.

The oddest of all the scares was the *Daily Telegraph* crossword puzzle of May 22nd. When this puzzle was solved, it included the name Omaha, which was the code name for one of the beaches where the Americans were to land, and the word *dives*, which might have been the River Dives, on which the left flank of the whole invasion was to rest. Another vaguely suspicious name in it was Dover. It caused some concern to staff officers who still retained the English middle-class habit of doing the *Telegraph* crossword after breakfast, and in after years it provided a story with unlimited scope for growth. Everybody enjoyed stories against the security forces, and stories of narrow escapes from disaster, and sooner or later most of the dozens of code words in the invasion plans were said to have been revealed in this puzzle.

After Eisenhower had extended the original COSSAC plan, the area of the landing covered sixty miles of the coast of France, from the River Dives near Caen to the east side of the Cherbourg peninsula. At each end of the area, large forces of airborne troops, Americans at the west end and British at the east, were to land by parachute and glider during the night to protect the flanks of the seaborne forces. In the first light of dawn, great fleets of naval ships and aircraft were to bombard the coast, and as the bombardment stopped, the seaborne forces were to land on five separate stretches of beach, each three or four miles long. Again, the Americans were on the west and the British on the east. The Americans had two stretches of beach, one on each side of the estuary of the River Vire; it was these which had the code names Utah and Omaha. The three other beaches were known as Gold, Juno and Sword. Gold and Sword were British objectives; Juno was mainly Canadian. The British and Canadian troops for the first assault were about equal in number to the Americans. The air forces were also equal. About three quarters of the naval forces were British.

Everything about the plan was superlative. The fleet of 5,333 ships and landing craft was the largest ever assembled anywhere; so was the fleet of 9,210 aircraft.* No landing either from the sea or air had ever been attempted on anything like such a scale. The bombardment before the landing was the heaviest and most concentrated ever planned. The logistics and staff work were by far the most complicated that any armies had ever undertaken. Dozens of new devices, from artificial harbors to tanks that swim, had been invented to solve new problems. The naval operation orders, three inches thick on foolscap paper, were the fattest and probably the most indigestible ever printed.

But individual soldiers and sailors were only vaguely aware of these superlatives. Nobody could see five thousand ships or ten thousand aircraft at a glance, and nobody, not even the highest commanders, had any first-hand impression of the whole of the tremendous undertaking at the time. Each man who dropped from the sky or plunged into the surf that morning was aware only of what was happening within the short distance he could see, and of the hope and fear and resolution within himself; and it is from that point of view, rather than in terms of enormous figures, that the only true impression of the morning can be given.

Several of the senior officers who commanded the forces of invasion—Eisenhower among them—have commented that the first assault was a soldier's battle, and not a general's battle. The plans were completed in the utmost detail, and explained with meticulous care to the men who had to carry them out; but once that was done, and the order was given for the operation to begin, and the aircraft had taken off and

*Figures like these always need explanation. The number of ships includes landing craft carried on larger ships, and some vessels which did not cross on D Day. On D Day itself, 2,727 vessels crossed the Channel on their own bottoms. The number of aircraft, on the other hand, does not include the heavy bombers and other aircraft indirectly supporting the invasion. Including these, 25,275 sorties were flown between 9 P.M. on June 5th and 9 P.M. on June 6th: on the average an aircraft took off from England every 3½ seconds all through that night and day.

the ships sailed out from the English harbors, there was absolutely nothing more, for the time being, that the high command could do. Not one of the famous leaders went ashore on D Day. Events had passed out of their hands. The beaches were attacked, the Atlantic Wall destroyed, and the Allied armies led ashore on the continent mainly by officers and men from the rank of colonel downwards. While they were doing it, they had neither the apparatus nor the time to send any full reports of what they were doing to England, and the few reports which did come back, mostly from ships off shore, were delayed because the system of signals was overloaded. So it happened that Eisenhower himself, in his headquarters in Southwick House near Portsmouth, knew practically nothing of what was happening until well after the first phase of the battle had been completed. At the moment when the seaborne forces began to storm ashore, the Supreme Commander, according to his aide, was in bed reading a cowboy story, and in the circumstances, that was much the wisest thing for him to do.

The names of the high commanders therefore have very little place in the narrative of the landing. But when everything was ready, one final act remained for them to do. That, of course, was to give the order to go; and this order was fraught with unexpected anxiety and drama.

Absolutely everything was organized except the weather. For a landing on Monday, the fifth of June, some naval units had to sail on Friday the second; these included the heavy ships for the bombardment which were starting from Scotland and Northern Ireland. The movement of men and materials out of the camps and into the landing craft and transports also had to start on that day. It would still be possible on the third to postpone everything for twenty-four hours; but by dawn on the fourth, the leading ships would have gone too far to be recalled. Weather which was reasonably calm and clear had been regarded all through the planning as absolutely essential for the landing; and thus, accurate weather forecasts forty-eight hours in advance were needed to ensure success or twenty-four hours in advance to avoid disaster.

A committee of meteorologists had been assembled for what was certainly the most important weather forecast ever made. All through May, forecasting had been successful, and the weather had given no reason for worry at all. But on June 1st, it turned dull and gray; and on June 2nd, the meteorologists reported a complex system of three depressions approaching from the Atlantic. On June 3rd, they forecast high winds, low clouds and bad visibility for the fifth, sixth and seventh—the only three days when low tide was at the right time in the morning.

This forecast, and the grim problem which it caused, were presented at 9:30 P.M. on June 3rd in Southwick House, at a conference of Eisenhower, his deputy, his three commanders in chief and their chiefs of staff. The first ships had sailed; tens of thousands of men were cooped up in discomfort in landing craft and transports; the camps they had left were being filled by follow-up troops; the whole immense machine was in motion. The problem at that moment was whether to let it go on, or to stop it for twenty-four hours; and either way, the possibilities of disaster were very clear.

Many accounts have been given of this all-important meeting, and of three which followed it in the next thirty-six hours. In their details the accounts are all different; and that is not surprising, because only nine men were present at the meetings, and even the most junior of them carried a fearful responsibility. Nobody was there as an observer. However high a rank a man achieves, his capacity for thought and feeling is only human, and one may imagine that the capacity of each of these men was taxed to the limit by the decision they had to make, so that none of them had the leisure or inclination to detach his mind from the problem and observe exactly what happened and remember it for the sake of historians. The men were General Eisenhower, Air Chief Marshal Tedder, Admiral Ramsay, General Montgomery and Air Chief Marshal Leigh-Mallory; and the four chiefs of staff, Lt. Gen. Bedell Smith, Rear Admiral Creasy, Major General de Guingand and Air Marshal Robb. It seems strange in retrospect that only two of them were American, and seven British; but for the moment, the British could only advise; the ultimate responsibility was Eisenhower's, and he carried it all alone.

In looking back at that moment of decision, one may also glance back further at the life of the man who had to make it. The story of Eisenhower's rise to fame is a typically American romance. He came of German stock, and people often commented on the irony that the Supreme Commander bore a German name; but his family had been in America for over two hundred years, and nobody could have been more purely American in character. An irony which was less widely known at the time was that his family had always been strictly pacifist; his mother, who was still alive in 1944, was a member of the Jehovah's Witnesses, and was a conscientious objector.

Eisenhower was born in Texas in 1890, and brought up in modest circumstances in Kansas. His father was a night watchman at a creamery, and his biographers describe a boyhood which might have been the story of any of the less privileged of the hundreds of thousands of Americans who were to come under his command: a story of working a way through high school, of interest more in athletics than in classes, of boyish fights and minor disgraces, and of only the vaguest of plans or ambitions for the future. Yet the marriage of David and Ida Eisenhower, his father and mother, was one of those strange and rare unions which produce children far more brilliant than their background would lead one to expect. All of their seven sons, except one who died young, hauled themselves up from obscurity to achieve considerable distinction, each in a different profession. The influence which made their third son choose the army came from outside the family and shocked his mother; but she had made it a principle never to stand in the way of her sons. He obtained an appointment to West Point from his representative and passed the competitive entrance examination at the top of his class. After that, his career in the military academy was not very distinguished, and when he graduated at the age of twenty-four, he was sixty-first in a class of 168. That was in 1915. During the First World War, he was never sent overseas, and never saw battle, and between the wars, his promotion was very slow. He remained a major for no less than sixteen years, and only just over three years before the invasion of Normandy, he was still a lieutenant colonel. At that time, his highest hope was to end up as a colonel.

His quick rise through the ranks in those three years was largely due to General Marshall, the American Chief of Staff. Of course, Marshall did not push him up without reason. During all his years as a junior officer, Eisenhower had collected an enormous fund of miscellaneous military knowledge, and he had the clear and analytical brain which high command requires. But probably another reason for his appointment to the European command was that everybody liked him. An American general in command of British armies—and especially of British generals—not only had to have military judgment which everyone would respect; he also needed exceptional tact and charm and a sense of humor. Eisenhower certainly had those qualities. He could be strict and tough, as generals have to be; but in spite of his position he still seemed a modest and even humble man. He never considered himself to be a genius. He had no pretentions, and none of the flamboyance which generals find so irritating in other generals. The British liked him as much as the Americans. At the time, they said he really might almost have been British; and afterwards, General Morgan wrote that his grin was worth an army corps.

This was the man who, after fifty years of obscurity, had to preside over the meeting of his British commanders in chief at Southwick House, and balance their opinions, and make the decision on which the course of history and the lives of countless men could clearly be seen to depend.

At the meeting on Saturday evening, June 3rd, the report of the meteorologists and the advice of the commanders in chief made him almost certain that the operations would have to be postponed. It was a most unwelcome prospect. Plans had been made by which everything could be brought to a standstill for twenty-four hours, but Eisenhower was sure that postponement would be hard on the morale and the physical condition of the troops already at sea; and any delay would add to the risk of the secret leaking out. The decision was none the easier because at that moment, outside the windows of Southwick House, the skies were clear and there was hardly any wind at all.

He decided to hold another meeting at 4:30 the next morning, Sunday, June 4th, in the hope of some improvement in the forecast. In the meantime, some of the convoys of American landing craft sailed from their ports in south Devon and Cornwall, and began their voyage along the English coast.

The next morning, the forecast was just as bad, though the weather outside was just as good. At this meeting, Montgomery was willing to go ahead in spite of the forecast, but Ramsay doubted whether his smaller craft could cross the Channel in the seas which were predicted, and Leigh-Mallory was certain that the air forces would not be able to play their full part in the plan. By then, the main forces were due to sail in two hours' time. But Eisenhower gave the order to postpone the sailing for twenty-four hours and recall the ships at sea. The fleet of big ships steaming south down the Irish sea turned about, to steam north for twelve hours. A flotilla of minesweepers was only thirty-five miles from the Normandy coast when it got the order to return, and a convoy of landing craft on its way to Utah Beach did not receive the signal and plowed on southwards. Destroyers were sent to turn it back, but they could not find it. At nine o'clock, it was spotted by a naval seaplane a third of the way across the Channel. The landing craft from Devon, which were then off the Isle of Wight, put back towards harbors which were already full. At Portland, there was the most tremendous traffic jam in maritime history. During the morning, in rising wind, it seemed that the landing craft would have to go back to Devon to sort themselves out and start again, and if they had, they would not have been ready for at least two days. But order was restored, in a struggle which lasted all day, and not very much damage was done except that one tank landing craft drifted into the tide race off Portland Bill and foundered.

But the postponement had not solved Eisenhower's problem. On Sunday evening, he faced the same terrible choice in a different and even more difficult form. Instead of good weather outside and a bad forecast, the weather outside was then visibly impossible, but the forecasters offered a chance of a slight temporary improvement on Tuesday morning. Ramsay reported that the convoys which had been recalled could only make one more attempt without refuelling. The choice was therefore between launching the invasion on Tuesday the 6th, in weather which was nothing better than a gamble, or postponing it for two weeks till the tides were right again. Once more, Eisenhower put off the final decision till early the following morning.

During the night, he carried as heavy a burden as has fallen to the lot of any man. Everyone who had been at the evening meeting remembered one phrase he had used: "The question is, how long can you hang this operation out on a limb and let it hang there?" The troops could not stay in their ships for a fortnight. But they had been briefed, and had now even been told the real names of the places they were to go to; and if all the tens of thousands of them were brought ashore again—even supposing it were possible to accommodate them—it was impossible to hope that the secret would not leak. So far, the German air force only seemed to have spotted a small proportion of the fleet, and had never attacked it. That luck was too astonishing to last. The Germans were known to have secret weapons (soon to be given the familiar name of doodle-bugs) which were nearly ready and might be used, with effects which nobody could foresee, in attacks on the crowded harbors. In postponement for a fortnight, there were such risks of confusion, of loss of security and of counterattack that the whole plan might have to be abandoned. These were possibilities which Eisenhower himself had said were almost too bitter to contemplate.

But the alternative of launching the invasion in uncertain weather was almost equally risky. If the forecast was exactly right, all might be well; but if it was only slightly overoptimistic, landing craft would be swamped, naval and air bombardment would be inaccurate, German bombers might be able to take off while Allied fighters were grounded, and the invasion might end in a slaughter of troops and the greatest military disaster which either America or Britain had ever suffered.

And finally, if it failed, whether it had been postponed or not, it would be impossible to try again that summer, perhaps impossible ever to try again. All the hopes and power of America and Britain had been put into this one attempt to bring the Germans to battle in western Europe. If it failed, hope might also fail, not only in America and Britain but in the countries which the Germans had occupied; the Russians might decide their allies were useless and make a separate peace. The ordinary troops, and the ordinary people, had never wasted time on the thought that the war might be lost, but Eisenhower, with expert and dispassionate knowledge, knew that if the invasion failed it might be impossible ever to win the war.

He himself, being a soldier, has never described his own feelings on that night of decision, but perhaps some indication of them is given by the announcement which he drafted, without telling anyone, some time on June 5th.

Our landings in the Cherbourg-Havre area have failed to gain a satisfactory foothold and I have withdrawn the troops. My decision to attack at this time and place was based upon the best information available. The troops, the air, and the navy did all that bravery and devotion to duty could do. If any blame or fault attached to the attempt it is mine alone.

When he had written this, he put it in his pocket in case it was needed. Six weeks later, he found it again, still in his pocket, and showed it to his naval aide, who kept it as a souvenir.

By the time he wrote this announcement, he had already decided to commit his forces to the hazard of landing, whatever the weather might bring. All through the meetings, Montgomery had been willing to start. Ramsay had agreed, but reluctantly. Leigh-Mallory, speaking for the air forces, had wanted to wait; but at the last meeting, just after 4 A.M. on Monday, he also had agreed that the chance must be taken, and Eisenhower had launched the invasion with the words "O.K. We'll go."

That evening, when the ships had sailed and there was nothing more that he could do except wait for the result of his decision, he drove to an airfield fifty miles inland near Newbury, where American paratroopers were waiting to take off. He had a particular interest in these men, a particular concern for them. Some thirteen thousand of them were to drop that night in the Cherbourg peninsula, while British parachutists dropped near Caen. Ever since the outline of this plan had first been made, four months before, Leigh-Mallory had opposed the American drop because it had to be made in wooded and well-defended country; he had predicted that 50 to 80 percent of the troop-carrying aircraft would be lost. Only a week before, he had come to Eisenhower again to protest against what he called the futile slaughter of two fine American divisions.

Eisenhower had never agreed with his pessimistic view, but it was no light matter to disregard the advice of his air commander in chief. At Leigh-Mallory's insistence, he had retired alone to his quarters and analyzed the airborne plan again with the greatest care, and then—again carrying the burden alone—he had decided to overrule him. But the doubt still remained in his mind that his air adviser might be right, and his own judgment might be wrong, and of all his personal worries that day, the worst, he said afterwards, was the thought that his own conscience might find him guilty of the blind sacrifice of these thousands of young Americans.

At the airfield, concealing this thought, he strolled round among them, talking cheerfully to anyone who caught his eye. They were full of confidence, and knew nothing of his fears. One of them, who had a ranch in Texas, offered him a

job when the war was over. As darkness fell, they embarked
in their aircraft, and Eisenhower waited and watched the
aircraft take off into the gathering night; a Supreme Commander
is always a lonely man. At the same time, others were taking
off from airfields all over England, and soon the sky overhead
was full of the sound of them.

Probably Eisenhower had hardly noticed the countryside
around the airfield, but the parachutists knew it well. When
they left their camp at Fort Bragg, North Carolina, England
had been described to them as a combat zone. Many of them,
after crossing the Atlantic, had arrived at their camps in
Wiltshire in the dark, and had had a surprise at what they
saw the next morning: gentle green hills, ancient stone pubs
and churches, thatched villages with incredible names—Chilton
Foliat, Straight Soley and Crooked Soley, Ogbourne St. George,
and the place which was written Mildenhall and spoken of as
Minal. There was no sign of combat, but every symbol of
ancient peace and calm. One of the parachutists said he felt
as if he had passed out and awakened on a Hollywood movie
set.

It was true that almost nothing could change the peaceful
ways of those English villages. Most of their young men and
women had gone away. All through the years from Dunkirk,
the people who remained had plodded on, working rather
harder than they ever had before, urged on by government
officials, and by their own consciences, to grow more than the
land had ever been made to produce, and spending what
leisure time was left in the Home Guard, the civil defense,
the first aid, or the fire watchers. When the Americans came,
the people of the villages watched the most extraordinary
activities with interest, but without very much surprise. Mass
parachute drops on the neighboring parks and farms became
such a common sight that they hardly bothered to go outside
to watch.

But when the Americans suddenly disappeared, the villages
seemed very strange without them. On the evening of the
fifth, when Eisenhower was at the airfield, the bar of the
Stag's Head in Chilton Foliat a couple of miles away was a
desolate place. Nobody was in, except the local regulars
sitting over their mild and bitter. The bottled ale and the
strictly rationed whiskey, which had usually all gone by nine
o'clock, were left on the shelves that night. The landlord and

the regulars, in desultory conversation, wondered where the Americans had gone, and agreed that they really rather missed the noise and hustle, and reflected how dead the place would have been all winter if they had never been there.

At closing time, with these thoughts still in his mind, the landlord locked the bar, and washed up the few glasses, and then went out to shut up his chickens; and it was while he was out there in the meadow behind the pub that the airfield came to life. The aircraft came up over the elms in the park where the American camp stood empty now and silent: in twos, in dozens, in scores, they circled overhead and took up formation, and others came over from farther north in hundreds. Standing there in awe, he called to his wife to come and listen. "This is it," he said.

Even in London, veterans of the air raids were wakened by the sound. There in the capital, there were many staff officers who knew the secret and had known it for months, but Londoners in general had known less of what was going on than country people. Out in the countryside, there was hardly a village without its own local airfield or camp or dump of equipment, in which the people had taken a personal interest and pride; but in London none of the preparations could be seen, except down the river where some of the colossal concrete sections of the two artificial harbors had been built—the harbors which were to be towed across the Channel and put together on the coast of France within a few days of landing. In villages, there were still some things which people could gossip about, because there were things which everyone in the village had seen; but in London security was such an ingrained habit by then that even people who had seen some clue to the invasion told nobody else about it. Invasion was in everybody's mind, but was seldom discussed at all.

It was not till nearly dawn that the aircraft began to cross London. Then they flew over the city without a single pause for two and a half hours. Nothing like this had happened before; the fleets of aircraft which had been bombing Germany had normally kept clear of London so that its defenses were not confused. Some people wakened by the noise thought at first, half asleep, that they must have missed hearing the siren; but then they woke more, and remembered that the days were past when Germany could send such fleets of aircraft over, and realized that London was hearing for the very first time a bomber fleet without an air-raid warning. People got up and looked out of their windows across the blacked-out city, but the sky was cloudy and there was nothing to be seen.

Down on the coast, everybody knew, even before the planes came over and flew in formation out across the sea. In the coast-guard hut on the top of St. Alban's Head, the watch had just been changed, and a man called Wallace had come off duty; and during the day he had been witness of a spectacle vaster and braver than had ever been seen on that historic shore, or on any sea in any age of history. St. Alban's Head is high, and from the top of it the view extends across the Channel to the south; to the east across Weymouth Bay to Portland; to the west across the approaches of Southampton Water to the Isle of Wight; to the north, through the gentle folds of the Purbeck Hills to the gray stone village of Worth Matravers.

The village and the coast-guard cottages and the hut on the top of the cliff had been home for Mr. Wallace for many years. He knew everyone in the place, and he was the sort of man whom everyone in the place, from the smallest children upwards, called by his Christian name, which was Percy. He was a veteran of the Dover Patrol of the First World War. Originally, he had come from Bristol, but his wife had been born in Worth Matravers, and it was on her account that he had come home there in his middle age, and settled down to a perfectly contented life as a coast guard, a churchwarden, a chairman of the parish council and an organizer in general of most of the activities of the village.

That was before the war, before Worth Matravers had become in a sense a front-line village, and before the coast-guard hut had become an outpost looking over no man's land. In those days, the village had been peaceful and even sleepy, but the part of the Channel off St. Alban's Head had always been busy with ships. In 1940, both village and sea had changed. Tired men without weapons, straight back from Dunkirk, had been put into camps among the hills. Farmers had sharpened pitchforks, the Local Defense Volunteers had paraded with pikes, the coast guards had armed themselves with knobbed sticks to repel the invasion; and the sea, for the first time in centuries, had been absolutely empty. For week after week, that year, not a single ship had been sighted from the hut, and the only entries in the coast-guard log were of German aircraft patrolling the English Channel unmolested.

Ever since those days, four years before, Mr. Wallace and the three men who alternated the watch with him had seen increasing drama as the Channel, from being a German preserve, became a battlefield. They saw the first coastal convoys, attacks by E-boats, sinking ships, crashing aircraft, deaths and rescues. And all through those years, they had the sense of standing on the very edge of the world; for the known, orderly, civilized world ended then within gunshot of the cliffs of England. It was plain to see that anyone who ventured beyond the edge took his life in his hands; while over the south horizon was implacable and impersonal hostility, as hard to visualize as the terrors which the ancients imagined beyond the Western Ocean.

This feeling, which was widespread in England, of an uncrossable frontier which hemmed the country in, made the sight which Wallace saw on the fifth of June more wonderful.

E-Boat

For several weeks, the harbor at Portland, seventeen miles to the westward, had been filling with ships. In the past week, when he looked at it through glasses, the whole of its area had looked black. Then it had begun to overflow, and all the seventeen-mile sweep of Weymouth Bay had begun to fill. A screen of destroyers had been thrown across the bay. The destroyers turned close in below his hut, and steamed in a straight line, back and forth, all night and day, across the mouth of the bay to Portland Bill; and inside the screen, ever more and more ships had anchored. Then, on the day before, between the squalls of rain, he had seen still hundreds more come in: these were the landing craft and escorts which had come up from Cornwall and Devon and then, on Eisenhower's orders, turned back to shelter.

And that morning, the fleet had sailed. He could not possibly count the ships, or even guess the numbers; in fact, much more than a thousand ships were before his eyes. Close under the cliffs of the headland, he looked down on landing craft, and could see the troops on board. Beyond them, line after line of tank landing craft passed by, escorted by motor launches. There were armed trawlers, and ocean tugs, and far out and ahead, there were echelons of minesweepers. Hundreds of ships were flying barrage balloons. Destroyers and frigates took up their stations out to sea; French, British and American cruisers; tank landing ships and infantry transports carrying small landing craft in davits; and on the horizon, coming up from the west beyond Portland, battleships and monitors and heavy cruisers. Fighter planes wove patterns overhead. Then in the east, more landing craft and escorts emerged from Poole, and in the far distance another separate fleet steamed out of the Solent and turned south in silhouette against the white cliffs of the Isle of Wight. Wallace stood on the head of the cliff, entranced and exalted by a pageant of splendor which nobody had ever seen before, and nobody, it is certain, will ever see again. Before evening, the last of the ships had gone, hull down on the southern horizon, and once more the sea was empty.

He was on his way home when dusk had fallen and the sound in the sky began. At home, his wife was listening. "This is it," he said to her. And later that night, when they were ready to go to bed, he said: "A lot of men are going to die tonight. We should pray for them." They knelt by the side of the bed.

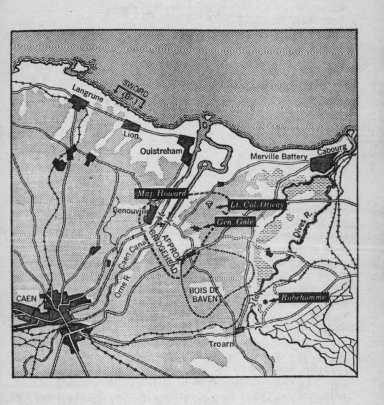

PART TWO

THE
BRITISH
AIR DROP

In the dark cloudy sky above the lush pastureland of Normandy, at twenty minutes past midnight, the first of the parachutists jumped and the first of the glider pilots cast off from his tug and the vanguard drifted down in silence on the wind.

At the eastern end of the invasion shore, there are three waterways: first the Caen Canal, which runs from the sea to the city eight miles inland; then the River Orne, which is close to the canal; and then, five miles farther east, the River Dives. The main German armored reserves were in the area east of Caen, and the role of the British 6th Airborne Division was to drop in the five-mile strip between the two rivers and protect the seaborne forces against armored counterattack while they were landing.

This task called for speed and good timing, and for novel and daring techniques. The division was not allowed to take off from England before dark, in case its aircraft were detected; and before dawn it not only had to win a territory of twenty-five square miles and demolish its main defenses, but also be ready to fight off German tanks. Its antitank guns and other defensive equipment were too massive for parachutes, and could only be carried in gliders; but nobody before had ever attempted an accurate landing in enemy country of large numbers of gliders in the dark. Nevertheless, under Maj.

Gen. Richard Gale, the division evolved a plan which it was confident could lead to success. The keys to it were seven small bridges, five over the River Dives, one over the Orne and one over the canal.

The Dives is a small river, which winds gently among flat water-meadows and willow trees; but the Germans had flooded its valley as part of their scheme of defense and made an impenetrable marsh from half a mile to two miles wide. No doubt they assumed that control of the five bridges which crossed it would be in their hands; but Gale decided to destroy them by surprise attacks, and so turn the barrier of the marshes to his own account. With these bridges down, a German armored counterattack from the east would be impossible, and he could concentrate his antitank defenses to the south.

The Orne and the Caen Canal, on the other hand, lay between his own landing zone and the British beaches from which he would ultimately be reinforced; and therefore, while the Dives bridges had to be destroyed, the Orne and canal bridges had to be captured intact. Only one road crossed the Orne and the canal between the city and the sea.

When the division's plan was completed, the main events of the night appeared as follows:

12:20 A force in gliders to land on the Orne and canal bridges.

12:20 Pathfinders to drop by parachute, to mark out dropping zones for the main parachute forces.

12:50 Main parachute drop to begin. Objectives: to demolish the Dives bridges, reinforce the defense of the Orne and canal bridges, capture a coast defense battery, seize the territory between the rivers, and clear landing zones for the main glider force.

3:30 Main force of seventy-two gliders to land with antitank armament, transport and heavy equipment.

Each of these separate actions depended on the quick success of those before it. The division's defense depended on the gliders. The gliders depended on the parachutists to clear their landing zones within one hour and forty minutes. The parachutists depended on the pathfinders. The final relief and reinforcement of the whole division depended on the capture of the Orne and canal bridges. And dawn began at 5:30. Much had to be accomplished in the seven hours' darkness of the summer night.

Since that night, there has been plenty of argument, mostly lighthearted, between units which claim to have been the first to land. It is an argument which can never be decided. The pathfinders and first gliders of the British army came down in groups, here and there between the rivers, with no more than a minute or two between them; and at almost the same moment American landings started fifty miles away. But whoever was the first to land, the first troops in action were probably three platoons of the Oxford and Buckinghamshire Light Infantry, and certainly they were the first to achieve their objective; for this was the force assigned to capture the bridge on the Caen Canal. At midnight these platoons were already close to the coast of France, each platoon cooped in the pitch-dark inside of a Horsa glider towed by a Halifax bomber. In the leading glider everyone was singing. "Abie, my boy" was the most successful song. Almost all that first platoon were Cockneys, and wisecracks flew around. Somewhere over the Channel, somebody dropped a machine gun magazine with a loud metallic clang on the steel floor; "Old so-and-so's dropped 'is false teeth," a voice said cheerfully. It seemed tremendously funny at the time, but heaven knows what doubts and fears were hidden behind the laughter; for apart from the apprehension of the coming battle, these men all knew that their glider was going to crash.

Most passengers in aircraft think of a crash as the end of everything; to begin the day with a deliberate crash appears a

Horsa Glider

bizarre conception. But logic, and the situation of the Caen Canal bridge, demanded this desperate measure. The bridge is a large steel structure which can be raised to let ships go through. At its western end there are a crossroads and the first houses of the village of Benouville. A quarter of a mile down the road in the other direction is the bridge across the Orne.

British Intelligence had learned from the local amateur French spies that both these bridges were wired for demolition and defended by permanent guards. Air reconnaissance had shown trenches and barbed wire on the approaches to the bridges, and during March concrete pillboxes had also appeared on the photographs. Nobody knew precisely what orders had been given to the German guards, but as they had wired the bridges it was only common sense to assume that they intended to blow them up, rather than allow them to be captured. To capture them intact was therefore a matter of split-second surprise. It had to be done before the guards knew what was happening or had time to make up their minds to press the button to explode them.

That was why the attack on these bridges was the first action in the airborne plan; and it was also the reason for the decision to use gliders for the attack, rather than parachutes. Parachutists are always more or less scattered when they drop, and take at least a few minutes to assemble. A glider provides a possibility of landing up to thirty men together on a given spot, ready for action within a matter of seconds of their landing.

But it remained no more than a possibility. First, the glider pilots had to find the bridges in the dark. Secondly, the bridges were surrounded by fields too small for a normal landing; and that was why a crash was inevitable. But the Glider Pilot Regiment, upon whom this duty was to fall, took pride in achieving feats with gliders which seemed impossible, and they confidently promised to try to do what General Gale demanded: to crash six gliders within three minutes of 12:20 A.M., three at each bridge and all within a few paces of the abutments—and to do it without killing their passengers.

The passengers in this deadly experiment were led by Major John Howard, one of the company commanders of the "Ox and Bucks"; and on the flight across the Channel, while his men were so cheerfully singing, Howard sat in the seat next to the door in the leading glider, keyed to the utmost

pitch of tense anticipation; for much of the plan of attack was
his own creation, and he had looked forward to and yet
dreaded this moment throughout the past three months.

Howard was a regular officer of thirty, and he had volunteered
for airborne duties, like many other men in the division, as a
matter of self-respect. For the first year of the war, he had
commanded a training company, but in 1942, when he had
begun to feel he could not stand it any longer, he heard that
the Ox and Bucks were going airborne, and he had made up
his mind to join them. Nobody he had asked knew very much
about airborne warfare, but it sounded the sort of thing he
needed to counterbalance that year which he was beginning
to feel had been ignominious. He lived in Oxford, so it was
only a matter of getting transferred to his county regiment.

But not very long before he made that decision, John
Howard had married a very pretty girl called Joy; and on the
day when he told her he had decided to become a parachutist,
she told him she was going to have a baby. That was an
unpromising beginning for an airborne career; but Joy
understood his professional pride, and did her best to hide
her anxiety from him. A month before D Day, their second
child was born; and all through the months of training,
Howard's wife and children had never been far from his
mind.

The flight across the Channel was scheduled to take one
hour and twenty-four minutes. It was a curious pause, between
the end of the preparations and the beginning of battle, in
which a man's thoughts—unless he could stifle them with
songs and laughter—were all too prone to dwell uselessly on
the possibility that something essential had been forgotten.
Howard's thoughts were a mixture of the personal and the
military. He thought about Joy. He thought with surprise that
it was a wonder he was not being sick; for he had always been
sick on training flights, even when nobody else was, so that it
had become a standing joke in his company. And he thought
with pride of his 160 men. Many of them were hardly more
than boys, and most of them had never seen action. Before
they had embarked, he had thanked them for their patience
in the long and tough and often boring training; and his voice
had not sounded like his own to him, because he felt the
emotion of the moment very keenly. They had always done
everything he told them, and so he felt responsible for their
fate. Next to him in the glider, for example, was Lt. Den

Brotheridge, the platoon commander. Brotheridge had been a cadet in Howard's own training company, and Howard himself had persuaded him to join the airborne forces. Howard reflected now that without his persuasion, Brotheridge would not have been there at all; and he knew that Brotheridge, like himself, had a young wife, and that she was expecting a baby any day. But in fact Brotheridge had no regrets, and would never have thought of Howard as responsible for his fate. He had bet Howard fifty francs he would be out of the door before him when the glider crashed, and so lay claim to be the first Allied soldier to land in the invasion.

On the other side of Howard, at the controls of the glider, was his pilot, Staff Sergeant Wallwork of the Glider Pilot Regiment. It was Wallwork who had done most to calm Howard's worries in the last few weeks. For Howard, the whole three months of planning and training had been a worrying time, and his worry had reached a climax on May 30th. On that day, he had been shown new aerial photographs of his bridges, and in all the fields round them, white spots could be seen which had not been there before. These, he was told, were holes for posts which were intended to make it impossible for gliders to land. The interpreters of photographs could not tell him whether posts had been put in the holes yet or not. Gloomily, he had shown the photographs to his pilots. They seemed delighted. "That's just what we needed," Wallwork had said. "We'll land between the posts. The posts will break the wings off and slow us down, and we shan't hit the bridge so hard."

It was impossible not to trust a pilot who could say a thing like that. Yet Howard, on his way across the Channel, was still wondering whether he had asked Wallwork and the others for something impossible. He had told them he wanted the first glider to stop with its nose inside the wire defenses on the bridge, and the others to stop ten yards behind and five yards to the right. He had no idea how such precision could be achieved, but they had made light of it, and his troops had caught their mood of confidence.

Sitting there in the dark, half listening to the singing and to the rush of air, Howard thought over these special worries of his own, and also the worry which beset almost every man who was crossing the Channel that night: did the Germans know they were coming? Would the surprise come off, or were they running their heads into an ambush? In a pause between songs, he heard a friendly anonymous shout from the back of the fuselage: "'Asn't the major bin sick yet?"

12:16: Wallwork half turned in the pilot's seat and shouted back to him, "Casting off." Howard called for silence, and the singing and talking died as the order was passed down the two lines of men who sat facing each other on each side of the body of the glider. The glider checked. The tow rope was gone. As the speed fell off, the roar of the wind on the flimsy structure also died, to a hiss which seemed like silence; and in the silence fears rose up which the cheerful noise had held in check till then. The nose dropped, and the glider swooped, bumping through the torn clouds. Brotheridge undid his safety belt and stood up, with Howard and the platoon sergeant holding him, and swung open the forward door. Cold air streamed in. The glider leveled out from the dive and banked steeply to the right and peering down through the open door into the darkness of space beneath, Howard glimpsed for a second a dimly gleaming ribbon: the Caen Canal. But the sight of it only elated him for a moment, because he was not really thinking of what lay below him and ahead. He was thinking of Joy and the children asleep in bed at home in Oxford, and he was thankful they did not know what he was doing.

"Hold tight," Wallwork said; and all the platoon linked arms and lifted their feet off the floor and sat there locked together, waiting.

The concussion was shattering. The glider tore into the earth at ninety miles an hour, and careened across the tiny field with a noise like thunder as timber cracked and split and it smashed itself to pieces. The stunning noise and shocks went on and on for a count of seconds; and then suddenly for a split second everything was perfectly still and silent. But even in the stunned silence, training worked. Howard found he had undone his belt and was on his feet. The doorway had crumpled into wreckage. But in front of him was a jagged hole in the glider's side and he went through it head first and fell on the earth of France, picked himself up and felt his limbs for broken bones and looked up; and there against the night sky, exactly and precisely where it should have been, twenty paces away, was the steel lattice tower of the bridge. Brotheridge came running round the tail: he had got out of a hole on the other side. "All right?" he said. "Yes," Howard said. "Carry on." Brotheridge shouted his platoon letter,

"Able, Able," to rally the men who were tumbling out of the wreckage, and the action began which they had rehearsed on bridges all over England. A phosphorus smoke bomb was thrown at the pillbox by the bridge. A machine gun opened fire from it, but one man ran forward under cover of the smoke and dropped a Mills bomb through the gun port, and the platoon scrambled across the wire which the glider had demolished, up an embankment onto the road, and with yells of "Able, Able," they dashed across the bridge against the fire of a second machine gun on the far side. Howard made for the spot he had named as his command post, followed by his radio operator, Corporal Tappenden, and as he ran he heard a crash behind him, and then another, the other two gliders coming in. Soon above the noise of small-arms fire he heard his second and third platoons come running through the darkness, shouting "Baker" and "Charlie," not only to identify

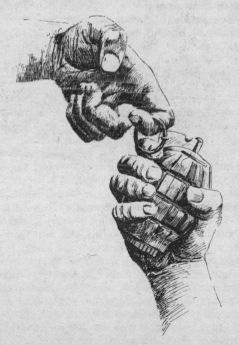

Mills Bomb

themselves, but also because men shout by instinct when they charge into a battle.

The sentry on the bridge was a young German called Helmut Römer, and when he saw the first glider crash, he naturally thought it was a bomber, because there were heavy air raids going on in Caen and along the coast, and he had been watching the antiaircraft fire. Nobody had told him anything more than an airraid was expected. So when men with black faces charged across the bridge at him, he was totally taken by surprise. He dived for the trenches: it was the only thing he could do. There was no time for the guard to turn out, much less for the whole platoon to be called from their billets. But the NCO of the guard fired the machine gun and shot down the first of the men who were coming across the bridge. Then the wave of them broke into the trenches, and the garrison scattered and ran.

Within three minutes of the crash, the attack had succeeded. Engineers searched for the demolition wiring and disconnected it. The charge itself had not been put in place. They found it afterwards in a cache by the bridgehead. With the bridge in their hands, the infantry went on to clear out the houses beyond it. One man from the leading platoon came back across the bridge to tell Howard the job was done. "But Mr. Brotheridge is hurt, sir," he said. By Howard's side, Corporal Tappenden was trying to call the other half of the company, which by then should have landed at the Orne bridge down the road, but he could not get an answer. A man was struggling up the steep bank to the road, and Howard bent down to help him and saw a face which was a red mask of blood. It was Wallwork, the pilot, injured but still bringing up ammunition from the glider. Men came back over the bridge carrying Brotheridge on a stretcher. Howard looked at his friend. He was still alive, but unconscious, and Howard knew by instinct that the man he had persuaded to go airborne, the man who had bet him he would be first to land, was going to be the first to die in action. Howard called for the doctor, and he was found wandering dazed across the bridge, for the second glider, in which he had traveled, had broken in half in the middle, and many of the men in it were injured. One had been thrown out of it into a little pond and drowned. Tappenden looked up from his radio and shouted: "I've raised them, sir. They got the other bridge."

The attack on the Orne bridge had been a walkover. The

landing had not been so precise as the landing at the canal. One glider was close to the bridge, but the next was a quarter of a mile away. The third was cast off from its tug in the wrong place, and landed beyond the marshes of the Dives. Even the first of the three was a minute or two behind the first at the canal, and the leading platoon, commanded by Lieutenant Fox, got to the bridge just in time to see the German defenders running for their lives. One of Fox's NCOs jumped into an empty machine-gun post and turned the German gun against the retreating Germans; and his commander of the second platoon, running breathlessly onto the bridge some minutes late, found Fox in the middle of it, staring down at the dark water of the Orne. "How's it gone?" he asked anxiously. "It's gone all right," Fox said. "But where the hell are the umpires?"

The code words which Howard had been allotted to signal the success of his attack had none of the air of modest triumph which might have suited the very first success of the invasion. The capture of the canal bridge intact was to be reported by radio to brigade headquarters by the word "ham." For the Orne bridge the word was "jam." Corporal Tappenden could not get an acknowledgment from brigade, and for half an hour, squatting by the roadside, he broadcast those pregnant words: "Ham and jam. Ham and jam. Ham and jam." Meanwhile, the six platoons, weakened now by the losses of the crash and the fighting, attended their dead and wounded and prepared to defend what they had won; for a counterattack was expected as soon as the Germans had recovered from their surprise, and until Howard's men could be reinforced by the main body of the parachutists, they were in a perilous position.

Nobody at Brigade Headquarters heard Howard's signal because the brigade signal equipment had all disappeared in the drop—the first symptom of a difficulty which was to bring the whole airborne attack to the edge of disaster.

The pathfinders of the division were a company of parachutists carried in six aircraft. Their job was to land at the same moment as Howard in his gliders, but farther east, and to set up lights and radio beacons on which the main parachute forces would be dropped. Their navigators and pilots, of course, were picked men, but even they had trouble, in the wind and cloud, in dropping their troops exactly. The parachutes themselves were carried by the wind. The errors accumulated, and when the pathfinders landed they found they were scattered and much farther eastward than they should have been. But they only had half an hour to prepare the dropping zones. There was no time to march back to the zones which had been planned, and so they had to set out their beacons where they were, although one of the zones which they improvised was dangerously close to the woods called the Bois de Bavent, and another was near the floodlands of the Dives.

Close behind the aircraft of the pathfinder company were those of the 3rd Parachute Brigade, whose mission was to destroy the five bridges across the River Dives and a powerful coast-defense battery at Merville, near the mouth of the Orne.

The capture of the Merville battery was important, because it commanded the beaches on which the left flank of the British 3rd Division was to land, and the anchorage where by dawn the fleet would be assembled. If it were still in action at the break of day, it would certainly cause havoc, and might even prevent the landing of the 3rd Division. The job of silencing it was given to the 9th Parachute Battalion, whose commander was Lt. Col. T. B. H. Otway; and when the brigadier had first given Otway his orders, he had described the job, quite rightly, as a stinker.

Reconnaissance had shown that the guns of the battery, in their bombproof emplacements, were surrounded first by machine-gun positions and a belt of barbed wire. Outside this was a minefield thirty yards wide, and outside that a second barbed wire entanglement. Beyond this again was a further hundred yards of mines surrounded by a wire fence. Intelligence estimated that it was held by two hundred men with ten machine guns and two dual-purpose cannons. Otway's battalion had to drop at ten minutes to one, assemble, march a mile and a half to this stronghold, and capture it by 5:15; for at that moment, if they had not fired a signal of success, the navy were to begin to shell it. The only support which Otway was offered was a bombing attack, in the early hours of the morning, by one hundred Lancasters of the RAF. But neither shelling nor bombing was expected to destroy the battery, which of course had been built to withstand that kind of attack. The only way to destroy it was to get inside it.

Lancaster

Terence Otway was twenty-nine, and looked younger; and at that age he commanded 750 of the toughest of British troops. He was slim and lightly built. His face was lean and gave an impression of keen intellect and an ascetic and sensitive character. One might almost have been forgiven for putting him down, at first sight, as an artist rather than a colonel of paratroops. But such appointments are more than a matter of chance. Otway's father had been killed in the First World War, and his mother had had a long struggle to bring up her son on a war widow's pension. When he left school he was nearly apprenticed to an attorney in Brighton; but he had hated the idea of settling down in an office before he had seen the world at all, and so, when he was nineteen he had entered the Royal Military College, Sandhurst, and been commissioned into the army, only intending to stay for five years. The army took him to the northwest frontier of India and to China. The five years expired a few months before war began. By then, he had come to despise a good many things about army life, especially life in an officers' mess in India, and he had tried to get out. But he had not been allowed to go; and so, by D Day, he had served for ten years and had revealed—perhaps to his own surprise—an extremely acute and incisive military brain.

When he had been told, four months before the invasion, of what his battalion was expected to do, he had set to work to prepare his plan and train his men with fantastic thoroughness. He went out with the secret maps and photographs of Merville to find a stretch of the English countryside which resembled the surroundings of the battery, and he found one near Newbury in Berkshire. Within two days, he had had it requisitioned, and persuaded the government to pay for

£15,000 worth of crops which he had to destroy, and he
fenced the place in with barbed wire and began to build an
exact replica of the battery and its defenses. When the
surrounding fields and woods did not exactly fit the maps and
photographs, they were bulldozed till they did. On this
artificial stage, in the strictest secrecy, the battalion rehearsed
its attack again and again, using live ammunition, first by day
and then by night.

Otway had heartily agreed with his brigadier from the very
beginning that the job was a stinker; and studying its details
and watching his rehearsals, he began to doubt whether it
was possible for his men with their light armament, to break
open the defenses within the short time they were allowed.
At best, there was a risk of failure; and logical analysis made
him decide that there was only one way to make reasonably
certain of success: to put sixty of the men in three gliders and
crash-land them inside the defenses, right against the walls of
the gun emplacements, at the moment the attack began.
This, he thought, would tip the balance; but it was obvious
that the sixty men would have even less prospect than the
rest of living through it. He chose his A company, and told
them what he had planned, and called for volunteers. As
usual, this procedure was no more than a formality, because
the whole company took a smart pace forward, and it was left
to him and the company commander to select the sixty men.

By the time this glider attack had also been rehearsed, and
the battalion had moved into its closed embarkation camp,
Otway's military mind was satisfied that his plan was as good
as it could be. But he was young, and perhaps too intelligent
and introspective to find life easy as a military commander;
and as D Day came nearer, he began to torture himself with
doubt. The lives of his 750 depended on his clear reasoning;
and he had also been told that a large and essential part of the
invasion itself, and therefore the lives of innumerable other
men, would hang on his success. It was a fearsome responsibility
for a man still in his twenties. On the night of June 3rd, the
night before he expected to embark, he had not been able to
sleep at all, and had walked round the camp all night in a
state of nervous tension which he had had to hide from his
officers and men, turning over and over in his mind the
utmost details of the operation, trying for the hundredth time
to weigh imponderable chances, glancing from time to time
at the familiar unworried faces of the men who were on duty,

and wondering how many of them would live to another dawn.

For him the postponement had been a godsend. By the night of the fourth, he had worried himself into exhaustion, and that night he had gone to bed and slept soundly. On the fifth, he was himself again, calm and confident; and when his men had assembled that evening to embark, he had walked round and exchanged a few words with every one of them. In the aircraft, by midnight, he was sleeping.

For the twenty-four hours before the attack, Otway had put a ban on drink, in case anyone, under the strain of waiting, drank too much and went into battle with a hangover. But he had broken his own rule to the extent of taking a bottle of whiskey with him, and somewhere over the Channel he woke up and passed it round the twenty men in his aircraft. They did not drink much, or perhaps they had quietly thought of providing themselves with something. The bottle came back to him before it was empty.

Soon after this interlude, the antiaircraft fire began as they crossed the coast of France; and not many seconds later, Otway had his first warning that the drop was going to go wrong. The pilot began to throw the aircraft about in violent evasive action. The effect on the drill of the parachutists was chaotic. When they tried to move down to the door to jump in the quick compact succession for which they were trained, the sudden lurches threw them off their balance. Some fell on the floor, encumbered by their heavy equipment. Others tripped over them in struggling, cursing heaps. Out of the mêlée, Otway shouted to the pilot, "Hold your course, you bloody fool."

"We've been hit in the tail," one of the air crew shouted back.

"You can still fly straight, can't you?" Otway asked angrily. But before he was given an answer, the signal came to jump. Otway's turn was early. He clambered along to the door, and found he was still clutching the half-empty bottle of whiskey. He thrust it at the RAF dispatcher. "You're going to need this," he said; and with that parting shot, he jumped.

In those few seconds of heavenly quiet which reward a parachutist between the shock of the jump and the shock of the landing, Otway looked down at the familiar land below him. He could see it quite clearly in the diffused moonlight and the gleam of searchlights reflected from the clouds.

There was the dark square of the wood which was his rendezvous. Beyond it, the sodden marshlands of the Dives, which the Germans had flooded, gleamed where the bog was wettest. Below him were fields with thick black hedges, and across the fields, down wind, a farmhouse which he knew particularly well. It was the last place he wanted to land, for it was ringed with blue on his map and marked as a German battalion headquarters.

Otway was still angry at the way his men's training had been nullified by the pilot's tactics. He was made angrier by finding now that the aircraft had been off course, and angrier still by seeing that somebody was shooting at him. Tracers were passing him; looking up, he saw them tearing through his parachute. It struck him as damned impertinence, but there was not much time to worry about it because the wind was drifting him straight to the German headquarters. He tried to manipulate his parachute to keep clear of the place, but there was nothing much he could do. Inexorably, as he fell, the wind took him, at fifteen miles an hour, across the last field and then across the farmyard. He hit the wall of the house itself, some feet above the ground, and dropped out of his harness into what seemed to be a garden. Two of his men were there already. A German threw open an upstairs window and leaned out. One of the men with Otway picked up a brick and threw it. It was a good shot. There was a crash of glass and the German put his head in, and Otway and his companions—he never knew who they were—ran by instinct to the back of the house and got out of the garden while the German headquarters staff poured out of the front door.

Otway learned later that only seven of the twenty men in his plane had managed to disentangle themselves in time to jump while it was over the dropping zone. It had to make three more runs to get them all out. Among the seven who jumped with him was his batman, whose name was Wilson. Before the war, Wilson had been a professional boxer and a professional valet, and nobody could have had better qualifications as an airborne colonel's batman; but his drop was even unluckier than his colonel's. In fact, no parachutist could have dreamed of a more grimly humorous landing; for the German headquarters building had a greenhouse attatched to it, and Wilson went plumb through the roof of it and landed in a shower of broken glass among the pot plants. At that moment, the Germans were rushing out of the building, and he rushed out behind them, and found himself being shot at by some Canadians. None the worse, he set off for the rendezvous alone.

As Otway hurried on towards the rendezvous, he picked up a few men heading for the wood in twos and threes. Before they got there, they had an experience which was harrowing even to the toughest of them. Strangled cries came from the darkness of a shallow valley, and following them they found in the valley bottom one of the tentacles of the flooded bogland of the Dives. There in the mud, not far from the bank, was a parachutist, struggling, sunk to his shoulders in the ghastly slime. They reached his parachute, and hauled in the lines till they were taut. Half a dozen men were on the lines before the end came; but fighting for a foothold themselves, they could not overcome the suction of the bog. Still shouting for help, the man sank lower. They never saw who it was. He gave a last cry of anguish before the mud silenced him.

When Otway got to the wood, the first man he recognized was his second-in-command, who said, "Thank God you've come, sir."

"Why?" Otway asked him.

"The drop's bloody chaos. There's hardly anyone here."

This was no exaggeration. It was nearly two o'clock. Otway himself was late, but only a few men had reached the wood before him. Glancing round at the group of them, he became aware of Wilson, ever the perfect servant, standing at his side, proffering a small flask as if it were a decanter on a silver salver.

"Shall we take our brandy now, sir?" Wilson said.

As time crept on, in the darkness below the trees, more men arrived, but only a few at a time; and Otway began to force himself to face a disaster worse than anything he had imagined. His plans had been flexible; no parachute commander expects a drop to be perfectly successful. But nobody could have planned for a drop in which only a handful of men survived and only a few odds and ends of equipment could be found. There was very little encouragement in the reports which were brought to him. By half past two, 150 men had come in; six hundred were missing. They had one machine gun. Their mortars and antitank guns and mine detectors and all their heavy equipment had disappeared, and so had their radios and all their signal equipment except, ironically, the Very lights which were to be fired to signal the success of the

attack. There were no engineers and no doctors; but six
medical orderlies, who were conscientious objectors, had
arrived with first-aid kits. There was no sign so far of a
reconnaissance party which had been dropped a little earlier
than the main body to penetrate the first belt of wire and the
minefield.

Otway was in a terrible dilemma. He had to decide whether
he ought to throw his remaining men into an attack which
seemed to be suicidal and doomed to failure, or whether he
ought to preserve their lives for the other secondary objectives
which they were supposed to tackle later in the day, and
leave the Merville battery to the air force and the navy. And
if he decided to attack, he had to decide exactly when to
move. There was still a mile and a half to go, and the
Germans were thoroughly alerted. If he moved too soon, he
would lose the help of any men who might still turn up at the
rendezvous. If he left it too late, he would not be ready when
the gliders came in, and their troops would probably be
captured. It was a problem he could not discuss with anyone,
for the only thing which might still save the day was the
self-confidence of his men, and a hint that he was in doubt
would have destroyed it. So for an hour, in the solitude of
command, Otway prowled round the groups of men who
were waiting in the wood, and wrestled with his conscience
all alone. The only man to whom, for a moment, he showed
his fears was Wilson. At a quarter to three, the time of final
decision had arrived.

"What the hell am I going to do?" Otway said.

"Only one thing to do, sir," Wilson answered. "No need to
ask me."

Otway laughed. "Yes, I know," he said. "Get the officers
and NCOs. We'll move in five minutes."

Wilson's confidence had settled the problem for him. The
officers and NCOs gathered round him, and he told them
they were going to attack with exactly one-fifth of the battalion.
None of them gave the slightest sign that they thought he
might order the attack to be abandoned. At ten minutes to
three, they moved out of the wood in single file.

Otway had ordered secrecy and silence on the march, but
some of the men were tempted by an antiaircraft battery.
They skirted round it, still in single file, a hundred yards
away. It was firing at gliders of their own division, which were
passing overhead to land further in from the coast. Every

time a gun fired, its crew were revealed, caught in mid-
movement like a flashlight photograph, an easy target for a
quick shot from a Sten gun. Otway's officers went back down
the line of men, grabbing guns which were leveled at the
Germans and shoving men back into file.

Sten Gun

Soon after this Otway, at the head of the file, saw a figure
and challenged and got the right reply. It was the commander
of the reconnaissance party, coming back to report to him.
Some of his news was good, and some was bad. He had cut
the outer wire fence and crossed the large minefield, and had
lain by the inner belt of wire for half an hour listening to the
conversation of the Germans inside the battery. There was no
sign of any tougher defenses than Intelligence had expected.
The wire was not so bad as it might have been. The engineers
who had landed with him to clear a path through the mines
had lost their mine detectors and the tape with which the
path was supposed to be marked; but they had got through,
searching for the mines with their fingers and "delousing"
them one by one, and they had marked the path as well as
they could by scratching two lines in the earth. But the attack
by the hundred Lancaster bombers had been a washout.
Their pathfinders had put down their markers not on the

battery, but half a mile away on the dropping zone of the reconnaissance party. Consequently, the reconnaissance party's drop had been very alarming. Some of them drifting down on their parachutes had heard bombs whistling past them and seen them explode below their feet. One man said he had been swung above the level of his own parachute by the blast of a bomb below him, but he had got down alive. So far as they knew, not a single bomb had hit the battery.

The 150 men reached the outer wire without any other incident, except that a herd of terrified cows alarmed them by stampeding through their file; and there, when he could actually see the casemates of the guns against the sky, the final blow awaited Otway's plans. It was 4:30. His gliders were due. Until the last moment, he had clung to a hope that somebody would turn up with the mortar flares with which, in accordance with his plan, he should have signaled the gliders to land. But nobody came. Precisely on time, he saw two of the three gliders and their tugs approaching. The tugs flashed their headlights—a private signal to him that they were casting off their tows. The gliders circled down. But he had no way whatever of telling them he was there and was ready to attack. Without such a signal, he knew they would conclude that his force had got into trouble and would land anywhere they could, except on the battery. He saw one glider skim over the battery, a hundred feet up: but he could only watch it as it turned away to come down in the countryside behind him. With this last hope gone, he gave the signal to attack.

The battle was short and terrible and bloody. Otway had no romantic idea of leading his men in the charge. The logical place for the command post was at the rear, where anyone could find it, and logic was always his guide. His first post was beside the gap in the outer wire, and there he waited, in a bomb crater with Wilson and his adjutant and signal officer, while the first men crept forward to blow gaps to the inner wire. He saw the explosions, and at once, a fury of fire burst out from the battery defenses. Silhouetted against the streams of tracers, his men were moving across the minefield, running and dropping down to shoot, or else to lie where death had found them. In the flashes of mortar bombs he saw the first of them fight through the gaps and into the trenches beyond.

That was his own moment to advance. Like many men with imagination, Otway had no great fear of being killed, but a horror of being mutilated. That horror attacked him when he had to get out of the crater and run forward into the flood of fire. Irrelevantly, the thought flashed through his head of what Wilson would think of him if he hesitated. He shouted, "Come on," and ran for it. Running, he forgot about the minefield which had become a minor danger. In the gap, the officer beside him, his adjutant, fell, shot through by a machine gun. He flung himself down inside the wire. The remnants of a company he had kept in reserve came through behind him, and dropped down, waiting for his orders.

He had planned that the leading companies were to go straight in for the guns, without wasting time on any troops outside the casemates. This they did. In a few minutes, he could see them right up against the casemates, pouring their fire through the openings. He ordered the reserve company up to clear the trenches. Soon shouts in German were heard— "Paratroops!"—and Germans began to surrender. In twenty minutes from his first order, it was over. His men were in the casements and had done their best to blow up the guns by stuffing German bombs into the breeches, since they had no more explosives of their own. The very light to signal success was fired. A spotting aircraft, circling over the battery, saw it and passed on the signal to the navy, fifteen minutes before the shelling was due to begin. Otway's signal officer extracted a battered pigeon from the blouse of his battledress and set it free. Back across the Channel, below the host of aircraft, this solitary bird flew through to its loft in England with the news that the Merville battery had fallen.

Otway's gallant remnant of a force had won by nothing but the unhesitating fury of their hand-to-hand fighting. But victory gave them no feeling of elation. On the contrary, when the men assembled they were pale and silent; for of the hundred and fifty who had charged twenty minutes before, seventy-five, exactly half, were now lying dead or wounded, and of the two hundred Germans in defense, only twenty-two could still rise to their feet to surrender.

There was no time for rest. As soon as the battery had fallen, another German battery to the west began to shell it. Otway set everyone to work to carry the wounded away from the shellfire to a barn beyond the minefield. Among the German survivors was an elderly doctor; and in the barn, this man started with impartial care to attend to the worst of the wounded, both British and German. Before long, both British and German medical supplies in the barn were finished. The German doctor knew where extra supplies had been stored in the battery, and he set off alone through the fire to get them. On the way, he was hit by a German shell.

The battalion had other assignments to carry out that morning, and before dawn Otway marched off, with one out of ten of all the men who had embarked with him when the night began. This skeleton of a battalion was extremely angry with the air force for the chaos of their drop, and later, when they began to hear what had happened to their comrades who had vanished, the news did nothing to calm their feelings. Some had been landed twenty or thirty miles away. Navigators had mistaken the river Dives for the River Orne, and without identifying the countryside below them had cast out their troops on the wrong side of the marshes. Some of these scattered men got back to their unit in the end. One of them swam along the shore for two miles, with all his equipment and his Sten gun, to get past the mouth of the Dives. One sergeant turned up four days later, bringing with him the whole of his planeload of men who had dropped thirty miles island, and bringing also, like scalps, the paybooks of a number of German officers. But a great many of the scattered troops were killed or captured; and of Otway's 750, no less than 192 men were never heard of again alive or dead. Perhaps they were dropped in the sea; but more likely the ghastly quagmires of the Dives closed over their heads and their bodies lie buried there today.

The parachutists were inclined to blame the pilots and navigators, but that was not fair. They had done their best. It might have been fairer to blame the RAF commanders who had sent them out with training which was clearly inadequate; but of course the size of the efforts of the Allied air forces that night had strained their resources to the utmost. The army's analysis of the drop suggested that one of the two RAF groups which took part in it had been much more successful than the other. Conditions were the same for both groups, and the difference certainly looked like a difference of training. Probably all the navigators could have found their targets if the night had been calm and clear, but on the evidence they had not been taught enough to cope with wind and cloud. As for the pilots, some had been sent on bombing missions to give them experience of antiaircraft fire; but others had never been shot at before, and had to make their own assessments of how dangerous the fire might be. Many of them, in their anxiety to get their passengers through, flew too high and too fast, or disorganized the jumping drill by "weaving." Yet the fire was not really intense; of the 373 aircraft which dropped the 6th Airborne Division that night, only nine were reported missing, from all causes, and seven damaged. On the other hand, to be fair, it must be said that the night was difficult for aerial navigation; for even some of the best trained men of Bomber Command, the pathfinders, missed their targets—like the Merville battery; and the Americans fared no better.

The dispatch of the air commander in chief which described this airlift afterwards ended with a very curious statement. Leigh-Mallory wrote: "The accuracy with which these forces were delivered to the allotted zones contributed greatly to the rapid success of their *coups-de-main*." Otway and his seventy-five survivors would have had a word for that; but it was not published till three years later, and by that time their tempers had cooled. Meanwhile when these men, soon after dawn, were marching wearily along a road on the way to their next objective, they were bombed by the American Air Force. That only confirmed their opinion of all airmen.

Fortunately, Major General Gale, the divisional commander, took a less gloomy view of the scattering of his forces, and was not in the least depressed. His equanimity probably had two causes: one was that he saw the division's landings as a whole, and knew that no other battalion had suffered quite so much as Otway's; the other was that he was an old soldier, used to the setbacks of war.

Age, of course, is a matter of comparison. Richard Gale was forty-eight; much older in years than his subordinate commanders, but no older in mental and physical agility. Thirty years in the army had molded his appearance and character; he had fought in the bloodier battles of the first world war, and had won his Military Cross in 1918. He was six feet three in height, stood as straight as a ramrod and wore a fierce, bristly mustache; and he would have been delighted to think that his juniors feared his displeasure—as they did—much more than they feared the Germans. But his martial appearance and manner seldom quite hid his robust sense of humor, and it never hid the quickness and originality of his brain. Among the qualities which helped to make him a great airborne commander were a passionate hatred of red tape, and, more subtly, an understanding of human frailty; for he had made a study of fear, and knew it is impossible to predict how a man will behave in a battle before he has been tried.

The general himself landed with the main glider force at 3:30. With him in his glider were his ADC, his jeep and driver, a dispatch rider with a motorcycle, and two or three headquarters staff. Before the action, Gale was confident, and elated at the greatness of the occasion. Privately, he was also delighted, in an almost boyish fashion, at being the first British general to land in France, and so stealing a march on his contemporaries. When his glider was airborne, he told his ADC to call him when they crossed the coast of France, and then he went to sleep. His landing was rough. The glider ran across a sunken lane, and the bump rammed the undercarriage up through the fuselage. But nobody was seriously hurt, and the general stepped out to a scene which in less experienced eyes appeared disastrous.

The parachutists had cleared the glider landing zone in time, removing the posts which the Germans had planted, and most of the natural obstacles, with two airborne bulldozers which had been brought by isolated gliders earlier in the night. The mass-landing was amazingly accurate. Seventy-two gliders were dispatched. Forty-nine of them landed on time, and right on the meadow which was cleared. For two or three minutes before and after 3:30, they converged from all directions in the dark. Almost all of them crashed. Wheels, undercarriages, wings were torn off. Some buried their noses in the soft ground, some collided. One went right through a small cottage and emerged bearing with it an old-fashioned double bed; rumor said that a French couple were still in the bed when everything came to rest. Troops who climbed out of the earlier gliders seemed in danger of being mown down by others swooping in; the headquarters staff had to duck as a latecomer swished over their heads. By 3:35 the meadow was covered with wrecks grotesquely silhouetted against the sky. At a glance, one would have expected a terrible deathroll. Yet most of the passengers survived. Upwards of a thousand men scrambled out, and dragged with them their jeeps and ten out of eighteen of the all-important antitank guns.

The general's jeep was stuck in the wreck of his glider, and rather than wait, he set off for his headquarters in Ranville on foot.* As soon as he was established, reports began to come in of tremendous casualties among the parachutists. They seemed alarming, but Gale remained unmoved. He knew that the immediate aftermath of a big night drop would seem chaotic, and he was convinced, through his own long experience, that casualty reports on the battlefield were always twice as high as they should be. And besides, he knew his own troops, and firmly believed they would carry out their missions whatever their losses had been.

The night passed without any news of the demolition of the five bridges on the River Dives, by which the division's flank was to be protected. Blowing bridges is work for engineers, and detachments of Royal Engineers had dropped to do it. By the time the general landed, several small isolated parties were out to the eastward; and they were justifying his faith by tackling jobs which he had allotted to much larger, more powerful units. One troop of the engineers, assigned to destroy a road bridge in the village of Robehomme, had fallen mostly in the marshes, and one of their aircraft had taken such vigorous evasive action that the men in it were thrown flat on the floor and jumped in a line which was over two miles long. The survivors of this troop struggled through to their bridge after seven hours in the marshes; but they found it had already been blown by a solitary sergeant who had happened to drop very near it and had borrowed explosives from some Canadians who had also come down there by mistake.

The most important of the bridges, and the farthest away, was the one where the main road from Caen to Rouen and Le Havre crosses the river, just beyond the small town of Troarn. This bridge was four miles outside the area which the division intended to hold. It was planned that a troop of engineers under Maj. J. C. A. Roseveare, protected by infantry, should dash for this bridge while the Germans were still confused. They were to carry their explosives in jeeps with trailers, which were to land in gliders. But this plan also went astray.

The troop dropped on time, at 1:50; but when Roseveare came to earth he could not see any landmarks which he knew. It seemed to him, as he stood in the dark in a field which he could not recognize, that aircraft were coming in from every

*In the height of the battle which followed, supply headquarters in England are said to have received an urgent request for a horse.

direction and dropping parachutists from every unit in the division. Some gliders were landing nearby, but not the gliders which were carrying his jeeps. A mile away to the southwest there were sounds of fighting, and he guessed rightly that the last men out of each of his aircraft were already involved with the Germans.

However, he rallied what men he could, and they collected all the equipment they could find. At length, he had six officers and about forty other ranks; but of the protecting infantry there were only twenty men and no officers at all. Between them, they gathered up plenty of explosive, but there was nothing to carry it in except carts, hauled by hand.

This rather forlorn and yet determined party set off about half past two, under mortar and machine-gun fire, to haul the handcarts up a steep hill in one of the winding Norman lanes. Many of them were already limping from injuries of the drop. Before long, they came to a crossroads with a signpost which confirmed what some had already come to suspect: they had dropped two miles too far north, and the Troarn bridge was seven miles away. There was very little hope of hauling the carts so far before dawn, and no hope at all, of course, of hauling them through the town in daylight.

In this unpromising situation, a motor was heard approaching, and a jeep with a trailer appeared from the darkness. It was not an RE jeep, it belonged to the Royal Army Medical Corps, and it was full of medical stores; but if the RAMC men had wanted to argue, they would probably not have had much chance. They surrendered their jeep, and the engineers turned out the medical stores in a timber yard, and loaded it with explosives. By then, it was four o'clock: just over an hour to dawn, and five miles still to Troarn. There was no time to think about anyone on foot. Roseveare dispatched the greater part of his force across country to another nearer bridge. He himself took the wheel of the jeep, and piled on the jeep and trailer one officer and seven other men. Including them, the load was a ton and a quarter. They drove off alone down the lane, into country where no British troops had landed.

Their first encounter was at a level crossing. The gates were open, but there was a barbed wire barrier across the road, and Roseveare drove into it before he saw it. A German sentry fired a single shot and ran away. The jeep was so tangled in wire that it took twenty minutes work to cut it free: a tense twenty minutes, for it had to be assumed that the sentry had gone to call a guard. Clear of the obstacle, they reached the main road on the edge of the town, and Roseveare sent two scouts ahead. As the scouts reached the crossroad, a German soldier rode past it on a bicycle. They pulled the unlucky man off his bicycle, and because he began to shout they killed him; but they foolishly did it with a Sten gun and so gave the alert to the town.

Bren Gun

Stealth was useless after that; Roseveare stepped on the gas and they went into town at full speed; but the overloaded jeep and trailer would only do about thirty-five miles an hour, and it seemed to be crawling. Soon they were under fire from the houses. One man by then had dropped off somewhere and been left behind. The remaining seven passengers all fired back with Sten guns and a Bren. At a bend in the road they saw the long, wide, straight main street of the town stretched out for a mile before them, downhill towards the bridge. There the firing was intense. Every doorway seemed to be hiding a German with some sort of gun; a cone of tracer came up the street towards them. Roseveare drove on, with his foot hard down on the floorboards. The overloaded jeep ground slowly forward. The passengers blazed away in all directions. It was the hill which saved the situation. On the downward grade, the jeep picked up speed, went faster and faster, swerved from side to side of the road as the trailer swayed behind, and tore out of the town and down to the river valley pursued by shots of a heavy machine gun. They came to the bridge, and found it had not been guarded. A man, who had acted as rear gunner with the Bren, had disappeared; none of them knew if he had been shot, or had lost his balance and fallen off the trailer. They unloaded their charges, and five minutes later the job was done and the center span of the bridge had dropped in the river. They drove the jeep up a side track as far as it would go and then ditched it, just as the sun was rising; and by wading through bogs and swimming over creeks, they reached the airborne perimeter again that afternoon.

By dawn, in spite of the scattered drop, the division had achieved every one of its immediate objectives. All the five bridges on the Dives were blown up. The canal and Orne River bridges, intact, were in Howard's hands, and parachutists were approaching to relieve him. The Merville battery would never fire again. The territory which the plan demanded was all under control, although there were plenty of Germans still at large inside it; and in the south, facing Caen, a tenuous line of antitank defenses was in position. It was a fine feat of arms.

Not all this news had yet reached Gale's headquarters. Even if it had, it was still too soon for him to congratulate himself or his commanders. The ground which was won still had to be defended until the seaborne forces were ashore. For the moment, the Germans were showing no signs of anything but confusion, but a counterattack was sure to come.

The achievement had not been cheap in terms of suffering; nobody had expected that it would be. Men were still creeping lost through the hedgerows and forests, or lying alone in pain. Many who had started the night in hope and vigor had already watched their own death approaching and surrendered to it. But at dawn the living heard a sound which encouraged them; beyond the sound of aircraft and bombs and small guns close at hand, an even deeper thunder from the north which shook the earth. On the canal bridge, one of Howard's corporals paused and listened. "Hear that, sir?" he said. "That's the navy."

Before long, the enormous naval shells were passing overhead, ranging on targets ten miles inland. One could hear them rumbling across the sky from north to south. The corporal, hearing this extraordinary and distinctive noise for the first time, looked up as if he hoped to see the shells. "Cor," he said, "what next? They're firing jeeps."

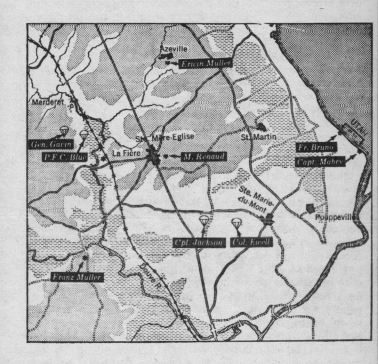

PART THREE

THE
AMERICAN
AIR DROP

Fifty miles to the west of the scene of these events, in the peninsula of Cherbourg, the German 709th Infantry Division had been waiting for a year, scattered in farms and villages along thirty miles of the Channel coast and in the countryside behind it. It was a force without much pride or much cohesion. It had been formed eighteen months before, with a core of German veterans from the Russian front and a large proportion of more or less unwilling conscripts. Most of its men were too young or too old or too unhealthy to fight on more active fronts. Its average age was thirty-six. Some of its private soldiers were Germans who had been living abroad when the war began, in France, Holland, Belgium, Denmark and other countries which since had been overrun. They had been dragged into the German army when the authorities caught up with them. There were also Poles and Russians who had fought for Russia and been captured and agreed to fight for Germany. Most of these were merely ignorant men dazed by events, who hardly knew one authority from another and would have fought dumbly for anyone in power over them. Others, captured at the height of the German successes in Russia, had declared themselves anticommunists, but as the Germans retreated, their anticommunist zeal had quickly cooled, and now they were rated officially as unreliable. In short, the 709th Division was a third-rate fighting unit, far from typical of the German army. But the German army, defending Hitler's vast perimeter, and weakened by its losses in Russia and Africa, was stretched too far and was forced to use motley divisions like this to man the static defenses of the Atlantic Wall.

The division had been where it was for much too long. It grumbled at boredom and bullying and apparently useless chores, as all soldiers of all armies grumble from time to time; but it grumbled with a venom seldom known in American or British armies, because it was not allowed to grumble; grumbling, in itself, could be called disloyalty. It was divided from top to bottom by an uncrossable rift: on one side, the men who still believed in the Nazi ideals and in Hitler as a leader, and on the other, those who had never believed, or had lost their Nazi faith; on one side, keen soldiers still ready to die for Germany, and on the other, the men who thought the war was lost already or should never have been started, and were only interested in coming out of it alive. Neither side trusted the other. The believers spied on the doubters, and the doubters were afraid. Newcomers to the division were treated with care and suspicion till they made their opinions known.

The whole division knew that invasion was coming, and knew there was a chance it might come on their stretch of the coast. Probably very few of them thought they could stop it if it came, with the weapons and organization they possessed. They were given pep-talks by their brigade commanders, aimed not at increasing their faith in themselves, but at persuading them that they could count on good support. They were told that the coastal artillery batteries were powerful enough to control the whole shore, and that secret weapons existed which would not be used unless an invasion came, but then would destroy it before it reached the land. Some of them—but only some—believed this.

These unhappy men, divided against each other, far from their homes in an alien land among resentful people, were scattered as usual in their posts and billets on the night of the fifth of June, with no suspicion that their doom was already approaching; for nobody had warned them.

About midnight an air-raid alert was sounded in their district. That was nothing unusual. There had been one already, earlier in the evening, which had only lasted for half an hour; and indeed there had not been many nights in the past few weeks without a warning. It was merely a nuisance. But in one section of an infantry platoon, stationed on a farm southeast of the town of Montebourg, the alert was almost welcome, because it put an end to an argument which was becoming dangerous. The argument may not have been typical, but it was symptomatic.

One of the antagonists was a private called Friedrich Busch, who had been a schoolmaster in Dresden. He was in a mood of desperate depression that night, and rashly said that he was fed up with soldiering for a cause he had never believed in, and wanted nothing in the world except to go home to his wife and baby. He was overheard by an NCO, who told him that the only thing he was fit for, and the only thing he could do for Germany was to get himself killed as soon as any fighting started. The argument grew angry, and Busch's friends were afraid he was heading for arrest and a charge of sedition. One of the men who listened anxiously was a German called Erwin Müller. His wife was Danish, and he had lived in Denmark for twenty years and thought of himself as a Dane; but he had never thought of applying for Danish citizenship until it was too late. So after Germany invaded Denmark, he was called up for the German army; and he went quietly, for fear of getting his wife and children and his parents in Germany into trouble.

Müller wholeheartedly agreed with Friedrich Busch, but he thought it was foolish to say so. When he left home, he had promised his wife he would come back to her alive, and fulfilling that promise was the only thing he really cared about. Long before, he had made up his mind what to do: to keep out of trouble and to hide his own thoughts, except from the friends he could trust. If it ever came to fighting, he intended to fight, if that was the only way to save his own life, but to let himself be captured if that seemed a better chance. He expected to fight, because he expected to find himself up against paratroops, and the division had been told that American and British paratroops never took prisoners. But he did not care in the least about fighting for Germany. There was Jewish blood in his family, and under the Nazis his father, still living in Germany, had led a difficult and precarious life.

When the second alert sounded, Müller felt relieved for the sake of Busch. As the section turned out for its air-raid posts, he heard Busch fling a parting shot at the NCO. "I

hope I'll see you in a battle," he said. "I wonder which of us
will be the first to get himself killed."

Sheltering in their trenches and bunkers, the platoon
began to wonder whether something more than an ordinary
air raid might be brewing, because there seemed to be so
many aircraft overhead, and because some of them were
showing lights. Soon after midnight, an order was passed
round to fall in on the road and march to a village called
Azeville. Few of them had ever been to Azeville, although it
was their battalion headquarters. The order surprised them,
but it also reassured them. On exercises in the past, they had
always carried blank ammunition in their rifles and the pouches
of their equipment; their live ammunition was stowed in their
haversacks. They had always supposed they would know the
real thing when it came because they would get the order to
load live rounds. But nobody gave them the order that night,
so they set out on their march with blanks still in their rifles,
believing the whole thing was another boring and ill-timed
exercise. The first shock and disillusionment came on the
outskirts of Azeville. They were shot at from the churchyard
in the middle of the village, and the ammunition was
unquestionably live.

The whole platoon dropped into ditches beside the road,
and without waiting for orders they delved in their haversacks
and reloaded their pouches and guns; and then, led on by
their NCOs, they crept forward by devious routes to surround
the churchyard. An eerie battle of hide and seek began
against the unknown enemy hidden among the gravestones.
Men with their nerves on edge fired at any shadow which
seemed to move or to have a human shape, and sometimes,
the shadows returned their fire. Very slowly, from grave to
grave, the Germans crawled in towards the church. As they
closed their ranks, dark figures dashed out between them and
escaped, and the firing died away; but by the church porch a
man was lying dead; and Müller, looking down at him,
recognized the equipment of an American parachutist and
knew the day had come.

Events moved swiftly in Azeville after that, towards a dawn
which Müller was to remember with horror all his life. The
platoon was posted round the village to defend it, under the
disadvantage that the men had never seen the place in
daylight and did not know their way about it. They wondered,
but never discovered, what had happened to the headquarters

platoon which should have been billeted there. Müller and another man were placed at a garden gate in a hedge and told to keep watch; and peering nervously over that gate, entirely ignorant of what they might expect, they witnessed a spectacle which they had never even imagined, for all of a sudden the whole night sky to the south and west was filled with uncountable parachutes.

Müller and his companion stood there and watched them, with awe and with a certain admiration for an army and air force which could launch an attack of such a majestic size. They believed from the moment they saw it that they were beaten, for the force and efficiency which they knew must lie behind it was far beyond anything they had ever experienced in their own inferior division. Some of the parachutists drifting down were within easy rifle shot, but the two Germans, inexperienced as they were in total war, were held spellbound by an instinctive feeling that it was unfair to shoot a man on a parachute. So they simply watched them come to earth. Only one of the parachutes came down in the village itself. That one was carrying not a man but a large container with a red light on it. Some of the Germans gathered it in and opened it, and found it was full of delicious things to eat.

It was not very long before the first Americans entered the village. Probably this was not a planned attack, but merely a group of men on their way to their rendezvous. They got into a farmyard opposite Müller's garden gate, and his section was sent to clear them out again. The NCO went first, through an archway into the yard, and nothing happened. Friedrich Busch went second, and a single shot was fired and killed him instantly.

Müller was shocked by the first death he had ever seen in battle; the more so when he remembered what Busch had said about his wife and baby. It was the first of a series of terrible events of that night in Azeville which haunted his mind for years afterwards as nightmare memories. They were memories of skirmishes in the dark; of a white-faced man who dashed through the village shouting that all his section had been killed, of the writhing body of a friend of his, not yet quite dead, being pushed down the road on a handcart by somebody looking in vain for a casualty clearing station; of a man, American or German, who screamed and screamed in an orchard not far away; of a rumor that Americans were shooting from the church, and of searching the church, and of a priest who watched him in silence as he committed this sacrilege; and of confusion and moments of paralyzing fear and the belief that nobody in command knew what was happening. The fighting in this insignificant village went on till dawn; and Müller fought as best he could all through the night, because there seemed to be no alternative.

By dawn his platoon was cut off and the village seemed to be surrounded. They had no radio, and the telephone had gone dead. The platoon commander told the sergeant to take a patrol to try to get through to brigade headquarters and ask for orders; and the sergeant picked Müller and a couple of younger men. There was an angry argument, because the platoon commander told them to go on bicycles and the sergeant told him that that was lunacy—as it certainly was—in daylight. But soon after dawn the four men stole out of the village on foot across the fields. As they crept along beside a hedge out in the no man's land of the open countryside, they had a most strange encounter. They heard voices, and saw two American soldiers in a meadow. Leaving the two young men to cover them, Müller and the sergeant crawled down a ditch until only the thickness of the hedge divided them from the Americans, who seemed preoccupied. Looking through the branches, Müller was astonished to see that one of the parachutists had a large painting of a pin-up girl on the back of his tunic, and the other had the words SEE YOU IN PARIS on the back of his. Müller, who had learned to speak English in Denmark, poked his rifle through the hedge and said "Hullo." At this surprising greeting, the Americans wheeled round. "Hands up," Müller said; and he and the sergeant broke through the hedge, and then saw a third American, lying badly wounded.

"I'm sorry, but we must search you," Müller said.

"O.K., if you say so," the younger of the two Americans answered; and as Müller began to go through his pockets he added: "But don't take the picture of my girl."

"I take nothing but your weapons," Müller said.

The collection of stuff which he found in their pockets surprised him again. It included chocolate, silk stockings and elegant lingerie. "What's this for?" he demanded, rather shocked at this flippant equipment.

"That's for the little girls in Paris," the prisoner said. "And the candy's for me. Have some? Say, how far is it to Paris, fella?"

"I don't know, I've never been there," Müller said, and accepted the chocolate.

"Don't eat it, it might be poisoned," one of the young Germans shouted.

"What does he say?" the American asked, and Müller told him.

The American laughed. "It's not poisoned," he said; and their eyes met, and Müller felt a bond with this casual, self-confident young man, who seemed to take war so lightly, as if they shared decency and sanity and could laugh together at mad suspicions and enmities. He ate the chocolate.

When the second of the prisoners was disarmed, Müller turned his attention to the man who was lying wounded. He was very badly hurt, and it was only a minute or two before he died.

"I'm sorry," Müller said; and he said it sincerely, for the body of this enemy lying there seemed as pathetic to him as the body of Friedrich Busch.

The young American knelt down and closed the dead man's eyes and crossed his arms on his chest; and then he began to say the Lord's prayer. Müller and the other American joined in; and then the sergeant and the two young German soldiers, recognizing the rhythm of the words, took up the prayer in German, and the six men in their two languages prayed together, grouped round the man who had died.

Müller and his sergeant got their prisoners back to the village in the end, and handed them over to their platoon commander. Probably they escaped very soon. Müller himself was taken prisoner after a week of wandering, and so, years later, he returned to his wife alive.

Suspended from one of the multitude of parachutes, which Müller had watched with such awe through the garden gate, was a farmer's boy from North Carolina, and his name was James R. Blue. Blue looked down, as they had taught him, while he dropped, and tried to make the countryside fit his recollection of the map of the dropping zone; but nothing fitted. Below him he could see tracers from machine guns, not aimed upwards at him but criss-crossed along the ground. To one side was a darker patch of land without any visible signs of battle, and he was glad to find he was drifting towards it. He manipulated his parachute as well as he could to hit this quiet area, and as the ground came up to him he got ready for the bump.

It was not a bump, it was a splash—a psychological more than a physical shock. Expecting the solid earth, he fell into three feet of water. It closed over his head and in panic—not knowing what had happened, thinking the water was deep— he struggled and lashed out with his arms and legs, felt the muddy bottom and came floundering to the surface. Before he found his balance, his parachute dragged him over backwards and he went under again, weighed down by his seventy pounds of equipment, fumbling at the buckles of his harness.

Blue was a man of exceptional strength; and the bottom of the marsh where he fell was hard enough to stand on. Without those two advantages, he would have drowned as so many Americans and British drowned that morning. Even with them, he was half dead when he got clear of his harness and stood up, waist deep in the stinking soupy water. He was sick from the water he had swallowed, and trembling from the shock. He peered round at the empty menacing countryside and felt quite lost and desperately lonely. And then he heard a familiar angry voice which filled the night with good rich American curses, the voice of a buddy of his who had jumped just before him.

"Hi there," Blue shouted when the other man paused for breath.

"Is that you, Blue?" the voice said in the night. "I've lost my goddamn helmet."

The journey from the Carolina farm to the marsh in Normandy had started when Blue was twenty-one, and had taken two years. It was quite a straightforward journey which he had made of his own free choice; and he had never regretted his choice, except perhaps in those seconds when he thought he was drowning.

He had volunteered as a parachutist because Gen. William C. Lee, the outstanding pioneer of American airborne forces, was a native of North Carolina like himself, and had been quite a near neighbor of his family in the small town of Dunn. The general had been the hero of his boyhood; and in a slightly more grown-up way, he still was.

Army life suited Blue very well, and he enjoyed it. It came easily to him, because he had been brought up to hard work; and because he was an amiable, kind-hearted, friendly young man who nevertheless enjoyed a good fight from time to time; and because he was six feet three and invariably won a fight once it had started. He had a reputation of making a good friend or a dangerous enemy, which is a useful reputation to have in any army.

Blue had a good measure of that unexpected humility and capacity for wonder and admiration which the British—perhaps because if flatters them—find so endearing in Americans whenever it comes to the surface. He always knew and sometimes said that in spite of being a private first class, he was still just a farm boy inside. Let loose on a pay day in Nottingham or Leicester, he was amazed at the luck which had brought him on a free trip to Europe—a thing he had never dreamed of as a boy—and had put money in his pocket and extended his horizon so far beyond the streets of Dunn and the fields of Carolina. He was ready to appreciate everything he saw, from quaint pubs to quaint policemen. It was inevitable that he should fall in love with an English girl, and perhaps equally inevitable that the love should not outlast the war. His three months in England had been a riot of new experience and excitement. He had won in fights, and won at cards, and won in love, and he went to Normandy in just the same spirit, expecting still to carry all before him.

This supreme self-confidence, for one reason or another, was typical of the American airborne forces. Perhaps it had its roots in a national characteristic, but it was also cultivated in the men by their senior officers. It is the policy of all successful armies to assure their men that they are the finest soldiers in the world. The German soldiers had always been told it, and so had the British in a less flamboyant way. But in the Americans, the belief in their own prowess sometimes took novel forms and induced the light-hearted attitude to war which had shocked Erwin Müller. The more callow youngsters among them wore slogans on their backs, or warpaint on their faces, or shaved their heads except for a scalplock, like red Indians; or relished daredevil names for their units, believing for example that the Germans often referred to American parachutists with awe as the Devils in Baggy Pants. This exuberance shocked plenty of people in Europe besides Erwin Müller, but it certainly did some good. For one thing, it provided the French with a welcome contrast to the grim formality of the German army. The American forces looked like liberators.

Blue himself, with a majority of the parachutists, was rather embarrassed by these eccentric signs of courage, because they offended his pride in his regiment, and because he suspected that the braver a man is, the less he needs to say so. All the same, as he flew the Channel, he was perfectly certain his outfit was on its way to lick hell out of the Germans. Perhaps, through no fault of his own, he was almost too certain; for in one respect, American confidence had been carried a little too far. Some senior officers, unnecessarily trying to encourage men who had plenty of native courage, had made them believe the invasion would be easy. Some men, new to battle, suffered for this when they found themselves face to face with horrors they had never been led to expect. But with that exception, self-confidence carried the Americans into France with an irresistible momentum.

As soon as Blue heard his friend's voice, his moment of panic and loneliness ended, and he was himself again. The two men waded toward each other, sloshing through the mud. The level surface of water covered with weeds stretched as far as they could see in all directions, and there was nothing to show the way to the nearest dry land. But tracer bullets were still flying about to the westward. Neither of the two, with a rifle full of water, was in any condition to fight; so they waded away from the shooting, hoping to find somewhere to dry their equipment, if not themselves, before they joined the battle. Blue regretted this afterwards, because he heard that the first fight going on just behind them had been led by Brigadier General James A. Gavin, the assistant commander of the 82nd Division, a man whom Blue admired next only to General Lee.*

General Gavin, who at that moment was leading only a few dozen riflemen, was the very model of the young intelligent officer to whom the American army often successfully entrusts its high command. He was thirty-six. His appearance was youthful, almost boyish, and his manner was the reverse of the pompousness which sometimes afflicts high officers; and he had a way of taking a military problem to pieces and deducing its answer, and expressing it so perfectly clearly that

*For General Gavin's own account of the invasion read the Bantam edition of ON TO BERLIN.

his listeners all felt they were strategists. He had started his army career as a private; soon after the invasion, at the age of thirty-seven, he was promoted to major general. This extraordinary rise in rank was a measure of his energy and brains, and of the passionate interest and belief in airborne warfare which he had held since its earliest days under Lee.

Gavin had jumped with the 82nd Division in Sicily, and since then he had worked with COSSAC as an airborne adviser on the plans for the Normandy invasion. This must have been a frustrating task, because the plans for the use of American airborne forces in Normandy had often been changed. At one period of the planning, there was talk of a landing near Paris. At another, the parachutists were to land all along the invasion beaches, and attack the shore defenses from behind. Then they were assigned to capture Bayeux, and occupy a river valley at the back of Omaha Beach. In March, in a plan which seemed at last to be final, two airborne divisions were employed, the 101st to land behind Utah Beach, on the east coast of the Cherbourg peninsula, and the 82nd to land near the west coast, so that between them they could cut the peninsula and isolate Cherbourg. But even this plan, after the intervening months of detailed work, was abandoned just over a week before the invasion started.

These changes, hard though they were for the airborne commanders, were nobody's fault. The eastern end of the invasion area, all through the planning, had been fixed at Caen and the River Orne; but the western end was limited by the forces which were available. When Eisenhower was appointed in January and supported Montgomery's demand for more forces, the extra forces were used to extend the invasion area to the west, into the Cherbourg peninsula. Thus the objectives for the British airborne troops were fixed from an early stage, but those for the Americans were moved as the plans expanded.

However, the final change of plans was caused by the Germans. For a long time, two divisions of Germans had garrisoned the countryside of the Cherbourg peninsula. One was Erwin Müller's, and the other was also a static division of something less than first-class quality. But during May, French railwaymen reported through their underground that a new and better division was moving into the district of St. Sauveure-le-Vicomte; and this was the very area where the 82nd was to drop. The German move was not due to any leakage of Allied plans, it was simply a matter of strengthening an area which was more weakly held than most; but the 82nd, in the face of this new opposition, might easily have been cut off and tied down in self-defense. So on May 27th, at a meeting of the American high command in Bristol, a new plan was devised: to drop both airborne divisions close to Utah Beach.

One result of these changes was that the American airborne commanders never had enough time to study and rehearse their attacks on specific targets. There was no chance of the elaborate tactical training which the British had leisure to apply to the Merville battery and the Caen Canal bridge. By comparison, the American airborne attacks were improvised, through necessity; and although the airborne divisions fulfilled their general role of protecting the landing on Utah, their successes, with one exception, were not so quick or so spectacular.

The ultimate last-minute plan, like the British plan, was based upon rivers and floods, and the bridges which crossed them. The floods which the Germans had made in the Cherbourg peninsula were even more extensive than those in the British zone. Behind the sand dunes on the coast, they had flooded a long strip of low-lying meadows and tidal marshes roughly a mile wide. These were crossed by half a dozen causeways; and the capture of these causeways was essential to get the seaborne forces off the beach. To the south, and about seven miles inland, they were also known to have flooded the valley of the River Douve. The seven-mile gap between the two belts of floods was the rich, lush pastureland which is typical of Normandy, a maze of tiny fields, thick hedges and winding lanes; and here the majority of the parachutists were to drop. The 101st Division was to capture the inland ends of the causeways which led from the beach; to capture or destroy the bridges and a lock on the River Douve, and so protect the southward flank of the area; and to form a defensive line towards the north. The 82nd Division was to drop on both sides of the River Merderet, a small tributary of the Douve. It was to capture the town of Sainte-Mère-Église, and so cut the main road and railway from Carentan to Cherbourg; and to capture intact two bridges across the Merderet and a wide area beyond it, which could be used by the seaborne forces in a westward drive to cut the peninsula itself. It was this latter force of paratroops which General Gavin commanded during the night of the landing until his divisional commander, Major General Ridgway, had built up a headquarters staff.

In the space of two minutes before he jumped, Gavin had to adjust his mind to yet another sudden drastic change in the prospects and plans of the assault. Crossing the Channel, absorbed in the kind of problems which concern a high commander about to give battle, he had glanced back in the clear moonlight and had seen the twenty aircraft which were flying in close formation with his own, and beyond them, as far as the eye could reach, the stream of other formations which carried his seven thousand men. All was well. The host of aircraft passed through the Channel Islands, where ineffective fire came up from Guernsey and Jersey; and it reached the mainland coast, on the west side of the peninsula, and turned east to fly across it. The antiaircraft fire was heavier there, but that had been expected. Gavin watched it with detached interest from the open door of his aircraft, and guessed that one dense array of flashes was the town of Barneville, where a concentration of guns had been reported.

But suddenly the view was blotted out. One minute beyond the coast, the aircraft flew into cloud, so thick that Gavin could not see the wing tips. He thought of the chances of dropping blind. In seven minutes and thirty seconds, they ought to be over the drop zone. In eleven minutes, they would be over the sea again, on the other side of the peninsula. But before he had come to terms with that idea, the aircraft was in the clear again. He looked down and ahead, and saw with surprise a wide gleaming sheet of water. By its size, he thought it could only be the flooded valley of the Douve, but it seemed to run from north to south, instead of from east to west, and he could not recognize it or find his bearings. And then he looked astern, and saw something worse. The tight formation of planes had disappeared. In the few seconds while he watched, two stragglers came out of the cloud bank, wide on either side; and that was all. At that crucial moment, he did not know where he was, or what had become of his troops. The green light flashed. For three more seconds, he searched the ground for a landmark; and seeing none, he jumped.

He landed unhurt in an orchard full of cows, and looked up through the branches of apple trees at the empty sky which should have been full of parachutes. There was nobody to be seen on the ground, neither German nor American nor French. He started to walk to the eastward, to round up at least the twenty men who had dropped from his plane. That took longer than usual, because of the hedges, but he found most of them in the end; and the search brought him to the edge of the water he had seen before he jumped.

The water still puzzled him, and it was a couple of hours before he discovered where he was. He saw a flashing light on the far side of the water, and sent an officer to try to get across to find out who was there. The officer came back to report that he had waded for an hour, sometimes up to his neck, and had found a railway embankment. That identified the place. There was only one railway embankment in the district, and that was in the Merderet Valley just north of Sainte-Mère-Église. The water must be the Merderet; and yet the Merderet had appeared on all the aerial photographs as a narrow winding brook.

Gavin was very surprised that the ample floods which he saw before him had never been spotted by air reconnaissance; and this is still one of the many minor mysteries of the invasion. The explanation seemed to be that grass and weeds had grown up through the water and lay in a mat on the surface, so that most of the valley looked solid. From the air, it looked solid to Blue, but it looked liquid to Gavin, who perhaps had chanced to see the direct reflection of the moonlight. But whatever the explanation, the important facts, as Gavin soon discovered, were that the bank of cloud and the antiaircraft fire had broken up the close formations of planes, and that most of the regiment which should have dropped with him had overshot its dropping zone by a few seconds, and had fallen with its equipment in the water. Many of the men were able to save themselves, like Blue; but it was much more difficult to salvage the equipment.

During the night, 150 men from different units attached themselves to Gavin. Many were soaking wet, some injured, and a few wounded in skirmishes with a German patrol which was approaching. Not one of them had a weapon heavier than a carbine or a rifle. Gavin assembled all comers in a meadow beside the water, placed some along the hedges for defense, and set the others to search the flood waters for equipment— especially for any weapon which could be used against a tank. The German patrol closed in, and began to attack. For the moment, the General was acting as a company commander.

M1 Rifle

*   *   *

Blue and his friend staggered on through the marsh till they also saw the railway embankment ahead, and they dragged themselves up it while water poured out of their pockets and the legs of their uniforms. On top, by the railway track, were a dozen sodden men from different regiments, under the command of a lieutenant. Blue had never seen any of them before, but he was glad of their company; and at dawn he followed them southwards, stumbling across railway ties, still very wet but still as full of confidence as ever, sadly regarding with his farmer's eyes the waste of good land beneath the floods on both sides of the railway. A mile or two down the track, they came to dry land, and then to a bridge where the railway was crossed by a lane. This was the road from Sainte-Mère-Église to the river bridge at the hamlet of La Fière, the capture of which was one of the principal aims of the division.

A good many other men had collected near the road. The lieutenant handed over his dozen to a captain; and then, about forty strong, in open order in both the hedges of the lane, a party began to advance towards the bridge, and Blue went with them. The party had one bazooka and one machine gun, which brought up the rear. At last, Blue thought, things were getting interesting. This was what he had come for.

Then he saw his first German. A motorcycle and sidecar came up from the bridge, and the rider did not seem to see the parachutists before it was too late to stop. He came on, and succeeded in passing all forty riflemen at point blank range, because none of them could fire without a risk of hitting their friends on the opposite side of the road. He nearly got through with his life, but not quite. The machine gunner shot him in the back as he rode away towards Sainte-Mère-Église, and the motorbike crashed into the hedge. It was terribly easy.

A hundred yards farther on, the party was shot at from a group of farm buildings just before the bridge, and a short sharp fight developed—the first for Blue, and for most of the men who were with him. The officers told them not to use the bazooka, because they only had a few rounds for it; but they fired at the windows with their rifles and machine gun, and soon a white flag appeared. A paratroop lieutenant walked up to the door of the farmhouse and pushed it open, and a single shot was fired from inside it. He ran back holding his ear, for the bullet had gone through the lobe of it, and he angrily called for the bazooka, after all. Two rounds were fired through the downstairs windows. They exploded inside and set the house on fire. In a minute or two, a German officer and fifteen men came out with their hands up.

Blue was elated with this quick and easy victory; so much so that he believed the bridge was won and the war as good as over. But then his high spirits were dashed. Two elderly Frenchmen slowly hobbled out from the back of the burning house, and one of them was pushing a wheelbarrow; in the wheelbarrow was a very very old woman.

That glimpse of another aspect of war went straight to Blue's heart, and hurt him deeply. She looked just like an old country woman from Carolina. He suddenly pictured this happening in a farmhouse at home, and for a moment it made him ashamed of the brave intentions and the military pride he had brought with him to France. What sort of liberators must they think we are? he wondered. Surely somebody should tell the old people they were sorry they had set their house on fire? But instead, the order came to cross the bridge.

Quite a force of parachutists walked unmolested over the bridge and a causeway four hundred yards long which crossed the marsh beyond it. Most of them spread out and vanished on the other side, and Blue was left to look after the bridge with three or four officers and half a dozen men. The position did not worry him; like any good private, he expected somebody else to do the worrying. He sat in what little sun there was, to get dry.

A German armored counterattack caught them with overwhelming strength. Blue saw the tanks come down the lane, but then his awareness of what was happening shrank to a confused impression of hellish noise and violence and a feeling of utter frustration as he pressed himself into the sweet-smelling grass by the side of the lane, because he had no weapon to hit back with. The man with the bazooka did some damage but not enough and Blue heard an officer shout "Every man on his own." He ran crouching towards the tall reeds in the marsh beside the causeway and plunged in and began for the second time to wade through the flood, keeping his head down among the reeds while tanks came roaring along the causeway close behind him. He reached the abutment of the bridge. The river was deeper there. He wondered whether to swim, but decided to try the bridge. He lay on the steep slope of the abutment while some of the weight of water drained out of his clothes. Somebody shouted "Run soldier!" and he got up and ran like a snipe across the bridge, the bullets whipping past him, and fell down gasping on the other side, back where he had started just over an hour before. The farm was still burning. The three old French people had gone, and Blue never saw them again. But he never forgot them, any more than he forgot his first victory, or his first defeat.

Blue as a private never knew what had gone wrong; but just about the time when the bridge was lost, General Gavin arrived there with his 150 men, and began to sort out the dangerous situation.

Gavin had already fought a long defensive action while half of his men searched the floods for the lost equipment. By dawn, not a single antitank weapon had been found. Gavin was impatient to reach the bridge. He had the choice of fighting his way, ill-armed, down the western bank of the river, or crossing the flood and marching down the railway, where he had heard that his other regiments were in reasonably good shape. He decided to cross; and in the early morning light, leaving their injured and wounded, his body of miscellaneous men began to wade under fire from German snipers. Most of them made the crossing; but delayed by the unsuccessful search, they were too late to save the bridge.

Like General Gale fifty miles away on the British zone, General Gavin was not perturbed by the apparent chaos of the drop; he knew his men would get on with the job wherever they happened to be. But the loss of the bridge was more serious, because it split his division in two and left parts of two regiments to fight without hope of reinforcements on the other side of the river valley. It had been lost through a misunderstanding. The main body of troops who had crossed it were men who had dropped on the wrong side of the river and crossed over simply to get to the other side where they ought to have been. They thought others behind them were following to defend it, but nobody came, except the dozen with Blue. Gavin, however, was not concerned to find out what had happened; he set himself to try to force a second crossing, not only at La Fière but also at another bridge a little further south, and at an ancient ford. But without the

support of any heavy weapons, the parachutists could not
shift the Germans, and nobody crossed the river again till
seaborne tanks arived there four days later.

But although they could not take the bridge, they did
achieve something almost as important; they stopped the
Germans crossing it, and so held the German tanks not only
away from the beach, but also away from the town of Sainte-
Mère-Église, a mile behind the bridge, where another of
Gavin's regiments, in the very early morning, had won an
unqualified victory.

Sainte-Mère-Église is a little market town of gray stone
houses which stood on each side of the main road from Cherbourg to the south. It has relics of the time when Roman
legions marched up that road, and of William the Conqueror's armies; but for six or seven centuries it traded
humbly in farm implements and horses and cattle and
cheese, and had no military interest. Even on the night
when it suddenly formed the stage of high drama, its importance
was only fortuitous. It was the beach, the roads and the rivers
which were important. Sainte-Mère-Église just had the luck,
good or bad, to be there, at a crossroads on the map, in the
middle of the area of the airborne forces' drop, and so to win
the double-edged honor of being the first town in France
which the Allied forces planned to liberate.

For precisely four years, an enormous swastika flag had
flown from the flagstaff outside the town hall, and Sainte-
Mère-Église, patient and cynical, had watched the progress
of the German occupation. It remembered the early days in
1940 when the pick of the German army, proud and confident,
had marched up the road singing *Wir fahren gegen* England,"*
and promising that Britain in three weeks would be *kaput*.
These German soldiers compelled some grudging admiration
from the people who watched them pass; but even then, the
town's small boys had perfected a technique of making seasick
and drowning noises which ruined displays of military pomp;
and the town had witnessed the first tarnishing of German
pride when the invasion of England had had to be postponed.
Since then, the occupation of Sainte-Mère-Église had mirrored
the creeping defeat of the German army. Little by little, the
finer troops had disappeared to face their doom in Russia or

* We're sailing against England.

North Africa or Italy; old men and boys replaced them, men who were sick or partly disabled by wounds, and finally the dregs of the foreign conscripts.

In the meantime, the town submitted to the gloom of occupation: the nagging fear, the rising prices, scarcity, black markets, the occasional rumors of sudden tragedy. It never suffered acutely. Perhaps the worst of its hurts was humiliation; the thought that after all the centuries of good Norman husbandry, the present generation had surrendered to an upstart foreign power.

Through the BBC, Sainte-Mère-Église followed the news of the war and waited from season to season for its liberation. At first, it clutched at every hint that the invasion was coming, and so it often suffered disappointment. As early as the spring of 1943, the BBC told people to move from the coasts. A great spring offensive was expected. Churchill broadcast, and people understood him to mean that France would be invaded before the leaves fell in autumn. But the leaves fell, and no invasion came, and Sainte-Mère-Église found it hard to maintain its faith through another winter.

In March and April of 1944, there were signs of new German activity. Troops passed through the town at night, going north, using requisitioned horses and farm carts to carry their equipment. An antiaircraft battery moved into the town and a new battalion was stationed in the villages round about. Exercises were held continuously. These were the local results of the arrival of the new division which upset the airborne plan, and of Rommel's energy. In May, the Germans demanded the help of ablebodied Frenchmen in putting up their antiglider posts. Their demand was naïve. The quicker the job was done, they explained, the better it would be, because once it was finished the "Tommies"* could never land near Sainte-Mère-Église, and the town and countryside would be spared from destruction. The Frenchmen were astonished to learn that the Germans really thought the district might be invaded; for they themselves, by then, hardly believed that the British would ever invade, and were certain that if they did, they would go to the district of Calais, or else to Holland. Not even the increasing air bombardment of the coast in the first days of June made them change their

*This word for a British soldier, almost forgotten in Britain since World War I, is still in use in France.

opinion. The swastika flag had flown so long outside their town hall that people hardly dared to hope to see it hauled down again. But on June 5th, at an airfield in England, the commander of a parachute regiment showed his men an American flag, and told them it was the flag which the regiment had hoisted in Naples when it fell; and he promised them they would fly it in Sainte-Mère-Église before the morning.

The delicate task of representing the town in its relations with the Germans had fallen upon the mayor, Alexander Renaud. M. Renaud was proprietor of the chemist's shop in the square in the center of the town. Chemists usually know their townsmen well, and so do mayors; being both, M. Renaud knew almost everything there was to know about Sainte-Mère-Église. In his shop, behind his counter, intent on his prescriptions, with his glasses on his nose, he appeared such a gentle and scholarly person that no stranger would have suspected how shrewd or how tough he could be. But all through those four black years, he defended the rights of the townspeople, such as they were, and yet avoided provoking the Germans to violence; and that was no small achievement.

M. Renaud was a veteran of the great days of the French army. He was proud to have fought at Verdun. As an old soldier, he could still appreciate military standards of behavior, and found he could size up most of the German officers who followed each other as garrison commanders of his town. Most of them were only intent on carrying out their orders, were strictly correct in the demands they made on him, and never showed their feelings. A few were bullies, and a few were openly unhappy in the role of conqueror. The commanders of the two units, the infantry battalion and the antiaircraft battery, which were in the district in May, were of opposite types. The infantry commander was a swashbuckler who made the mistake of thinking the mayor was as meek as he sometimes looked. He tried to humiliate and frighten him; and when that only made him angry, he threatened him with instant execution if the "Tommies" landed. Perhaps the threat was empty, but Renaud was not at all sorry when the battalion moved away. Then only the antiaircraft unit was left in the town. Its commander was an elderly Austrian. It was said that before the war he had been the music critic of a newspaper in Vienna. If he was, it is easy to imagine why he seemed miserable, as he did, in his post at Sainte-Mère-Église. Gossip said that his only remaining interest was in wine. This man was in charge of the town on the night of the landing.

The night began with a house on fire on the opposite side of the square to the chemist's shop. M. Renaud had just gone to bed, uneasy in his mind, for he had spent the evening at an upstairs window, watching the flashes and flares of a tremendous air raid somewhere in the direction of the coast. He was roused by somebody banging on his front door; the fire brigade wanted all the men they could muster to help them by carrying water. He dressed quickly and put on his coat and hat, and leaving his wife to look after the children, he crossed the familiar square, beneath the chestnut and lime trees in front of the church. The house was blazing. Nobody knew how it had started. It might have been just an accident, but the sky was full of aircraft and it seemed more likely that something—not a bomb, but a flare perhaps—had fallen on the roof, which was well alight. The firemen in their bright brass helmets were trying to save the thatch of a barn nearby which was threatened by sparks, and volunteers were carrying water in canvas buckets from the pump in the cattle market. M. Renaud joined them. The flames lit up the belltower of the church, where German machine gunners, posted on the roof, were shooting aimlessly at the aircraft overhead, filling the sky with arches of tracer bullets. Other men of the antiaircraft unit, waiting the order to fire, watched the firemen from their positions in the square. The earth below the trees vibrated with the explosions of distant bombs.

Then above the sounds of war, the church bell rang. It continued to ring, urgently and quickly—the tocsin, the ancient signal of alarm. M. Renaud stopped on his way to the pump, with a new clutch at the heart as he asked himself what more disaster the clamor of the bell foretold. He instinctively looked up towards the tower, and so he saw what was coming; low over the rooftops and the trees, almost in silence, a host of aircraft sweeping across the town, their lights burning, their wings and bodies black against the moon; and then as the first of the waves of them receded, the giant confetti which drifted in their wake.

M. Renaud and the firemen stood amazed, neglecting the fire, unable to believe that the thing which they had thought about so long was really happening, and was happening in Sainte-Mère-Église itself. High up, the parachutes were seen in silhouette against the sky; as they fell, the men on them were also seen, in the light of the fire. The machine gunners

on the church tower and in the square saw them too and fired
lower. The watchers, horrified, saw the convulsion of a man
who was shot as he was falling. They saw a parachute which
draped an old tree; the parachutist began to climb down, the
machine-gunners saw him and left him swinging limply in his
harness. They also saw a man fall into the fire and crash
through the burning roof. Sparks spurted out, and the flames
blazed up afresh. More squadrons of planes were passing
over, the bell still ringing, shots cracking through the square.
The German soldiers ordered the Frenchmen indoors, and
M. Renaud, anxious for his wife and children, hurried home.
A German beneath the trees, pointing at the body of a
parachutist, shouted to him with satisfaction, "Tommies—all
kaput."

This fatuous optimism may have been shared, for the
moment, by other Germans in the square of Sainte-Mère-
Église, for the few parachutists who had the bad luck to drop
within the firelight presented easy targets. It was not the
intention, of course, to drop on the roofs of the town itself.
The men who did so were only stragglers from a whole
regiment which landed between the town and the river, and
this regiment had the most accurate drop of any parachute
unit that night. A thousand of its 2,200 men fell in the
dropping zone and assembled at once. Most of the rest were
not very far away, and came in before daylight. Within an
hour of dropping, the regiment had begun its first task of
clearing Sainte-Mère-Église and blocking the road to the
north and south of it.

The old soldier in M. Renaud made him sally forth before
long to see what was going on, and he happened to pass a
pond, which had once been the public laundry, in the nick of
time to seize the lines of a parachute and haul out a man who
had had a ducking there. But after that adventure, he spent
the rest of the night indoors with his wife and children,
listening and trying to interpret the sounds from the streets,
for the moon had set, and it was too dark to see anything
from the windows. The firing had died away, except for the
machine guns on the church. He heard cars and motorcycles
in the square, but saw no lights, and he guessed that the
antiaircraft battery was retreating. For almost an hour, from
two o'clock to three, there was a strange and ominous silence.
About three, he saw matches lit below the chestnut trees,
and the glow of cigarettes, and the light of a flashlamp, and

he and his family debated who was there, the Germans or the "Tommies." And at last, day began to break, and as the light penetrated below the trees, he was astonished to see that his square was occupied not by Germans or by "Tommies," but by men in the round helmets he had seen on American troops in German newspaper pictures. The people of Sainte-Mére-Église, through all their years of listening to the BBC, had never dreamed that their liberators, in the end, would be American.

Very soon after dawn, a parachute captain knocked on the door, introduced himself, and offered the mayor a piece of chewing gum. The new regime had started. The captain asked the way to the headquarters of the German commander of the town. M. Renaud escorted him there himself; but during the night, the Viennese music critic and all his men had gone. The swastika flag had gone too; the American flag from Naples flew instead.

So Sainte-Mère-Église received the honor of being the first town in France which was liberated; an honor which it proudly remembers still, especially at its annual fête on the sixth of June. But the honor was costly, and the price had still to be paid; for during the next two days, till tanks and reinforcements came through from Utah Beach, the Germans turned their batteries on the town and shelled it heavily; and many of M. Renaud's townspeople who had lived through the four dark years were killed in the first two days of the freedom for which they had hoped so long.

The capture of the town was the only specific objective which the American airborne troops achieved before dawn; they got off to a much slower start than the British. There were reasons for this. Through the changes of plan, their training had been shorter. Their drop, on the whole, was even more chaotically scattered; and their stretch of the Norman countryside was even more labyrinthine than the British. But quick tactical victories were not the only way to success. What did happen during the night, far out from such centers as Sainte-Mère-Église and the bridge at La Fière, away in the damp dark silent woods and meadows was equally important; it was a gigantic and lethal game of hide and seek. Over ten thousand Americans were taking part in it, and probably at least five thousand Germans. It covered an area over ten miles square, and grim isolated games were being fought twenty and twenty-five miles away from the center. In this unique contest, the Americans knew what was happening, but few of them knew where they were; the Germans knew where they were, but none of them knew what was happening.

At first, almost every parachutist was alone, lost in the dark in strange country where every rustle and shadow seemed hostile, like the forests of children's dreams. General Maxwell Taylor himself, commander of the 101st Division, spent his first half hour on the battlefield all alone, searching for even a single one of his seven thousand men. If he had given an order, he remarked afterwards, nobody would have heard it except the cows. And even he, when at last he did find an equally lost and lonely trooper, was so relieved that the two of them embraced each other warmly. The fact is that most grown men, even soldiers, of any nation, have traces of their childish fear of the dark; and when the dark forest is really full of enemies, the first thing that any man will look for is a friend. The Germans who were out alone that night, or in small groups on patrol, had just the same instinct: they tried to find other Germans, or to get back to headquarters and band together for self-defense and for moral support. So all through the four hours from the drop to the dawn, hundreds and hundreds of little groups and solitary men, American and German, were prowling about the country, trigger-conscious, but put on the defensive by sheer loneliness. Anything which moved or made a noise, and could not give a split-second answer to a challenge, was liable to be shot at; the cows and horses suffered considerably. No German who ventured out by car or motorcycle succeeded in traveling far; even a general was ambushed and killed that night. Here and there, where two groups met face to face, there were sharp exchanges of shots at close range. But both sides, with a few individual exceptions, felt they had enough trouble on their hands without looking for more, and these small engagements seldom lasted long.

This curious kind of red-Indian warfare had never been planned, and would never have happened if the drop had been more successful and concentrated; yet it was most effective. For about eight hours, it totally paralyzed the Germans. Their garrisons were in small units, like Müller's platoon at Azeville. They were not connected by radio, only by telephone and by dispatch riders. The parachutists cut telephone wires whenever they saw them—including the main cable from Cherbourg to the south—and dispatch riders were sitting ducks. When their telephones went dead and their dispatch riders vanished, the German small-unit commanders did not know what to do and were scared to move, while the higher command had no means of knowing what was happening, or which of their scattered units were still in existence. Of course, the German divisions were far more heavily armed than the Americans, but their artillery and even their tanks, in these early hours, were useless. Ten thousand Americans, spread over a hundred square miles of country and constantly moving, never offered a target worth a shell.

Among the Germans unwillingly wandering in the woods was a young man called Franz Muller—no relation of the Müller in Azeville. Franz Muller was a medical orderly in a mobile artillery regiment. His regiment had moved into the district only a fortnight before, for the specific job of opposing an airborne landing. It was cleverly or luckily placed; his own battery was on top of a hill which commanded most of the area where the Americans landed. It was also well equipped, and its morale was high; and yet it never fired a single artillery shot from the hill, because it never had a target.

Franz Muller, who was twenty-two, was in France like many other soldiers only because he had already been badly wounded in Russia, and was rated unfit for any more arduous front. He had entered the medical corps in a rather unusual way. He had always wanted to be a doctor; but his father was a monumental mason in a village on the edge of the coalfields of the Ruhr, and he had insisted that his son should follow him in the business. When the war began, Franz, who was then seventeen, was attending night classes in anatomy, and so the medical corps had been glad to accept him. That was a step towards being a doctor; and nobody knew that his father had only let him learn anatomy to qualify him for carving angels on tombstones.

Muller was not enjoying prowling in the woods, any more than anybody else; but at least he was doing it with a reasonable, humanitarian motive, which meant a lot to him; his officer had sent him out, with a couple of other men, to look for wounded, either German or American. From the top of the hill, Muller and his companions had watched the parachutes come down with a feeling almost of pity for the parachutists. They had seen their own machine-gunners dispatch a good many before they landed, and they had seen others fall in the floods of the Douve; they were sure the remainder would soon be rounded up. All the same, they had no intention of taking chances with them. They had been told that parachutists never took prisoners. Some of them had seen the ruthlessness of their own parachute corps in North Africa. Muller himself had seen German parachutists shooting their Russian prisoners. To go down from the safety of the hill and search the dark woods around it seemed risky enough in itself, and he had been surprised and rather aggrieved when the officer suddenly told him he would have to go unarmed.

All Muller's experiences as a medical orderly had been in Russia, where neither side had taken much notice of the Geneva Convention. He had worn a red cross, but carried a rifle too, and used it when he had to; and so he had brought it to France.

"But these are either British or Americans," the officer said, "and you can't carry arms against them."

Muller said: "That's like sending me into the lion's cage and telling me they won't bite."

Orders were orders, he decided, but common sense was something different. He left his rifle, but when nobody was looking, he put a revolver in his trouser pocket.

Down in the woods, it was eerie and quiet. Many of the trees were draped with parachutes. From some of them, corpses dangled, victims perhaps of the battery's shooting while they dropped. On others, the harnesses were empty, and the parachutists had disappeared. By and by, Muller and his two companions heard German voices, and pressing on, they came to a glade where an American was lying, dead or unconscious, on the ground. A German soldier was rifling his pockets and making lewd comments on the picture of a girl he had found in his wallet. Muller was rather offended, and he said so. The German told him to mind his own business. He finished the job by taking a ring from the American's finger, and then stood up and walked away. When he had gone a few paces, a rifle shot was fired from somewhere close at hand, and he fell like a log.

The medical orderly's work often needs courage. No doubt it needed it then. Muller walked across the glade to the German. He was quite dead. He went back to the American. He was still alive, although he was unconscious. Muller began his usual routine of first aid. No sooner had he started than a shower of cigarettes fell round him, apparently from the sky. Absorbed in his task, he was only a little surprised. So many amazing things had happened already that morning that his faculty of wonder was overworked. The Americans were dropping cigarettes, presumably from aircraft; that was all. He did not smoke himself, but most of his patients asked for a cigarette as soon as they came to their senses, so he picked up a few and put them in his pocket.

It was quite a long time before he thought of a rather less whimsical explanation: that parachutists had still been up in the trees around him, and had shot the robber, and then done their best to reward him for giving first aid to their friend.

Quite close to Franz Muller, completely lost, was another young man of exactly his age called Schuyler Jackson. The two men had quite a lot in common besides their age—the same youthful interests and similar senses of humor. Perhaps if they had ever met in normal life they would have enjoyed each other's company. But the only time they nearly met was in the Norman woods, and it was just as well that their devious paths did not quite cross that morning; for while Muller had come there from the Ruhr, Jackson had come from Washington, D.C., and was playing his part with some relish in the one-man battles which were disrupting the German system of defense. Already, with one other man who was also lost, he had come across a German antiaircraft gun whose crew of six were intent on targets overhead. It had been easy to creep up to them in the dark and throw grenades among them and kill them all, and with that success behind him, Jackson was ready to try his hand again.

All the same, that kind of chance encounter was not what he had come for, and he was worried and upset because time was slipping by and yet he could not find out where he was or get on with his proper job. He was a corporal in the 101st Division, and it was only a few hours since he had been face to face with General Eisenhower, just before the division took off. He had been so surprised to find himself so close to so much brass that he hardly remembered anything Ike had said, but he had a vague recollection of being asked: "You know your objective?" That had been an easy one to answer. He knew his objective as well as he had ever known anything.

The division was to capture the inland ends of the causeways which led through the floods behind Utah Beach. His own battalion was to attack a heavy battery which commanded the beach from a village called St. Martin-de-Varreville. According to the plan, he should have dropped within half a mile of St. Martin and it should have been easy to find. But now he had dropped and St. Martin was not there.

What especially puzzled him, as he hunted for landmarks in the dark, was not only that he was lost, but that he kept on meeting men from his own battalion, all going in different directions, and all as lost as he was. Evidently, the battalion had made a good concentrated drop; yet none of them could make head or tail of the maps and the countryside. Jackson simply could not believe the only feasible explanation: that the whole of the battalion, or nearly the whole of it, had been neatly dropped together in the wrong place. But that was what had happened. The leading aircraft, off course through cloud and antiaircraft fire, had spotted the pathfinder's lights on another dropping zone, three miles south of where it should have been, and dropped its passengers there; and twenty-seven other aircraft had blindly followed its example. The battalion was not only lost, it was leaderless. Its commander, Lt. Col. Steve A Chappuis, was in one of the very few aircraft which found the right dropping zone.

This mistake might have proved a serious one for the fleet which was assembling off the beach, for the battery at St. Martin had been powerful. Colonel Chappuis was in an even worse dilemma than Colonel Otway at the similar battery at Merville; while Otway had found 150 men of his British battalion, Chappuis could only find a dozen. With that forlorn force, he hurried to the battery to see what he could do; he found it ruined and deserted. Air attacks in the last few nights had been successful; the Germans had taken their guns away and abandoned the site.

Corporal Jackson, knowing nothing of any of this, went on searching for the battery till dawn, and then gave it up. About dawn, he came on a glider which had crashed. Dead men were lying in it and round about it. Only one man there was still alive, an officer who was sitting on the ground, apparently uninjured. Jackson asked him if he was all right. The officer said he had a few aches, but nothing serious. Jackson was getting tired, and he sat down beside him to rest. The officer started to talk and ask questions, not about the war or the glider or the immediate future, but about life at home in America. Jackson told him about Washington, and told him he had joined the airborne forces just to show he was as good a fighting man as his father, who was a naval officer. The irrelevant, friendly conversation among the silent corpses was macabre. Slowly Jackson began to understand that the officer had some very serious invisible injury and was in pain and had detached his mind from all the grim surroundings and was living in some time before the present. Jackson offered him morphine. "I've taken some already," the officer said. A few minutes later, he died.

Jackson left that somber scene and went on with his aimless journey. He joined up with a friend, and soon they saw another man lying in the middle of a field, and went to see if he was still alive. It was the colonel of their own

Thompson M1928

regiment, and he was alive and conscious, but he had broken his leg very badly in the drop, and had lain where he was for five hours. He told Jackson and his friend to drag him to the side of the field, where a little dip with a stream in the bottom gave some cover. They had hardly started when they were shot at, and Jackson had a glimpse of a German running behind a hedge. The two men dropped the colonel where he was, and gave chase. The German seemed to run down a farm track between thick hedges. Jackson followed him, spraying the hedges with his submachine gun. To his astonishment, screams and groans broke out, and a white handkerchief was poked through the upper branches. *"Kamerad! Kamerad!"* Jackson shouted. He hoped that would do as an order to surrender. It did. A dozen men came out from behind the hedge, some with their hands up, some staggering; and Jackson was shocked to see the result of his casual finger on the trigger. There was a man supported by others clasping his stomach in agony. There were men drenched with blood. There was a boy, who looked fifteen, shot by some evil chance through both his wrists; when he tried to put his hands up to surrender both hung limply down. Something in the faces of these men, together with their readiness to surrender, made Jackson think they were not Germans at all. Whoever they were, seeing them at his own mercy and in such distress, he found he could not hate them, as he had expected to hate the enemy. They merely looked human, and pitiable. Other parachutists who had heard his fusillade were coming along the track, and Jackson, half ashamed of the hot gun in his hand, and half ashamed of his unsoldierly feelings, let the others take charge of the prisoners and quickly went away. He did not want to look at them any more.

He went back to the colonel, and dragged him to the stream; but the colonal had a compound fracture and needed treatment. Jackson went to look for something to carry him on, and hit on the same solution which Blue's two Frenchmen had used for their similar problem: a wheelbarrow. He found one in a courtyard, and also found someone at last who could tell him where they were: four miles south of the battery of St. Martin. This placed them only a mile or so from a monastery building which had been designated as divisional headquarters, and the colonel, confronted with the wheelbarrow, told Jackson to take him there. Jackson hoisted the colonel into the unusual equipage and trundled him off down the lanes. "It must have hurt him like hell," he said with admiration when he thought of it afterwards. "But I'll say he could still bark out his orders."

The sight at headquarters of a sweating corporal pushing a colonel in a wheelbarrow, incongruous and unique as it was, caused no one to laugh. Everyone there was a parachutist, and had an inkling of the feelings of a professional officer who had broken his leg on jumping into his first—and possibly his last—historic battle. Still full of fight, the colonel reported to General Taylor, who ordered him, in spite of his protests, to the aid post.

Corporal Jackson seemed to be getting among the brass again. He retreated, to take it easy. One way and another, it had been a busy morning, and he felt he had learned a lot.

It was about 2:30 in the morning when General Taylor embraced the first man of his division whom he found. Now, about 2:30 in the afternoon, his divisional headquarters were still far from complete, and he was still out of touch with most of his command. Almost everything was still confused, and he did not yet know the important and comforting fact that the Germans were far more confused than the attackers. But during the morning, in his own travels, he had witnessed the outcome of the most important of his tasks: the attack on the first of the causeways which led to the beach.

The general had landed quite close to his correct dropping zone, which was west of the village of Sainte-Marie-du-Mont, and four miles southeast of Sainte-Mère-Église; but not even he had been able to find where he was in the maze of hedges. The fact was that to drop and assemble in the dark in that particular part of Normandy was a wholly impossible task. If a parachutist had been lucky enough to recognize a landmark— of which there were few—in the seconds while he was falling, all would have been well. But hardly any of them did so; and once they were down, they could seldom see more than a hundred yards, and all the woods and hedges looked the same.

The general worked his way laboriously eastward towards the coast, and picked up as he went a motley assortment of troops, including, by coincidence, far too high a proportion of officers. When dawn began to break, and the bombing and shelling of the coast to shake the earth, about eighty men were with him in the meadows, among them one other general—General McAuliffe, his artillery commander—and at least four colonels. As the light in the eastern sky increased, they saw silhouetted against it the only landmark which could have told them at a glance where they were: the tall beautiful and distinctive tower of the church of Sainte-Marie-du-Mont. They were not more than two miles from the end of the southernmost causeway. None of the officers or men belonged to either of the two battalions which should have been there and should have attacked the causeway; but one of the colonels, Lt. Col. Julian J. Ewell, was commander of a reserve battalion, and about half the men were his. The rest were staff officers, artillerymen without artillery, clerks, military police, the two generals, and a war-correspondent from Reuters. General Taylor put Ewell in charge of this curious outfit, and told him to do what he could at the southern causeway. Generals and colonels were nothing much more than observers. Majors and captains had sections to command. Lieutenants had nothing at all. As the troop began to move, General Taylor remarked to Ewell tha never before were so few led by so many.

Julian Ewell was a professional officer, a graduate of West Point, and young at twenty-eight to be a colonel. This was his first combat, an important occasion in his career, and he would much have preferred to go into it with his own well-trained battalion, instead of a lot of men who had never worked together and did not even know each others' names. Probably he would have preferred to try his hand a little less closely under the General's eye. But parachutists learn to be resourceful.

The two-mile march in the growing light brought minor excitement: the first shots, at a German guard post, the first sight of German dead; the first prisoner, who turned out to be a Pole; and the first American death in action—a medical orderly who ran out into the open to help an officer wounded by rifle fire. As the party skirted Sainte-Marie-du-Mont, it grew like a snowball, collecting wandering men in twos and threes. Some of them had landed in the village itself, and said they had already been captured and escaped.

On the road which leads to the causeway, just before the beginning of the flooded salt flats, there is a primitive little hamlet called Pouppeville. From the first few of its cottages, rifle fire brought Ewell's column to a halt. He deployed his forces to attack the place.

The fight which followed seemed a stiff one at the time, though later, when Ewell had more experience of fighting, he looked back on it as a very small affair. The Germans had to be fought from house to house with rifles and hand grenades. Ewell himself, intent on organizing a coherent attack with his ill-assorted force, was hardly aware of danger until he incautiously put his head round the corner of a wall and was smartly rapped on the top of his helmet by a sniper's bullet. Very slowly, as the Germans retreated, the fight began to converge on the village school; and Ewell, advancing more carefully now down the village street, reached the wall of the playground and looked over it. A German lieutenant ran out of the schoolhouse towards him, shouting. Ewell shot at him with his pistol and missed, and then realized that he was trying to surrender. Twenty or thirty Germans came out of the school behind him, and Ewell's first fight was over.

Beyond the school, the causeway could be seen, a narrow straight road with water on either side, and at the far end of it, the sand dunes of Utah Beach. There seemed to be nobody on it. But soon, in the reeds beside it, a few small orange flags appeared, and there were the signals of recognition which had been planned for this moment: the first meeting of airborne and seaborne forces.

Ewell sent a few men down the road, and they came back escorting an officer who reported to General Taylor: Capt. George Mabry, of the 8th Infantry Regiment, 4th Division. The parachutists looked at him rather like a man from another planet, for he had come by sea. The time was 11:05 A.M.

Colt .45 (1911A1)

PART FOUR

UTAH BEACH

Mabry had been ashore for four and a half hours, and had covered over two miles from his landing place; and so far, the seaborne infantry's losses had been astonishingly small. That was the real measure of the airborne troops' success. Although the scattered drop and the difficult countryside had made havoc of their plans of battle, they had reacted everywhere with spontaneous guerrilla warfare; and the all-important result of it was that the defenses on Utah Beach were cut off from the German army command, which was not even told till the afternoon that a landing had started there. No German reinforcements ever got near the beach. This result was achieved with nothing like the casualties which Leigh-Mallory had predicted to Eisenhower. The losses of American troop-carrying aircraft were twenty out of a total of 805, instead of the 50 to 80 percent he had feared. The losses of parachutists did appear to be very high at first. At dawn, five out of six of them were missing. By evening, less than half were in organized units. But many of the missing men were still wandering, and turned up in the next few days; and a couple of months later, when there was time to prepare statistics, it was found that about one out of ten of the airborne troops had been killed on D Day, or were still missing and presumed to have been killed or captured on that day. That was bad enough, but it was less than the paratroopers themselves expected, and by the standards of war it was a price well worth paying. By the evening of D Day, Eisenhower's worst anxiety for the airborne troops was over, although the 82nd

Division was still cut off from everybody else. On the next day, Leigh-Mallory wrote him a note to say that it was sometimes difficult to say that one was wrong, but that he had never had greater pleasure than to admit he had been wrong about the drop. He congratulated Eisenhower on his wisdom in deciding to go ahead with it, and apologized for having added to his worries. Captain Harry Butcher, Eisenhower's naval aide, regarded this as a typically British sporting gesture, and wrote in his diary: "You simply can't stay mad at people like this." So this remarkable difference of opinion ended.

It was only by chance that George Mabry was the first seaborne officer to report to the airborne general. Nobody had planned it. But his experience of the landing, and all that led to it, was typical of the experience of most of the six hundred men who landed in the first wave of troops on Utah Beach that morning. In fact, Mabry was typical in an even wider sense. It would be absurd of course, to describe him as a typical American, because there is no such thing; but his British acquaintances might have said—and meant it as a compliment— that nobody could have been more American than he was.

He was twenty-four, and he had lived all his youth in Sumter County, South Carolina, where his father, who had once been a famous baseball star, was a farmer on a fairly big scale. The farm grew cotton, the farm workers were descendants of slaves, and George's pastimes when he was a boy were fishing in the rivers and hunting in the woods around his home. When an Englishman heard George speak of his boyhood, it seemed unexpectedly familiar, and he felt that they must have met before; then he realized that he was thinking of his own boyhood recollection of Mark Twain.

George's greatest sorrow in his youth was being small. He overcame that disadvantage in the only way he could in such a he-man's country; by making himself go one better than the other boys, walk farther, swim longer, climb higher trees. He had never heard of complexes, but it became a habit in him to believe he would always have to do this sort of thing to keep his end up. When he left high school, he told his father he did not want to go to college, and his father shrewdly gave him the toughest job he could think of: he put him in charge of a farm which employed thirty men. George ran the farm for a year. By the end of the year, in a boxing ring, he had fought every able-bodied employee to prove, either to them

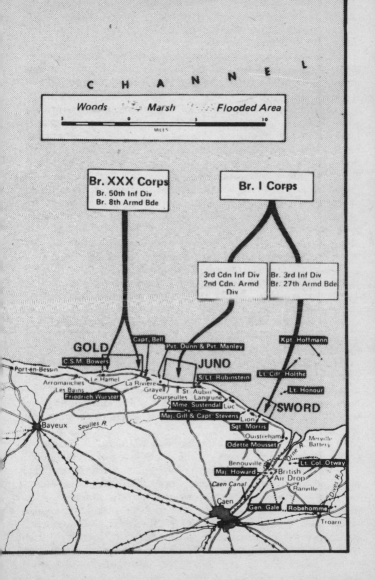

CHANNEL

Woods   Marsh   Flooded Area

5   0   5   10
MILES

Br. XXX Corps
Br. 50th Inf Div
Br. 8th Armd Bde

Br. I Corps

3rd Cdn Inf Div
2nd Cdn. Armd Div

Br. 3rd Inf Div
Br. 27th Armd Bde

Kpt. Hoffmann

GOLD   Capt. Bell
    Pvt. Dunn & Pvt. Manley

C.S.M. Bowers   JUNO
Port-en-Bessin   S/Lt. Rubinstein   Lt. Cdr. Holtke

Arromanches   Le Hamel   La Riviere   Lt. Honour
Les Bains   Grayell   St Aubin
Friedrich Wurster   Courseulles   Langrune   SWORD
    Mme. Sustendal   Luc
Bayeux   Maj. Gill & Capt. Stevens   Lion

Seulles R.   Sgt. Morris
    Ouistreham   Merville
    Odette Mousset   Battery

    Orne R.
Benouville   Lt. Col. Otway
Maj. Howard   British
    Air Drop
Caen Canal   Ranville

Caen   Gen. Gale   Robehomme
    Troarn

or to himself, that he was the boss; and having done that, he agreed to go to college. As if to complete this picture of an American upbringing, George played baseball as a professional during his college vacations.

He joined the army impulsively on a reserve commission in the period after Dunkirk and before Pearl Harbor, when people were beginning to believe that America would fight in the end. As a junior officer, his smallness made him adopt literally the age-old principle of never telling anyone to do anything he could not do himself. In training, it was sometimes hard for him to live up to that principle; even so, whenever he thought about combat, he pictured himself out in front, doing all the most dangerous jobs, because he knew he would never be able to tell anyone else to do them first. In the end, the mere fact of being small led him by these devious trains of thought to a belief which is rather unusual in a soldier; he believed he was sure to be killed. The idea did not worry him, once he was used to it. He would not have told anyone about it, but by then he was married, and he had to tell his wife. For one thing, there was the question of children; they both wanted children, but he thought they ought not to have them. When he was sent overseas, he asked his wife not to expect to see him again, and tried to make her feel as contented about it as he did. At the end of the war, he was surprised to be still alive, pleased at his luck, but a little disappointed in himself. He felt that if he had really achieved the standard he had aimed at, he would be dead.

But in the meantime, accepting the idea of being killed had saved him a lot of worry. For example, while he was waiting in England, he had worried much less about crossing the Normandy beach than many soldiers whose desperate hope was to put up an honorable show but to come through the war alive.

In England, Mabry's battalion was stationed at Seaton, a small old-fashioned resort on the south coast of Devonshire. The people of seaside resorts are more used to sudden invasions of strangers than the people of inland towns and to the people of Seaton, the American troops did not seem very much more foreign than the city holiday-makers who had come there every summer before the war. Commercially, they were a boon to a little town which had lost its tourist traffic abruptly four years before; but commerce apart, the people were glad to see them, and eager to do what they could to make them feel at home, because they knew that the invasion was coming, and that the Americans were there to take part in it, and that invasion would bring the first glimpse, after all those years, of an end of the misery and boredom of the war. The Americans on the whole felt the people's good will and appreciated it, although it could not cure their homesickness. They did not want to be on foreign service any more than any other citizen army, but if they had to be, there were worse places than Seaton and worse natives than the English, hard though their customs were to understand.

"Say, what kind of a bird is that?" a soldier once asked, looking in amazement at a swan on the small river which runs through the town.

"That's a swan," an elderly Seaton lady told him.

"Are they good to eat?"

"So I am told. But swans in England belong to the King, you know."

"Is that so? Well, whadda ya say we knock one off for dinner?"

The only memorable complaint from a local person was also concerned with birds. A landowner requested the American commander to put a stop to rifle practice on the shore, because it was disturbing his pheasants in the breeding season. At first, this made the American commander very angry. Then, for quite a long time, he laughed. Finally, he began to wonder if the landowner was right, and if it was the army which had lost its sense of proportion, and if breeding and shooting pheasants was not as important in the long run as shooting Germans. Anyhow, he had been told to humor the English, and he shifted the rifle range.

George Mabry had been in the same battalion ever since he joined the army, and had been a platoon commander and a company commander. In the waiting time in England, he was operations officer (S-3); and so, in the last few weeks after men of his rank had been told the secret, he was engrossed in the detailed plans of what his own battalion had to do. Two of its companies, three hundred men, were to land from ten landing craft on the left-hand end of Utah Beach, while two companies of another battalion of the same regiment landed on the right. At the same time, or as soon after as possible, thirty-two amphibious tanks were due to land. Five minutes later, the second wave was due: nine hundred men in thirty landing craft, including the rest of his battalion. After them, there were more tanks, and engineers to demolish the obstacles which the Germans had put on the beach, and to blow gaps in the seawall to let the tanks go through. And behind all this was the organization and power which was to put ashore twenty-one thousand men, and seventeen hundred vehicles, and seventeen hundred tons of stores, on that single beach by nightfall. In military language, the word spearhead is often used, and it was never more appropriate: the battalion in which George Mabry served was the head of a spear with a tremendous weight behind it in the shaft.

The battalion's responsibility kept him up, night after night, poring over the plans and trying to perfect them, although they were as perfect as military plans can ever be. But late one evening, to his surprise, the assistant commander of his division came stumping into his office and sat down and said: "What the hell are you up to, George? Quit worrying." This was Brig. Gen. Theodore Roosevelt, Jr. "Whatever you plan," the general went on, "the boys are just going right in there and throw in all they've got. So what do you want with all this paper?"

General Roosevelt was famous for outrageously unorthodox statements of this kind. They had a way of proving to be right, and this was not an exception. George stopped fussing over his plans; and as it turned out, the details went for nothing when the battalion landed, and it was the General himself who changed them on the spot; for in spite of his rank and his age—he was fifty-seven—he had volunteered to land with the first company and coordinate the attack.

Roosevelt was not only the most senior in rank, and probably much the oldest, of all the men in the first waves of the invasion; he must also be accounted its most striking personality. He was the eldest son of President Theodore Roosevelt, and a cousin—though not a close one—of President Franklin Roosevelt. Like his father, he had had a career of soldiering, politics and exploring. He had already seen action in North Africa and Italy. Whatever he did always seemed to be done with ten times the gusto and energy of most ordinary men. He was always completely oblivious of his own safety; he seemed to treat everyone, except laggards, with the same kind of affectionate disrespect; and he had a lightning wit, and an ability to see life from a private's point of view. He hardly ever looked like a general. All these qualities made him the kind of man—like Churchill—who has innumerable stories told about him, always with a tinge of admiration. In the first four day of the invasion, he was said to have had four personal jeeps shot to pieces. On one of those days, he came into a junior command post and sat down and took off his helmet and wiped his brow. A cook came in, and said "You look like you need a cuppa coffee."

"I certainly do," the general said. "What neck of the woods do you come from?"

"Pittsburgh," the cook said.

"Pittsburgh? Hell of a place, that. No pretty girls there, and if there were you couldn't see them for the smoke."

The cook clapped him on the shoulder and hotly defended Pittsburgh and its girls. Then he saw the helmet on the table, with the general's star on it, and rushed out of the room in confusion. "Goddamn it," he said later, "I thought he was some frazzle-assed old sergeant."

Roosevelt, in fact, was the perfect GI general.

George Mabry's journey to France was enlivened by several glimpses of this remarkable man. Indeed, every one of the six hundred men of the spearhead on Utah must have been aware of the General's presence on the beach, and have felt better for it; if the old man can take it, they thought, then so can we. One man whom he drove to mock despair was his aide. "The old feller'll get me killed," he lamented to Mabry. "He doesn't give a damn for anything." But it was not so. The General led the men ashore, inspired them through the first of their battles, saw the invasion succeed, risked his own life a hundred times, and fell dead of a heart attack six weeks later. They buried him at Sainte-Mère-Église.

The General was present when the day came at last for the embarkation. The battalion embarked at Torquay. George Mabry stood on the quay of the little harbor, which is normally used by yachts and by boats which take holiday-makers on trips along the coast, and he watched the men carrying their equipment aboard the tender which was to take them out to their troopship anchored in Torbay. At that important moment, he was confident and excited. After four years in the battalion, he knew every man in it by sight. He had helped to weed out and get rid of weaklings; and now, among those who were left, there was no visible sign of fear, only of a healthy tenseness as they packed themselves on board for the ultimate adventure. The months in England had been rather like a very long time in a dentist's waiting room;

boring, and full of slight apprehension. Now they were all
relieved, he thought, that the waiting was over. A small
soldier was staggering up the ramp, carrying the base plate of
a mortar, when Mabry heard the general's booming voice:
"The army hasn't changed in a hundred years. Always the
littlest guy gets the biggest load." The small soldier grinned,
and hitched his burden a little higher.

For the infantry in their large troopships, the channel
crossing was much less dramatic than for men in small
landing craft. They were quartered below decks, and most of
them saw very little of the sea, or of the armada on it—the
865 vessels on their way to Utah Beach—or of the forces at
sea and in the air which were deployed all round to protect
them. For all they could tell, they might have been sailing
north or west, instead of east and then south; they just had to
take it on trust that after a day and a night at sea, in the light
of dawn, there would be a coast; and that the coast would be
France. When the navy takes charge, soldiers are always
reduced to a state of suspended animation. On the crossing,
Mabry heard the general shouting to his aide: "Steve, where
in hell is my lifebelt?"

"I've given you four already," the aide replied, with a
delicate hint of reproach.

"Well, give me another," the general said. "I've lost the
whole damned lot."

"Did you notice his armament?" the aide asked Mabry. "A
pistol and seven rounds, and his cane. He says that's all he'll
need."

Drama began at 2:30 A.M., when the engines of the troopship
stopped. Mabry went up on deck. It was very dark, and very
quiet except for the sounds of the wind. They seemed to be
stopped in midocean. As his eyes grew used to the darkness,
he saw that there was a faint light in the eastern sky, and
reflections of it glinted on the waves. The waves looked large.
All round, he saw the shadows of other ships, unlit and silent.
Far away to the west there were flashes and flares; he guessed
they came from the Cherbourg peninsula, where the airborne
fight should already be going on.

The silence was unexpected, and seemed sinister. Nobody
knew why the Germans were not attacking; nobody could
believe they did not know the fleet was there. There was an
uneasy feeling of an enemy lying in wait, of an ambush, of
some secret danger which the planners had never foreseen.

By instinct, absurd though it was, men were talking in hushed conspiratorial voices, as though Germans might overhear.

The transfer to landing craft had been rehearsed so often that no orders had to be given. The landing craft were LCVPs, each of which carried some thirty men. A few were launched from davits on the troopship itself; others, carried across the Channel in special landing craft transports, were coming alongside Mabry's ship to pick up troops.

The LCVPs launched from Mabry's transport broke the silence by crashing and clanging against the sides of the troopship; it was certainly rough down there. At five minutes past four, the troops of the first wave scrambled over the side and down the net with hardly a word, so that something General Roosevelt said was plainly heard. Two soldiers offered him a hand over the gunwale. "Damnit," be said testily, "you know I can take it as well as any of you. Better than most."

Mabry, waiting his turn on the deck, watched the men ahead of him descending the net to the swaying landing craft beneath. And as he watched, one of the men nearest the bottom lost his grip and suddenly he was hanging head downwards, suspended by one foot caught in the net, in obvious and imminent danger of being crushed between the rolling LCVP and the larger ship. But the men around him managed to haul him to safety before the two ships met.

Mabry took his turn, and one by one the landing craft cast off to leave room for more, and began to circle round to wait till it was time to set course for the beach.

In this hour before dawn, it was cold and wet and rough; there was plenty of time for courage to sink, and for seasickness and cramp and discomfort to weaken the strongest will. The square-bowed open boats butted the waves and showered the troops with spray. Most men crouched beneath the gunwales, more or less miserable, heads down, trying to preserve a little warmth and present the smallest target for the spray, and not caring to get themselves soaked by trying to watch what was happening.

At 4:55, the landing craft were assembled and started their long run—an hour and a half—towards the beach. They were led by two 173-foot patrol craft, and one smaller boat specially fitted with radar. There should have been two radar boats, but one had suffered the most ignominious of nautical failures; at the critical moment, it had got a rope round its propeller and could not move. Mabry and the infantry knew nothing of this, but it was the first of a series of cumulative mishaps which were to upset every one of their calculations.

As the landing craft turned to the westward and plugged into the head sea, Mabry was so excited and so passionately interested in the military scene that he never thought about getting wet, and stood in the bows of the craft looking over the ramp. He was in a free boat—a boat which was not attached to any particular wave of the assault, but could make its own landing at whatever stage seemed best. It started behind the second wave, but soon passed through it and began to catch up with the first. The shore was still far out of sight, but already Mabry could see part of the concourse of ships: ahead, the battleship *Nevada* and a line of British and American cruisers lying at anchor; astern the command ship *Bayfield*, the transports and tank landing craft. As the dawn light increased, ships more and more distant emerged from the cover of night: destroyers, minesweepers, the ancient British monitor *Erebus*, the American cruisers *Quincy* and *Tuscaloosa*, incredible uncountable numbers of ships from horizon to horizon. They lay still and silent and unreal, though already the sound of distant guns was rolling in from the northwest, where American destroyers, still out of Mabry's sight, were under fire from the coast, and the British cruiser *Black Prince* was fighting a duel with a German battery which had shelled some minesweepers.

The column of boats—a core of them ahead of Mabry's and a hundred more astern—went on towards the line of heavy ships, steering for a gap in the line to the south of the *Nevada;* and as they approached the gap, the hands of clocks moved on to the minute for which the ships were waiting: 5:40. Mabry saw the muzzle flashes and the smoke, and then the spitting crash of the first salvos of the bombardment came across the water like a wall of sound. From then, for forty-seven minutes, there was never a pause in the roar of naval gunfire.

The boats crept past the warships, underneath the shells. Before six o'clock, Mabry could see the shore; or if not the shore, the smoke and the dust of shellbursts which spouted from it. He peered at the coastline he knew so well from its maps and photographs, but so far there were no landmarks to be seen. He saw the bombers come down through the low gray clouds, squadrons and squadrons of them, and the antiaircraft fire go up to challenge them. The firing looked to

him so fierce and thick that he could hardly believe an
aircraft could fly through it. Ahead, he saw a bomber explode
in an orange flame, the sound of the explosion drowned in the
sea of noise. The shore erupted again and again, the bombs
being added to the shells.

His attention was diverted from the shore by events which
were closer at hand. A solitary German fighter broke through
the clouds and dived towards the landing craft. A Spitfire fell
from the sky like a hawk and pounced on it and blew it to
pieces with three bursts of fire. The German's propeller, still

Spitfire

spinning, crashed into the sea nearby. Ahead, a small ship
was floating bottom up. The landing craft passed close to it,
and someone identified it as one of the two patrol craft which
were guiding the boats to the beach. Two men were lying on
the keel. One seemed to be dead—the first dead American
Mabry had seen. The other was waving, and they could see
but not hear him shouting for help, but of course they did not
stop. Soon after they passed, the ship sank. Beyond it, an
amphibious tank was on the point of sinking. Its crew had
escaped, and were swimming round it; but as the landing
craft passed it, Mabry saw an officer, struggling half out of the
turret. It was a man he knew. The tank wallowed, a final wave
broke over it, and it sank, dragging the man down with it.
Mabry thought of him sadly, drowning there so near the
surface. (But long after, he met him again; he had been
trapped by his foot, but when the tank hit the bottom he
freed himself and floated up again.)

The shore was now close. Landing craft armed with 4.7-inch
guns were closing in on either side, shooting at close range
against the dunes. Seventeen tank landing craft fitted with

rocket launchers fired salvos of fifty-pound rockets with a noise which was fearsome even above the gunfire. Mabry could see the sandy beach, heaving, drenched with explosives. But smoke and dust and fine sand were drifting out to sea, and he only caught glimpses of the outline of the dunes behind the beach. There should have been a windmill, and a small patch of dunes called Les Dunes de Varreville which were higher than the rest. But he could not identify anything. The first wave of landing craft were just ahead of him, steering for the shore in line abreast, leaving white wakes in the water. Four hundred yards out, two of them fired black smoke signals into the sky: the sign to the navy that the moment of climax had come. Instantly, the barrage lifted; the beach lay still. The landing craft drove onto the narrow line of white where small waves broke quietly on the shore. To within a minute, the time was H Hour: 6:30 in the morning.

In the last minutes, Mabry glanced back at the men in the boat with him. The colonel's bodyguard, a very small man—smaller than Mabry—whom everyone in the battalion knew as Smoky David, was being sick in his helmet. Some others were grinning, watching him out of the corners of their eyes; but several looked green themselves. Looking at all their familiar faces, each with a hint of serious anticipation or else of exaggerated calm, Mabry had the sense of solid companionship; and besides that feeling of *esprit de corps*, he was aware also of himself, an individual, the real George Mabry beneath the grotesque helmet and the uniform, equipment and insignia of rank; aware of home, the farm, the cottonfields in the sun, the hunting and fishing, his father and mother and wife, all the people and things which had made him the person he was. He wondered at seeing George Mabry as a witness of such great events, and like the bowmen of Agincourt he knew he would remember this day and this hour for the rest of his life, whether life was short or long. There was no time for these thoughts to be put into words, but he knew they were there, in the back of his mind. Something like them was in the minds of most men who landed that morning in Normandy. If Mabry had spoken at all, in those few seconds before the boat's engine slowed down and the bottom grated gently on the sand, he might only have said that this would be something to tell the folks back home in Carolina.

*　　*　　*

The beach was about three hundred yards across, and on the other side of it, lurking in their dugouts in the dunes, were some hundreds of men of the German army. Looking back on it now, no soldier would deny them a little sympathy. In front of them was the sea, behind them the flooded meadows. On the narrow strip of dunes between the two, the most concentrated bombardment of history had just fallen. Now the survivors, emerging dazed from the deepest of their shelters, saw the invaders storming up the beach, and behind them tanks rising from the sea, and behind them again the largest fleet which man had ever seen. They had been promised ample support, if this thing ever happened, from artillery and the air force and the secret weapons. But so far, the artillery had not fired, because its batteries were bombed or captured by the parachutists; the air force had not come, because what was left of it was busy defending Germany itself; and the secret weapons were not ready yet. The telephone lines to headquarters had gone dead in the early morning; nobody knew why. Men who had been sent with messages had never come back; nobody knew what had happened to them. It was impossible to ask for help or for orders.

In these circumstances, some of the defenders whose discipline was strongest fired their guns. Some tried to escape by running along the causeways through the floods, where they were quickly shot down by the parachutists lying in wait for them. Some saved their lives by surrendering, and these incurred the rage of Hitler himself, who called them traitors and deserters.

Mabry went down the ramp and felt the sand under his boots in about four feet of water. Smoky David was on his left, and he saw him go over the side of the ramp and disappear entirely. Perhaps he had fallen in a shell-hole. Mabry had never wanted so badly to run, but of course he could only wade slowly forward. Looking back, he was glad to see Smoky David's head come up again. It was most of a hundred yards to the edge of the sea. Perhaps it took him two minutes to reach the shallow water where he could pick up his feet and splash onto the hard wet sand. But it seemed a long time, because he knew he was an unprotected target in the field of fire of the defenses he had studied so carefully, and because he had gone a long way before he realized, to his astonishment, that there was far less shooting than anyone had expected.

Once on the beach, he only paused to see his companions close behind him with expressions of incredulous relief on their faces, and then he set off for the dune lines. Even on the beach, he could not run. His sodden clothes were heavy, and his legs were cramped and numb from the coldness of the two hours journey in the boat. There was a man lying on the sand. He went to him; it was a corporal he knew, wounded in both legs. He bent down to him and said he would drag him up to cover in the dunes. "No, I'm all right," the corporal said. "Keep going, Captain." (But he died of his wounds, or was drowned when the tide rose.)

On the seaward face of the dunes there was a concrete seawall about four feet high, and there in the dry sand above the tidemark, among such familiar seaside holiday things as shells and seaweed and corks washed up from fishing nets, the leading two companies were pausing; and there Mabry learned why he had not seen any of his landmarks. So far the battalion's landing had been easy; but it had landed in the wrong place. General Roosevelt, who perhaps knew the terrain even better than Mabry, had already been up on the dunes to find out where they were, and had discovered they were over a mile too far south.

This mistake at the culmination of all the months of planning was the result of the series of mishaps which had started with the rope round the screw of the radar boat. The sinking of the patrol craft which Mabry had passed had left only two of the four guide boats in action. One of the two had turned back to help tank landing craft which were delayed by the head sea; and that left only one. The off-shore wind had hidden landmarks by blowing the smoke and dust to seaward; and finally, no allowance, or not enough, had been made for the tidal stream which flows at two to three knots to the southward, into the bay of the Seine, on the flood tide. It was this stream which had carried the whole fleet of landing craft a mile off their course.

But nobody on the beach was caring how the mistake had been made. The urgent question was what should be done about it: write off the first waves of troops, and allow the following forces to land in the right place, or change the assault plans and bring in the whole force to the wrong place. The mistake might have led to totally disastrous confusion, but the situation was saved by the presence of General Roosevelt. He not only had the quickness of mind to make the decision at once, he also had the authority to enforce it. In the lull so luckily caused by the weakness of the German troops, he consulted the two battalion commanders and for better or worse, he signaled the navy to send in all the succeeding waves to the place where the first had landed.

By then, heavy shells had started falling on the beach, and desultory mortar fire was coming from somewhere beyond the dunes. A man close in front of Mabry was blown out of existence by a direct hit. Something small struck Mabry in the stomach. It was a thumb. Some of the men thought the navy were shelling them, and they were complaining furiously. Mabry watched a few shellbursts and guessed rightly that they were coming from the south, from the heavy batteries five miles away on the other side of the estuary of the Vire, but the men would not be convinced and wanted him to fire another smoke signal. To satisfy them he had a spare signal fired, but of course the shelling went on. And then he saw the general, striding along the beach, waving his cane in the air and roaring at everyone to get moving across the dunes.

Mabry went through a gap in the seawall which led to a path. His job, as he had no command of his own, was to join G Company and keep them in touch with the battalion command post; and G Company's job, in the plans he had worked on so carefully, was to turn left along the dunes and attack the defenses to the southward till they came to a highway which was known as Exit 1.

In the gap in the seawall there was a dead German, the first he had seen; through the gap, on the left, were the remains of a barbed wire fence. A sergeant and three other men were scrambling through the fence, and the sergeant was from G Company—he knew him by his red hair. He followed them; a heavy explosion threw him off his feet, and he stood up again to see all four men lying dead or wounded. It had not been a shell; perhaps the sergeant had touched a trip wire and fired a mine. Rather shaken, he went through the fence himself and took off southwards through the dunes to try to catch up with the rest of the company.

Mabry's legs were working all right by then, but perhaps for the moment, after the explosion, his head was not very clear. At all events, he went on for a long way scrambling up the hillocks of sand and sliding down them, before he noticed landmines. As soon as he saw one, he saw dozens, lying about on the surface, uncovered perhaps by the bombing. He reckoned they must have been duds; but he was certainly in a minefield, where there might be others still covered and still alive. He wondered whether to go back or go on, and went on, hurrying because he thought he was left behind; and there was another bang and he fell and rolled down a dune. The sand rained down on him and he lay there and wondered if he was dead.

Far from being dead, he was not even hurt, except that the breath was knocked out of him; but as his senses came back, he felt sick with mortification and rage at himself. All these years, he had meant to be out in front in combat, if only to prove to himself that he could do as well as anyone in spite of being small; and now, he thought, in his very first combat, he had got left far behind all alone, just following on the tail of the company. So he got up again and ran on, and went over the top of a dune and came face to face with five Germans. One had a grenade in his hand and raised his arm to throw it, so he shot him, and the others threw down their rifles and put their hands up.

This was queer and unexpected. He wondered why four of them should surrender to him alone; they could easily have got him before he got all of them. But glancing round, he saw what they had seen; through a gap in the dunes, there was a view of the sea, and almost all the horizon was hidden by

Potato Masher Grenade

ships. The sight was enough to make anyone glad to surrender.
He did not want to be delayed by prisoners; but luckily, he
saw an American soldier just then—the first he had seen
since he started through the dunes. He called him over, and
gave him the prisoners, and also asked him if he had been
with G Company. The man said that so far as he knew they
were still on the beach. Even then, Mabry went on believing
they were still in front of him.

What brought him up in the end was a pillbox, from which
a machine gun fired at him. By then he was through the
dunes, in a flat meadow behind them. He took cover in a
convenient drainage ditch and tried to crawl along it; but he
was shot at again whenever he showed his head. At last, this
personal attention convinced him that the company had not
already passed that way.

Once he had made up his mind to that fact, Mabry began
to enjoy himself. It was true that he had failed to do the job
assigned to him in the battalion plan, but he was much
happier to be in front of the company than behind it, and he
never thought twice about going back to look for it. Instead,
he lay in the ditch and studied the little tactical problem of
the pillbox. While he was there, several other men came up
behind him, and quickly dived into the ditch when they came
under fire. But even with their support, he could not figure
out any way of capturing the pillbox; so he sent one of them
back to look for a tank.

Mabry had rather lost count of time by then. Probably it
was after nine o'clock. At all events, the engineers, who
landed in the third wave, must by then have blown a new gap
in the seawall and bulldozed a track through the dunes,
because Mabry's rather imperious demand for a tank was
soon answered. One of the twenty-eight amphibious tanks
which had reached the shore came roaring along at the back
of the dunes, fired four shots at the pillbox and roared away
again, leaving him and his followers to collect the two dozen
Germans who had come out waving the white flag which the
defending forces seemed always to find at short notice.

With them out of the way, Mabry went on a little farther.
After a while he was rewarded by the irresistible sight of a
causeway across the floods which seemed to be intact and
totally undefended. This was Exit 1, the most southerly of all
causeways, the one which led to Pouppeville, and thence to
Sainte-Marie-du-Mont. There was a little bridge in the middle

of it; and while he advanced towards it, a few Germans came running from the other end, jumped off the road by the bridge, and disappeared beneath it. They might just be looking for a hideout, he thought; but they might be laying charges to blow up the bridge. The sight of them decided him. He collected his followers—a dozen or so by then, stragglers like himself—and began to stalk the Germans. It was while he was crawling towards the bridge through the flat wet meadows that he heard shooting from Pouppeville. He rightly guessed that there could not possibly be any Americans there unless they were parachutists, and hoisted the small orange flag which he had been given to use in that very situation, the flag which Colonel Ewell's men saw and recognized when they finished their battle in the village school.

The parachustist came down the causeway, Mabry and his men went up it, and the Germans at the bridge were caught between them. An airborne lieutenant greeted Mabry as if he had not seen an American for years, and told him that General Taylor was there and would certainly be glad to see him.

The whole thing had not been at all the sort of combat which Mabry had always imagined. From a military point of view, he had made rather a mess of it. But even though it had happened by mistake, he had fulfilled an ambition; he was certainly out in front.

The whole landing had been much easier than anyone had anticipated. The confusion caused by landing too far south had not lasted long; the plans had been flexible enough to stand the strain of this sudden change, and most of the infantrymen, like Mabry, had used their own common sense and initiative, and made for their objectives as soon as they found where they were. The battalion as a whole crossed the floods in safety and joined up with the airborne men soon after midday; and of all the thousands who landed on Utah that morning, only twelve were killed and just over a hundred wounded. For this comparatively easy passage, the seaborne troops were indebted to the parachutists, and to the bombarding forces of the navy and the air force.

Many men on the ground on D Day, American and British and German, took it upon themselves to criticize their air forces. Some of them—the Germans in particular—had some reason to be annoyed, but most had none at all. In retrospect, it is too easy to accept the soldier's view; few of the critics were pilots, and few of them had any idea of the difficulties of flying on that day. The weather and the antiaircraft fire were obvious difficulties; but another, less obvious, was the unprecedented congestion in the air. The crews of the Marauder bombers, which Mabry had seen as he approached the beach, thought much less about the German opposition than about the risk of collision with one another.

Martin B-26 Marauder

These crews had not been briefed till two o'clock that morning. It is strange to reflect that even after the parachutists were in action and the fleet was assembled off shore, men who had such an important part to play were still in bed in England and had never heard of that stretch of beach or been told that the invasion was beginning. But they had to be kept in the dark. They were flying every day over France, and any of them, any day, might have been shot down and captured; so they could not be told the secret. In its organization, their part in the invasion was very much like any other raid.

However, the whole of the tactical air force had known since the previous day that something unusual was brewing, and had guessed pretty well what it was, because all their aircraft had suddenly been painted with black and white stripes of distemper—a kind of paint that can easily be removed. Someone had foreseen that when there was such an enormous number of aircraft in the sky, both the troops and the fighter pilots would need a very quick and infallible method of distinguishing enemy from friend. New identity marks were needed; and they had to appear for the very first time on the morning of D Day, so that the Germans could not possibly have time to copy them. Broad stripes of distemper were a good answer; they could be put on quickly, and scraped off without much trouble when the need for them was over. But even this simple plan was not very easy to execute on the scale which was required. Ten thousand aircraft had to be painted in a single evening. To make sure of the job, one hundred thousand gallons of distemper were ordered. In the whole of Britain, there was nothing like that quantity. The distemper industry was mobilized, worked overtime, gave up its Whitsun weekend without ever knowing why its humble produce had suddenly become so important, and finally delivered the stuff in time. It was received without thanks on airfields where nobody, at that stage, knew what it was for. By comparison, the purchase and distribution of twenty thousand paint brushes was a simple affair.

One of the Bomb Groups of Marauders destined for Utah Beach was briefed by its colonel, Wilson R. Wood, and his briefing made such a deep impression on his crews that many of them never forgot what he said. Colonel Wood was rather an impressive person at any time, partly perhaps because he was tall and remarkably handsome, partly because he was a Texan and had the distinctive charm of a southerner, and partly because he was only just twenty-five. He himself had known of his group's invasion mission for nearly a fortnight, and he had not been allowed to fly since he had been told it. That morning in the briefing hut on his airfield in Essex, northeast of London, he stood up as usual and began to speak in his unemphatic sleepy Texan voice.

"This morning's mission," he said, "is the most important mission you've ever flown. Maybe the most important mission anyone has ever flown. This is the invasion. Our job is to bomb the beach, and right after our bombs go down, thousands of Americans just like us will be landing there from the sea."

This introduction had his crews on the edge of their seats. "I don't care if any of your aircraft are not a hundred percent," he went on. "You'll fly them this morning, and you'll get over that beach whatever happens, and you'll take any risk to get right on your targets and give those boys in the boats every bit of help you can."

After that, he gave the crews his usual meticulous details of timing, targets, routes and tactics. The targets were seven of the centers of defense on the narrow strip of dunes. The timing was more critical than usual, because the whole operation had to start after dawn and end by the clock immediately before the landing craft reached the shore. When Wood sent his men out to their aircraft, they were certainly imbued with his own conviction that the safety of a few aircraft and even the lives of a few crews were of small importance beside the help they could give to their fellow-countrymen in the boats. In this spirit, they took off at 4 A.M.

Wood led his own group very low across the Thames below London, over Kent and Sussex and out across the Channel, flying all the way below the cloud base. As usual when he was flying, he was happy. One might say that he was a born airman. His father was an engineer, his home was four hundred acres of virgin land in Texas, and from his earliest boyhood in the era of Lindbergh, flying had been his dream and his delight. He had joined the air force as soon as he left college, when he was twenty, and had risen from enlisted man to colonel in five years simply because he was a natural leader and had a single-minded love of aircraft. Like most American bomber pilots, he did not particularly hate Germans, or particularly like dropping bombs; but he would have said that the only way out of a war was to fight your way out of it. Somehow, he had managed to combine his intense preoccupation with flying with being happily married. It was typical that when he was made a colonel, four months before the invasion, he sent his wife a cable saying "Promoted—Wilson," and forgot in his excitement to send her his love; but she was sufficiently sure of it to forgive him.

Now he was in the middle of a tour of fifty combat missions; and he felt that this morning, whatever the future might bring, was a climax in his flying career. Over the Channel, this feeling was strengthened when he saw the countless white wakes of ships all pointing like arrows towards the coast of France.

Visibility was supposed to be eight miles, but it seemed to be less. There was broken cloud from two thousand up to seven thousand feet, and a fairly solid layer of cloud above that. It was not very comfortable to fly just under clouds into an area where German fighters seemed sure to be around; but that was the best way, he thought, to find a difficult target on a bad day.

He saw the coast less than two minutes before he crossed it—the straight featureless line of shore, so long that it vanished in haze in both directions. In those minutes, he flew into the most congested bit of air he had ever seen. The area of each of the seven targets was very small—perhaps a hundred yards square—and the air space above them was limited by the clouds and the small-arms fire which came up from below. Two hundred and seventy-six aircraft converged on these areas, all flying within a couple of hundred feet of the cloud base. Some had to make more than one run; some, which had approached above the clouds, came down through gaps at unpredictable moments. Wood had expected a crowd, but he found it distracting. The antiaircraft fire was a danger he could easily dismiss from his mind, because there was nothing much he could do about it; on the other hand, the risk of a collision was much more of a worry. Careful flying and a good lookout could have reduced the risk, but keeping a lookout for other aircraft was no help towards accurate bombing. Wood determined to concentrate his eyes and his mind on his target, and leave a collision to chance; but it needed all the self-control he had.

When his own bombs went down, he turned away towards the sea. He could not possibly have seen where they had fallen, for the whole shore was smoking and flashing like a firework; but he was satisfied. As he cleared the coast, he saw the sight which justified the dramatic words he had used to his group that morning; the landing craft, heading towards the beach in an endless column which emerged from the glare on the sea in the east where the early sunlight filtered through the clouds. He wished them luck. He had done all that an airman could to help them through.

Before eleven o'clock, the time when Mabry saluted General Taylor in Pouppeville, and Wood had had breakfast in England and was preparing for his second flight to France, the landing on Utah Beach had become a routine. Among the men who were pouring ashore, an outstanding figure was that of Chaplain Luechinger, a Capuchin friar and a native New Yorker, who was better known to his Manhattan congregation as Father Bruno. He waded ashore in a lull in the German artillery, and so far as he could remember afterwards, he was on the beach for an hour before he heard a bang.

To be a friar from Manhattan suggests a contradiction, since friars are reputed unworldly and Manhattan is best known for its worldly splendors. Father Bruno's church was a couple of blocks off Broadway, within sight of all the glitter of Times Square, and its spire reached less than a quarter as far towards heaven as the roof of a big hotel across the street. But the contradiction was only superficial. The brown hood and habit of a Capuchin often hides a remarkable amount of worldly wisdom; and Manhattan's famous facade, on the other hand, hides every kind of activity of the spirit and intellect. And for a Capuchin friar to wade ashore on D Day was no contradiction at all, because the order has provided chaplains for armies since the Middle Ages.

Even if he had not been a friar, Luechinger would have been a remarkable person; for he was not only a very learned man, but was also a master of the opulent slang which is the hallmark of the true New Yorker. Englishmen in Devon had been delighted by his combination of clerical appearance with Yankee wit, even when he used his wit to heap good-humored scorn on everything English. His own troops found it easy to confide in a priest who naturally spoke their own language, and spoke it more fluently than they did.

In the past few months in England, the padre had listened to a great many personal troubles, mostly arising in one way or another from homesickness, and so he had learned even better than before to understand and appreciate his countrymen, with their strength and their weaknesses. He crossed the Channel with apprehension for the men on whom the burdens of pain and death were so likely to be laid. Their almost carefree landing was therefore a surprise and a pleasure to him, as it was to them.

His landing had a touch of drama in it, as well as a touch of farce. While the fifth wave of landing craft were circling round before setting course for the beach, his own craft rammed the one in front of it. It was a boat of a British design, and nobody but a Limey, the chaplain remarked, would have put the helmsman right at the back where he could not see out. They had to go back to the transport to change to another boat, and before they had done so the wave of craft had started and disappeared; so they set off for the beach alone. The new helmsman had never been told that the landing was a mile too far south. The southerly tide had slackened, and he steered an accurate compass course according to his orders. Probably this craft was the only one in the landing at Utah which arrived off the right stretch of beach, where its passengers found, with no little consternation, that there was not a soul in sight. But they saw some activity to the southward, so they turned that way and cruised along the coast; and in doing so they passed the guns of a major German strongpoint. It shook them to hear, when they landed, that this strongpoint had not yet been captured: But by this time the Germans on Utah Beach, whether captured or not, had given up the fight.

On the beach, when he got there at last, the padre found a scene which was humming with activity but showed little sign of battle. The desolate shore had already been transformed. Roads had been bulldozed through the dunes, and tanks, artillery and supply trucks were rolling out of tank landing craft, assembling and roaring along the new roads towards the causeways, as if the embarkation on the Devon coast had been reversed. There were hundreds and hundreds of men on the beach, infantry landing, waiting for orders and moving inland, signalers, prisoners, naval units, medics; it was with these, in the aid posts, that a padre's work was found. He went from post to post, giving thanks in his heart that so few of his men were lying in need of the service of a priest, and perfectly confident, like every man on the beach, that the plan had succeeded and the army was there to stay.

But twelve miles to the eastward, at this same hour, on Omaha Beach, there was a man whose home was quite close to Father Bruno's; and he was crouching in a foxhole, bewildered and leaderless, looking out on a scene of terror and utter confusion.

PART FIVE

OMAHA BEACH

The man in the foxhole was Pfc. Henry Meyers. He felt he was looking at himself from outside himself, with sorrow and pity, as people sometimes do when events are almost too much for them. The real Henry Meyers, the I of his existence, the schoolteacher from Brooklyn, the man who was loved by Molly his wife, did not seem the same person as the soldier crouching like an animal in the hole he had scraped in the sand, made numb by the concussion of explosions, and staring aghast at the sand spurting from the strikes of bullets and the bodies dead and half-dead on the shore. His emotions were in disorder and his only clear thoughts were Why in hell am I here? What am I doing in this mad place?

The merely factual answers to those questions are easy enough to record, though of course they were not the answers which puzzled him. He had never wanted to be drafted. The draft call had interrupted his vocation as a teacher of mathematics, and his marriage which was only a few months old, and the placid life he enjoyed among all the bustle and noise of an industrial part of New York. The army had wrenched him away from all that, and discovered he was a mathematician and put him, by army logic, in the Signal Corps. Of course he knew the necessity for service as well as anyone else. He would not have dodged it if he could, and he had done his best at it; but he had never pretended he had any ambitions in soldiering for its own sake, or that he wanted anything more than to get it over as quickly and efficiently as he could, and go home and start teaching again.

In the army, he just made himself feel content to do what he was told. Whenever he was faced with some unpleasant chore he cheered himself up with the thought that if he did not do it, somebody else would have to. He had even made himself interested in the mechanics of signaling, but he could not help despising it as a mental exercise when he compared it with the beauty of pure mathematics.

When Meyers' small unit had been packed on board a troopship and told that this was really the invasion, he had been glad. He did not need to be told that invasion was the quickest way to end the war, or that any minute degree of help he could give would be help in the right direction. On the channel crossing, this glad resolution had been almost swamped by seasickness—he was so sick that he wished he were dead; but he felt better again when he boarded the landing craft, where at least the air was fresh; and as it pitched and rolled on its way to the beach, he felt ready for anything. The companionship was encouraging: all his own unit grouped together joking and shouting, men he knew well, all very literally in the same boat together, all keyed up for the adventure.

Henry Meyers could not see much from his position in the boat, wedged in among other men who were taller than he was. He could not move much either. Apart from his equipment and his rifle, he was carrying a heavy coil of wire over his shoulder. It was telephone wire, and he and a couple of friends were supposed to lay it from the beach to some place inland which somebody would show them. He could not see, but he could hear. There was a tremendous noise, and as the boat came nearer to the beach the noise grew louder. He had never heard such a noise before. It was infinitely worse than the practice runs with the live ammunition, but he supposed it was all right and was only what had to be expected. In the last few seconds, above the ramp of the boat he had a glimpse of shell-bursts and of clouds of yellowish smoke and the crest of a green hill showing dimly through it; and at that same moment he heard a different noise, alarming and very close: the unmistakeable splatter of bullets on the ramp itself. And then the boat grounded, the ramp went down, the men in front ran forward.

Meyers knew he hesitated, but for such a short time that nobody would have seen it. It was not the danger which made him hesitate, because he still could not see very much and still had no real idea of what he was in for; it was just an instinctive ridiculous reluctance to do anything so unnatural as to jump in the sea with his boots and trousers on. But then he was in, and it was warmer than he expected; and he could see.

He could see men in front of him falling—and not just stumbling, but falling limp face-down in the water and making no effort to rise. On the edge of the sea where the waves were breaking, he could see bundles washing in and out, rolling over and over: bodies. Beyond, he could see the sandy beach, very wide, and bodies lying there too, and a tank burning, men clinging to its shelter like a cluster of bees, and here and there, all the time, the beach was erupting in sprays of sand and debris where shells or mortar bombs fell, while small flicks of sand from machine-gun bullets ran across and across it like wicked living things. Far away up the beach was a bank of stones, and behind that in the smoke the low hills, flashing with fire, but whether from shells bursting or guns firing he could not have told, because he had seldom seen either before. And the noise was so terrible that he could not think; his brain stopped dead.

They had told him to run. Instinct told him the same. But instinct would not allow him to run up the beach; he could not, simply could not run that way. He turned to the right and ran along the water's edge, splashing through the little rims of foam.

It was difficult to run in wet clothes, the rifle and the coil of wire jolting awkwardly on his shoulder. He had an impulse to throw the wire away. But that brought him up; the wire. The wire was what he was there for. They would be stuck without it. He had a job to do, and if he didn't do it somebody else would have to. He stopped and stood still for a second, every inch of his body expecting the horrible whack of a bullet; and then he started to run up the beach.

He ran terribly slowly in spite of his utmost effort, like another childhood dream, the one in which one runs and runs to escape from a monster but cannot move at all; and while he was running he was only conscious of a little area of sand around him, a yard or two on each side and ahead. It was such ordinary sand, he thought. It was so like the sand on the beaches on Long Island where children built castles and ran and shouted, and he and Molly had sunbathed; sand of bathing suits, suntan lotion, ice cream, Coke in bottles with straws; sand that got into the picnic basket. Things came into the little circle of his vision as he ran: a German obstacle, a mangled body in uniform, blood, wreckage, rifles, torn equipment. He ran over them or round them, and hardly knew they were there.

Then the high-water mark, the line of seaweed, and then the dry sand where he could not run any more but only drag his feet forward; and then the stone bank. They were big stones, three or four inches, like cannon balls; and men were lying elbow to elbow, hugging the steep face of the bank for cover, or squatting in holes in the sand, some wounded. He dropped down there, aware for the first time of the rasping of his own breath and his heart thumping, and he peered at the men near him, hoping to see his friends and his officer. But there was nobody there that he had ever seen before.

What ought he to do? Above the dreadful noise, he heard thin screams, and shouts which might have been orders, but if they were he could not understand them, and nobody moved. What ought a good soldier to do? With nobody to tell him, the answer could only be: keep alive, if you can, till they need you. So he started to dig. He was trembling from the shock of what had happened; and that is no wonder, because that same shock, the shock of the instant transition from the companionship and shelter of the boats to the very whitest heat of war, where every man is always alone in spirit, had strained every man who landed to the limit of what brain and will can stand. Some had run up the beach, as he had in the end, and they had a chance to survive; and some had been unable to make the decision, as he had at first, and they lingered on the edge of the water and died.

Desperately digging in the loose dry sand, Meyers threw down his coil of wire beside the hole. There it lay, half a mile of it, and something must have gone wrong, he thought, the landing could not have been meant to be like this; because he was meant to go on and lay the wire to some place a mile inland, but nobody, so far as he could see, had even been able to cross the stone bank.

He was right; since the very beginning, an hour before he landed, almost everything had gone wrong, and at that moment the landing on Omaha was only being saved from total failure by blind tenacity and the last shreds of courage, and by the very impossibility of the idea that it could have

failed. In calm analysis the causes which led to this situation
can be listed and understood: the weather was bad, the
bombardment had failed, the beach was naturally a good
position for defense, the German forces manning it were
better troops than had manned it when the attack was
planned, and finally—though this may still be a matter of
opinion—there were basic mistakes in the plans. But the men
who were suffering on the beach that morning were only
aware of two of these causes: the weather, and the formidable
hills they were expected to assault.

Omaha Beach is five miles long, and very slightly curved,
and like Utah Beach it has sand which is firm and yellow and
slopes so gently that the tide runs out for three or four
hundred yards. But that is its only resemblance to Utah.
Behind it, instead of dunes and flat meadows, there is first
the bank of stone which Henry Meyers reached, and then a
stretch of marshy land two hundred yards across, and then
green grassy hills or bluffs, 150 feet high, which are easy to
climb but too steep for trucks or tanks. At each end of the
beach, the bluffs run out into vertical cliffs which extend for
nearly ten miles in each direction. There are four small
valleys in the bluffs, with trees and bushes in them. Before
the invasion, one of them, the most westerly, had a good road
in it, which led down to a few seaside villas on the flat strip
behind the stone bank, and the other three had lanes. The
military importance of these otherwise insignificant little
valleys was equally obvious to the attack and the defense;
except for one isolated gap at Port-en-Bessin, the four valleys
were the only possible ways for a mechanized army to move
inland on the whole of the stretch of twenty miles of coast
from the mouth of the River Vire to the village of Arromanches.

From almost anywhere on the bluffs, the whole length of
the beach can be seen. On flat beaches like Utah, the
Germans had to build their pillboxes and emplacements close
to the edge of the sand; attacking infantry did not have very
far to go before they could get to grips with them. But on
Omaha, the gun positions were built on the sides of the
bluffs. Overlooking the beach, they had an enormous field of
fire, and to reach them, infantry would have to cross not only
the beach itself, but also the stone bank which had barbed
wire on top, and the flat strip behind it which was mined; and
then they would have to climb the slopes. For the whole of
this journey of five or six hundred yards, they would be

plainly visible from the bluffs, except in the couple of yards
where they could hide behind the stone bank.

The Germans had grouped their defenses mainly round the
mouths of the valleys, but the whole of the beach was
covered by their fire. The heavy guns were in concrete
emplacements from which they could only fire along the
beach, not straight out to sea, the seaward sides of them
being protected by fifteen to twenty feet of concrete which
made them almost proof against naval gunfire. Each group of
emplacements was connected by trenches and tunnels with
underground magazines and living quarters. It was estimated
that the beach was covered by over sixty pieces of artillery,
besides mortars and a very large number of machine guns.

In addition to these manned defenses, the Germans had
made great use on Omaha Beach of the underwater obstacles
which has occupied so much of the energy of British and
American reconnaissance. Aerial photographs had shown four
different kinds. About 250 yards out, not far from low water
mark, there was a row of what the reconnaissance men had
called Element C. These were like very large and heavy
field gates of steel, facing the sea and buttressed behind by
girders. Further up the beach, there were rows of wooden
ramps, with their pointed ends towards the sea, and of stout
wooden posts driven into the sand with contact mines on top.
Finally, on the upper part of the tidal flat, steel hedgehogs
were scattered about. They were made of three lengths of
angle iron or railway line, welded together in the middle so
that they formed a kind of double tripod, with spikes sticking
up whichever side they lay on. These obstacles were laid so
thickly that a landing craft which tried to go through them
would stand perhaps a fifty-fifty chance of getting in, but a
smaller chance of getting out again by turning or going
astern. The first step in the plan of attack was to remove the
obstacles before the tide rose over them.

The plan had been as follows. H Hour was 6:30, which was
soon after low water. From 5:50 till 6:27, a tremendous naval
bombardment had been arranged. From six o'clock till 6:25,
over four hundred bombers were to attack the shore defenses.
At 6:29, sixty-four amphibious tanks were due to land; at H
Hour itself, thirty-five ordinary tanks and sixteen armored
bulldozers; and one minute later, eight companies of infantry,
1,450 men in thirty-six landing craft. Two minutes behind the

infantry were a special demolition task force, to clear and mark lanes through the obstacles before the tide rose up and covered them.

After these demolition men, a pause of half an hour was left in the planned landings to allow them to finish their work. Then bigger waves of infantry were due to arrive, with the first artillery units beginning to come in at eight o'clock.

The demolition men were really the crux of this plan. There were 270 of them; rather more than half of them were naval men. They would have a delicate and fiddling task in attaching explosive charges to the obstacles and connecting them with fuses and detonators, and they would be much too busy to protect themselves. For defense, and for conditions sufficiently quiet to allow them to work, they had to depend for the first half hour on the infantry and the tanks. But 1,450 men and ninety-six tanks were no match for the German defenses, unless the bombardment had already largely destroyed them or stunned the men who manned them.

Not one of these plans was fulfilled. The air bombardment missed its targets. The naval shelling had little apparent effect on the defenses. Most of the tanks were lost at sea or quickly destroyed on the beach, and the infantry were scattered and decimated. The demolition lost nearly half their number almost at once, and the remainder struggled to carry out their orders under conditions which were all but impossible. The beach became a chaos; the program of landing was abandoned.

And the whole of this chain of disaster was started by the weather.

The conditions of cloud in the early morning varied from place to place, but there is no evidence that they were worse at Omaha than they were at Utah. The difference between the air bombing on the two beaches was a difference in policy and aircraft. At Utah, medium bombers, Marauders, carried out the last-minute bombardment; at Omaha, the job was done by heavy bombers, Liberators. These heavy bombers could either bomb visually or by instruments, which in those days was a much less accurate method. The decision was taken the night before, on the basis of the weather forecast, to use instruments, and this decision was endorsed by the Supreme Command.

The infantrymen, who had hoped and expected to find the defenses in ruins, knew nothing of this decision, or of its

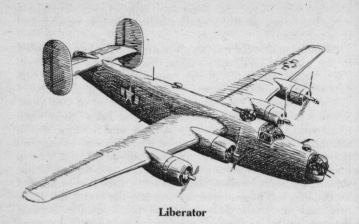

Liberator

implications. Because of the inaccuracy of the instruments, there was thought to be a risk that the bombing would hit the landing craft. The aircrews were therefore ordered to delay their drop after crossing the coast, the length of the delay to vary inversely with the length of the time before H Hour until it reached as long as thirty seconds. This meant inevitably that the center of the weight of bombs fell at first a few hundred yards inland, and crept further away until just before H Hour it was three miles beyond the beach; and none of the bombs, except a few which were badly aimed, fell near enough to the beach defenses to do them the slightest harm.

The results of the naval bombardment were also meager; but this is not so simple to explain. The bombardment looked heavy on paper. There were two American battleships, *Texas* and *Arkansas,* three cruisers of which one was British and two were Free French, and eight destroyers. They were to fire thirty-five hundred rounds of calibers from 5 to 14 inches. Army artillery was mounted on landing craft so that it could fire while it was waiting to go in, and was scheduled to fire nine thousand rounds in the thirty minutes before H Hour. Finally, nine rocket craft were each to fire a thousand high-explosive rockets. What happened to 21,500 projectiles? There are many answers, and none of them conclusive. Only quite a small proportion of the volume of fire was real naval gunnery. The rockets were notoriously inaccurate under the best of conditions. The aiming of army guns in small landing craft could only have been uncertain, because the sea was rough. The morning was rather misty and the beach was soon covered like Utah with smoke and dust, which made spotting difficult for the larger ships. The Germans had taken care to make their emplacements difficult to see and almost impregnable by fire from seaward, and intelligence and reconnaissance had not detected them all. Part of the naval effort, especially of the battleship *Arkansas*, was directed against heavy German batteries far out on the flanks which threatened the sea approaches but did not affect the beach. A naval historian, summing it up, believes the bombardment was simply too light and too short; no more ships could be used, because there was no more room for them in the sea, and the navy needed more time to do the job thoroughly. It was the army, he implies, who restricted the length of the shooting to thirty-five minutes.

Nobody can be certain either exactly how much damage the shelling had done before H Hour, and the guesses vary. The only certain thing is that it did not do nearly enough, and that when the troops started to cross the beach the greater part of the German defenses were still intact and went into action against them.

The weather which had rendered the aerial bombing useless and distracted the gunners' aim caused its greatest havoc among the infantry landing craft and the amphibious tanks. The conditions of cloud at Utah and Omaha were much the same, but the conditions of sea were quite different. The wind was blowing at ten to eighteen knots from the northwest. At Utah, the wind was off-shore, and the closer one went to the beach, the calmer the sea became. At Omaha it was on-shore; and the waves were four feet high, and sometimes six feet. Neither the landing craft nor the amphibious tanks were designed to work in such a rough sea as that. The very first of the victims of the tragedy at Omaha were the crews of the tanks.

Amphibious tanks were a new invention then, and were used on all the beaches. Those for Omaha were carried across the Channel in sixteen landing craft commanded by a reserve naval lieutenant named Dean L. Rockwell. So unpredictable are cause and effect in war that it could truly be said that Rockwell was in the navy, found himself in this curious command, and became the first man to put landing craft ashore on Omaha simply because he had been a professional wrestler. He came from Detroit. Before he joined the navy, he had never seen salt water except on his honeymoon in Florida; but many excellent naval men had had even less experience of the sea. In Detroit, he heard that Gene Tunney, the heavyweight boxer, was making a recruiting tour as a naval lieutenant commander; and out of admiration of Tunney, Rockwell hurried off and joined the navy as an instructor in physical education.

But this proved a disappointment. He did not approve of the way the navy ran its physical education, and his criticisms gave him a reputation as a "bolshie." As a punishment, or as a fitting fate for bolshies, his senior officers managed to post him to landing craft, which they regarded as the navy's suicide squad. But there Rockwell found his vocation. Men brought up with ships might think that landing craft were ugly, or unseamanlike, or unhandy; but Rockwell loved them, and because he loved them he became exceptionally clever at handling them and understanding their sometimes strange behavior. He was only a petty officer then, but he was soon given a craft of his own to command. By the time he reached England, destined, he knew, to take a front seat in the invasion of Europe, he was an officer and commanded a flotilla, and was perfectly happy about it. Then in March he was summoned to the naval base at Dartmouth and told he had been chosen for a new job in cooperation with the army. He was disgusted at first, but he soon changed his mind. He was let into the secret that amphibious tanks existed. His job was to study the technique of launching them from landing craft at sea. In good time for the invasion, he had made himself expert at that as well; and in doing so he had developed the deepest respect for the men who manned the tanks.

The idea of a tank which would float and propel itself in water, and yet still remain an efficient tank on land, had interested and baffled engineers in every army, mainly because tanks had grown in size and weight between the wars until they were too heavy to cross rivers by most of the ordinary bridges. The solution of the problem, the invention of the DD tank, is attributed to a Hungarian-born engineer called Nicholas Straussler who was working in Britain. The Admiralty condemned his design as unseaworthy; but the War Office,

Sherman M4-A4 DD (Duplex Drive)

caring less about standards of seaworthiness, saw the possibilities of the tank as a weapon of surprise in invasion. They took up the idea, and as soon as Eisenhower and Montgomery saw it demonstrated, orders were given for hundreds of Shermans to be converted.

Straussler's basic idea had the simplicity of many great inventions. A kind of canvas screen was fastened round an ordinary tank. Tubes in the canvas could be blown up like an air mattress, and when that was done, the canvas stood up to make a primitive sort of open boat, of which the canvas formed the sides and the tank itself formed the bottom. The tank's own engine was connected by extra clutches to two propellers. DD stood for Duplex Drive, and not, as many tank men surmised, for Donald Duck.

The beauty of this invention, from a tactician's point of view, was that when the tank was swimming it was a small and insignificant target which looked like a boat and not like a tank at all; but at the very moment when it touched shore, the air could be let out of the tubes and the canvas collapsed, and within a couple of seconds the tank was in action. The sight of full-sized tanks rising out of the sea was expected, quite rightly, to surprise and alarm the opposition. A second advantage was that if tanks could swim ashore themselves, there would be no need to risk the large vulnerable tank landing craft in the first waves of landing.

But beautiful as the DD tank appeared to tacticians, from the point of view of the men inside it, no more unpleasant means of going into battle could be imagined. Even the top of the tank was several feet below water level. The tank commander could stand on a platform behind the turret, and from there he could see out above the canvas gunwales; but the rest of the crew were down inside the tank. The driver had a periscope, but the others—the codriver, radio operator and gunner—could neither see nor hear what was going on outside. They did know, however, that their thirty-ton tank was suspended from a flimsy structure which would collapse if it was punctured or could be swamped by a moderate wave, and that if that happened, the tank would sink as quickly as a stone, with them inside it. They also knew, because they had tried it in training, that it was possible to get out of a sunken tank, using submarine escape apparatus; but that a good many people, in emergencies, had failed to do so. And they learned, from Rockwell's experiments with this landing craft, that once they were in the water, there was no going back. The tanks could go down the ramps of the landing craft, but they could not go up. Once launched, they had to reach land or founder.

When the experiments in launching these tanks were completed, Rockwell's flotilla assembled in Portland Harbor in Dorset; and while they were waiting there for the day, an incident occurred which perhaps deserves a place in history. The King came to inspect them, escorted by Admiral Stark, the senior American naval officer in Europe, and a formidable array of brass. On one of the craft, the King asked the ensign in command if he was all ready for sea.

"No sir," the ensign replied, to everybody's stupefaction.

The King asked him why not.

"Well, I've asked time and again for an extra fresh water tank, but I've never got it and I know what'll happen, it was the same in the Mediterranean air, the army drink you dry and you're left out there for days—"

The King suggested to Admiral Stark that he might look into the matter. Admiral Stark told a vice-admiral to investigate. The vice-admiral told a commodore to see to it, and the commodore told a commander, and the commander told a supply officer, and the ensign, no doubt, thought his water tank was as good as installed. But he was wrong. Too much brass can be as bad as too little. They all forgot.

The crossing was hard for the landing craft crews; perhaps harder for the tank crews. After the false start on the previous day, they finally sailed from Portland at 9:15 in the morning with a voyage of twenty hours in front of them. The further they went, the rougher the sea became. The tank landing craft were built in three sections, bolted together, with all their heavy machinery in the after end. Loaded with four tanks, they worked in the waves and gave an ominous impression of being liable to buckle in the middle. The decks where the tanks were lashed were often awash. Even Rockwell had to admit that they were showing their worst behavior. Steering a course was difficult, and keeping station in close convoy was worse. There were a good many collisions. None of them was serious, but every now and then a craft which was trying to avoid a crash would be caught by the sea, and yaw, and career off the course of the convoy all by itself, the helmsman wildly spinning its wheel.

Many of the tank crews and many of the naval men were sick all the way. Between their bouts of sickness, the tank men speculated endlessly about the prospect of the weather in the morning, wondering whether they would be able to launch their tanks at all, or whether all their amphibious training would be wasted.

This worry was on Rockwell's mind as well. Everyone knew the tanks could not swim in rough water. It was so obvious that nobody had ever risked a tank and his life by trying it. Rockwell's orders were that if the sea was too rough for the tanks to swim, the landing craft should take them right in to the beach and land them. The decision had been left to the men on board, but the orders about it were vague. The sixteen craft were to divide, before they reached the area for launching, into two groups of eight craft each. The senior naval officer and senior army office in each group were to consult and make a joint decision whether to launch or not. It is unusual for any military decision to be left to two officers of equal authority, and nobody had told them what they were to do if they disagreed.

Nightfall on the stormy sea threw the convoy into even worse confusion, and offered no chance of rest to Rockwell and his skippers, who had been on their bridges all day. At dawn, Rockwell was pleased and secretly rather surprised to find all his sixteen ships still afloat and still in sight. He led them through the lines of the infantry transports, anchored ten miles off shore, along the lane of buoys which had been laid by the minesweepers, and past the heavy ships which were waiting to open their bombardment. The groups divided, his own eight craft towards the western end of the beach, the others towards the east.

From the first moment when it was light enough to see the waves, Rockwell himself had no doubt in his mind that the tanks would never make it. It could not be anything more than a hunch, but he was sure he had never seen a tank launched in such a sea, and he did not believe it could be done. The senior army officer of his group was in another craft. Prepared to argue, Rockwell went down to one of the tanks and called him on the tank's radio. He was thankful to hear him echo his own thoughts: "I don't think we can make it. Will you take us right in?" Rockwell said he would. It meant that his eight large, unarmored, vulnerable craft would be in exactly the position of danger which the DD tanks had been meant to obviate; but of course he had been prepared in his mind for that ever since he had handled a landing craft, and the prospect did not dismay him. The important thing was to get the tanks ashore; what happened to the landing craft was of minor consequence. At that moment, in the early dawn, his ships were steaming in line to the eastward, waiting to launch. He signaled them to prepare to turn 90 degrees to starboard in line abreast and beach. At 5:30 he gave the executive signal, and saw them all turn together with perfect precision towards the shore, the van of the landing on Omaha. It seemed a proud sight to him.

The other group decided to launch. At the crucial moment, the extraordinary order that the army and navy should share the decision caused the confusion which might have been foreseen. The result was terrible. Each of the landing craft dropped its ramp, and on each of them the four tanks moved forward to enter the water from which they could not possibly return. Some of them went off the ramps successfully and traveled a hundred yards or so before they abruptly vanished below the waves. Some never floated at all. There was a certain gallantry, however unwise, in the way they went. Commanders of the second, third and fourth tank in each craft could see the leaders founder; but the order had been given to launch, and they launched, one by one, each of them hoping perhaps for better luck; and once they had started, the navy could not stop them, but only watch each one till the moment when a wave broke over it, or the canvas collapsed, and the tank instantly disappeared and nothing was left on the sea but one man swimming, perhaps two, but seldom more. Within two or three minutes, twenty-seven of the thirty-two tanks were at the bottom of the Channel; 135 men were drowned, or swimming for their lives. It was difficult, in the large tank landing craft, to rescue survivors, the best that most of the crews could do was to throw out extra lifebelts and leave the swimmers to wait for smaller craft.

On one of the landing craft, the fourth tank tore its canvas on a gun mounting as it moved along the deck. Its commander was a sergeant called Sertell. He stopped to see what damage had been done, and while he was stopped everybody on the landing craft, including him, watched the three tanks in front of him go under. The naval officer on the bridge advised him to stay on board, and told him that his orders had been that if the last tank was damaged he should land it later in the day. But Sertell insisted on going. He said he thought his bilge pump could keep down the water from the leak. He drove down the ramp and sank. Later in the day, the same landing craft was hailed by a small patrol boat which handed over a body to be taken back to England, and the body was Sertell's.

Two of the tanks reached the beach under their own power. Three more were saved by an accident. One craft launched its first tank and watched the tank commander and gunner desperately bracing their backs against the bulging canvas to try to keep it from collapsing under the pressure of the waves. Their struggle only lasted half a minute. But the landing craft had lurched when the first tank went off it, and the second ran backwards into the third and fourth and all three of them tore their canvas so badly that they could not possibly have floated. The ensign commanding the landing

craft decided on his own responsibility to make for the shore;
and he fought his way in all alone, and landed the three last
tanks.

The infantry on the eastern half of the beach thus had the
support of five DD tanks, out of the thirty-two they had
expected.

Rockwell did not see this tragic proof that his own decision
had been right. His own eight craft were some distance to the
westward, and he was intent on watching the beach ahead,
and the clock, and the crowds of other craft all round him.
The clock was important. If he was two minutes too early, he
would run into the tail end of the bombardment. If he was
two minutes too late, the infantry would not have the help of
the tanks at the moment they needed it most. The time and
position for launching had been decided to suit the speed of
the tanks; but the landing craft were faster, so they had to
waste time. It was a navigational problem which was elementary
enough, but it needed concentration because so many things
were happening. The battleships and cruisers behind him
were shooting over his head. On each side of the aisle
reserved for the landing craft, the destroyers and army artillery
were banging away. Threaded through the racket of guns,
there was a continuous noise of aircraft engines, although the
bombers were hidden by clouds. And as he approached the
shore, the rocket ships began to let loose their own particularly
horrifying roar, and the tanks of his own craft started up their
engines.

From far at sea, the shore had been dim in the early
morning haze. Now as he came nearer, it almost disappeared
in smoke, and only the level top of the bluffs could be seen
against the sky. For a time, Rockwell and his skippers lost
sight of their landmarks. But a shift of wind rolled back the
smoke for a minute from the mouth of one of the valleys and
the group of villas underneath the bluffs, and Rockwell saw
they were being set to the eastward by the tide. All of them
changed course to starboard and increased their speed. At
precisely the time when the barrage lifted, they were exactly
opposite the points for their landings, ready to run the last six
hundred yards to the water's edge.

This was indeed the scene which Rockwell had always
imagined, ever since he had been thrown out of physical
education and steered his first landing craft. It was the
moment for which a landing craft existed. But he had always

expected, and been trained to expect, to land under heavy
fire. So far, he had not been aware of any opposition. With all
the noise and the smoke, he had not been certain whether
German guns were firing at all. The only missiles anywhere
near him were rockets falling short. Even when the close
barrage stopped, there was plenty of noise; but it came from
the revving engines of his own four tanks and the gun of the
first which was firing over the ramp; and the wide beach,
covered with obstacles, looked quiet. The villas were ruined,
the bluffs deserted, smoke rising here and there from burning
grass. Within his view, there was no human being alive or
dead, and the whole desolate scene had the air of a place
deserted in the face of disaster. In those last two minutes,
from 6:27 to 6:29, while the tank landing craft approached the
breakers, stopped engines and grazed the sand of Omaha,
there was a fleeting hope that the bombardment had done its
work and the defenses had been destroyed.

The ramp of Rockwell's craft went down, the first of the
tanks lurched forward, dipped its nose to the slope, crawled
into five feet of water and ahead through the breakers to the
sands fifty yards away, the water washing over its back and
pouring off again. In that same moment the Germans came to
life. Perhaps they had waited on purpose; more probably,
their gunners had just come up from their shellproof shelters
of which the strength had been so badly underestimated.
Rockwell saw the muzzle flashes from casemates on the bluffs.
For the first few seconds their shooting was ill-directed. His
second tank got away. Then three of the landing craft on his
right were hit in quick succession: an 88-mm gun was enfilading
the beach from an emplacement at that end. He watched his
third tank go out, and waited with an interest which was
almost detached for the German gun to raise its sights to him,
for the landing craft, lying still and almost broadside to the
gun, was a target which it could not possibly have missed.
But the last of his tanks went into the water, and the moment
it was clear the ramp was raised and the engines put astern.

The work of a landing craft was dangerous but short.
Rockwell's own job was finished on the stroke of H Hour. The
tanks were ashore, and his only duty then was to get his craft
away in safety, if he could. Seven of the eight backed out from
the beach, two burning; one was left there wrecked. But the
German fire which had concentrated on them for the first few
seconds seemed now to be random. Many more guns on the

bluffs had begun to shoot, but they had shifted their targets.
Rockwell saw the first of his tanks start to pick its way
between the obstacles on the beach. Before it had gone ten
yards from the water, it burst into flames. And looking astern
as his craft got under way, he saw the new targets which had
drawn the German fire; the infantry landing craft, ploughing
their way towards the breakers, running the gauntlet through
the spray of shell-bursts.

The first of these landing craft should have been carrying
infantry, with the Navy-Army Demolition Force close behind
them; but on some parts of the beach they all arrived
together, and on some the demolition men were in the lead.
This letter was written by one of them. He was a seaman.

". . . We stood looking over the side at the beach we were
to go in at soon. We were all happy and smiling, telling jokes
and yelling. Six o'clock came and we went in. . . . There
hadn't been a shot fired from the enemy yet. But soon as we
dropped our ramp, an 88 mm came tearing in, killing almost
half our men right there, the officer being the first one. We
all thought him the best officer the navy ever had. . . . From
then on things got hazy to me. I remember the chief starting
to take over, but then another one hit and that did it. I
thought my body torn apart. When I woke I seen a big hole in
the bulkhead between the sergeant and me. He was dead, it
must have been instant. I was blood from head to foot but
didn't know it at the time. Later I found the shrapnel had got
me in the left leg and arm. I looked round and seen no one
else alive. The explosive was on fire and was burning fast, so
I went overboard and headed for the beach. The surf was
filled with soldiers trying to get ashore. But the bullets in the
surf from the enemy were thick. They were getting killed
fast. I reached the obstacles and got behind one to shelter.
Just then the landing craft blew up, that got me, not caring
whether I lived or not I started to run through the fire up the
beach. Which was plenty far to run, it probably seemed
longer at that time. That's when I found my leg and arm stiff.
After a while the soldiers were pouring in thick. I did a little
rifle firing with them. . . ."

A great many of the 1,450 men of the eight companies of
infantry suffered this kind of experience. One company, landing
on the western end of the beach, a little to the right of
Rockwell's tanks, had one of its six craft sunk half a mile from

shore; men were seen jumping overboard and being dragged down by their equipment, which was too heavy to allow them to swim. A second craft was blown to pieces by mortar fire. The other four grounded and the men scrambled out, but there were deep channels there, and some men were out of their depth. Intense machine-gun and mortar fire enveloped them. Many were wounded in the water, and fell down and were drowned. Those who struggled to land took refuge behind the German obstacles, or went back into the sea for cover. A few formed a firing line on the water's edge; but soon all the officers of the company and most of the sergeants were killed or wounded, and the men, without leaders, gave up any hope of advancing across the beach. Within fifteen minutes, the company was out of action. Some of its survivors stayed in the water all the morning, and succeeded in reaching safety in the end by crawling up the beach as the tide came in.

This company had landed in the right place. The only other infantry who did so were a small company of rangers, who had a special mission on the right-hand end of the beach. All the rest of the eight companies were carried eastward by the same tidal stream that had upset the landing at Utah. It had not mattered at Utah; the infantry had landed at the wrong place but in good order, and the weakness of the opposition had given them time to organize. But here at Omaha, all order was lost before the soldiers even reached the shore. Some craft were only two hundred yards to the east of the places where they should have been; some were a mile. One company, after two of its craft were swamped, approached the shore two miles away, and had to come back against the wind and tide, and landed ninety minutes late. All the others were mixed up together. Two stretches of the beach, both half a mile long, had no infantry at all; other parts had too many. Men found themselves pitched onto the shore in single boatloads, cut off from their officers, faced with defenses which were not the ones they had studied in their briefing, under a terrible gunfire which they had never been warned to expect, and with nobody to tell them where they were or what they ought to do. Almost all the heavier weapons were lost in the struggle through the surf; and most of the men who succeeded in crossing the beach and reaching the temporary safety of the stone bank were so shaken by the ordeal that for the time being, no organized action was possible.

Not even the heaviest gunfire puts such a strain on a
soldier's morale as not being told what to do. In this respect,
the demolition men were better off than the infantry. They
had a specific job to do, and they could do it, or try to do it,
wherever they landed. There were the obstacles in front of
them; and each team of them, one officer and a dozen men,
had to clear a fifty-yard gap right through to high-water mark;
and they had to do it quickly, because the tide was rising. To
move and work on that beach would have seemed impossible
if they had stopped to think; but none of them had time to
stop or think.

The training of the demolition force, on the sandy shores near
Barnstaple in Devon, had been hurried and incomplete. It
was hurried because obstacles on Omaha Beach had only
been seen in reconnaissance photographs for the first time in
April, and then, under Rommel's pressure, had multiplied
very quickly. And it was incomplete because nobody knew
exactly what the obstacles were like. They could not tell from
the photographs what the things were made of, or how they
were put together, or whether they were mined. Perhaps the
American demolition men were not well served by their
liaison with the British; for British commandos had landed on
different parts of the coast of France and inspected at least
three kinds of obstacles—steel "hedgehogs," and wooden
ramps and stakes—and had taken measurements of them at
their leisure. But only part of this information filtered through
to the Americans, and their plans for getting rid of the
obstacles had to include an element of guesswork.

Even the organization of their teams was rather an
improvisation. They had started as a naval force, divided into
teams of one officer and seven enlisted men—sixteen teams,
to blow sixteen gaps in the defenses. But whenever new
photographs were taken of Omaha Beach, the belt of obstacles
was seen to have grown more complex; and not long before D
Day, the naval command concluded that a team of eight men
was too small to blow a gap during the half hour which the
plan allowed them. The navy had no more explosives men to
spare, so the army lent them some. Five army men were
added to each of the naval teams.

The commander of this peculiar composite force was a
naval reserve officer called Joseph H. Gibbons, and in their
six weeks of training, Gibbons had managed to make his men

sure that nothing could stop them from doing the job they
had been assigned to do. He himself was prepared for the job
to be tough, but a tough job suited him well; and indeed he
had probably been chosen more for his character than for his
knowledge of demolition, which was small. He was a powerfully
built man of moderate height with a bulldog's tenacity and a
habit of saying exactly what he thought no matter who was
listening; strict, outspoken, fair, a man to whom right was
right and wrong was wrong, and no shades existed in between.
He was very much aware of his responsibility to the navy and
especially to his men, towards whom he behaved like a very
stern, old-fashioned and yet affectionate father. These qualities
probably dated back to his upbringing in the woods and the
bluegrass country of Kentucky, and perhaps they owed
something to his training at the Naval Academy at Annapolis;
for he had graduated there in the twenties but then had left
the service, which seemed a dead end to him, and taken a job
in a telephone company. Whoever discovered Gibbons and
appointed him to his command had made a wise choice. He
was exactly the man to give his forces the moral impetus they
needed to carry them through the ordeal on the beach.

Gibbons himself landed exactly in the middle of the beach.
As he was in charge of all sixteen teams, the job he had
planned for himself was simply to walk along the beach and
see how they got on and help them when help was needed;
and that is what he did, absorbed by his technical problems.
The thought was certainly there in the back of his mind that
something must have gone wrong and that conditions were
very much worse than anyone had expected; but the gunfire
tearing down the beach worried him first and foremost for the
effect it might have on the job.

The first two of his men he met told him the whole of the
rest of their team had been killed while they were landing.
He told them to take cover behind the stone bank till he
found a job for them. Next he found a team which had landed
intact and started already to fasten its charges to the obstacles.
Each man had landed with a string of two-pound blocks of
explosive round his waist, and each team had an extra supply
in a rubber boat which it was supposed to haul ashore from
its landing craft. Gibbons had always expected the best of his
men. Watching this team, he was very proud to see how well
they justified his confidence. He saw them moving methodically
from one obstacle to another, taping the charges onto the

stakes and angle irons quickly but not hastily. One of them was running out the instantaneous fuse which was to connect all the charges together. One had laid out the two buoys which were to mark the gap, and was going up the beach carrying posts with triangles on them which he had to set up as additional markers in line at the top of the beach. None of them was showing any visible sign of fear.

Gibbons moved on. Absorbed as he was, his walk was not without incident. Once, suddenly aware of shells bursting all round him, he dived into a hole in the sand. Another man, a moment later, dived in on top of him shouting furiously, "Get the hell out of my foxhole." Gibbons got out, ashamed of himself, and did not go to the ground again. Somewhere along the beach, another thing penetrated his consciousness: a scream, a long terrible dying scream which seemed to express not only fear and pain, but amazement, consternation and disbelief.

He found other teams at work, and other teams decimated on the water's edge; and he found a gap blown, and the bodies of the men who had blown it scattered among the wreckage of the obstacles. He watched the tide rising. At half tide, it rose a foot in eight minutes, and within the first few minutes of the landing it was among the outer obstacles, swirling into the channels and advancing at an average of a yard a minute up the gentle slope of yellow sand.

On the beach, he only gained a rough impression of his men working against time under conditions which he vaguely knew were terrible. It was not till later in the day, when the tide put an end to their efforts, and their survivors took refuge at last behind the stone, that he began to learn the extent of their successes, and heard of the accidents that had overwhelmed the teams which had failed.

Five gaps had been blown, and two partially blown, out of the sixteen which had been planned. Two or three teams had been lost before they landed, or been landed so late that the tide was up before they got to work. At least two had been slaughtered in landing. One had had its rubber boat hit by a shell while the whole team was gathered round it dragging it ashore. It blew most of them to pieces. One team had laid all its charges and connected them, and the men were still standing by them preparing to fire them when a shell hit the fuse and ignited it and set off all the charges prematurely and wounded or killed them all except the man with the markers.

One team had everything ready when some tanks, arriving late, drove over the fuses and cut them to pieces so that the charges could not be fired at all.

The remaining teams were all delayed by a humanitarian consideration which nobody could possibly have thought of: the infantry, desperate for cover, who huddled in groups behind the slenderest obstacles. One of the warrant officers, his charges laid and ready at the cost of the lives of two of his own twelve men, ran round frenziedly kicking the soldiers to try to make them move so that he could fire the charges. Another team leader, when every persuasion had failed, lit his fuse and then ran round from one obstacle to another shouting to the men that it was burning and they had half a minute to get out. For some teams, the difficulty was worse, because wounded men had been dragged into the imaginary shelter of the obstacles, and they could not move. Some teams wasted so much time in trying to clear men off the beach that the tide rose and drowned their charges and their gaps were never blown. None of them could bring themselves to do what the logic of war demanded; blow the gap and kill their own countrymen.

In the face of all these difficulties, the blowing of five gaps was a wonderful achievement, although it was only a third of the number planned. Gibbons might say he had never been brave himself, but his unit action could well be judged the most gallant of all on D Day. Of his 272 engineers, 111 were killed or wounded, almost all in the first half hour. Yet their gallantry was largely wasted, by hastiness in planning. The fault lay with the markers they had been given. Some of the buoys and posts they had brought to mark the gaps were lost or broken in the landing. The posts which they set up at the top of the beach were easily knocked down, and were not conspicuous enough to be seen through the smoke from seaward. The buoys, which they laid on each side of each gap, were ordinary metal can buoys with a spar and a flag on top; but they could be punctured and sunk by a single rifle bullet, and instead of being port and starboard buoys they were all the same color, so that when one was sunk, nobody could tell which side of the gap was marked by the one which remained.

So when the tide had risen and covered the obstacles, the gaps which had been made by such sacrifice were practically impossible to find. All the morning, landing craft skippers milled around offshore looking for buoys and posts, and most of them, knowing that gaps had been planned, hesitated to trust to luck and charge the obstacles.

Two other cumulative disasters helped to deprive the stricken infantry of the support they had the right to expect. A large proportion of the artillery intended to land in the first few hours had been loaded in the amphibious trucks called DUKWs. This plan had simply not made enough allowance for the rough sea which can be found in the English Channel even in June. With guns, ammunition, sandbags and men on board, the DUKWs were top heavy and the great majority were swamped or rolled over in the sea.

DUKW

Secondly, it was a long time before army engineers succeeded in making any gaps in the bank of stone, which was too steep for vehicles or even tanks to cross; and so the tanks were not able to lead the infantry in any advance beyond the beach itself. The reasons for this delay again were losses of equipment. Explosives had been lost in the surf. Sixteen bulldozers had been provided, but only three survived, and one of those was unable to maneuver because of the infantrymen who clung to its shelter. No gaps were made in the bank until ten o'clock. By then, it was nearly high tide. The tanks which were still in action had been penned into a strip of beach which was only a few yards wide. Other kinds of vehicles, jeeps, trucks and half-tracks, had started to land, and as the tide rolled up to the stone all of them were caught in a dense jam of vehicles, men and wreckage, from which nothing could escape towards the gaps. This concentration of material was still under fire from German guns at close range; and an order had to be sent, by a naval radio which had been landed in working order, to suspend all landings of vehicles till something could be done to clear the beach.

Into this scene of confusion and death, just before the landings were halted, a landing craft disgorged a unit of antiaircraft guns mounted on half-tracks, the 467th AAA battalion, of which one section was commanded by a sergeant called Hyman Haas; and Haas's experience was typical of that stage of the battle except for the very unusual fact that he brought his whole section and his guns and vehicles through it with hardly a scratch on the paint.

Hyman Haas's job was making frames for ladies' handbags. He was Jewish and came from the Bronx, and he was cheerful and friendly and efficient. This was his first combat; and all through it, and for months afterwards, he remained so cheerful and turned out to be so lucky that his section might well have looked on him not only as a sergeant but as a mascot.

Haas's unit were principally trained as antiaircraft, but they had also practiced on surface targets; and that was lucky in itself. Even while they were still out at sea, he knew they were out of a job as antiaircraft gunners, because the sky was full of planes with black and white stripes of distemper, and there was never a single German to be seen. But the moment they hit the beach they found a job which was very much more important; to help to take the place of the artillery which had foundered in the DUKWs.

Like everybody else, Haas was shocked and amazed at his first close sight of the beach; and like everybody else, he found that his orders were impossible to fulfill as they had been planned. He was supposed to drive his half-tracks straight across the beach and up one of the valleys to the village of St. Laurent at its head, and then set up his guns on the top of the bluffs. He was landed in the right place. The water was deep. It came up to his waist in the cab where he was sitting with his driver. But his waterproofing held, and the half-track wallowed through the water to the sand. There was the valley, just where he had expected it to be; but there also, only a few yards ahead of him, was the stone bank, still intact and impassable, and between him and it were the debris, the wrecks of tanks, the corpses and the hundreds of crouching men. There was no room to go forward at all. To let the rest of his unit squeeze onto the beach behind him, he had to tell his driver to turn to the right and try to move out of the way between the wreckage and the water.

The sight of the 37-mm gun coming ashore just behind them must have appeared as a godsend to the infantry, some of whom had been there for two hours without any artillery at all. An officer ran towards Haas before he had even stopped, shouting and pointing out a pillbox on the side of the bluff about three hundred yards away. Haas looked at it and saw it fire. His own gun was mounted so that it could not fire forward on low elevation. There was no room to turn round on the beach. He told his driver to turn to the right again, and drive back into the sea. That pointed the half-track's stern at the bluffs; and there, half submerged in the surf again, Haas trained his gun and laid it on the pillbox. He fired ten rounds. So far as he could see, they all went through the aperture and exploded inside. Anyhow, the German gun was silent after that.

By then, the whole of the unit was ashore, and for a long time nobody showed Haas another target. There was nothing for him to do but to sit and wait, and hope that somebody somewhere would punch a hole in the stone bank and let him move before his gun was destroyed.

Few people had the opportunity that morning to see the landing at Omaha as a whole; but to all who did, it seemed for several hours that the attack was going to fail. A German officer in the fortifications on the cliffs at the west end of the beach counted ten tanks and a great many other vehicles burning, and saw the American troops taking cover behind the stone and the dead and wounded lying on the sand; and he reported that he believed the invasion had been halted on the shore. The German divisional commander, receiving this and similar reports, was so confident of the outcome that he sent a part of his reserves to counterattack the British farther east. General Bradley, out on the cruiser *Augusta*, could do nothing at that stage to influence events; the battle, he wrote later, "had run beyond the reach of its admirals and generals."

All the morning, he was extremely anxious at the alarming and confused reports which came in by radio. About nine o'clock, he sent an observer close inshore in a fast patrol boat; but his first-hand report was no more reassuring. He had been able to see the shambles on the beach, and another staff officer who was very close in at the same time reported landing craft milling around "like a stampeded herd of cattle." At noon, a further radio report told Bradley that the situation was still critical, and he began then to contemplate diverting his follow-up forces from Omaha to Utah and to the British beaches—a decision which would presumably have meant writing off the landing at Omaha as a failure, and abandoning most of the forces already ashore to be killed or captured. For the next hour and a half, this terrible prospect remained in the general's mind, so near did Omaha come to defeat. And then, at 1:30, seven hours after the landing, he received the message, "Troops formerly pinned down . . . advancing up heights behind beaches."

Something had tipped the balance which had been swinging towards defeat, and inclined it slightly at last towards victory.

It was partly the slow effect of the almost irresistible weight of American arms. The American forces could lose all the tanks and all the artillery in the first waves of their attack; there were still enormous quantities of tanks and artillery to follow in later waves. They could even lose their infantry; manpower was no problem, for tens of thousands more men were waiting and ready to go in. But the German defenses, strong though they were, were limited and immobile. From time to time, a lucky shot like Haas's wrote off a pillbox, and nothing could replace it. Time was bound to wear the static defenses down.

This process was certainly quickened by the navy's intervention. The naval bombardment had been scheduled to stop three minutes before the troops landed, for fear, of course, of hitting them while they advanced. But when it became obvious that the soldiers were not advancing at all, but were penned on the beach, and that the situation was desperate, destroyers were ordered in as close as they could go, to shell whatever targets they could see. Some of them went in till they scraped their keels on the sandy bottom.

By this naval fire, aided by the remnants of artillery on the beach, German guns were silenced one by one, and German fire against the beach slowly slackened. But none of the men on the beach were aware of any slackening. It is nearly as bad to be shot at by ten guns as by twenty.

What really turned the balance was a final stubborn reserve of human courage. It came to the surface quite independently, at several different places on the beach. The shock of the landing had numbed the willpower of a great many men, not because their morale or their courage was particularly weak, but simply because the shock was too great for any ordinary human being. The loss of leaders and lack of orders had created a feeling of hopelessness and lethargy. But here and there during the morning, officers and NCOs of more than ordinary moral strength, recovering more quickly than others from the shock, began to take stock of the situation and to rally whatever men they happened to find around them.

It is impossible to say how many of these natural leaders were discovered by the very horror of the position on the beach; perhaps there were a score, perhaps a hundred. None of them had any example to follow, or knew that anyone else was even trying to break the deadlock, because in general nobody knew what was happening beyond the very limited distance he could see. Sometimes a single man's action inspired others; sometimes men had to be bullied or persuaded; sometimes a single concise remark stuck in men's minds long afterwards as the turning point, and was repeated in recollection after the battle was over, and so found its way into official records. On one bit of the beach, a lieutenant and a wounded sergeant quite suddenly stood up among the men who were lurking behind the stone, and walked over the top of it—the very thing which nobody had dared to do. They looked at the wire entanglement just beyond the bank, and then the lieutenant came back and stood on top looking down at the cowering men and said to nobody in particular: "Are you going to lay there and get killed, or get up and do something about it?" Nobody moved, so he and the sergeant found explosives and blew a hole in the wire; and then men began to stir. An infantry colonel, on another part of the beach in the same situation, expressed the same thought: "Two kinds of people are staying on this beach, the dead and those who are going to die. Now let's get the hell out of here." In the largest and most effective advance which was made from the beach that morning, it was actually a private soldier who was the first to go over the bank and set a bangalore torpedo in the wire.

Before he could fire it, he was killed. A lieutenant went over next, and fired it and blew a gap. The first man to try the gap was shot; but others made it, in twos and threes, and found shelter in some empty German trenches; and little by little the numbers increased till the remnants of a whole company were following.

In this way, several small groups of men, mostly ill-armed and mostly unsupported, began to creep inland behind a leader. The groups varied in size, from half a dozen men to a company, and each of them, so far as its members knew, was alone in trying to penetrate inland. Nobody will ever know how many groups started and failed. Roughly a dozen succeeded. None of those which succeeded were opposite the strongly defended valleys; they were all in between them. There, they began to find that there was really more cover beyond the beach than on it. There were ruins, and bushes, and small folds and hollows in the face of the bluffs. Once they were clear of the beach, they found the German fire less dangerous than the minefields. None of them had time to clear the mines, and few of them had the knowledge or apparatus. One engineer lieutenant, who was trained in mines but had no mine detector, led men through a minefield in the marsh below the bluffs by crawling on his stomach and probing with a hunting-knife. Most of these tentative advances were made in single file, each man treading in the footsteps of the man in front, stepping over the bodies of men whom the mines had killed. In some minefields, wounded men were left lying where they fell while a column walked over them, because the column could not be stopped and there was no room, on the narrow track which was proved to be safe, to carry them back to the beach. It was through these hesitant columns of shocked and weary men that the advance from Omaha began. The landing there, one-fourth of the whole invasion, had stood on the verge of failure; but a few brave men, mostly of junior rank, had refused to acknowledge that it had failed, and had begun to lead their companions to success.

But for the whole of the day, success remained uncertain. By noon, a few of the infantry were up the bluffs, and began to attack the defenses from behind. But no tanks or artillery could follow them, because the valleys were still being strongly held. Sergeant Haas saw soldiers on the skyline of the bluffs above him but he still had to wait for a gap in the stone through which he could drive his half-track, and until he could move, he could not find any targets for his guns. Almost all the beach obstacles were still intact and were still a menace to the landing of reinforcements. Gibbons was still waiting impatiently for the tide to go down again so that he could renew his attack on them. Communications hardly existed at all. Most of the radios which had been landed were full of salt water, and it was long after nightfall before anyone had any use for the telephone wire which Henry Meyers, the mathematician from Brooklyn, had carried ashore and was waiting to lay inland. Through all these hours, a strong counterattack could have pushed the whole of the American forces off Omaha Beach and back into the sea again.

But no counterattack was made, and for this reprieve, as for so much else, the thanks of the troops on the ground were due to the air forces which had won complete supremacy in western Europe. Allied aircraft that day were delaying the movement of German reserves far and wide over France; and before that day, they had already played their part in disrupting communications and in sowing confusion in the minds of the German commanders.

From the first moment when parachute landings had been reported, the German command had been reluctant to believe a real invasion was beginning, because of the weather. The Germans were far less well equipped than the British and Americans with weather stations in the north Atlantic area. This was partly, of course, a matter of geography, but partly also because their air force had been worn down to a point at which it could hardly risk long-range aircraft on weather reconnaissance. As a result, their meteorologists failed to forecast the temporary break in the weather which had been spotted by Eisenhower's advisers. They predicted nothing but bad weather, and on the strength of a forecast which seemed to offer safety from invasion for several days, Field Marshal Rommel had gone to Germany to spend a day at home and then report to Hitler, and in the invasion area itself, all the divisional commanders had been summoned to a meeting in Brittany which was to take place on the morning of the sixth. Even when the landings had started, it seemed unlikely to the German high command that the Allies would have launched a full-scale attack with such a forecast.

To this unwillingness to believe the truth, the Allied air forces had added uncertainty, by keeping German reconnaissance aircraft away and by successfully attacking German radar stations. German reconnaissance flights in the previous week had reached the Dover area and reported the dummy fleet which was lying there, but had not been able to penetrate to the English harbors farther west where the real fleet was waiting. The early warning radar stations along the coast of France were sufficient, in theory, to detect ships or aircraft over most of the English Channel; but in that same week, the stations had been bombed, and on the night of the landing those which remained were jammed. However, enough of them were deliberately left in working order in the eastern part of the Channel to ensure that the dummy fleets approaching the Calais area were detected.

To the high command, a full-scale landing anywhere that morning therefore seemed unlikely; the information which reached von Rundstedt's and Rommel's headquarters was meager; and what there was of it seemed on the whole to confirm von Rundstedt's belief that the main attack would come in Calais, and to suggest that the action in Normandy was a mere diversion. At the crucial moment, they hesitated to throw in the whole weight of their reserves.

Their reaction was also delayed by the fact that their command was divided between the army and the Nazi party. The army had one armored division close to the invasion shore. It was stationed near Caen, and was in action against the British early in the day. There were two more first-class armored divisions between Normandy and Paris, but they were SS divisions—Nazi party units which were not under the army's direct command—and von Rundstedt had been forbidden by Hitler to commit them to battle without consulting him. Before dawn, von Rundstedt's chief of staff asked for Hitler's permission to move them up; but Hitler, at home in Berchtesgaden, refused to let them move to the west, in case it should be true that the main attack was still to come in the east. Having made this decision, Hitler took a sleeping draught (according to Chester Wilmot) and went to bed, and his decision was not reversed till the afternoon. By then, it was much too late for the two divisions to play any part in opposing the first assault; and when they did begin to move, they found movement by daylight made almost impossible by Allied fighter-bombers which patrolled the roads and even hunted out tanks which tried to advance across country.

These armored divisions were the nearest strategic reserves.

The tactical reserves close to Omaha Beach had already been dissipated. There were two infantry brigades; but before the landing at Omaha had been reported, part of this force had been dispatched to the west to tackle the American airborne landing, and during the morning, most of the rest of it was moved east, to a point where the British were quickly advancing inland. The Atlantic Wall at Omaha was tough, but it was thin.

PART SIX

THE
BRITISH
BEACHES

As the tide came up the Channel from west to east, the British army, half an hour later than the Americans, began its assault on the three beaches which had been given the code names Gold, Juno and Sword; and on Gold Beach, fifteen miles east of Omaha, the experience of a captain of the Westminster Dragoons called Roger Bell provided a contrast in character and technique with the Americans and their landings.

Bell was not unlike a good many young officers in the British wartime army, at least in his attitude to the army and to the war. He had been twenty when the war started, apprenticed to a chartered accountant in the city of Coventry; and he had joined up at once, partly in a fit of patriotism, but partly also because he was afraid he was going to fail his next examination in accountancy, which was due in a month or two. What had followed had not been at all what he expected; not gallant action, neither death nor glory, but four and a half years of solid training and exercises, and much less danger than was suffered by the women and children in the terrible air-raids on his native city.

The reversal of the roles of civilians and soldiers in Britain in the four years between Dunkirk and Normandy had affected the outlook of everyone in the army who had had the misfortune to be stationed there all the time. Throughout history, armies had gone to the wars with bands playing and the population lining the streets and cheering. Physical courage had been the soldiers' pride. The bombing of Britain had exploded an agelong myth by showing that courage was not confined to soldiers but, on the contrary, was a virtue which almost everybody had when it was needed. Courage did not need bands, or uniforms or traditions or drill, or any of the pomp and ceremoniousness of armies. It was not even an exclusively manly virtue any more. Most soldiers who had been in Britain all through the war must have had the experience of feeling rather foolish, when they went home on leave from a secure and well-sheltered camp in the depths of the country, and saw what had been happening in the towns or found themselves secretly alarmed in an air-raid which their mothers and wives and neighbors and even daughters took as a matter of course.

This upheaval of the fundamental hypothesis of war may have been the cause of the widespread fashion in the armed forces to make light of courage and pretend to be a coward. During his training, Roger Bell had never been able to bring himself to take the army quite seriously, and he would not have known whether to feel flattered or not if anyone had ever told him he was a good soldier; but probably no one ever did. When their divisional commander told the Westminster Dragoons they were to have the honor of being among the first to land in France, Bell and most of the other junior wartime-only officers agreed it was an honor they would gladly have done without. But that was not much more than a pose. Bell was glad, at a rather deeper level, that he was going to have a chance at last to do something really dangerous. Apart from the patriotic feelings which he would hardly have dared to confess, he was tired of feeling faintly ridiculous. Having joined the army, it would have been a final blow to his pride to have gone right through the war in perfect safety.

So on the whole, he had been perfectly happy when the years of training ended with the final embarkation in a landing craft in Southampton Water—an embarkation not just for another practice landing round the corner in Studland Bay, but for the real thing at last. The landing craft carried a team of six tanks, and he was second-in-command of the team and had a tank of his own. When the tanks had been reversed on board and the small ship backed off from the shore, there was a holiday atmosphere which lasted all through the extra

Sherman "Crab"

day of waiting. Bell sighed with relief to think that all the worries and annoyances of preparing were over, and that if he had forgotten anything there was nothing anyone could do about it. He and all his men knew exactly what they were supposed to do, and they were sure they could do it, or at least have a go at it. Meanwhile, it was up to the navy; the army could relax.

What Bell was going to try to do was something which the Americans did not try at all. His tank was a flail, specially designed to open tracks through minefields, and his team, which was a mixture of Westminster Dragoons and Royal Engineers, included three different kinds of the peculiar tanks which were officially known as specialized armor, and less officially but more usually as "funnies."

These tanks were the products of a tremendous fund of ingenuity, and of a study of the problems of invasion which went back to the raid on Dieppe in August 1942. They were developed by the 79th Armored Division under the command of Maj.-Gen. Sir Percy Hobart, a pioneer of armored warfare who had retired and become a corporal in the Home Guard but was dragged back into active service by Churchill.

The experience of Dieppe had persuaded the British—and Churchill in particular—that army engineers, in a seaborne assault on prepared defenses, could not efficiently demolish obstacles, lay roads, clear minefields, fill antitank ditches, or destroy fortifications while they themselves were under heavy fire. The funnies were designed to provide the engineers in the forefront of the landing with armored protection and mechanical means for carrying out their tasks.

The DD tank was one product of the 79th Division. Others were flails, such as Bell commanded, bobbins, fascines, roly-polys, petards, crocodiles, self-propelled ramps, and tanks which carried bridges. The whole of the British plan of assault was based on the use of these tanks and a description of the British landings must start with an explanation of what was hidden by their code names.

The flail tanks were designed to supersede the slow and dangerous process of clearing landmines by hand. A flail was an ordinary Sherman tank with two arms in front of it which carried a revolving drum. On the drum, there were short lengths of chain, and when the drum revolved the chains flew round and flailed the ground in front of the tank, exploding mines before the tank had reached them. The tank left a wide visible track which other tanks or infantry could follow.

Bobbins and roly-polys unrolled various kinds of matting or steel mesh, drove over it and left it behind them to form a temporary roadway. They had been designed for laying roads across dunes, or over the patches of clay which reconnaissance had revealed in some of the Normandy beaches.

Fascines each carried an enormous bundle of logs which they could drop into an antitank ditch so that they themselves, and other tanks, could cross it. Self-propelled ramps were tanks without turrets, which could lay themselves against a seawall or an antitank wall so that other tanks could climb up them and get over. The bridging tanks carried thirty-foot bridges for the wider ditches or craters; they laid their bridges and then drove over them. Most of these machines reverted to the functions of ordinary tanks as soon as they had finished their special missions.

Petards and crocodiles were tanks for destroying gun positions. The petard threw an enormous bomb from a short-muzzled mortar, sufficient to blow a large hole in a concrete emplacement—and the crocodile threw flame, much more and hotter and further than the flamethrowers which were carried by infantry.

For the invasion, these products of inventive minds concentrating on destruction were assembled in teams to suit the terrain and defenses they were expected to have to face. Each team fitted into one landing craft. Bell's piece of beach, for example, was not complicated by dunes or a seawall, but it was defended by mines and gun emplacements, and wire and obstacles on the sand. It also had a patch of soft clay on it. The first tank in Bell's team was therefore a bobbin, to lay a track across the clay. Then there were three flails, to clear the minefields. The fifth was a fascine, in case of craters on the roads which led inland, and the last was an armored bulldozer to push the beach obstacles out of the way. Other teams, to land on each side of him, included armor to deal with the gun emplacements. There was no need for ramps or bridges on his sector.

All these gadgets had been offered by the British to the American high command, but they had politely refused them excepting the DD tanks, which unfortunately, when the day came, were the least successful of all because they were dependent on the weather. It has puzzled military historians that Americans, usually regarded as the most mechanically minded people, should have preferred to try to do by hand the work which the specialized armor could do by machinery. Possibly there was an element of national pride involved in their not wanting to accept British inventions. By the time the offer was made, which was after Eisenhower and Montgomery were appointed, the American engineers had made up their minds how they were going to tackle their problems and had started to train their men; and they could not bring themselves to scrap the planning and training they had done and start again. It was also characteristic of American military planning to be more spendthrift with the lives of their soldiers than the British, perhaps because they had a much bigger population behind them, and perhaps because the British still remembered more vividly the loss of a generation in World War I. But whatever the reason, American instinct, confronted with defenses like those at Omaha, was to go for them bald-headed with their bare hands, and to support the action with the argument that this was the quickest way to achieve success, so that although it might cost more lives at the time, it would save them in the long run.

It would have been difficult to support this argument after Omaha. It is usually uncertain in military affairs to say what might have been; but it does seem likely that if the American commanders had accepted the British equipment and been able to land it on Omaha in sufficient force, it would have punched gaps at once in the stone bank, and cut the wire and rolled up the minefields, and so let the infantry and tanks get off the beach without the lethal and paralyzing delay which they suffered. The outcome of the battle would never have been in such doubt, and many of the three thousand men who were killed or wounded there would have been saved.

As soon as the landing craft which carried Bell and his tanks got under way on the morning of the fifth, and out of the lee of the Isle of Wight, the rough weather took the edge off the party feeling. Most of the thirty men on board were sick, in spite of the pills of hyoscine they had taken. There was nothing for them to do, and not very much to see. Peering out over the high wet bulwarks, the tank crews saw the other landing craft of their own flotilla, but no other shipping at all, and some of them wondered gloomily whether there had been a ghastly muddle. Perhaps, they thought, the whole thing had been postponed again and the naval types who were running the flotilla had missed the signal. Nothing seemed more likely. Perhaps they were crossing the Channel all alone. As dusk began to fall that evening, they were a little cheered up by the sight of two cruisers. They were a long way off, but they were going in the right direction: south.

Bell was a fairly good sailor, and managed not to be sick. He did not feel the slightest apprehension either, or fear for what was coming in the morning. He had never seen battle. He had never even seen a dead man. But as darkness fell, and the landing craft plunged onwards, he felt a tremendous elation at taking part in such a great adventure. It never crossed his mind that the invasion might fail. He had read the personal message which Montgomery had circulated; and Monty said he had complete confidence, and so that was that. It had never occurred to him either to think very much about the cause he was going to fight for. If he ever paused to think of it at all, he would certainly have thought the battle was right and just.

At nightfall, he encouraged his men to lie down on the steel decks and get what sleep they could. There was only one army officer on board besides himself; and the skipper of the landing craft, who had to be on the bridge all night, had offered them his cabin. There was that much to be said for being an officer. At midnight, two-thirds of the way across the Channel, with a clear conscience and no worries in the world, Roger Bell was fast asleep.

* * *

At that same hour, in a gun battery on a hill behind the exact part of the coast which was Bell's objective, a young man called Friedrich Wurster was on duty as a sentry; and his thoughts were wandering, as the thoughts of sentries do. He was listening to heavy bombers going over on their way, he imagined, to bomb the towns of Germany, and he was thinking of the air-raid sirens sounding at home, and his mother waking and having to get up and go down alone to the shelter again; alone, because his father was stationed as a soldier in the north of Norway, and his brother was in the air force. The thought of it made him both sad and angry, exactly as similar thoughts of home made British soldiers in outposts sad and angry.

Wurster, however, was spared the feeling which Bell had found so hurtful to his pride; the feeling that while the civilians suffered, he was safe in the army. His army career had been far from safe. He was twenty-one, and he had been a soldier for four years. At seventeen, he had marched into France with the conquering army. At eighteen, he had marched into Russia. At nineteen, he had been wounded within a hundred miles of Moscow. Before he was twenty, he had been patched up and sent back to Russia and witnessed advances

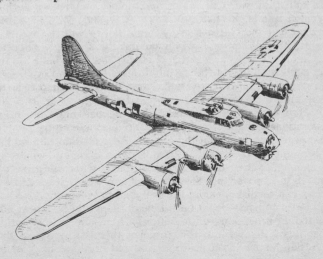

and then retreats; and he had been wounded a second time, so badly that they could not make him fit for Russia again but sent him to the Atlantic Wall instead, a semi-invalid at twenty-one.

So he knew a lot about war; and in fact, as he sometimes admitted to himself, he had not had much time to learn about anything else. On his solitary nights as a sentry, he often wondered how it would end, whether it would ever end, whether he would survive it, whether he would ever live at home with his family again, and he dreamed of all the things he would like to do, now that he was grown up, and if there was peace and he was free.

But although he longed for the war to end, he had never imagined its end as anything but a German victory. He was the son of a farmer, and he had been ten when Hitler came to power. Like every boy and girl he knew, he had automatically joined the Hitler Youth; and practically the whole of his education had been at the hands of Nazis or under the control of Nazism. It would be inaccurate to say that he believed in Nazi doctrine; it was not a question of belief or disbelief. Nazism was truth. It was the only social system and the only philosophy he knew; for he had not learned anything of democracy in France or communism in Russia, except that he was told they were decadent and almost laughably inferior. Even in Russia, he had never had to consider the idea that Nazism and the German army might fail to win the war.

But still, Wurster was fundamentally a simple, decent peasant, with normal feelings of charity. So far, what little he had come to know of the dreadful degradation and cruelty of the system he represented had always been explained away to him, either as something right and necessary, or as a lie invented by enemies. The character he had inherited from generations of hard-working and God-fearing country people was quite different from the character driven into him by his upbringing, and it may be that he was doomed, whatever happened, to a revulsion sooner or later, when he grew up enough to discover that these parts of him were irreconcilable. When the revulsion came, it was bound to be painful for him, and to turn upside down the whole of the world he knew; but the sooner it happened, the better for him, and for the world. That night, he was on the verge of the first spasm of the revulsion, as he stood unsuspecting and bored at his post in the dark, looking out towards the glimmer of the sea.

At two o'clock he was relieved, and he went back to his quarters to turn in; but before he had finished undressing, the alarm bell rang and the battery loudspeakers called everyone to the first state of alert. His companions crawled out of bed grumbling sleepily, and slowly began to grope about for their clothes. There had been so many false alarms in the last few weeks that they were fed up with them and did not take them seriously any more. Before any of them were ready, the second state of alert was sounded, and through the loudspeakers an officer told them that parachutists and gliders had landed beyond the River Orne and attacked the battery at Merville, which all of them knew at least by name because it was manned by their own regiment.

But still they did not worry or feel that things were urgent. They had been told by their leaders time and again that the Atlantic Wall was impregnable, and they believed it. The artillery had more reason to believe it than the static divisions of infantry. Their own positions and armament were good, and so was their morale, and they did not know of the doubts and inefficiency of some of the infantry units on whose cooperation they depended.

So they went on dressing in a leisurely manner, discussing the news. Merville was twenty miles away, and the general opinion was that this was a local raid. Wurster's companions had been told it would be crazy for the British or Americans to make a serious attack on the Atlantic Wall, and they did not believe they would try.

When Roger Bell woke up and looked out at the break of dawn, what he saw was astonishingly different from the scene of the evening before: the same gray turbulent sea, but full of ships from horizon to horizon. Bell had been cynical—or pretended to be—when General Hobart had talked of the honor of being among the first to land. Now he began to see for the first time exactly what the general had meant. It was the first time he and his tank crews had ever seen a fleet prepared for action, and the first time they had had any real impression of the fantastic size and power of the force which had been assembled to support them. As their flotilla steamed through the lines of battleships and cruisers and destroyers towards the smudge of the shoreline of France, they did feel proud at last of being among the first performers in such a drama.

On board the landing craft itself, as it passed inshore of the
fleet, the scene was almost domestic—the tank men finishing
breakfast, stowing away their blankets, washing their faces,
some trying to shave. Some, after a miserable night, had not
been able to face the British army compo tea—a ready-made
mixture of tea and sugar and powdered milk which made a
fairly nauseating drink at the best of times. Bell, as part of the
pretense that he would be scared out of his wits, had stowed
a bottle of navy rum in his tank to give himself Dutch courage
for the landing; but now that the moment had come, he was
so excited that he forgot all about it and swallowed his tea
with enjoyment. Everyone was cheerful, now that the crossing
was nearly over. Whatever was going to happen on the beach,
they looked forward to being on land again.

Bell saw to the clearing of the chains and chocks which
held his tank, and then from his turret he looked out at the
shore ahead—the shore which he knew, from maps and
photographs, almost as well as Friedrich Wurster knew it.
This was Gold Beach. It was a straight stretch of sand about
three miles long, which had a small village at each end of it:
at the west end, Le Hamel, and at the east, La Rivière.
Beyond Le Hamel, a line of hills ran out to the coast and
ended in cliffs which separate the beach from the little town
of Arromanches. Beyond La Rivière, at the other end, the
shore was protected in 1944 by a very high seawall of
concrete, with a road on top of it—an obstacle which was
even beyond the powers of the specialized armor.

But between the two villages, there were only dunes
behind the beach, with a few holiday houses and wooden
bungalows. Beyond the dunes there was a narrow strip of
marshy ground, and a road which joined the villages, and
then a line of gentle grassy hills. The hills were not so steep
as the bluffs of Omaha, and they presented no obstacle for
tanks; but they commanded a view of the whole of the beach,
and Wurster's battery, among others, was built on top of
them.

Bell was to land at the eastern end of the beach, just clear
of the seawall of La Rivière, and one of the landmarks he had
been told to look out for was a large emplacement on the top
of the seawall, which was believed to contain an 88-mm gun
which was sited to enfilade the beach.

So far, as Bell advanced, like Rockwell with his tank

landing craft at Omaha, under the arch of the gunfire from the heavy ships behind him, he had not seen any activity from the German batteries. The smoke of the bombardment hid the hills and hung over the village; but as the craft drew in, the beach itself was clearly visible. It looked dead and perfectly deserted, as if nobody had set foot on it for years; and that was no wonder, because La Rivière itself, which was no more than a score of houses defended by a single platoon of Germans, had just been bombed by six squadrons of heavy bombers and was now being shelled by the sixteen 5-inch guns of four destroyers, and by twenty-four 25-pounders of the Royal Artillery in landing craft, and by two thousand rockets.

The bombardment, striking just before dawn, was the first warning Friedrich Wurster had that anything really serious was happening. It did very little structural damage to the battery, but while it lasted the artillery was paralyzed. Not even the veterans like himself from the Russian front had ever known anything like it, and not even the best trained soldiers could stand up and keep a lookout or lay a gun. Even after dawn, they could not have seen anything through the smoke and flame, and they could not have heard an order. Wurster dived into an armored emplacement, and so did everybody else who could; and in the only glimpse he had outside in the whole of that awful hour, he saw cows and horses in the meadow beside the battery felled by the high explosives and set on fire, some still alive, by incendiary bombs.

Before it stopped, the trained hearing of the artillery men had detected the sound of shells among the other noise, and shellfire could only have come from a ship, improbable though that seemed; and so, when suddenly there was silence, or what seemed by comparison like silence, and Wurster stood up and looked out, he was partially prepared for what he saw. But it was still an overwhelming shock. He had half expected ships, but he had never expected or even dreamed of six hundred ships, and at least that number must have been in sight from his battery at dawn. Nor had he ever heard of landing craft; yet there they were, already in the surf, and men and tanks were pouring out of them and advancing across the beach to the foot of the hill.

*   *   *

Bell's was among them. Still surprised that he was not being shot at, he had spotted the end of the seawall and the 88 emplacement on top of it, and he knew his skipper was going to succeed in putting him down at exactly the right place and the right time. The map of the shore was clear in his mind's eye, and his job was simple; to flail a track through the minefields, across the road, and straight on up the hill. He was intensely excited. The supreme moment of all his training was approaching; and like Mabry, like Gibbons, like thousands of other men, he knew it was a moment he would remember all his life.

The crews of the other tanks, the bobbin ahead of him and the other flails astern, were starting up their engines. Bell gave the order to start up too; and then something terrible and quite ridiculous happened. The starter motor whined, and whined again. He shouted to his driver. They tried again and again: no good. At the moment of moments, his engine would not start.

No motorist stalled in a busy city street ever felt such a fool as Bell. He had to move, to let out the four tanks behind him. The line of breakers and the beach were just ahead. There was only one hope: a tow. He jumped down and seized the towing cable from the bobbin tank ahead of him and shackled it on to his own. The Royal Engineers in the bobbin were not at all pleased at the idea of entering battle towing a derelict 30-ton tank of the Dragoons. In the excitement and argument, Bell had no time to look around him and before he expected it the landing craft was aground and the ramp banged down into the water. The bobbin lurched forward and jerked the cable taut.

Bell's tank moved a few yards along the deck, and that did it. The engine started. Bell signaled O.K. to the bobbin and cast off the tow. As he climbed back to his turret, the bobbin roared down the ramp and almost vanished into deep water. His turn had come. Thinking of nothing but his engine, he followed, and in a few seconds waves were breaking against the turret and splashing over him, and the tank was crawling towards the shore. For the minute or so while he had fumbled with the tow, he and the bobbin had been easy targets; but if anyone had fired at them, he had been too busy to notice it.

As the tank rose up from the sea and the water streamed

Churchill AVRE "Bobbin"

off its hull, Bell in the turret had an impression of stakes on each side of him with landmines fastened on top of them: and he glanced along the beach to his right, and saw through the eddying smoke that the beach was no longer deserted; all along it, as far as he could see, tanks were rolling out of the water and making for the dunes. Even in that momentary glance he saw two of them hit: two of the flails of his own regiment which had landed a little to his right. And then a petard tank of the Royal Engineers a few yards ahead of him exploded with a sudden appalling crash and a gush of flame. At almost the same instant, Bell felt his own tank shudder and felt rather than heard an explosion just behind him. He looked round. Flames were pouring from the stern, just behind his head.

A tank only starts to burn if its gasoline is alight. Shermans had the reputation of burning often and quickly; British tank men called it "brewing up"—the phrase also means making tea. The Germans grimly but aptly called them Tommy-cookers. When they brewed up, the crew had a matter of split seconds to get out before they were burned alive. Seeing the flames, Bell ordered his crew out and began to get out of the turret himself. Then a large lump of flaming twisted steel fell off the stern of the tank and lay blazing on the sand, and he realized that he had not been hit at all; a piece of the exploded tank ahead of him had landed on him still burning and then rolled off again. He shouted to his crew, above the din, that it was all right. But what, he wondered, had hit the three tanks ahead? Accurate and powerful fire was coming from somewhere, but he did not know where it was. And then he saw a small puff of smoke; it was the 88-mm gun in the emplacement a hundred yards away which was still in action in spite of the bombardment and was enfilading the beach and picking off the advancing tanks at point-blank range.

The emplacement of La Rivière, like many others, was built so that it could only fire along the beach, and not out to sea. On its seaward side it was protected by 17 feet of concrete, as defense against naval gunfire; and the concrete had held. Bell, landing almost in front of it, was out of its field of fire, but to advance anywhere he had to cross almost under the muzzle of the gun. Indeed, all the armor on the beach was having to run the gauntlet of its fire, and the outcome of the whole of the first assault in that sector was likely to depend upon somebody doing something about that gun.

At the sight of it, Bell's reaction was immediate; an instinctive reaction much deeper than all the superficial talk about being frightened. He did not pause to think that it was somebody else's job, but drove on full speed to the place where the others had been hit, so that he could see the embrasure in the side of the emplacement and the muzzle of the 88 sticking out of it towards him. There was a steel shield over it. He stopped, and brought his own gun to bear. He was a sitting target, and he knew it, a hundred yards in front of a gun which could knock him out at twenty times that distance. He fired the two rounds of HE but they seemed to have no effect. The German gun fired again, but it fired past him at one of the dozens of other targets down the beach. He fired three more shots with armor-piercing shells. He could not have missed, but he could not see whether his shots had gone through the shield. Before he could fire again, another tank which had not seen what was happening drove up from the beach between him and the gun and masked his fire; he watched it fascinated, waiting to see it brew up, as it crossed the field of fire within 50 yards of the emplacement. Nothing happened. The 88 was dead. He and his tank crew had done what all the bombardment that morning had failed to do.

Ahead of him now was the wire and the first of the minefields. He crashed through the wire, and started his flail and began to flog his way across the minefield towards the road, the whirling chains churning the soft sandy earth like a gigantic cultivator. At this point he had been ordered to light a green smoke grenade and throw it overboard as a signal to somebody—he could not remember whom—who was coming in behind him. It was the kind of grenade which is lit by a striker like a matchbox. He lit it; and at that moment the tank gave a lurch and he dropped the grenade and it fell inside the turret. Immediately, the tank was filled with a lurid green smoke. As it flogged on across the minefield, he was groveling in the bottom of it for the grenade and smoke was pouring out of the turret top. He found it at last and came up gasping and dropped it over the side. The flail did not seem to be exploding any mines. The ground was very wet, and it got worse towards the road; and just before the tank reached the road, she stuck in the mud.

While the tracks of his own tank dug themselves deeper, the two other flails of his team went past him on luckier patches of ground, and climbed the embankment onto the road, hesitated, and then turned left and roared off into the ruins of La Rivière. Annoyed with himself, Bell got out of his tank and climbed carefully down into the minefield. His gunner laughed, and he looked at himself and found the grenade had dyed him bright green all over. He looked back at the beach. The infantry were pouring ashore, and crossing the tidemark where the German gun would have decimated them a few minutes before. All kinds of tanks were following the tracks of the flails through the minefield. Bell began to laugh too; and still beautifully green, he walked back to the beach, down the path which he had flailed, to find a tank recovery vehicle, or anyone else who would pull him out.

Almost everything, he thought, had gone ridiculously wrong with his landing. Well, what could they expect? He had always said he was no good as a soldier. It simply never occurred to him, till they gave him a medal long afterwards, that he had gone and done something brave at the very first opportunity he had had in all his five years in the army. But he had; and his moment of blind courage, and his five unerring shots, had been worth the best part of a battalion.

The flail tanks on this end of Gold Beach had not had much to do in their primary task of cutting paths through minefields. The first minefield, in which Bell and several others were stuck, turned out to have been sown with Belgian mines which did not explode, either because they had been badly made to begin with, or else because they had lain too long in the wet earth. The second minefield, beyond the road, was much wetter than air photography had suggested. There were reeds and standing water in it. Only one of the flail tanks tried it, and that one was damaged immediately by a mine because the ground was too soft for the flail to work. The commanders of all the other flails which reached the road decided at a glance that the bog was impassable, whether it was effectively mined or not; and they turned left, towards the ruins of La Rivière, and began to drive inland by road. One minefield had been too easy, and the other too difficult for the flails.

Nevertheless, in their secondary role as ordinary tanks, the flails and the other funnies had largely cleared this beach for the infantry, by many such actions as Bell's, and made up to a great extent for the absence of the DD tanks, which had not been launched because of the weather and were brought ashore behind the infantry; and as soon as the flails were safely on the road, they set to work to force the exits from the beach inland.

Beyond the minefields, there was an antitank ditch; and soon the first of the flails, rumbling down the road which led inland from La Rivière, came to the point where the road crossed over the ditch, and the tank commander saw to his surprise that the crossing had not been blown up. He reported by radio to his squadron that he was going to try to cross. "If you hear a loud bang," he said, "you'll know what's happened." But there was no bang. The tank crawled safely over. A little further on, the road was blocked by an enormous bomb crater. One of the RE's bridge-carrying tanks was called up, and quickly laid a bridge across it. The flails went on and flogged a track for half a mile further. Within half an hour of

Churchill Mk. III AVRE (SBG)

the landing, the specialized armor had broken a route right through the Atlantic Wall; and other tanks and the infantry—the Green Howards—began to pour along it into the open country, while the East Yorks cleared out the village.

Further west, in the center of Gold Beach, out of the point-blank range of the gun at La Rivière, the attack went in with even more precision; but at the opposite end of the beach there was serious trouble in front of the village of Le Hamel. The Germans there had fortified a sanatorium on the seafront, and the bombardment had left this strongpoint still in good working order. The aerial bombing had missed it, and the shelling from the sea, though it had wrecked the sanatorium, had not done any important damage to the guns because they were heavily protected, like the one at La Rivière, on the seaward side. But, again like La Rivière, the main guns of Le Hamel could not fire straight out to sea. They were sited to cover the high-water mark along the beach, and so at low tide, close under the strongpoint itself, there was a small area of beach which was almost safe but was surrounded by other areas almost impossible for a man to cross alive.

Here other teams of the Royal Engineers and Westminster Dragoons went first, followed seven minutes later by the infantry of the 1st Battalion, the Hampshire Regiment. Among the veterans of the Hampshires was Company Sergeant Major H. W. Bowers, and his landing may be taken as an example of the experience of the foremost companies, or at least of their survivors.

Company Sergeant Major Bowers was the opposite kind of soldier to Captain Bell: a Cornishman, a regular with seventeen years service, the son of a soldier, whose army service was both his profession and his pride. At the age of thirty-six, he was not only an old soldier, he was almost an old hand at assault landings, for the landing in Normandy was his fourth. His first had been the invasion of Sicily, and the next two were on the Italian coast. He had won the Military Medal in one of them, and been mentioned in dispatches in another. So, unlike the great majority who crossed the Channel, he had known what he was in for. It had scared him, more than it had scared Bell, who knew so much less about it. All the way over, his stomach had been doing what he called the butterfly hop. He had felt the same on his way to the other landings. The trouble was having too much time to think. He knew he would be all right when he got his two feet on dry land, because then there would be no time to think at all, and because he was quite convinced that man for man, and hand to hand, a British soldier was more than a match for a German; but meanwhile, on the landing craft, being a sergeant major, he had to take care to look much tougher than he felt.

Besides that lurking fear, there had been another private thought at the back of Bowers' mind all through the crossing, a somewhat less somber one. His British army boots were killing him. Whatever else happened in the invasion, what he meant to win was a nice soft pair of German boots to give his feet a rest.

In the last mile towards the beach, Bowers and his boatload of men had been encouraged and roused from the lethargy of seasickness, like so many others, by the majestic scope of the bombardment. Above the roar of the shells and rockets going overhead, somebody shouted, "Fancy having that lot on your breakfast plate." It was hard to imagine that anyone could still be alive on the receiving end, so the shock was all the greater when the Hampshires ran ashore straight into a deadly counterfire.

On the beach, as Bowers waded ashore with his company, the noise and concussion were so stunning that he was unconscious—like Henry Meyers on Omaha—of anything more than the few men close beside him and the few yards of sand ahead. But he knew exactly what he had to do, and so he did it. He ran blindly up the beach to the first of the rolls of concertina wire above high-water mark, together with other men carrying bangalore torpedoes. They thrust these into the wire and fired them, and Bowers went through the first of the gaps which they blew and reached the low concrete seawall which lay beyond it. Breathless in the illusory shelter of the wall, he looked round and saw that desperately few of the company had made it: most of them were lying far back towards the water's edge, dead, or wounded, or shocked into immobility. But his company commander, Maj. D. J. Warren, had got through. The two of them could see their company being slaughtered, but time passed before they saw that the bulk of the fire was sweeping along the beach from right to left, and more time before they spotted its source in a pillbox built on the seaward end of the sanatorium. An attack on the pillbox was imperative, but only four men close to Bowers were fit to move: the major and himself, and his runner, who carried a walkie-talkie radio, and one other soldier.

These four crawled along below the wall towards the pillbox; but a hundred yards away from it the wall petered out, and they found themselves pinned down on open ground, looking into the muzzles of three or four machine guns and an 88 mm which was firing close over their heads at the tanks along the beach. While they searched for a way of moving nearer, the radio operator received a message for Major Warren to take over command of the battalion. The major began to crawl back. The radio operator shuddered in the sand and died without a sound. At this, the other soldier turned back and followed the major, and Bowers was left all alone. He was not feeling too good himself. But there was no way forward, so he also crawled back to where he had started; and there he found his colonel with a badly smashed arm.

"What, Bowers, you still alive?" the colonel said.

"Just about, sir," Bowers said; and he told him about the pillbox.

The colonel listened, and then Bowers understood him to say, "Well, go and see what you can do about it."

"Very good sir," Bowers replied; and he thought, "Christ, he expects me to take on the whole bloody Jerry army."

Bowers had lost his sense of time by then, but a lot had happened while he had been alone. More of the Hampshires had made their way across the beach, but he did not recognize any of his company. For the moment, in fact, the situation was the same as at Omaha, the infantry being shocked and shot to pieces; but the specialized armor had broken the deadlock. The armored force had lost its commander, who was killed by a sniper very soon after he landed, but the petard tanks had blown breaches in the seawall. At least one of the flails, though Bowers had not seen it, had turned along the beach to fight a duel with the pillbox and had got the worst of the encounter; but several more had gone through the gaps in the wall just to the left of the village and started to clear lanes through the minefields up to the coastal road. In the first of these flails was the second-in-command of the armor, Capt. B. Taylor. The second was commanded by a sergeant called Lindsay. Captain Taylor's tank was damaged in the minefield, but Sergeant Lindsay reached the road and turned right towards the center of the village where, according to his orders, he was to find the command post of the Hampshires. Captain Taylor knew the Hampshires were not yet in the village, and with consternation he saw Lindsay accelerate and charge into the village street. He tried to warn him, but his radio was out of action; and Lindsay disappeared into the enemy village and was seen no more that day.

Churchill Mk. III AVRE (Petard)

Lindsay, in fact, had soon discovered he was out on his own, ahead of anybody else, but he went on methodically with his business. Finding no infantry at the rendezvous, he shot his way right through the village and round the back of the sanatorium and began the second task in his orders: to clear the road which led out of the village to the westward. He was foiled in that by a tank trap of steel rails planted in the road and by an antitank ditch on the inland side of it; so he turned round and went back into the village, and found a place where he could cross the ditch, and started his third task of flailing a lane through a minefield beyond it. Slowly flogging his way across open country, he was an easy target, and before he had gone far his tank was hit twice by an 88-mm gun on the cliffs above Arromanches, half a mile away. On the second hit it brewed up, and Lindsay and his crew bailed out, all more or less burned, and hid in a cornfield. Lindsay and two of them waited there till midnight, and then rejoined the British forces. The other two had the experience, unusual on that morning on the seafront, of being taken prisoner by the Germans, but they escaped a few days later and joined the Americans.

This solitary escapade behind the sanatorium distracted the Germans' attention for a time and probably diverted some of their fire from the Hampshires. It probably also helped Bowers as he started to carry out the order which he thought he had been given.

Bowers was armed with a Sten gun, some British hand-grenades, and a haversack full of Italian grenades, for which he had formed affection and respect in Italy. With this equipment, the only way to "do something about" a pillbox was to get within arm's length of it and that was impossible head-on along the beach; so he went through the gap which the tanks had made in the seawall, and plotted a possible course through an open space which might have been a garden or a playground.

In the gap he met two sailors of the RN Commandos. They had been with him on the landing craft, and he knew them as Paddy and Taffy. "Hey, Harry!" they shouted. "Where are you going? Can we come and have a bit of fun?"

"Some people have a queer idea of fun," he said, glad of their company and of their tommy guns.

The three men worked their way across the devastated space behind the seawall, fighting it out with some Germans who threatened to take them in the rear, and won a position behind the pillbox, close to the ruins of the sanatorium. A grenade was thrown at them there. It rolled along the ground, rolled so long that Bowers shouted "All right, it's a dud"; whereupon it exploded and wounded Paddy in the leg. The others patched him up. Bowers put the two sailors in a position to cover the pillbox with their tommy guns, because he had spotted a way to get to grips with it. They poured a continuous fire at the openings they could see, and under the protection of their fire he climbed into the ruins, and through them, and found an empty window above the pillbox and jumped down onto the roof of it. He ran across the roof, and lay down on his stomach and leaned over the edge with a grenade in his hand. Through the firing slit below him, somebody was pushing a white sheet of surrender, but he thought "Hell with you, mate, after all this trouble," and he dropped his grenade through the slit.

After the explosion, the door of the pillbox was opened and the survivors ran out. They had their hands up. From his perch on the roof, he looked down at them with interest, partly because they seemed to be shouting that they were Russian, and also because some of them were wearing nice soft German army boots.

As soon as Friedrich Wurster and his companions in the battery on the top of the hill had recovered from the bombardment and the shock of seeing the fleet and the landing craft, they started to fire, with their 105-mm French guns, against the beach; but the firing was interrupted again and again by low-flying aircraft which drove the gunners to shelter with machine guns and cannon shells. Several men had been killed by the bombing. Now the number of casualties grew till the aid post overflowed. It was not very long either till they lost their forward observation post, which was down by the shore. The battery commander was down there, and everyone in the battery heard his last call on the communication system.

"They're coming right in the post," he cried with a frantic note in his voice; and he added "*Lebt wohl, Kamaraden,*" and the line was silent. Soon after, the last call came also from regimental headquarters, which was near Merville. It said that Merville had fallen, and headquarters itself was under fire from tanks and infantry. Then that line went dead too, and the battery was isolated.

But Wurster could see the British tanks still coming ashore in what seemed to be limitless numbers, and disappearing into the folds of the hills and the countryside around; and one after another, the neighboring German strongpoints were falling silent. Wurster knew the battery must be surrounded by tanks already, and that an attack was sure to be made on it very soon; and he heard somebody say there were only three antitank grenades left in the battery because they had used the rest in an exercise three days before and they had never been replaced. On the verge of despair, the men looked up for help; but the sky was full of enemy aircraft, and not a single German could be seen. The position was terrible and hopeless; the only choice, if it was a choice, was death or surrender. It had happened so quickly that Wurster could hardly believe it, and yet there was the proof in front of his very eyes; the Atlantic Wall had crumbled away into ruin as soon as it had been tested, and the air force had abandoned them to their fate.

The attack soon came, but it was short. The gunners managed to bring three of their 105s to bear against the tanks and hit two of them, and then the rest broke off the fight and disappeared inland; and Wurster knew what that meant. The battery was so securely trapped that the British would not waste time in fighting it, but would leave it to be captured at their leisure—the technique which the Germans had taught them in 1940.

It was Bell's squadron of the Westminster Dragoons which captured Wurster's battery in the end, though Bell and Wurster probably never saw each other and certainly never

Churchill Mk. VIII "Crocodile"

heard each other's names. It did not happen till the next morning, and it happened in a rather peculiar way. After an exciting day, made even more exciting by a totally false report that forty German Tiger tanks were about to attack them, Bell and the squadron of flails settled down for the night in an orchard. Their resting place was within a couple of hundred yards of an outpost of the battery, but neither side knew the other was there and both spent a quiet night. At dawn, the German gunners saw the tanks, and defiantly opened fire. The Dragoons, with two of the flame-throwing tanks of the Engineers, then roused themselves and quickly overran the battery and took a hundred prisoners.

A squadron of flail tanks did not expect to take prisoners, and these—after nearly five years of war against Germany— were the first German soldiers that Bell and his men had ever seen on a field of battle. Naturally, they regarded them with tremendous interest and considerable pride, and finding themselves so unexpectedly in the role of victor, they treated their fallen enemies with old-fashioned courtesy and honor. This made a deep impression on Wurster, who would have been much less surprised to be bullied or even shot; and he remembered this first impression a few days later, when he heard of Hitler's denunciation of him and his fellow-prisoners as traitors. This contrast, between the off-hand chivalry of his enemies and the shocking injustice of his own leader's accusation, was often in Wurster's mind in his imprisonment. It forced him to face the bitter alternative that his own high command had either been deceived itself about the strength of the Atlantic Wall and the air force, or else had deliberately deceived its own troops. So he began to think critically about the German conduct of the war, and to question the cause for which he and his family had suffered and so many of his friends had died. It was the events of D Day which started the revulsion in Friedrich Wurster's mind, the revulsion of the man he had been born, against the man that Nazism had made him; and the same could be said of very many Germans.

Long before Wurster's battery fired its last despairing shots against the tanks, the issue on Gold Beach had passed beyond any doubt. The Germans in Le Hamel had held out till the afternoon, and the Hampshires had suffered badly; but already, in the middle of the morning, seven exits from the beach had been cleared by the armor, the followup forces were pouring through them, and the advance had carried over three miles inland and was going strong.

Bell and Bowers, and probably everyone else who fought his way ashore on Gold Beach, believed they were the first Britons to set foot on it in the past four years, but they were not. Two soldiers had been there, on New Year's Eve. They went ashore at precisely the spot where Bell landed and made a survey of the beach in the dark; and although this escapade happened five months before D Day, it had an influence on what happened that day, and so it deserves to be mentioned. The men were two commandos called Logan Scott-Bowden and Bruce Ogden Smith; the first was a major and the second a sergeant, and they were the chief exponents of the curious art of swimming ashore by night and crawling out of the water unobserved.

A small unit for the reconnaissance of the beaches had existed for years. Like many odd little fighting units, it owed its existence to the passionate belief of one man. The man was a naval navigator, Lt. Comdr. Nigel Willmott; and his belief was that it was stupid to land an army anywhere on a hostile shore using only charts and photographs, because there were so many things which neither charts nor photographs could show. One of these things was the hardness of the sand—a matter of obvious interest in landing tanks and trucks.

Willmott had always said that the only way to find out such important details was to go and see, and that this was not nearly so difficult or dangerous as it sounded; but he had had a hard time persuading anyone to let him do it. He himself had swum ashore and reconnoitered Rhodes in 1942; but then the projected invasion of Rhodes had been canceled and the value of his observation had never been tested. Before the invasion of North Africa, his men had been forbidden to land for fear that they would be captured and the plans of the landing would be compromised. In Sicily and Italy, they had had some success; but his unit, and his theories, only came into their own at the end of 1943, when photographs of the beaches of northern France showed dark strips here and there, which might have been mud or soft clay. The plan of the whole invasion was suddenly seen to depend upon whether these strips would carry tanks or not, and none of the usual sources of intelligence could answer this question. After years of half-hearted support, Willmott found his ideas received with enthusiasm in the highest quarters. Although it was midwinter, he was told to go ahead and get samples of the material of certain French beaches as quickly as possible. Now that his chance had come, he himself was ill and not fit for winter swimming; but he had trained other swimmers. Scott-Bowden and Ogden Smith were two of them.

Sergeant Ogden Smith was the son of a family which had made fishing tackle for nearly two hundred years and sold it in a formidably dignified shop among the hatters and boot makers in the neighborhood of St. James's Palace. He had had the kind of education which makes it easy, in the British army, to become an officer. When people asked him why he was not one, he explained that he was quite happy as a sergeant. This was an attitude which had been fasionable, in the first year of the war, among the intelligentsia of the territorial army, of which he had been a member; but few men stuck to it as a principle, as he did, and resisted the comfort and prestige of being an officer right through the war. Once, he had given in to temptation and started an officers' training course, but he had only been half-hearted and he had been returned to unit when he wrote rude words on an intelligence test which he thought was a waste of time. When he was asked why he made a practice of swimming ashore on hostile beaches, he simply said that he liked it—it was not too bloodthirsty, and yet was quite exciting. In short, Ogden Smith was one of those brave but eccentric soldiers who can be a great asset to an army if it does not have too many of them: a square peg who had luckily found a square hole. Very few people knew of the job he had made his speciality. He had not even told his wife, who only knew that he sometimes got weekend leave when he had been on an expedition somewhere, and that she could expect a summons any moment, at the factory in Wales where she was working as welfare supervisor, to join him for a night out in London.

Through most of the winter and spring before the invasion, whenever there were moonless nights, Scott-Bowden and Ogden Smith were taken across the Channel to within a few hundred yards of the shore of France by small landing craft or midget submarines, usually navigated by Willmott. The equipment they took was simple; a lot of thought had been needed to make it so simple. They wore loose-fitting waterproof suits, and each of them carried a flashlight, compass and

watch, an underwater writing tablet, an auger with which to
bore holes in the beach and bring up cores of the material it
was made of, receptacles for carrying the cores, some meat
skewers, and a reel of fine sand-colored fishing line with a
bead on it at every ten yards. The fishing line and the reel
had been made in Ogden Smith's father's workshops. They
also took a fighting knife and a .45 Colt, which they had
found to be one of the few firearms which still work when
they are full of salt water and sand; but they relied more for
their safety on the hypothesis that only an exceptionally
wakeful sentry would see a man swimming in surf or crawling
on a beach at night.

When the shore was in sight on these expeditions, and
Willmott had fixed their exact position, they slipped over the
side of their boat and struck out for the breakers together. It
was always extremely cold. When they felt bottom, they
waded to the edge of the surf and lay there to get their
bearings and study the skyline till they were sure of the
movements of the sentries; and then, if everything was
reasonably quiet, they stuck a skewer in the sand with the
end of the fishing line tied to it, and started to crawl on their
stomachs up the beach, probing for mines and unwinding the
line as they went. At each bead on the line, they bored a hole
and took a sample, and skewered the line again and crawled
on, on a compass bearing.

In this way, they made passably accurate surveys of a great
many beaches. A large proportion of the places they landed
were not in the invasion plans at all, but they were sent to
them to ensure that if they were captured they would not be
able to tell from their own experience where the invasion was
going to be. They found it difficult, after several months, to
remember which beach was which; but they did remember
their landing at La Rivière because it was there that Ogden
Smith had suddenly remembered the date, and noticed that
it was midnight, and had taken it into his head to crawl to
where the major was lying listening to the conversation of
two sentries on the seawall, and in a stage whisper had
wished him a happy and prosperous New Year.

Sometimes they did other work besides looking for mud
and clay. They measured the gradients of the beaches, and
charted sandbars off shore where landing craft might have
stranded; and here and there they went inland to measure
and investigate obstacles beyond the beaches. They crossed

the minefield and the road where Bell's tank stuck, and had a
good look at the gun emplacement there. In the middle of
January, they were on the top of the fatal stone bank at
Omaha. They made an entirely uneventful tour of Utah; but
on a second visit to Omaha, a sentry came along the beach
between them and the sea and tripped over their fishing line.
It was through this accident, exciting at the time, that the
American army was able to land with the assurance that the
beach had not been mined; because if it had, the sentry
would not have been there. The two men bore a charmed
life. They were not only never seen, but every time, when
they had finished their probing, they waded out through the
waves again and swam three hundred yards to sea and flashed
their torches away from the land and waited; and every time,
before cold and cramp and exhaustion crippled them, their
boat came in and picked them up again. In the quest for
mud, they swam ashore on thirty beaches.

The result of this unique performance was to be seen in the
plans of the specialized armor, in Bell's landing craft, for one.
The tank in front of Bell's was a bobbin, placed there to lay a
track across a patch of mud on the beach. Probably the
bobbin's crew never guessed how anyone knew the patch of
mud was there. On many other parts of the British beaches,
track-laying tanks were sent in first on the evidence gouged
out by Willmott's swimmers.

This was the final vindication of the ideas which Willmott
had pressed forward so long. But even before the invasion, an
event occurred which must have given him the greatest
satisfaction. General Bradley had been worried by a suspicious
patch on photographs of Omaha. He had never heard of
beach reconnaissance, but he asked British Intelligence whether
anything was known about the texture of the beach. The
enquiry was passed to Willmott. Without telling the general,
he sailed across and landed Scott-Bowden and Ogden Smith;
and the next day he attended an American conference and
produced a sample of sand from his pocket, with an elaborately
casual air, explaining that his unit had fetched it the night
before, and that the beach was firm and would carry tanks all
right. This achievement amazed General Bradley, and he
generously said so. Perhaps he perceived the pride which
Willmott believed he was hiding.

As for Ogden Smith, his wife received an invitation to an
investiture at Buckingham Palace, where he was to receive

the Military Medal, though nobody had told her what he had done to earn it. The date of the investiture was June 6th. On June 5th, she had already put on her best hat and was on her way to the railway station in Wales when she had a telephone message to say that her husband was unavoidably detained and would not be turning up to meet the King. Nothing surprised her by then. She went home, and sadly put the hat away again, hoping she would need it to go to the palace one day.

It would have been quite in character for this curious soldier to have been late for his own investiture, but in fact it was hardly his fault. He and Scott-Bowden were on Omaha Beach again—this time not alone. The American army had taken them there as guides. They were the only people in England, so far as anyone knew, who had ever been there before.

Others of Willmott's men were playing an important and peculiar part in the invasion. They were lying about a mile off shore in midget submarines, one at each end of the British sector; and at H Hour they had already been there for three nights and two days and were not far from being dead of suffocation.

These submarines had the distinction of being the first of the whole invasion fleet. The code name of their operation was Gambit. Their crews, uneasy about this name, had looked up the word in the dictionary, and found it meant an opening move in a game of chess in which the player deliberately sacrifices a pawn. As they suspected, the name was shrewdly chosen. They were the pawn.

The submarines were the type called X craft, about fifty feet long and five and a half feet in diameter. Each of them was commanded by a naval reserve lieutenant with a crew of two, and each of them carried two of Willmott's specialized navigators; and their job was to place themselves as lightships. It was a simple and commonsense idea, because in the light of dawn on D Day, and in the heat of battle, it was expected to be difficult for the first landing craft or their escorts to fix their exact positions from observations of the shore, and mist or an off-shore wind which blew the smoke of the bombardment out to sea might make the shore invisible, as it did in fact at Utah. The X craft, on the other hand, were meant to arrive off the shore thirty-six hours before anyone else, so that they would have a whole day, if they needed it, to put themselves exactly in position by periscope bearings and anchor there. The fleet could then home in on them. The American navy rejected the idea. If it had not, it might have succeeded in landing the troops at Utah and Omaha in the right places; but still, its decision may have been wise. The reason for turning down the idea was that the X craft might be spotted and draw attention to the beaches, and there certainly was such a risk. On the British sector, the X craft mission was successful and useful; but the bad weather and the postponement made it far more risky than the British themselves had foreseen.

Of these two humble vanguards of the fleet, X23, commanded by Lt. George Honour, RNVR, had the more easterly position, a mile off the port of Ouistreham. His craft was unarmed, and was fitted with a radio beacon, a flashing light on an eighteen-foot telescopic mast, and an underwater signaling device, as well as extra navigational equipment and marked charts. It could not have been anything but a lightship. If the Germans had captured it, or its sister ship at the other end of the beaches, they could not possibly have missed the implication. These two obvious clues to the exact position of the British assault lay for fifty-six hours within a mile of the German army—and lay there in an onshore wind and in weather worse than any they were designed or built to stand.

But the responsibility of his job had not weighed too heavily on Lieutenant Honour before he sailed; it was only afterwards that the risk he had run began to make him lie awake at night. He knew all about X craft. Two years before, when he was skipper of a landing craft running stores into Tobruk, he had impulsively put his name down for a job which was only described as hazardous; and ever since then, he had been training with X craft at Rothesay on the Clyde, and in the deserted sea lochs in the west of Scotland. At Rothesay, he had mainly distinguished himself by marrying one of the Wren drivers at the base, and on the evening of June 3rd, when he sailed his small ship out of Portsmouth harbor and through the fleet which was waiting off Spithead, his wife was working as a censor officer in HMS Victory, the naval base ashore; and she guessed, although he had never told her, exactly what he was doing.

All through the night of June 3rd, X23 and her sister ship X20 were towed by trawlers southward across the empty Channel. At 4:15 the next morning, Saturday, the trawlers slipped them and went home, and an hour later, in the dawn, the submarines submerged and each set course alone towards its assigned position.

Inside an X craft, there was not much room to move. A short man could stand upright in the control position; elsewhere was less than five feet of headroom. There were two bunks, one amidships and the other on top of the batteries. The crew breathed oxygen, but after a time, especially with five men on board, the atmosphere became almost unbearable, and the smell of diesel oil, although it was harmless, gave a feeling of suffocation. There was no conning tower, and at sea, even when the submarine was surfaced, waves often washed right over it. At sea, therefore, the hatches could not be opened, and the only way out was for one man at a time to enter a watertight compartment, shut the door behind him, and then open a hatch above his head. If the compartment flooded, it had to be pumped out before the next man could use it. Many of the men who volunteered for X craft had to give up because they could not stand the sensation of being shut in.

From five in the morning on Saturday till half past ten at night, Honour and his crew, shut down in the darkness below the surface, drove slowly on towards the coast of France. At dusk, they had reached the edge of a German minefield. They surfaced, and crossed it in the dark; and at four o'clock on Sunday morning the echo sounder showed only ten fathoms below them, and they could see the coast as a shadow in the moonlight. They went down to the bottom then, and lay there to wait for daybreak.

At eight they came up to periscope depth, and the navigator, who was a regular naval lieutenant called Lyne, roughly fixed their position from landmarks ashore. They set course to the east for two hours, and lay on the bottom again until five in the evening, when they came up a mile off shore for a final fix. This was easier said than done. One of the submarine's pumps had gone wrong, and so had the gyro compass. It was two hours before Lyne was perfectly satisfied that he had identified landmarks ashore and taken accurate bearings of Ouistreham lighthouse, and the church towers of Ouistreham, Langrunes and La Delivrande; and all that time Honour and his crew, short of one pump, were in the utmost difficulty in holding the craft four feet below the surface. None of them had much doubt of what would happen if she broke surface, for through the periscope Lyne could see German soldiers bathing and playing with a ball on the beach below their artillery observation tower.

At about this time, Honour's wife, back in Portsmouth, heard another Wren officer say "We've lost those two midget subs." But she was not supposed to know anything about them, so she could not ask questions.

After dark on Sunday night they surfaced, thankful to be able to breathe fresh air and blow out the submarine, and they anchored in a position which Lyne was confident was within fifty yards of the spot assigned to them. By then, a considerable sea and swell were running, and waves were breaking over the submarine all the time. All the men were tired and dizzy from breathing the artificial atmosphere, and several of them were washed overboard; but they were wearing frogmen's suits and had made themselves fast with lifelines, so that did not matter very much. Their weariness was overcome by the thought that there was not much longer to wait; and so it was a bitter blow when at 1 A.M. they heard the radio signal which meant a day's postponement. That morning at dawn they were all extremely gloomy as they battened themselves down again and sank to the bottom for another nineteen hours' incarceration.

All day, they lay and sat around, moving and talking as little as they could, because they were listless and because they had to save oxygen. Even at sixty feet, the submarine began to rock and bump gently on the bottom. That implied a rough sea above, and each of them, lost in his own thoughts and depressed by semisuffocation, wondered whether there would be a second postponement and, if there was, whether they could get back to England before their oxygen failed. Two or three times during the day they heard propellers, always an ominous sound in a submarine submerged in enemy waters. By evening, their third evening off the invasion shore, they felt that their luck had been too good to last, and when they surfaced, it was with more than the usual apprehension that an C-boat would be waiting for them there. Honour crawled into the watertight compartment, and shut himself in and opened the hatch above. A deluge of water fell on him, and filled the whole compartment. He clambered out, and hanging onto the casing he shut the hatch and waited alone until the pumps could clear it. There was nothing to be seen on the darkening stormy sea, but the ship was pitching and rolling heavily and tugging the anchor rope. Every sailor knows the fear of being anchored off a lee shore in worsening weather. That was Honour's fear that night; and no lee shore was ever so menacing. If X23 had been wrecked, no shipwreck would ever have had such terrible consequences.

That night, they heard the signal that the invasion was on, and they went to the bottom again where they could lie more safely. At 4:45 in the morning they came up, started the radio beacon and the underwater signal, and raised the mast and flashed their light to seaward; and at dawn, in the last extremity of exhaustion, they saw the sight which was ample reward for sixty-four hours' submersion: the host of ships converging towards their light. They had the Germans' view of the fleet approaching, and it was terrifying, even before the start of the shelling over their heads. At 6:55 the first wave of landing craft, led by a launch equipped to receive the sound and radio signals, passed by the solitary submarine, and its job was done. At eight, Honour cut the anchor rope because he and his crew were much too weak to raise it; and twenty-four hours later, he was back in Portsmouth, to explain to his wife exactly what he had been doing and—which was much more difficult—explain to his base ship why he had lost the anchor.

Among the ships which bore down on Honour's submarine at dawn, the only naval engagement of D Day was fought, and was quickly ended.

The bombardment fleet for the eastern beaches had been led, in the latter part of the crossing, by two Norwegian destroyers, *Stord* and *Svenner.* This position had been meant as a compliment by the British naval authorities, and the Norwegian crews appreciated the honor, uncomfortable though the position might have been.

The captain of *Svenner* had particular reason to be proud of the place which his ship had been given, for she was brand-new. He was a thirty-year-old lieutenant commander from Trondheim called Tore Holthe; and he had been in the Norwegian navy before the war and had seen it grow, from the humiliatingly feeble state in which the country's neutrality had kept it, to a force whose destroyers had sailed and fought in British flotillas all over the north Atlantic. His own story had run parallel to his navy's development.

When the Germans invaded Norway in 1940, Holthe was captain of a torpedo boat. At that time, the Norwegian

merchant fleet was one of the largest and most modern in the
world; but Holthe's torpedo boat, a vessel of about one
hundred tons, was coal-fired and had been built before the
First World War. It was a museum piece among warships. The
German invasion caught him, as completely surprised as all
Norwegians, in Arendal on the south coast of the country.
Before anyone knew what had happened, the Germans were
in all the south and west coast ports, and as the torpedo boat
could only steam a negligible distance before it needed more
coal, there was absolutely nowhere that Holthe could take it
to keep it out of the hands of the Germans. So he sent his
crew home, and scuttled his pathetic ship, and set off to look

for some more efficient means of fighting against the Germans. He made his way to the west coast, and requisitioned a fishing boat and set sail for Britain, with three even younger naval officers, to an exile which was to last for exactly five years.

His first command in Britain was better, but not by much: a Norwegian destroyer, so called, of the vintage of 1909. But that was just after Dunkirk, when the British were glad of the help of anything that would float, to help to repel the invasion which they in their turn expected every night; and for eighteen months, Holthe coaxed his ancient vessel up and down the east coast of England.

Hunt Class Destroyer

But his next appointment was a big step forward: first lieutenant of a new Hunt Class destroyer, the first modern ship of its size which the Norwegian navy had ever owned. After that he became first lieutenant of *Stord*, when she was also new; and he sailed with her as far south as Gibraltar and as far north as Murmansk, and was serving aboard her when she played her distinguished part in the sinking of the German cruiser *Scharnhorst*.

And finally, after nearly four years in Britain, he got a new ship of his own: *Svenner*, straight out of the builder's yard, a fleet destroyer of eighteen hundred tons, four 4.7-inch guns, eight torpedo tubes and a complement of over two hundred men. No captain can ever have had more pride in a new command; Holthe's pride in *Svenner* was national as well as personal.

By then, it was already the spring of 1944, and even while *Svenner* was working up, it was clear she was destined for a part in the invasion. Most of her practice shoots, up in Scapa Flow, were at targets ashore, and most of her fleet exercises were rehearsals of landings. In May, she sailed to the Clyde; and there Holthe received the orders for her first action, and his own first action in command of a modern ship. *Svenner* and the flotilla to which she was joined were to escort the capital ships to the area off Ouistreham where they would anchor to start the bombardment; and then she was to go farther inshore, to three thousand yards if necessary, to engage the coastal defenses at short range.

The fleet sailed on June 2nd: the battleships *Warspite* and *Ramillies*, the old monitor *Roberts*, the cruisers *Mauritius*, *Arethusa*, *Danae*, *Dragon* and *Frobisher*. Holthe was free then to tell his crew what they were going to do. Most of them, like himself, had been completely cut off for years from their own country and their homes and families. The only thing they really wanted in life was to help to win the war and get home again; and the scope of the plan he described elated them because, indirect though it was as a route to Norway, it was so clearly a positive step in that direction. The sight of the fleet of which they were part had inspired them too, and their excitement increased as they steamed down the Irish Sea, and were joined by American, British, French, Dutch and Polish warships, and by the scores of old merchant ships whose fate was to be scuttled to form the first breakwaters of the artificial harbors off Arromanches and Omaha.

This was the force which turned round, on Eisenhower's postponement, and steamed north for twelve hours to waste the extra day; and so it was on their third day at sea that they rounded Lands End, and steamed up Channel, and reached the area south of the Isle of Wight which the navy called Piccadilly Circus, where all the convoy routes converged to turn south through the ten channels which minesweepers had already cleared ahead.

At 11 P.M. they entered the easternmost channel, between the lines of lighted buoys which the minesweeper flotillas had laid like streetlamps across to France. *Mauritius*, the flagship of the eastern bombardment fleet, was in the van, with *Svenner* 30 degrees on her port bow at a range of a thousand yards. At midnight, Holthe ordered his crew to action stations, and felt for the first time in *Svenner* the intense aliveness which pervades a ship before an important action. A little after midnight, the force moved into line ahead, with *Stord* leading and *Svenner* second. A stream of reports was reaching Holthe from the radar and hydrophone watches; the sea was full of the sound of propellers, and the ether full of echoes; so full that Holthe could only assume that all the ships were friendly and that the worst risk he was running was the risk of collision. The air also was full of sound—the sound which had already wakened England—of the endless fleets of aircraft overhead. Towards dawn, from *Svenner's* bridge, Holthe and his lookouts saw the flashes of bombs on the coast ahead, and the flicker of fires reflected by the clouds.

At 5:30, in the gray of dawn, the battleships and cruisers anchored. By then, the shore could be seen, and certainly the fleet could be seen from the shore but the Germans were silent. The fleet was not only in range of the shore ahead, but also of heavy batteries at Le Havre, which was seven or eight miles away to the east; and to protect the ships from that direction, aircraft began to lay a smoke screen. *Svenner* and the other destroyers stopped to the west of the capital ships, to wait for the minesweepers to open a channel even closer towards the shore. This moment was a climax of the first ten years of Holthe's career: the fleet poised for action, the scene set for a battle of supreme importance to his country, and he with the most perfect of modern ships and a well-trained crew at his command. It was in that moment that he saw, three hundred yards away, the unmistakable track of a torpedo.

Three German torpedo boats had emerged from the smoke

screen, on the far side of the fleet from the spot where *Svenner* lay.

At that stage of the war, the German navy had only three ships larger than destroyers that were fit to go to sea; its U boats were fighting a losing battle, and its coastal forces that night had failed even to detect the invasion fleet until it was within gunshot of the shore. The navy, in fact, was a spent and ruined force; but its regular officers would not have admitted that, even to themselves, and when the commander of the torpedo boats was ordered to sea that morning, he acted as any good officer of any navy would have acted. His name was Heinrich Hoffmann; his ship was of fourteen hundred tons, the size of a small destroyer; and perhaps no other officer of any navy has ever found himself facing such odds or offered such a target.

Hoffmann had been in the Channel since 1940, except for occasional sorties to Norway and the Bay of Biscay, and he had been in action against the British raids on Dieppe and St. Nazaire. After those four years, there was not very much he had still to learn about quick night battles between naval forces. He felt respect and a kind of sporting affection for the British navy. But experience of the last year or so had taught him to care more about air than surface opposition, and he believed it was a useless risk to go to sea on moonlit nights, when aircraft had the advantage over ships. So on the night of the 5th of June, he had decided to keep his flotilla in harbor at Le Havre, not because of the roughness of the sea, but because of the moon.

It was about 2 A.M. when the first warning of enemy forces reached him from the naval operations staff ashore. The report was of six large ships in the Bay of the Seine, steering a southerly course. It probably originated from a naval radar station at Cherbourg which had not yet been put entirely out of action by the bombing and jamming which had destroyed the defending army's radar chain. Hoffmann had six ships in his flotilla, and he called his captains together at once. Only three of the six, including his own ship, were ready for sea. At about half past three, he led his half-flotilla out of harbor.

So far, Hoffmann had no idea that his three small ships alone were challenging the greatest force which Britain and America had ever put to sea. But as he left harbor and set a westerly course, he heard the fleets of aircraft. He did not bother about them, because he knew that if they had been out for attacks on shipping, they would not have flown so high; but the quantity of aircraft, together with the report of ships, soon made him suspect that the invasion was beginning. In spite of that suspicion, he held his course and speed. He personally believed at that time that if the invasion could be held off, the war might yet be won, but that if the invasion succeeded, nothing then could save Germany. So he was perfectly ready to sacrifice himself and his flotilla if he could help to defeat the invading forces.

When he first saw the smoke screen, he thought it was a natural bank of fog; but then he saw an aircraft dropping smoke floats, and he suddenly recognized that the whole mass of it across his course was artificial. That finally confirmed his belief that a major operation was under way. His ships had no radar, and so he had no means of knowing what he might find beyond the wall of smoke; but he went into it, at 28 knots in line ahead.

The sight which he saw when he came through the smoke amazed him, prepared though he was for something extraordinary. Straight ahead of him, in the early light of dawn, he saw six battleships or heavy cruisers, and so many minor warships that he had no time to count them; and yet, to his further surprise, not one of them opened fire. He signaled his base that he was going to attack, set course to present the smallest silhouette, and had time to maneuver his ships into a textbook approach. Between them, they fired seventeen torpedoes into the mass of ships ahead.

When Holthe saw the torpedo, he instantly gave the order for full ahead and full port rudder, and the telegraph rang and the engine room acknowledged the order; then time seemed to stop. He stood on the bridge and watched the wake of the torpedo tearing through the choppy sea towards him, and he knew it was going to hit his ship, because she was lying stopped and there was never a chance to get steerage way on her. And he had a moment's astonishment because the torpedo was coming from the port side, right out of the middle of the fleet of friendly ships. And then for a fraction of a second his heart lifted because the wake always follows behind a torpedo, and the wake came so near that he thought the torpedo had gone under her. Then it hit. It hit her amidships, and oil went up in a great fountain and covered the whole ship from bow to stern.

For Holthe himself on the bridge the physical shock of the

explosion was small. His emotions were numb. Immediately, *Svenner* was visibly buckling amidships. He knew she was doomed. Probably less than two minutes passed before he gave the order to abandon ship. The boats were wrecked; the crew got some rafts overboard, and began to jump. She broke in two and sank, and as she went down Holthe jumped from the bridge itself.

When he came up and began to swim, men of his crew were scattered all round him in the water as far as he could see, and he was confident most of them had got clear except for the engine room watch who must have been instantly killed. He saw the canopy of his motorboat floating, and he swam to it and held on, and then looked back at the beautiful ship which had been his pride. To seamen, the sinking of a ship is like a death, and the death-throes of *Svenner* were grotesque. Her bow and stern rose high out of the water, and her broken midships section stuck on the bottom of the shallow sea; and there she stood, a gigantic ironic V for victory. Holthe watched her with the most intensely bitter disappointment. She had not lived to fire a single shot.

At the moment when Hoffmann fired his torpedoes, the first British salvo of shells fell in front of his bows, so close that his ship, still moving at 28 knots, steamed into the spouts of water before they fell and a flood came down on the foredeck and the bridge. The concussion put out all the lights on board, and cut off the radio. He altered course abruptly to avoid the fire, and returned it impudently with his 4-inch guns. By vigorous evasive tactics, all three of his ships got back into the smoke screen, and not one of them was hit.

Emerging again on the homeward side of the smoke, Hoffmann met a forlorn and almost pathetic sight. Three armed fishing boats, the only other German naval units which had reacted to the report of enemy ships, were steaming purposefully at 8 knots towards the sounds of battle. He could not tell them what they were up against, because his radio was gone; but his sudden appearance was sufficient warning. The British gunfire, controlled by radar, followed him through the smoke, and then transferred to the leading fishing boat. All three turned back, and he crossed their bows to try to draw the fire back on himself; but one fishing boat was hit and sank. British fighter bombers appeared then, and escorted Hoffmann's flotilla back to port.

From Hoffmann's point of view, it was the most extraordinarily bad luck that *Svenner* was the only ship he hit. His seventeen torpedoes went right through the close-packed British fleet. Two of them passed between the battleships *Warspite* and *Ramillies*. A third headed straight for *Largs*, the headquarters ship of the area, which only avoided it by going full speed astern. The destroyer *Virago* reported a near miss. The torpedo which hit *Svenner* had already gone through the fleet from one side to the other; *Svenner* was on the west of it, and Hoffmann on the east, and they were never in sight of each other.

Nobody would deny that the spirit and execution of Hoffmann's attack would have been a credit to any navy. He succeeded because the British smoke screen protected him, and because the British radar was confused by the enormous number of echoes from British ships. But his was the only action of any kind whatever that the German navy took on D Day, and *Svenner* and the American destroyer *Corry*, which was hit by a shore battery north of Utah, were the only warships of their size which were lost that day.

Thirty-two of Holthe's crew were killed, and two of the British liaison men who had been on board with him. After half an hour, the stern of *Svenner* rolled over and disappeared, but the bow stood there for a long time, and thousands of troops on their way to the beach saw it projecting above the surface, like a tombstone. Holthe was picked up, while the bombardment in which he had hoped to take his part roared overhead towards the beach and the town of Ouistreham.

The bombardment was an ordeal for the French people in the towns and villages on the coast. It was short, but it was far more intense than any air raid, and every house which was close to the shore was destroyed or badly damaged; but the number of civilians injured or killed was smaller than might have been expected. All of them, of course, had been warned for at least a year, by the Germans and by the BBC, to go away from the coast, and more than half of the original population had left. Some areas had been forcibly cleared by the Germans; and many of the houses were seaside villas which had only been used in peacetime in the summer. So most of the ruins which lined the shore by the morning of D Day had already been empty, or full of German soldiers, before the bombardment started. Far greater numbers of French people were killed in the towns inland—Caen,

Montebourg, Valognes, Pont-l' Abbe—which remained on the
perimeter of the bridgehead for several weeks.

On Utah and Omaha, there were not many houses, because
the coastal villages were a mile or more inland. Probably no
Frenchman witnessed the landing on Omaha, and very few
on Utah. One of the few on Utah had a nightmarish experience
which yet—since it ended happily—had some comedy in it
too. He lived in a cottage just behind the dunes, and his wife
had just had her first baby. Early in the morning of D Day, he
heard things going on outside, and went out to see what was
happening. While he was out, his cottage was hit by a shell,
and he saw it collapse, with his wife and the baby inside it.
Distraught, he ran back and began to drag away the wreckage
with his hands, but before he had moved very much of it the
first American troops came storming over the dunes and he
was seized and marched over the beach and hustled into a
landing craft. He protested and shouted and tried to tell
everyone about his wife and baby; but nobody understood a
word he said, and before he knew what had happened he was
hoisted into a troopship and taken across to England. Perhaps
they thought anyone so near the beach was either a collaborator
or a German. He never knew.

Later in the day, some other Americans passed the ruined
cottage and heard the baby crying, and paused long enough
in the battle to dig out the mother and child, both of them
still alive; but by then, of course, the first lot had moved on,
and nobody knew what had become of the father. It was a
long time before either the man or his wife discovered that
the other was still alive and much longer still before anyone
could spare the time and transport to send the outraged
Frenchman back to France.

But in contrast with the deserted dunes of Omaha and
Utah, the British and Canadian beaches were on a stretch of
coast with small towns and villages, almost continuously
joined together by a line of villas and hotels and boarding
houses where middle-class French families, in summers before
the war, had taken their children to play on the beautiful
sands. The names of these insignificant seaside resorts are
famous now, with the peculiar immortality which wars confer
on the places they ruin: Le Hamel and La Rivière, the two
small hamlets at the ends of Gold Beach; the oyster port of
Courseulles and the town of St. Aubin, where the Canadians

landed; Langrune and Luc-sur-Mer, where the Royal Marine Commandos fought from house to house; and Lion, and the port of Ouistreham, with its seaside resort called Riva Bella. In all these places, the French people who still remained suffered like the people of Coventry and Rotterdam and Hamburg; and yet on the whole, through the worst of the bombardment, they were buoyed up by the thought that the four years of German rule were ending. Perhaps they did not think very closely about the liberation of their country; if they had, it might have seemed bad luck that the process of liberation had begun on their doorsteps, instead of somebody else's. But for most of them, liberation had some more personal importance. To mention a single example, Mme. Sustendal, who lived on the sea front at Luc, ran to the garage of her house when the shelling started, and pushed her two small boys underneath her husband's car, and got her own head and shoulders underneath it too, and she lay there quite happily and almost without any fear, illogically certain that British bombs and shells would never harm her. The reason for her happiness was this: her husband, the village doctor, had made plans of the local defenses and sent them to England, and he had been arrested and sent to a concentration camp. To her, liberation meant simply that she could begin to hope she might see him again alive; and no fear could dim the dawning of that hope.

It was in Ouistreham that people suffered most, because it was the largest of all the towns along the invasion coast, and because the defenses of its little port at the mouth of the Caen Canal were right in among its houses. Ouistreham and its smart beach of Riva Bella had a population of four thousand before the war began, and something like twenty thousand in the summer holiday seasons. All of these had moved inland except four hundred; but of the four hundred, one third were killed on D Day and another third were seriously injured.

A young man called Raoul Mousset was a native of Ouistreham. As it happened, he was in Caen on the night of June 5th, but his wife Odette was in Ouistreham where they had bought a small hotel six months before. The sound of the bombing and shelling woke him, and soon after dawn Caen was full of rumors of what was happening on the coast. Mousset had a truck, and he set off to join his wife. But only a little way beyond the town, the road was blocked, and he heard the sounds of battle close at hand. German soldiers stopped him and told him he could not go any further, and one of them said that Ouistreham was burning.

"Did you see the Hotel de Normandie?" Mousset asked him.

"No, I didn't," the German said. "It isn't there any more. It's gone."

Odette had looked out when the antiaircraft fire had started just about midnight and she saw the parachutes coming down, beyond the River Orne. She thought at first it was a German exercise; but the town was awake, the firing was very heavy, and rather than go to bed, she stayed downstairs with one or two late customers in her café, uneasily discussing what was happening. About two o'clock two German army truck drivers rushed in. They had been in for drinks earlier in the evening, and their trucks were still parked outside. Perhaps they had been impressed by Odette, who was a remarkably pretty young woman. Now they had come to urge her breathlessly to get away while she could. The English were coming, they said, and they were getting out. But of course she refused to leave her hotel. She heard the trucks drive away towards Caen.

She was still in the hotel when it was hit by a British bomb about four o'clock in the morning. She ran out through the back door unhurt and crossed the yard and took refuge in a little wood on a patch of waste ground between the houses. From there, distraught and shocked, she watched the hotel begin to burn, and flare up till the roof crashed in, and then die down till only the walls remained.

About twenty of her neighbors had joined her in the wood. At seven o'clock a naval shell fell on this group of anxious women and killed thirteen of them. Odette was appallingly wounded.

The carnage in the wood was discovered by Leon Tribolet, the local barber, and a young civil servant called Pierre Desoubeaux, who were both wardens in the Ouistreham civil defense force. They sorted out the wounded and the dead, and carried Odette away to the first-aid post.

The civil defense had been on the alert since the previous evening, because Pierre Desoubeaux, for one, was connected with the resistance movement and knew a code message which the BBC was to broadcast when the invasion was coming. He had listened in secret for months, and among the hundreds of code sentences on the evening of June 5th, he had heard it at last: The arrow pierces steel. He had gone round the town warning the rest of the civil defense men to stand by; and so when the bombing started, they were as ready as they could be. But there were only ten men in the first-aid squads, and the size of their disaster overwhelmed them.

The post was in the village square, next door to the Mairie and the eleventh-century church. The only French doctor in Ouistreham was Dr. Poulenc, who was seventy-three years old. He was still an efficient doctor in spite of his age, but early in the day a bullet went through the palm of his right hand, and after that Pierre Desoubeaux and others who had a little first-aid experience had to take a share of the heaviest jobs, like amputations. Early in the day also, the chemist's shop was destroyed, and the only reserve of drugs and dressings was lost; but mercifully, there was plenty of morphine. It was Pierre who gave Odette an injection and silenced her screams, but there was not much more they could do for her.

From five o'clock onwards the rows of injured grew on the floor of the first-aid post, and so did the rows of dead in the yard outside. More and more people brought in their wounded relatives, and the uninjured stayed to help, or to pray with the curé, or just to lament. At eight o'clock the mayor of the town, Charles Lefauconnier, a civil defense man himself, burst in on this terrible scene, and people noticed an expression of joy on his face. "They're landing," he shouted. "They're landing." The shout was taken up all through the post. Dr. Poulenc was told, in the middle of an operation. People murmured it into the ear of wounded men on the edge of unconsciousness. It lifted their hearts.

Pierre Desoubeaux went out again soon after this, on his search for more wounded, and as he passed through the square, in a lull in the thunder of battle, he heard an unexpected sound: men whistling the Marseillaise, rather badly. And round the corner, in single file, came a dozen British soldiers. Pierre did not think he was an emotional man, but after the tension of the night, at the sight and sound of this symbol of liberty, he burst into tears. Ashamed of himself, he shook hands with the first of the soldiers; and the soldier, perhaps feeling that this was a moment in the

Frenchman's life which called for a souvenir, felt in his battledress pockets, and took out his pipe, and presented it to Pierre, who cherished it for years.

The first Allied soldiers to come to the first-aid post caused even more surprise. People greeted them with joyous shouts of "Tommy!" The Tommies, however, answered in the dialect of Brittany, for they were men of the Free French troop of No. 4 Commando—the first French soldiers to land that day in France.

Towards the evening of D Day, the Royal Army Medical Corps got through to the first-aid post in Ouistreham, and helped Dr. Poulenc to repair the damage which British shells had caused. They brought penicillin, which was still unknown in France. For many of the patients, this help had come too late; but Odette Mousset was still alive, and sometimes conscious. A British medical officer examined her and told her she would have to go to England, because her wounds were far too bad to be treated on the battlefield itself. But she refused to go, because her husband Raoul, so far as she knew, was still in Caen and would not know where she was.

But Raoul, after hearing that their hotel had been destroyed, was quite determined to get home to see if his wife was all right. By the time he had reached the front line, on the German side, the battle was raging in its full fury between Caen and Ouistreham. Naturally, the Germans were ready to shoot any Frenchman who tried to cross to the British side, on suspicion of being a spy. All day on D Day, Raoul prowled round unhappily, turned back whichever way he tried to go, either by German patrols or by British artillery fire. By nightfall, anxiety drove him to desperation. He came on a dead German soldier, and beside him a bicycle. He stole the bicycle, and pedaled furiously down the main road to the coast; and by the kind of miracle which is sometimes the reward of determination, he went right through the German front, and the no man's land, and the British perimeter, and nobody tried to stop him. At length, he found Odette. By then, the English doctor had said she would be dead the next day if she still would not go to England.

Few of the stories of Ouistreham had a happy ending, but this one had; for Odette was put in a DUKW, and taken out to a landing craft which was full of wounded soldiers; and the British army let Raoul go with her. She was in a hospital in

England for eleven months, but then they both went home to the ruins of Ouistreham.

At the village of Graye-sur-Mer, at the present day, there is a bridge where the road from the village to the beach goes over a stream in the marshy land behind the dunes. Families on holiday use the bridge to go down to the beach to bathe, and carts drive over it to bring up sand and seaweed; but many of the local people have forgotten its history and do not know that a British tank is buried underneath it.

Graye is three miles east of La Rivière, where Bell landed. Graye and the oyster port of Courseulles, and the villages of Bernières and St. Aubin, all lie close together on the next stretch of shore which was attacked: Juno Beach, where Canadian infantry and tanks made the first assault with the help of the British specialized armor. The bridge, or most of it, was built between eight o'clock and 9:15 on D Day, and it was a masterpiece of improvisation under fire, and also a good example of the use of the specialized armor. To put its story in perspective, one must look back beyond that day at the lives of some of the humble British sappers who were there when it was built.

One of them was a coalminer from Sunderland whose real name was William Dunn; but as he was a north country man in a mainly southern unit, his army friends all called him George or Geordie, and most of them never knew he had another name. George was twenty. His twenty-first birthday was on June 9th, and for two or three weeks it had been a matter of argument whether he and his tank crew would celebrate it in an English pub or a continental café.

George Dunn, for his age, was a resourceful, adaptable, well-balanced kind of man; he had been trained to that in a fairly hard school. He had been born and lived all his life in a cottage in a row in a mining village. All the men he knew at home were miners. His father had been a miner; but when George was thirteen, he had been killed by a cave-in. Naturally, the very day George left school, when he was fourteen, he went to the mine and asked for a job and got it. He had never thought of being anything but a miner, and expected to be a miner all his life.

But the job had not lasted long. The mine exported most of its coal to France, and when France fell to the Germans in

1940, the mine was simply shut down and almost the whole
of the village was suddenly thrown out of work. George was
seventeen then. He had to go on the dole, like all his friends
and neighbors; and then of course he had to take whatever
job was offered him by the labor exchange. They drafted him
to an oil refinery far away. It was strange work and a strange
place, and he was unhappy; and so, although he had never
had any dreams of being a soldier, he was not at all sorry
when his army call-up came.

An outsider, looking at George's village and the life which
the British social system had given him so far, might have
thought he had not very much to be grateful for, and less
reason than most men to fight for his King and country. But it
was not in George's nature to think that way. The outsider
would only have seen the blackness and bleakness of the
village; but George had only seen the friendliness and kindness
and good humor of its people. It was home; and although he
may sometimes have felt that society had given his family a
raw deal between the wars, he was just as ready to fight to
defend his home as anyone else; more so than many men who
had far more material possessions but had never been taught
to value them.

Anyhow, the army struck George as a very lazy life compared
with mining, and he set himself to get as much out of it as he
could. He soon found there was plenty of fun to be had in it,
and plenty to learn. With that attitude, he made a good job of
it. By D Day, he was driver of a Churchill tank. But he still
did not want to do anything when the war was over except to
go home and start in the mine again.

The radio operator of George's tank was even younger. His
name was Roy Manley. His father had also died when he was
young, but apart from that coincidence, the two men were
almost as different as two Englishmen could have been. Roy
came from the opposite end of England, from Devonshire.
When he left school, he had got a job with a builders'
merchant on the edge of Exeter; and when he first met
George, the two of them could hardly understand each
other's language.

George's first impression of Roy was that he was rather a
mother's boy; and perhaps by George's hard standards, there
was some truth in that. George had taken his place as head of
his family when he was still very young; but the dominant
personality in Roy's family was his sister Ruth, and when

Churchill Tank

their father died it was Ruth who grew up to make the family decisions. Roy had always been quite content with that. He and Ruth were very close in more than just age, and he had grown to depend on her and not to care very much about making other friends outside his home. Before he was called up, he had never been away from home at all. Almost his only independent interest was going shyly to the local Saturday night dances, and his ambition was to save enough money to buy a motorbike.

Roy had been miserable on the day his call-up came; he had dreaded the army. Ruth also hated the thought of his going away, but she had the good sense and courage not to say so, because she knew, when she came to think of it, that

he was young for his age and admitted reluctantly to herself
that the army might do him good. She was right. For the first
few weeks, he went on being miserable, while the army
roughly shook him out of his shyness and forced him to stand
on his own feet. But then he began to make friends who had
nothing to do with the narrow circle of his life in Exeter, and
he began to discover new pleasures and interests. Radio
began to interest him; learning about it was much harder
than any job he had had to do before, and finding that he
could do it gave him self-confidence. The tank fulfilled some
of his wish for the motorbike. People like George gave him a
new and more grown-up and masculine view of life. Roy
admired George as a man of the world who could always get
things done, and always knew his way around, and was always
at ease in company. George liked Roy because he was quiet
and patient and kind-hearted and unselfish, and perhaps also
because he was so eager to learn from George's worldly
wisdom.

Ruth never met George; but each time Roy went home on
leave, she saw more and more of the effect that the army in
general, and George in particular, were having on him. It was
certainly not a bad effect at all. When he had left home so
unwillingly in his civilian clothes, he had really been only a
boy; but now she began to discover that this young brother, of
whom she had always been so fond, was also a young man
whose good looks and new assurance any sister would have
been very proud of.

The rest of the crew of the tank were not much older than
these two, except the commander, who was a sergeant called
Jim Ashton. Sergeant Ashton seemed almost middle-aged to
his crew: he was nearly thirty. Most of the time, except when
they misbehaved, he treated them with fatherly benevolence,
and he succeeded in making them proud of themselves and of
the job they had to do together.

Their tank was a fascine—the kind of specialized tank that
carried a bundle of logs eight feet in diameter. Before D Day,
all the crew had studied the photographs and models of their
beach, and they had seen the obstacles on the beach, and a
gap in the sand dunes behind it, and the marshy ground two
hundred yards wide at the back of the dunes. In the gap,
they had seen a tank trap, and in the marsh a winding stream
and a place where a culvert across it had been destroyed.
Sergeant Ashton and George and Roy and the others all

understood exactly what they had to do: to follow the flail tanks through the dunes and along the road to the culvert, drop their fascine in the gap where the culvert had been, drive over it, and hold a road junction just beyond it while the Canadian infantry followed across the open ground. That was just the kind of thing they had done over and over again on exercises, and they were sure they could do it again. Each of them knew his own job and a good bit of the jobs of the others as well, and each of them knew he could depend on the others whatever happened; for they had not only worked together but lived and slept and eaten together for eighteen months in getting ready for this day. Sometimes their friendly arguments on the tank's intercom sounded more like a family party than a tank crew, except for the language. They argued about a lot of different things, but more than anything else perhaps about the sergeant's singing. Jim Ashton was always singing, and the microphone in the turret seemed to inspire him. His favorite tunes were "Kiss me, kiss me again" and a sad Australian ballad with the refrain:

Churchill AVRE "Fascine"

> "Why do I weep
> Why do I cry?
> My love's asleep,
> So far away."

George and Roy used to beg him, not always as respectfully as they should, to sing something new if he had to sing at all; but he took the view that a tank commander could sing what the hell he liked on his own intercom, and if the crew didn't appreciate it they were just an ungrateful unmusical lot of bastards.

Sergeant Ashton was singing as the landing craft went in to the beach. As soon as Roy had established radio contact and switched on the intercom, the familiar tune came out of the headphones. To the crew, it seemed no more beautiful than usual, but this time they did appreciate it, because they knew he was doing it to remind them of all they had done together and to make them feel less alone down in the bowels of the tank where none of them except George could see any daylight at all; and absurd though it may have been, it did pull them together.

George's first impression of the beach, when he peered at it through his narrow visor, was the impression shared by everyone else who landed on the eastern beaches in the early hours: it was much narrower than it ought to have been. This was true. The tide was higher than the British Admiralty had predicted, either because the prediction was wrong or because the wind had piled the water into the Bay of the Seine, or perhaps from a combination of both these causes. His second impression was of dead or wounded men lying so thickly on the beach that he wondered how he would manage to drive between them. But there right in front of him was the gap in the dunes which he had seen so clearly on the photographs; and beyond it, he knew he would see the road and the tank trap and the broken culvert.

Jim Ashton had stopped singing and opened the turret and put his head out, and he guided George up the beach, avoiding the corpses as best he could. There was much less shooting than they had expected; and that was because one of the landing craft of their troop had had engine trouble and had made them all late, and the Canadian infantry and the DD tanks had already been there for twenty minutes and had crossed the first line of the German defenders. The flails which had landed ahead went up through the gap, churning a track which was easy to see and follow and George went after them till he could see over the marsh to the crossroads and the houses beyond it. The tank trap barred the way, a ditch fifteen feet wide and nine feet deep. That was not their job, and George pulled aside while another fascine tank which should have been in front came past, and paused on the edge of the ditch, and released its great bundle of logs which fell with a crash in the hole, and then immediately crawled on again across its own logs. The flails queued up and followed it over the tank trap which, far from trapping the tanks, had hardly delayed them a second.

There on the back of the dunes it was not so quiet. There was no artillery, but mortars and machine guns were firing from the houses on the crossroad; safe enough for tanks, but not for infantry. George drove across the logs, and followed the flails which flogged the road to the broken culvert fifty yards beyond; and then they drew aside, and let him take the lead, with the tank of the troop commander close behind him.

The last twenty or thirty feet of the road surface before the culvert had been destroyed. Beyond the broken end of the road, George saw through the visor a few yards of sand and weeds, and then a narrow strip of water where the stream flowed through.

"Crater's filled up," he said.

"Looks all right," he heard Ashton say; and on the radio the troop commander told them to carry on.

George eased the tank forward on to the patch of weeds; her nose dipped, and he saw the weeds part, and water gleaming through, and she started to slide. He had stopped the tracks, but she went on sliding, and then she fell, and the daylight through the visor was cut off, and she stopped with a crash. Water fell on him, and before he could catch his breath it was over his head, and with the gasp that he gave it went down in his lungs and choked him. He struggled to get out of his seat and somebody, Ashton or Roy, grabbed him by the back of his neck and hauled him up; and then he was on top of the turret, lying on his stomach being sick, and the turret was only just over the surface and it was still sinking. Ashton got him onto the bank and shouted, "Run for the dunes," but he hardly had the power to run. The troop commander turned his tank to give cover from the machine-gun fire, and the crew made for the dunes, and got over the top of the first of them, and threw themselves down on the sheltered seaward side; and before they were there, the tank had disappeared except for the top of its fascine. The crew never saw what happened after that.

The weeds on the top of the water had looked so solid— like those on the floods where the American parachutists fell—that nobody who saw them from the tanks had doubted there was dry land underneath. Blown sand had been lying on top of them. But after the tank had fallen in and broken the surface, it was seen that the gap in the road was sixty feet wide. The bridges which the specialized armor carried were only thirty feet long. Perhaps nobody would have thought of sinking a tank in the middle of the gap if George had not already done it by mistake, but that was the only possible way to bridge the gap. A bridge-carrying tank was ordered up, and it dropped the far end of its bridge on top of the sunken tank. The troop commander and two other men scrambled out to it, still under fire, and stood on the turret which was under water, and blew off the wire strop which held the fascine, so that it dropped in the water ahead. There was still a gap beyond it. More fascines were put into place; more tanks were brought up to give covering fire, and troops from the beach carried up some logs which the Germans had left there and threw them in as well. At 9:15, an hour and a quarter after the troop had landed, the first tanks and infantry crossed the bridge and rushed the houses by the crossroads from which the machine guns and mortars had harassed the whole operation.

Jim Ashton and his crew, not knowing the use which was being made of their derelict tank, were lying close together on the back of the dunes, fed up with themselves for having lost the tank when the battle had hardly started, and thinking of the eighteen months of training which had culminated in less than eighteen minutes of action. George blamed himself. Ashton reassured him. Roy, from his radio position, had not seen anything at all till the water poured in. Ashton was the first to get over the shock; he was the only one of them who was really quite grown up, or had been more than a small boy when the war started. He began singing again to cheer them up a bit, singing quietly against the sound of the machine guns and mortar bombs:

"Why do I weep,
Why do I cry?
My love's asleep,
So far away."

He was singing it when he died. A mortar bomb fell right among them. George did not know what happened. Something terrible happened, that was all he knew, and cut a few seconds out of his life in utter oblivion. Roy was lying on top of him. He pushed him off, and saw he was dead, and glanced and saw Jim Ashton was dead and the others were lying half-buried and still. He stood up, and fell, and rolled down the steep face of the dune, and opened his eyes again in agony and saw a rough board above his head with a skull on it and "ACHTUNG—MINEN" and he got up again and ran, as a desperately wounded animal can run, till he fell again with his left leg crumpled under him. The doctors would never believe he had run on it, it was so badly shattered, but he knew he had. His other leg was wounded too, and he lost his left arm. He never became a miner, but he got a good job in the mine which a one-armed man could do.

In Graye-sur-Mer, at the present day, they talk of the famous people who landed there in the first days of the liberation, and entered France by way of the bridge when it had been tidied up at leisure. Some say Churchill came that way, some say Montgomery, and others claim King George VI and Eisenhower and General de Gaulle. But of course nobody there has heard of Jim Ashton or Roy Manley, and underneath the bridge, even when the stream is low in summer, only a few inches of metal, red with rust, can be seen above the surface of the mud.

The pattern of the assault on the Canadian beach had been different, in its successes and failures, from any of the beaches farther west. In one respect, it resembled Omaha: the bombardment, owing to the poor visibility, mostly fell inland and left the beach defenses intact and the men who manned them shocked but still alive. The weather, on the other hand, had a different effect on the landing. The troops were put in at the right places, but the rough sea delayed the landing craft; the first waves of infantry were up to half an hour late, and some of the specialized armor was even later. As the tide was higher than had been predicted, and was still rising, the outer lines of obstacles on the beach were under water before anyone arrived at all. There was no chance for the demolition teams to get to work on them until the tide fell in the afternoon, and meanwhile the landing craft had to take their chance and drive blindly into them or through them. Most of the craft succeeded in reaching the shore, but many were damaged or sunk when they tried to go out, and the accumulation of wreckage added to the difficulties of the later waves.

The delay had given the defenders extra time to recover from the stunning effects of the bombardment, and the Canadian infantry crossed the beach under very heavy fire. In some places, the slaughter in the dash across the sand was as terrible as at Omaha. But here there were no hills behind the shores; the defenses were close to the back of the beach, among the dunes or the houses of the villages; and once the Canadians reached them, these defenses very quickly fell. Fifteen minutes after the initial attack, the first line of defenders had been killed or disarmed in short furious hand-to-hand battles, and the firing on the beach, as Jim Ashton had found, had died away to mere sniping, and mortars fired at random.

The tanks and infantry tore through Courseulles and Bernières, and only met the first check to their progress in the meadows and orchards beyond the villages. They were held up there for a couple of hours before they broke out and continued an advance which carried them farther than anyone else on D Day; and during this delay, more armor and trucks had piled ashore behind them, and a tremendous traffic jam built up in the village streets and on the narrow beach above high-water mark.

On the left-hand end of the beach, at Saint Aubin, a force of the Royal Marine Commandos landed a few minutes behind the Canadian infantry. Among them was a man called Anthony Rubinstein. He was nineteen, the son of a distinguished family of lawyers, and his childhood in England in the 1930s had been carefree and comfortable and sheltered. When the war began, he was in his second year at Cheltenham College. For three more years, he had led the cloistered life of an English public school, and when he was seventeen he had gone straight from the sixth form to the army, because it was the accepted thing to do. By the pure chance which governs most peoples' fate in wartime, he was transferred to 48 Royal Marine Commando, and on June 5th he sailed as a second lieutenant in command of a section of thirty men. In some ways, he was still young for his age.

The Royal Marines, seagoing soldiers, have a tradition as a disciplined force which is older than the navy's and more continuous than the army's. Their commandos were new formations of the Second World War, but they inherited the marines' strict standards of discipline and toughness. They were small elite forces of three to four hundred men: six troops in each commando, and two sections in each troop.

A social theorist might have expected that Rubinstein's thirty men would resent their section commander's youth and his privileged upbringing; nearly all of them were older than he was, and most of them had more experience, not only of war but also of life in general. But it did not work out that way. During their training in Scotland and in the bombed streets of southeast London, he had found them very easy to get on with. He liked them, and enjoyed their company. On their side, they must have felt that his liking was sincere, because all of them, and especially the NCOs, helped him to avoid mistakes which he might have made through his lack of experience. Far from being cut off from his men by wealth and youth and education, he became more friendly with them than the convention of the Royal Marines allowed. In the end, he was reprimanded for being too friendly, but he was not in the least repentant. The reprimand might have been more severe if anyone had known that while they were in training his sergeant, whose name was Blyth, had given him lessons in ballroom dancing, and that he and another young officer called Yates and the NCOs and men of the section had all frequented the same local *palais-de-dance*. It is hard to believe that friendliness was anything but a help to Rubinstein and his section in the events which awaited them in Normandy.

The Royal Marine Commandos, true to their independent spirit, crossed the Channel all by themselves in vessels called Landing Craft, Infantry, Small; and these were, in fact, the smallest landing craft to carry troops across under their own steam. Each of them was crammed with a troop of sixty to seventy men. Rubinstein's boat had cabinlike hutches fore and aft for officers, and he spent most of the night inside one

ɔf them, taking a drink from time to time to keep the cold
ɔut, with Captain Perry, the troop commander, Lieutenant
Curtis, the second-in-command, and one or two others. He
thought it was absurd that the officers should be segregated
in a cabin of their own; he felt he ought to be out on deck or
squatting in the forepeak with Sergeant Blyth and the rest of
the section, but he had the good sense not to say so. But
otherwise, he was quite content. The briefing before they
sailed had given him a fairly clear idea of what the Commando
was meant to do. It was to land at St. Aubin, on the left of the
Canadians, and capture the coastal defenses in the four-mile
gap between the Canadians and the British beach to the
eastward. Halfway along, it would meet another Commando
which was to land on the British right and come up the coast
in the opposite direction. The toughest obstacle in the gap
was expected to be a German strongpoint on the seafront in
the village of Langrune-sur-Mer.

So far, his idea of the impending battle was right enough;
but he had also understood from the briefing that everything
was going to be easy. The Commando would not be landing
till half an hour after the first of the infantry and armor. By
then, the underwater obstacles would be cleared away and
the beach would be under control. The whole coast would
have been bombed and shelled so heavily as to crush the
defense and leave nothing much for the marines to do except
to clear up the mess.

It is hard to say how much of this impossibly rosy picture
was due to over-optimistic briefing, and how much to
Rubinstein's own misunderstanding. He had never seen a
battle, and he had never seen anyone die except in Western
movies. He had no conception at all of what it would be like,
and very little of what it was all about, except that he firmly
believed what everyone had told him since he was a child:
that the Germans were a menace to the world and had to be
beaten. So he did not worry. The chain of command protects
a second lieutenant from worry; and he knew he was in good
company. His dependable Sergeant Blyth was in the same
boat with him, and his friend Yates was in another just astern.
He felt that his section trusted him, and he and all of them
trusted and admired Captain Perry. If he had worried at all,
he would have reassured himself with the thought that Captain
Perry would tell him what to do, and Sergeant Blyth would
help him to do it; and if he did it wrong, he could depend on

Yates for sympathy. So he crossed the Channel and approached his first battle in cheerful and youthful ignorance, still very much the sixth-form schoolboy he had been two years before.

The spectacle of the bombardment did nothing to disillusion him: it seemed unreal. The first shock of reality came when the landing craft was a few hundred yards from the beach: and then, for a few dreadful minutes, reality crowded in upon him in quick impressions of horror after horror. Machine guns opened fire from the shore. Shells and mortar bombs began to fall in the sea all round. The briefing had been wrong; the defenses were far from crushed. He saw that the beach ahead was covered with wreckage. Then, one by one, he saw the Commando's other landing craft on either side hit hidden obstacles and explode or stop, impaled on the spikes below the water. But inexplicably, his craft sailed on and on undamaged, into the chaos among the breakers, and grounded under the flying tracers and the gunfire.

"Don't stop to help anyone; get ashore." That was what they had all been told. The ramps were lowered, narrow gangways on either side of the bow which men could only go down in single file. Waiting in the queue, Rubinstein had a glimpse of one of the sailors of the crew, standing right up in the open on the foredeck, blazing away with the boat's gun at the houses opposite. He admired him. Then his turn came; and on the ramp, the man in front of him was shot straight through the head, and fell back against him, blocking the way. Without a thought, he shoved the body over the side of the gangway into the sea, but as it splashed in he felt revulsion at what he had done; had the man been dead? But the men behind were pushing him on, and he got to the water and waded ashore and ran across the narrow beach to a seawall and a low earthy cliff where men were taking shelter. He dropped down among them, and looked back.

The beach was a dreadful shambles of dead and dying men, of vehicles packed together, some wrecked, some burning, some trying to find a way through. It was much narrower than the briefing had said it would be; where he had come in, the waves were not ten yards from the wall. Beyond, in the sea, half the Commando's craft were still stuck two hundred yards off shore. Some of them were sinking. Men were trying to swim in, but the tide was running strongly and carrying them off to the east, to the beaches in the gap where nobody had landed. Sickened and yet fascinated, Rubinstein saw them struggling for their lives; and then he saw his friend Yates was going to drown. Human impulse conflicted with his duty. All his own instinct told him to throw off his equipment and swim out to help his friend, but orders had been to help nobody, and his duty still lay with his section. Fear and shock had confused him, and the moment when he could have decided passed. While he watched, his friend gave up the struggle and went under. He averted his eyes. And there, closer at hand, he saw the body of the man he had pushed off the gangway, washing limply backwards and forwards in the breakers. Reason said that he must have been dead before he fell, yet he felt he had murdered him.

While he crouched below the seawall towards the end of those terrible minutes, Rubinstein was very frightened and his feelings were in chaos. But as he began to take a grip on himself, his thoughts began to crystallize into unanswerable questions which were to remain with him for years. What possible use could there be in such destruction? What good could ever come of such slaughter?

The commonest cure for fear is action. Rubinstein and his men were not left long to brood on the disasters of their landing. Somebody came along below the wall to say that a route off the beach had been found, and the survivors crept out through a gap in a minefield, away from the stricken beach to a quieter place inland.

When the commando assembled there, it could count its losses. So many men were missing that two troops were combined to form one. Many were shot, and many more were drowned; but fifty of the missing men who were assumed to be dead were really still alive, for in the middle of all the stark tragedy they had suffered a fate which was ludicrous and humiliating. A tank landing craft had picked them up two hundred yards off shore, but its skipper had insisted, in spite of furious arguments, that his orders were to go straight back to England: and straight back to England they went.

As soon as it seemed that all the men who had landed alive had been collected, the Commando set to its work of clearing the defenses to the eastward, and for a little way it advanced along lanes without opposition. There were still a few Frenchmen lurking in their houses, and when the troops passed a café, Captain Perry told Rubinstein, as the last out of school, to go in and ask where the Germans were. There was a crowd of elderly men and women inside, and Rubinstein brought forth the best of his school French: *"Ou sont les Boches?"* The answer was a torrent of Norman dialect which he did not understand at all. But this was an incident more like normal life; it was the sort of thing he had imagined might happen, and it helped to bring him back to a more normal state of mind. So did the sight of a cow, standing perfectly calmly in a meadow chewing its cud. It must have been deaf, he thought.

But the lull of relief and normality ended soon. A barrage of gunfire came down on the troop, and it was British, not German fire. Someone had made a mistake, and the Royal Navy shelled the Royal Marines. The troop was forced to retreat, angry and frustrated, and the misunderstanding cost the life of Lieutenant Curtis, the second-in-command and Rubinstein's immediate senior. He was cruelly wounded by a British shell, and there was nothing they could do but give him morphine. When the barrage stopped and the troop advanced again and left him behind, he was still conscious enough to tell Rubinstein he would see him soon in London. But Rubinstein knew he was dying, and wondered again at the uselessness of such agony. The troop moved on to Langrune-sur-Mer.

The Commando's fight for the strongpoint there was the most prolonged street battle in the whole of the assault on Normandy. The strongpoint, as the briefing had said, was a complete block of houses on the seafront, with the seawall on one side and streets on the other three. The houses were reinforced and their windows were blocked up, and they were surrounded by trenches, minefields, barbed wire and machine-gun posts which were connected to the houses by underground passages.

At about eleven o'clock, Captain Perry's troop, with Rubinstein now acting as second-in-command, began to advance up one street while another troop attacked the other end of the block. As they dodged from doorway to doorway, a stream of bullets came down the street from a pit with a concrete cupola over it, in the middle of the crossroads by the strongpoint. Perry took the troops through the deserted houses into the backyards behind them; they climbed over or knocked down the walls between one yard or garden and the next, and quite quickly reached the house on the crossroads itself. So far, they had got on well; but the next step had still to be decided. Perry left Rubinstein in the house, saying he was going to have a look round; and only a minute later a man ran in saying: "Captain Perry's killed, sir."

The men in the house were shocked that the one man in whom they had put their trust was dead. The news went round among them of how it had happened: he had been shot by a sniper in a gateway beside the house. It was a shock to Rubinstein too, but he hardly realized the effect of it till somebody asked him: "What do we do now, sir?" It was a situation he had never remotely imagined. There was nobody senior left. The troop was isolated, a long way from headquarters, and as the only one of its officers left alive, he was in command. The survivors of sixty-five men were waiting for his orders.

When a boy is so suddenly forced to behave like a man, what he does is a matter of chance—the chance of heredity and upbringing. Rubinstein was lucky. He was not consciously prepared for responsibility, but when it came, something made him able to accept it. It took him a few minutes. His first reaction was natural but ineffective: he collected all his NCOs because he felt he needed their support. But that had a result which only made matters worse. They assembled in the porch of a house, and while they were discussing the situation a mortar bomb came through the roof. It blew Rubinstein down the cellar steps. He was not hurt, but when he got up again he found two of the sergeants wounded. That finally showed him that if life was to be so cheap, it was foolish and cowardly to depend on anyone else for moral support. While he was still alive and unhurt, the least he could do for the troop was to stand on his own feet and make his own decisions. Action had pushed his first fear into the background; responsibility killed it.

For the next nine hours, the troop fought a solitary battle under Rubinstein's command. Later on, when he had learned a bit more about soldiering, he saw for himself some mistakes which he made that day. He might have sent back for help and for more explosives, but communication with headquarters was tenuous, and he did not think of it. Instead of that, the troop doggedly hammered away at the strongpoint, hunting for an opening they could exploit with the weapons they carried. It was a battle of wits against an enemy they hardly ever saw; an affair of advances from house to house and from room to room, and of retreats when they found the way impassable, of snipers' shots and mortar bombs which fell unpredictably from invisible emplacements, and quick dashes over streets which were covered by machine guns. Rubinstein sent Sergeant Blyth to make a reconnaissance, and that added to his own loneliness and worry, because Blyth did not come back and Rubinstein could not possibly go to look for him. During the afternoon, Rubinstein and a few of the men got into one corner of the strongpoint, but they were held there by a concrete wall, over which the Germans threw a stream of hand grenades. A tank which turned up to help them used all its ammunition against the wall without knocking it down, and the troop had to retreat and try again. Rubinstein himself had been sent into battle with a .455 revolver, the conventional and practically useless weapon of an officer, but he had picked up a rifle. There was very little use for that either, but he did once see a German running along a trench, and he raised the rifle and fired. The German jumped like a shot rabbit and disappeared. Rubinstein felt no emotion at all, except surprise that it had been such a good shot. He had discovered by then that in battle the enemy seems impersonal.

By the evening, they had still made very little progress. No doubt they had worn down the strength of the defenders, but

Webley .455 Mk. VI

their own strength was flagging too. The fact was that the strongpoint was too well planned and too toughly defended for light arms to make any quick impression. Towards dusk, the commanding officer of the Commando came up to their corner of the battle. He told Rubinstein that a counterattack from inland was expected during the night. The Commando was therefore to break off the attack, and assemble outside the village to defend itself, and leave the strongpoint till the morning. Rubinstein was glad of the chance of a rest; he was tired, and so was his troop. But one worry was still on his mind: Sergeant Blyth had still not come back from his reconnaissance. Rubinstein asked his commanding officer if he could stay behind when the troop withdrew, to look for the sergeant.

So the troop went back by the way it had come in the morning, and left him alone on the ground it had fought for so long. Silence fell with the darkness on the wreckage round the crossroads, and shreds of the beauty of a summer night descended. Rubinstein walked all alone down the streets where men had only moved at the risk of their lives in daylight, and as he went along he shouted for Blyth; but he only heard the echoes of his own voice, and the sound of the sea, and gunfire in the distance. Blyth did not answer. The Germans must have heard him behind their walls, but they gave no sign of it.

When he had sadly given up his search and joined the troop again in their bivouac in an orchard, he found some of the men hysterically angry with the Germans, mainly because of the death of Captain Perry. They swore they would get inside the strongpoint in the morning, and kill any German who tried to surrender. Their unreasoned impulse seemed shocking to him. He had seen too much of death. He had watched his friends die, and rebelled at the waste of their lives; and he had tried to kill Germans himself, because it seemed it had to be done while they still resisted; but to kill men in anger, because they had done what he had done himself—that was worse than warfare, it was anarchy.

So he thought as he lay on the ground exhausted, under the apple trees. He had grown up a lot since the morning; but still, he was only nineteen.

Next day, they captured the strongpoint. Sergeant Blyth was found wounded but alive. They took thirty-one prisoners.

*   *   *

Most of the adverse conditions on Juno Beach in the early stages were also found on Sword Beach, on the eastern flank of the invasion area: the rough seas, the abnormally high tide, and the defenses which had survived the bombardment. On Sword, there was the added unpleasantness of German artillery fire from beyond the River Orne. Though Otway and his parachutists had captured the principal battery at Merville, other batteries over there, and mobile guns which were hidden in the woods, were still in action. Indeed, it was weeks before they were all overrun and the eastern end of Sword Beach was out of artillery range.

Sword was in an area aptly called La Breche—the Breach— on the outskirts of Ouistreham and the seaside resort of Riva Bella. It was also on the outskirts of particularly heavy fortifications. Ouistreham, on the mouth of the Orne and the Caen Canal, had a port large enough for small naval ships like motor torpedo boats and inshore minesweepers. The Germans had a minor naval base there. Some ships were caught in it and tried to escape by steaming up the canal; but when they came to the bridge which Howard and his glider force had captured, and signaled for the bridge to be opened, the answer was not at all what they seemed to have expected.

Round the mouth of this harbor and along the sea front of Riva Bella, there was a concentration of heavy emplacements, and the bombardment which had done so much damage in the town had left the emplacements still able to fire on the beach. The first to land on this formidable spot were some of the DD tanks of the 13th/18th Hussars.

The 13th/18th were a venerable cavalry regiment that had only left their horses behind in India just before the war. Some of them, it was said, still had their hearts in the stables. When tanks broke down or burned out under them, they still liked to refer to themselves, only half humorously, as unhorsed. In spite of this inclination, they had taken to tanks with efficiency; but when they had heard they were getting swimming tanks, their first reaction had simply been disbelief; the thing just wouldn't work, they said. Certainly that was not an unreasonable opinion; but it had worked, and remarkably well, in rehearsals.

One of their tank commanders was a sergeant called Harry Morris; and no doubt many of the other commanders shared Morris's feelings as they sailed across the Channel. First, he was secretly full of admiration for his own crew, who were all very young; compared with their jobs down inside the tank, he felt that his own, on top in the open air, was a soft spot. Secondly, like Americans in Rockwell's landing craft much farther west, he was very worried about the weather; he had never tried to launch a DD tank in such a sea. And thirdly, he and everyone else in his troop were suffering an extra refinement of the general misery of seasickness. It was their rations. They opened pack after pack, hoping to find something which seasick men could stomach, but every single one was full of tinned steak and kidney pudding—good nourishing stuff, no doubt, but almost the last thing that anyone would have chosen on a rough night in the English Channel. By morning, these Hussars were hungry and miserable, and when the time had come for launching, what they wanted most in the world was to get off the landing craft and onto dry land, no matter how or where. So they were glad when they heard their commander's decision: the swim was on, but from four thousand yards off shore instead of the five thousand which had been planned.

Perhaps the sea off Sword Beach was not quite so rough as off Omaha; or perhaps the Hussars should be given credit for their greater success. At any rate, the tanks did not sink at once. But from the moment when they were launched, they began to sink slowly. Whatever course they steered, waves broke over the canvas and washed about on top of the tanks and ran down through the turrets faster than the bilge pumps could empty them out. Sergeant Morris, trying to follow the leader of his troop and to steer his clumsy craft so that it dodged the waves, knew it was only a matter of time, a toss-up whether they would reach the shore before the tank went down. But out in the very front of the assault, there were other hazards too. The bombardment was reaching its climax, and the whole of it was going over the heads of the DD tank commanders. Morris found it impossible not to duck. The big shells from the fleet some miles behind were comfortably high, but the tank and infantry landing craft, which were almost on his tail, were firing their cannons at short range on a flat trajectory and their tracers seemed to be only just over his head. Worst of all were the rockets, because he could hear them coming from behind him; and in fact the rockets were partly to blame for a tragic mix-up which sent some of the tank crews to the fate which they must have feared.

In the rough sea, the tanks could not keep up their full speed. The tank landing craft, which should have landed two minutes behind them, began to catch up with them, until the leading tank landing craft actually passed the last few of the tanks. At that critical moment, when the ships and tanks were dangerously close together, a salvo of rockets fell short into the sea just ahead of them all. One or two of the landing craft captains, who saw the rockets falling, altered course abruptly and ran down two of the tanks. They sank at once. Their commanders were picked up, but their crews never came to the surface. Perhaps the tanks turned over as they sank.

But Morris was well in front, and did not know of this tragedy behind him. He was watching the deserted, empty beach, and calculating whether they would reach it. He called his driver on the intercom to ask how he was getting on. "All right, but—wet," the driver answered. In fact, he was sitting up to his waist in water. In the last few hundred yards, the heavy barrage lifted, but the lighter shot from behind was still going past, and now it was met by small arms and mortar fire from ahead as the Germans began to recover from the shelling. Between the two fires, Morris's tank ploughed on, and a couple of rifle bullets could have sunk it. But he hardly gave a thought to the stuff which was flying around, because now he could see his objective right in front of him—a gun built into the basement of a hotel above the beach—and now he felt certain he was going to reach the shore.

The tracks grounded a long way out, and he drove forward till the hull was half out of the water, and gave the order "Down canvas," and as the canvas dropped, his gunner fired a shot straight ahead without stopping to aim. With that shot, the DD tank achieved the first of its objects: surprise.

Morris had made it; but not all the commanders had been so lucky or so skillful. Five had not been able to launch at sea, two had been rammed. The survivors, on the final approach to the beach, had not attracted special attention from the German artillery because they were insignificant targets among the approaching landing craft; but as soon as they beached and dropped their canvas and the German gunners saw them for what they were, fire was concentrated on them and several were destroyed before they were out of the water.

Some other commanders, having never landed before in such a surf, made the fatal mistake, even after they reached the land, of dropping their canvas too soon, so that waves broke over their turrets and swamped them. Sergeant Morris dealt with his strongpoint, but immediately after that he was called back into the edge of the sea again to try to haul out another tank of his troop which was half full of water. Through all these causes, the force of DDs was halved.

Within two minutes of the landing of the DDs, the hitherto deserted beach was covered with tanks and hundreds of milling men. In fact, the mass of men came too close behind the tanks, because the tanks were late; and the first of the infantry found themselves on the beach before the armor had been able to cope with the strongpoints or start the job of breaching the dunes and minefields. To most of these men, the scene appeared chaotic, but in part at least that appearance was deceptive: every man knew what he was supposed to do himself, although nobody knew what all the men he could see were supposed to be doing. The confusion looked much worse than it really was.

Part of the job of the DDs was taken over, without any orders or hesitation, by flail tanks of the 22nd Hussars which had landed in the teams of specialized armor. Some of these teams were equipped to make exits from the beach, and others to clear the obstacles on it—the work which Gibbons' men had had to do by hand with such sacrifice on Omaha. But the obstacle-clearance teams could only do half of their job, because half of the obstacles were already under water when they got there. As the senior engineer of the sector, Col. R. W. Urquhart, came in to the beach in his landing craft, he saw that the outer stakes and ramps were only just showing their tops above the waves, and that all of them had either a landmine or a shell fixed on to them. Urquhart and his men dropped most of their equipment and went overboard, and swam from stake to stake cutting the mines away and letting them fall to the bottom where for the moment they could not do any harm. In the rough sea, under fire, and with landing craft blundering in among them, the swimmers felt, and were, extremely vulnerable, and there was a limit to what the most gallant of them could do; but this resourceful effort saved many landing craft, for the stakes and ramps, once the mines and shells were off them, were much less dangerous than they looked, and when landing craft hit them,

it was often the stake which suffered most. An engineer
lieutenant had the idea of mounting a tank and persuading its
commander to close his turret and drive into the sea, so that
he could stand on it to take the mines off the stakes. This also
worked well for a time. Some authority with an extraordinarily
economical mind had issued an order that the mines were to
be stored for future use; so the lieutenant, as he collected
them, stowed them dutifully on top of the tank till a sniper
hit him in the shoulder and the tank commander had to open
up and haul him out of the sea by his hair.

Above water, the armor got to work and cleared gaps at the
top of the beach according to plan. The wooden obstacles
were crushed where they stood, and the steel hedgehogs were
shackled to hawsers and towed out of the way—a simpler and
safer process than attaching charges to them and blowing
them up. But in spite of all efforts, it was impossible to get at
all the obstacles before the tide covered them, and the beach
became lined with the wreckage of landing craft. The engineers
on this job had lost one in five of their men by the time the
day was over.

The armored breaching teams, which had the job of forcing
exits from the beach, were also having a very hard time. At
the back of Sword Beach, there were dunes and then a row of
seaside villas and hotels; and behind them a road ran parallel
to the beach. In the gaps between the buildings there were
sandy tracks which led to the road, but they did not extend
through the dunes, and they were mined. Some of the houses
were fortified, and most of them seemed to shelter mortar
teams or snipers. The work of clearing exits through to the
road was therefore done at close quarters with the Germans
in the houses, often within the range of a hand grenade.

To this task, the engineers had brought sixteen flail tanks,
eight armored bulldozers, and twenty-four other tanks with
assorted implements—tanks which laid bridges against the
dunes, tanks which laid trackways, and tanks which were
fitted with pipes full of explosives which they thrust into the
dunes to blow the sand away. Without these machines, the
forcing of exits would certainly have been long and have cost
many lives; with them, it was quick, and the cost was in
machinery rather than lives. Within an hour, five exits were
clear and were connected together by the road behind the
houses. On the left-hand end of the beach, where the artillery
fire was heaviest, two more exits had been made but then

had been blocked by damaged tanks. In the second hour, at
least three more were opened. Traffic was flowing; but half of
the tanks which had done the job were out of action.

The control of traffic on beaches was a novel problem, and
novel units had been formed to solve it. By long tradition, the
navy's responsibility ends and the army's begins at the line
called HWOS: high water of ordinary spring tides. Both the
navy and the army were therefore involved in beach control,
and had groups of men on the beaches—the navy to organize
the approach of the landing craft and to tell them where to
come in, and the army to organize the exits from the beaches
and keep the traffic moving. Most people, before the invasion,
had regarded the beaches as death-traps to be crossed and
left behind as soon as possible, so nobody very much envied
beach control or anyone else who was expected to have to
stay on the beaches all day.

On the army side of high-water mark, each beach had its
beach commander, and under him a beach control group had
been assigned to each exit. Each group had a radio, and
beach control had its own network, so that as one exit was
blocked or came under heavy fire, the beach commander
could be told and could divert the traffic to the others. The
job was only expected to last until D + 1, and so most of the
officers and men who were to do it were chosen from
regiments which were not scheduled to land in the first week
or so. When the beaches were well organized and no longer
under fire, the beach control units were to hitchhike back to
England to rejoin their regiments and prepare to go over
again. On Sword Beach, the 3rd Reconnaissance Regiment
provided the men for this unpromising assignment; and among
them were Neville Gill and Ivor Stevens.

Gill and Stevens, rather like Roy Manley and George
Dunn, might be taken as an example of the way in which war
can throw together two men of different background and
temperament, and by giving them experience in common can
unite them in a friendship which they might never have
achieved in peace. Gill was thirty-one, a solicitor from
Newcastle, with the learned interests of his profession. Stevens
was twenty-five, the son of the landlord of a pub in Bradford-
on-Avon, and he had joined the Grenadier Guards as a
guardsman before the war. Gill had no interest in sport, and
preferred a quiet sedentary life. Stevens, on the other hand,

was an enormous athletic man, as strong as an ox, who rowed and played football and cricket. Both, it was true, were alike in being bachelors, but whereas Gill was destined to remain one, Stevens, on D Day, was in the middle of a whirlwind courtship of a Scots girl called Connie Bowes. He had met her only five times; but the fourth time they met, she had promised to marry him, so that to him the Normandy campaign was merely a job he had to get done before he could attend to much more interesting prospects.

Those were the obvious differences between the two men. What they shared was the experience of the past four years. Both of them had been at Dunkirk, Gill as a subaltern and Stevens as an unpaid lance-corporal, and they had both come out of it unhurt but feeling shattered by their first experience of war and determined that no power on earth would get them across the Channel again in wartime. But that feeling had worn off. Both of them had been in Britain ever since, endlessly training. By D Day, Gill was a major, and Stevens was a captain and his second-in-command, and both of them, if not exactly eager for death or glory, would have been disappointed if they had not had the chance to go.

Oddly enough, though neither of them was afraid of the landing, they had both been afraid of what would happen when they tried to take ship to come back to rejoin their regiment. They would be all on their own, and so far as they knew, beach control groups were the only people in the whole invasion force who had anything but a one-way ticket. If two army officers and a dozen men went to the captain of a ship on D + 1, and told them they wanted to go home, it was going to look funny, and the more they explained it the worse it was going to be. They had worried so seriously about being taken for deserters that Gill had procured a letter of authority, with a roll of his men, signed by the Corps Commander himself, and he carried it most carefully in the breast pocket of his battledress. Both of them regarded this letter as the most important possession they took with them, their passport to safety again.

Gill and his group were due to land nineteen minutes after the first wave of infantry. If anyone could have observed the small landing craft which carried them from their ship towards the beach, he might have discovered another difference between the two officers, for Gill was right in the bows, and Stevens was right in the stern. Gill took his command very seriously. It was a very small command for a major, it was true, only about a dozen men all told; but it was an unusually independent command, because his only link to any senior officer was by radio. And of course responsibility for the lives of a dozen men may weigh as heavily as responsibility for a thousand, because the commander of a dozen men can know them all as individuals and know, rather than merely imagine, the importance to them and to their families of their individual lives. So Gill had rather relished his duty to take the most vulnerable place in the landing craft and be the first to land.

But Stevens, the old soldier of twenty-five, took a down-to-earth view of gratuitous courage. He was one of those people who are brave as any but like to pretend to be cowards. A good soldier, he always said, did what he was told but otherwise took care of his own skin. Nobody in their senses did brave deeds unless they had to; people only won medals, he believed, because some circumstance compelled them to do what afterwards seemed to be brave. It is an arguable point of view, and Stevens liked arguing about it. The stern of the landing craft, as it happened, was the proper place for the second-in-command, but Stevens took it as if it had been his own choice. "You're welcome to the front, sir," he had said to Gill. "As far back as I can get, that's the place for me." He was rewarded, in the ninety minutes of the run-in to the beach, by the sight of the heaving backs of the men in front of him crouched miserably over the paper bags which the army had wisely provided; and soon he was using his own.

But Gill, peering out over the raised ramp, between the bursts of spray which broke over it, was too worried to be sick: worried not by danger but by the belief that they were heading for the wrong beach. The craft was commanded by a subaltern of the Royal Marines. He had a photograph of the beach, and so had Gill. As they drove on, they could see the row of seaside villas which were shown on their photographs, but by then they had been badly knocked about, and through the fog of the bombardment it was difficult to tell which villa was which. The marine was sure he was right. Gill was sure he was wrong, and grew annoyed. But while they were afloat, the marine was in charge, so Gill had to let him have his way. As the craft lurched in towards the end of the line of boats already lying in the breakers, Gill was miserably uncertain of himself. The crisis was coming, the very moment when his dozen men would depend on his leadership; and desperately searching the beach and his photograph, he could not discover for certain where he was. He felt he was going to fail them.

The dropping of the ramp gave each man in the boat, before he plunged into the sea, a momentary photographic glimpse of the scene he had imagined for so long—the few yards of breaking waves, lapping the shore in a thin line of foam, the almost level sand, two tanks burning, the stakes with mines on top of them, the swirling smoke, and far away, the line of the dunes and the ruins of the villas.

Gill found he was chest-deep, and he waded forward with only one thought in his head; to find out where they were, how far from the place where they ought to have come ashore. There seemed to be nobody moving on the beach ahead. He supposed the first wave of the infantry were across it and in the dunes: they should have been by then. Stevens and the others came splashing through the waves behind him. "Steve," he shouted above the din, "we're in the wrong place. Get the men under cover. I'm going to find out where we are." And he walked up the beach alone.

Stevens was amazed to see him go, because his first impression of what was going on was quite different. All along the water's edge to his left, as far as he could see, men were crouching or lying in the shallows. To his right, there was nobody at all. Evidently, they were on the very end of the area under attack. Tanks were coming ashore on the left, but the only ones he could see up the beach were burning. It looked to him as if the infantry were stuck and nobody so far had got across the beach. Wondering what on earth to do, he crouched in a couple of feet of water. He was still feeling giddy and weak from seasickness. In his left hand he was holding one end of the group's radio: the other end was carried by a corporal. Waves broke against their backs.

Gill went along the beach, puzzling over the photograph and the map and cursing the marine subaltern. Men were milling around the edge of the tide. Shells were falling and machine-gun fire was coming from heaven knew where and the noise was tremendous. In the fog and confusion, he met a man he knew but had not seen for years; he asked him where they were, but he seemed to have no idea. But one thing at least was perfectly clear to Gill, and that was his duty. Steve could look after the men; his own job, first and foremost, was to find out where to go. He never thought about the danger because everyone had expected the beach to be dangerous.

So he went further up the beach, to try to get a clear view of the dunes and villas. As he went up it, he met a crowd of Germans coming down it with their hands up. They all made for him, evidently wanting him to accept their surrender; but prisoners were no business of his, so he told them to stay where they were and walked on.

Stevens had soon lost sight of Gill. Staying in the water gave a feeling of being under cover, but he knew quite well it was no protection against the stray shots which were flying around and that he ought to get the men somewhere safer till Gill came back. He made up his mind to make for the nearest derelict tank ahead. And then, before they could move, the corporal on the other end of the radio was shot. He fell in the water. One of the others picked up the radio and Stevens shouted to them all to follow him. Dragging the dying man, the group ran forward to the tank. As they dropped down in this momentary shelter, one of the men called to Stevens, "There's the major." And Stevens looked as saw Gill all alone on the open beach; and in the same second, he saw him throw up his hands and fall down and lie still.

Gill felt something like an electric shock and felt himself falling. He fell flat on his back with his pack under him. He tried to get up again, but he could not move at all. His arms and legs lay where they were, and he could not pick them up. He felt very surprised. He thought, "I'm wounded," but it did not hurt after the first shock, and he did not even know where the wound was.

His brain was quite clear. Just before, he had seen some medical orderlies hiding behind a tank, and he shouted to them to come and give him a hand, but they did not come. He turned his head to look for them, and saw, crawling up the sand, head-on, a Sherman tank with an explosive charge on the front of it, the sort which he knew was used for blowing holes in sand dunes. It came straight at him. Had the driver seen him? he wondered. Did he know he was not dead? Would he drive over a dead man lying in the way? He tried with all his will to move, to get out of the way, to wave his arm to make the driver look; but nothing would move except his head. He had time to imagine most clearly what would happen if the track went over him, and time to wonder if there was clearance under the belly of a Sherman, if the tracks passed him one on each side. The roar of the tank increased, and he shut his eyes. And then above all the noise he heard Stevens breathless voice with its friendly familiar west-country intonation. "What happened, sir?" Steve said.

Stevens had left the lee of the burned-out tank and run alone across the open beach to where Gill had been shot. It had cost him an effort of self-control. He expected to be shot himself. Whether the infantry were in the dunes or not, there were obviously Germans still within rifle range. But he reached Gill unharmed and as he dropped down beside him the Sherman tank stopped dead and turned in its tracks and went round them. "Steve, I can't move," Gill said. "Where did it get me?"

Stevens could not see a wound, so he turned him over. There was blood on the back of his battledress. He rolled up the tunic and found a jagged wound below the shoulder blades. He got out a field dressing and started to put it on, and saw from the corner of his eye that the Sherman tank was butting its way into the dunes.

"Keep your head down," he said. "The tank's going to fire its charge." He lay down beside Gill and waited.

Once on an exercise, Gill had been with a man who was badly injured, and a medical orderly had asked him to hold the man's hand. He had felt a fool, but he had held it while the man's injuries were dressed. Now, as he lay with his face in the sand and the numbness began to recede and the pain to flame up inside him, a feeling of terror and loneliness overcame him like a shadow of death. Then he felt Steve's enormous hand take his and understood the strange comfort of this kind of human contact. The tank's charge exploded and sand showered down on them. "I'd better take the Corps Commander's letter," Stevens said; and Gill knew then that his battle was finished before it was even begun. "It's in my breast pocket," he said, and Stevens rolled him over again and took it out.

Then Stevens roused the medical orderlies from behind their tank, and made them come out with a stretcher. And there the two men parted—Stevens to find the beach exit which Gill had been looking for; and Gill to lie all day under morphine on the beach, to learn that a bullet had gone right through his chest from front to back and broken his spine, to spend a year in a plaster cast and a lifetime of intermittent pain. Fourteen years later, he died as a consequence of his wound.

Stevens never changed his low opinion of martial courage.

He never told anybody how he had gone out to help Gill; he would have been very upset if anyone had accused him of being brave. But Gill knew quite well what he had done, and understood his embarrassment. "Of course, you didn't care about me, Steve," he said when they met again. "All you wanted was the Corps Commander's letter."

The contradictory impressions which Gill and Stevens received when they landed were an example of a widespread dilemma. Men who landed in large units could usually follow the crowd, but for men in small specialized groups, suddenly pitched ashore in the midst of the battle, it was extremely hard, if not impossible, to judge at a glance what was happening, and there was never time to pause to think it out. If they had not been able to get their bearings before they landed, there was nobody, in the early stages, to tell them where they were. The most nightmarish experiences on all the beaches except Utah were not merely of being under fire, but of being lost: lost in a battle, perhaps in a minefield, among crowds of other men who seemed to know what they were doing but were much too busy to bother about the fate of one lost individual.

Stevens was not in that situation for long. He found his beach exit, and set to work on the job of controlling the traffic through it, and repairing it when it was torn up, and removing by brute force any tanks or trucks which stuck and threatened to jam up the stream. Sword Beach never became a comfortable place to work. German long-range artillery kept it under accurate fire—so accurate that the opinion spread that the gunners were ranging on the barrage balloons which were flying from the beach. As there were no German aircraft to be seen, the RAF men who were flying the balloons began to find themselves unpopular, and in the middle of the morning, the balloons were all cut adrift. By noon, the exceptional tide had risen to within ten yards of the dunes, and the narrow strip of sand above it was dry and soft. Trucks, jeeps, tanks and artillery began to get snarled up together so that none of them could even reach the exits, and landings had to be halted for half an hour while people like Stevens sorted out the jam. But by that time, great forces were already ashore and had passed inland, and the first assault on Sword could already be said to have succeeded. Ouistreham had fallen. The defenses of Riva Bella had been overcome in a fierce battle by a Commando force which included the two troops of

Free French who walked into the first-aid post in the town; and Royal Engineers and other Commandos were converging on the Caen Canal bridge, four miles inland, to join with Howard's glider force, and the parachutists.

There are still, and always will be, rival claims for the honor of having been the first to reach the bridge. A unit of engineers drove there in jeeps by a roundabout route, finding no opposition on the way except from snipers. Their mission was to build a new bridge, whether the original one had been captured intact or not. Their first reconnaissance officers got there at one o'clock and found the place still under shell and sniper fire; and like true technicians they set about their plans without ado. About the same moment, the first commandos arrived on bicycles, and crossed the bridge to join the airborne forces. An hour later, the main body of commandos under Brigadier Lord Lovat arrived at the bridge, and with a better eye for the picturesque and perhaps for history, they marched across it with Lovat's personal piper playing a cheerful tune.

With this meeting of seaborne and airborne forces, whoever got there first, the assault on the beaches of Normandy was complete.

PART SEVEN

THE
ANNOUNCEMENT

The announcement was the cause of intense excitement, and of intense anxiety.

The first news came from Germany. At 6:33 A.M., within five minutes, by chance, of the landings on Omaha and Utah, Berlin radio said Le Havre was being bombed, and then gave a reasonably accurate report of Hoffmann's flotilla's action against the British fleet. Every few minutes after that, it added more details, especially of parachute landings, some of which were right and some wrong. News agencies which monitored these broadcasts relayed them round the world, and radio news bulletins repeated them. In Washington, where it was just after midnight, people not in the know were sceptical, and thought they might be some kind of propaganda. For two and a half hours, rumors spread, and could not be confirmed. Eisenhower had refused to authorize any announcement at all until he was certain his troops were ashore. At 9:01, the first guarded official statement was issued. It did not mention any names of places; but seven minutes later, Berlin said the landings stretched over the whole of the area from Le Havre to Cherbourg. From that time onward, news commentators all over the world were on the air, but still most of their material came from Germany. On the eastern seaboard of America, the official news broke at 3:30 A.M. and the first comment came from Mayor LaGuardia of New York, who rightly foresaw the mood of his city and indeed of the whole of the Allied world: "We can only wait for bulletins and pray for success. It is the most exciting moment in our lives."

In America, people working on night shifts heard it. In England, the day had begun. In both countries, and even in Germany too, there was relief that for better or worse the waiting was over and the blow had been struck at last. But there were no outward signs of rejoicing; everyone everywhere knew the battle had only begun, and while people hoped for success, they feared that success would only come through dreadful slaughter. From New York, it was reported that men and women off night shifts were drifting into churches on their way home; a daily paper threw out its leading articles and printed the Lord's Prayer; a prayer meeting was held in Madison Square Garden. In London, services were held in St. Paul's and Westminster Abbey. Some people had a sense of anticlimax; it seemed wrong that life should go on as usual, that busses and trains should run and meals be served in restaurants and business be done while such desperate events, on which all this normal life depended, were happening so few miles away.

Personal anxiety was deeper and more widespread than it need have been. Rumor had said that enormous casualties were expected. The secret official belief was that ten thousand men might be lost in the first assault; but in fact, the cost in lives was less than a quarter of that. Censorship of letters from troops had been very strict for months, and for some time even men who had no dangerous part to play had not been able to write home at all; and so mothers and wives who had been waiting for letters and now heard the news of invasion imagined their sons and husbands to be fighting their way ashore at that very moment. Probably for each man in the first assault, ten families suffered the anxiety of believing their man was there.

Joy Howard, the wife of John Howard, who had led the glider attack on the Caen Canal bridge, was feeding her baby at home in Oxford, too busy to switch on the radio, when a kindly neighbor came in and asked her to spend the day with her, and said somebody had given her a brace of pheasants which they could have for dinner. Joy was surprised by this sudden invitation, and her mind flew to the problems of taking the pram for the baby and the highchair for the two-year-old. "We thought you'd like company on a day like this," the neighbor said; and then, seeing her bewilderment she added, "Oh, haven't you heard the news?"

John had told her weeks before that by the time she heard of an airborne attack, his own part in it would be over; and so it was, for the moment. Just about then, in fact, he was finding time to laugh. Two Italians had reported for duty at the bridge. They had been working for the Germans, digging the holes and putting up the antiglider posts in the meadow by the bridge where his gliders had landed. They had finished the holes, but not the posts. Now they did not know what to do, but after they had argued it out between them, they decided they had better carry on. So they went into the field and started putting up the antiglider posts, all round the gliders which were already there.

Connie Bowes, who had just got engaged to Ivor Stevens of the beach control group, heard the news on the radio in the factory where she worked at Hawick in Scotland. It was a stocking factory, turned over to making jettison fuel tanks for aircraft, and all the workers were women; and almost all of them had a son or a husband or a lover who had not told her for months what he was doing and had not written at all for weeks. Work stopped for a bit, and then went on with extra energy. Almost everyone in the factory was in tears. Connie Bowes kept her feelings to herself, but she wondered what Steve was doing.

Perhaps it was just as well she did not know, because just about then he was lying in a slit trench on top of another man and thought his last moment had come. All morning, since Neville Gill had been wounded, Steve had been looking after his exit from Sword Beach, not caring about anything except to see that traffic kept moving through it. Suddenly he saw men scattering for cover on the beach and looking behind him saw a row of German bombers tearing along the beach at the height of the villa rooftops. He dived for his trench and as he fell in on top of the man who had got there first, he saw the first plane hit and swerve towards him. It went over the trench so low that he felt the heat of it, and it hit the dune a few feet beyond him and burst into flames. Expecting to be burned alive, he jumped up to get out, but the first of the bombs in the aircraft exploded with heat, and he quickly lay down again. Bombs went on exploding one by one. It was a long time before Steve and the man underneath him agreed that the last had gone off.

Sylvia Ogden Smith, whose husband was the man who swam ashore to sample sand, was also at work in her factory in Wales when she heard the news and understood why Bruce was not coming to Buckingham Palace that afternoon to get his medal. She had been given notices to be posted when the invasion had started, urging the staff to work even harder to support the men at the front. She went round and stuck them on the notice boards, but they were not at all necessary. She saw a stout elderly mother sobbing over her capstan lathe, but the lathe was still running and her hands were moving as fast as ever. She went to talk to her, and found most of the other women weeping at their work. She tried to cheer them up, and then she went away to have a cry herself.

Her husband, just about then, was trying to help to rescue the crew of a landing craft which was burning furiously aground on Omaha Beach; and somewhere quite close to him, Henry Meyers, the schoolteacher from Brooklyn, who had landed in conditions worse than any of the women had imagined, was waiting to advance with his telephone wire; and his wife, Molly, who operated an accounting machine in a New York store, was given time off and went to church to pray for him, with her friends from the office who had husbands and lovers overseas in England.

For a few, the immemorial roles of men and women in war were reversed. In concentration camps in Germany, prisoners were not supposed to hear any news at all, but in some of them prisoners who were technicians were kept at work repairing radio sets which belonged to the guards, and they contrived to keep one in working order in the workshops. So Dr. Sustendal of Luc-sur-Mer, in prison in Germany for suspected spying on the Atlantic Wall, heard that his own village was on the invasion shore, at almost the moment when his wife and his two boys were seeking shelter from the bombardment underneath his car in his garage; and the news brought both hope and concern to him, hope which was justified; he lived through his ordeal and went home to his village in the end.

Some Germans, with special anxiety for men in France,

listened secretly, against the Nazi laws, to Swiss radio stations, for fear that their own would not tell them the truth; but the German radio, in fact, had a new sober air and did not make many extravagant claims that day. It was left to a Japanese spokesman to say "The Germans will now have an opportunity to begin new offensive operations."

In the morning, the House of Commons was packed by members waiting eagerly for a statement by Mr. Churchill; but nothing whatever disturbs the routine of Parliament. Question time was first. A communist member made a plea for the abolition of banks, and an independent asked the Secretary to the Treasury if he would arrange that members of the Government Minor and Manipulative Grades Association of Office Cleaners should be referred to in future as such, and not as charwomen or charladies. When many matters like these had been disposed of and Churchill rose to speak, he added to the atmosphere of impatient expectancy by talking for ten minutes about the fall of Rome which had been announced the day before. Of course that was only fair to the men who were fighting in Italy; but he seemed to members to be taking a mischievous delight in keeping them on tenterhooks, and his own account confirms that he enjoyed it. When at last he announced the invasion he added: "So far, the commanders who are engaged report that everything is proceeding according to plan. And what a plan! This vast operation is undoubtedly the most complicated and difficult that has ever taken place." That afternoon, in a second statement, he reminded the House: "It is a most serious time that we enter upon. Thank God we enter upon it with our great allies all in good heart and all in good friendship."

The annual meeting of the Channel Tunnel Company was held that day in London, and the chairman reported that the future of the tunnel was impossible to foresee.

By midday, the first eye-witness accounts were coming in from war correspondents who had flown over the beaches: "I feel it is a great privilege to be here. I'll be glad to get home all the same. . . . I can see the invasion craft out on the water . . . I feel detached, and that awful feeling that the great history of the world is unfolding before us at this very moment." All day, news from the shore itself was very meager. But while the public knew little of the progress of the battle, it might be said that the men who were ashore knew even less. There is a military phrase for their experience: battlefield isolation. All that they knew was what they could see, and what their own command radio network told them, and once they were across the beach and in among the lanes and villages and hedgerows, they could see very little. Few of them had the time or a suitable radio to hear what was broadcast from London; but one American airborne commander, out alone with his unit and wondering whether to attack or not, happened to hear a BBC bulletin which said the airborne operation was going according to plan; and on that slender evidence, he ordered his attack. All that most men knew was that they were ashore and still alive, and that surprised them.

By nightfall, the issue was decided. The foothold at Omaha Beach was still narrow, General Gavin's airborne troops were still isolated, and the landing of materials had lagged behind the plan; but the Atlantic Wall was decisively broken and the armies securely ashore. Eisenhower was satisfied, but unwilling to be overoptimistic. He was still worried about Omaha, perhaps more worried than he need have been, because the reports which were reaching him were still being delayed in the signals system; and he was chafing at being unable to do anything whatever to influence the battle. But in fact one question, the question of the assault, was already answered. Everything now depended on the answer to a second: could the Allies build up their forces more quickly than the Germans? The answer to this question depended on the weather, and the weather had already brought the project near disaster.

The Allied troops could not afford to be overconfident either. Over there, with the Channel behind them and unknown forces ahead, they felt their dependence on support and material which all had to come by the same long perilous route across the sea and the beaches.

The clearest assessment of the outcome of the day was made by the German front-line troops. They knew their own capabilities, and had also seen the fleet and the weight of Allied material thrown against them, and the more clear-headed of them knew they could not win.

The German commanders had not seen the fleet, and no mere military report could have conveyed to them the impression of irresistible power which it gave; but still, it is likely that before the day was over, they also knew in their

inmost thoughts that the invasion could not be defeated. It
was only eleven days later that von Rundstedt and Rommel
tried to suggest to Hitler that Germany should sue for peace
with Britain and America—though not with Russia.

Night fell, and the men who had been the first to land
were tiring. War may be mechanized, but battles are limited
by the stamina of the human body. Some of the men were
still in action, and some could try to sleep; but in the dark, a
hundred German bombers ventured over, and the night on
the beachhead was noisy with thousands of antiaircraft guns.
Where the first troops rested, the follow-up troops were
passing through. In the Channel, ships with more men and
more material were passing ships returning to reload. In
English ports, more ships were being loaded, and all over the
south of England still more men and still more material were
on the move, southward toward the Channel. The assault was
over; the battle of the build-up had begun.

On St. Albans Head the night before, Mr. Wallace, the coast
guard, had seen the fleet and heard the aircraft and knelt
down with his wife to pray; and now the prayers of the great
and humble were united. President Roosevelt broadcast, and
then went alone to his room and wrote a prayer for "a peace
that will let all men live in freedom, reaping the just rewards
of their honest toil." In Britain, King George VI broadcast,
and these were his final words: "If from every place of
worship, from home and factory, from men and women of all
ages and many races and occupations, our supplications rise,
then, please God, both now and in the future not remote, the
predictions of an ancient psalm may be fulfilled: 'The Lord
will give strength unto his people: the Lord will give his
people the blessing of peace.'"

ABOUT THE AUTHOR

DAVID HOWARTH was born in London in 1912. He attended Tonbridge School and Cambridge College, where in 1933 he received a B.A. in physics and mathematics. As his first job, he worked for John Logie Baird, pioneer in television, in the days when it was worked by a large revolving disk. He then joined the British Broadcasting Corporation, working first as a technician and then on news and editorial jobs.

Mr. Howarth served for the first eight months of World War II as a war correspondent for the BBC with the British and French Armies in France. During the evacuation from Dunkirk he joined the navy, and spent the next nine months in command of an old motor yacht patrolling the southeast coast of England hoping to repel German invasion. From 1941 to the end of the war in Europe, he was stationed in the Shetland Islands as second-in-command of a private navy, first of Norwegian fishing boats, later of American-built sub-chasers, which landed arms and agents in occupied Norway. This experience provided the material for his first book, *Across to Norway.*

After the war Mr. Howarth stayed on in the Shetland Islands and worked there for five years designing and building fishing boats and yachts. But as a result of the success of his first book, he decided to devote his full time to freelance writing. *D Day* is the fifth of his seven books to be published in America.

Mr. Howarth now lives in the country outside of London with his wife, Nanette, and their four young children.

The short, shaggy [ ] ged at the accusation [ ] int blank, "Who did [ ] here. Who?" he shut up entirely.

While in an American court the Fifth Amendment would protect him against self-incrimination, this was neither court nor America. It was a battlefield.

Gul punched the turncoat, a heavy, straight smash to his face that knocked him back against the rock. When he recovered, with a shake of his head that threw drops of blood from his nose, his attitude had changed. He turned to Kyle and spoke in English.

"It is a holy honor to die for Allah," he said. His eyes had that look of a true believer.

Kyle had had enough. "An honor indeed," he said. He wasn't opposed to torture for information in this case, but it would take time they didn't have. He snagged a grenade from his harness, flipped the pin out with his left thumb, and stuffed it down the coarse shirt of the little troll. He gave him a heartfelt knee to the groin, lifted his leg and drove his heel into the skinny little runt's chest. The man said "Guhhhh!" with a terrified look on his face as he bounced over the precipice and down. Precisely at the three-second mark, a horrendous BOOM! indicated that his body was splattered over the cliff face.

"Bon voyage," Kyle said. "Say hi to Allah for me."

MICHAEL Z. WILLIAMSON

THE
SCOPE OF
JUSTICE

AVON BOOKS
An Imprint of HarperCollinsPublishers

This is a work of fiction. Names, characters, places, and incidents are products of the author's imagination or are used fictitiously and are not to be construed as real. Any resemblance to actual events, locales, organizations, or persons, living or dead, is entirely coincidental.

AVON BOOKS
An Imprint of HarperCollins*Publishers*
10 East 53rd Street
New York, New York 10022-5299

Copyright © 2004 by Michael Z. Williamson
ISBN: 0-06-056524-1
www.avonbooks.com

First Avon Books paperback printing: July 2004

Avon Trademark Reg. U.S. Pat. Off. and in Other Countries, Marca Registrada, Hecho en U.S.A.
HarperCollins® is a registered trademark of HarperCollins Publishers Inc.

Printed in the U.S.A.

10 9 8 7 6 5 4 3 2 1

To Ray Chatterjee:
Thanks, Dood.

THE
SCOPE OF
JUSTICE

"YOU WILL USE TEN KILOGRAMS OF SEMTEX, which will be provided to you by another. Messages regarding it will be delivered to the safe house," Rafiq bin Qasim said to the man before him, concluding the briefing. "Are there any questions?"

"None, sir. I go with God!" replied the man. His name wasn't important. Allah knew his name. Soon he would be dead, then others would know it, too.

Bin Qasim's office was unusual. The brand-new computer and flatscreen monitor, fax, several TVs and radios, all wired into uninterruptible power supplies, set on modern desks and static-reducing mats, were in sharp contrast to the poured-concrete walls and hazed glass in the single, small window. Woven mats covered the rest of the floor, lit at present by the four-tube fluorescent can overhead.

"Go with God, brother," he agreed, dismissing the man to his fate. He was neither bright nor highly trained, but he was dedicated to the cause and that was enough. If all he could do to help was die, bin Qasim would send him to die.

There were others like that. There were also those who didn't want to die, who had to be led to believe such plans were nonlethal. But martyrs were necessary to the cause, and it was annoying that so few of them were intelligent enough to bother with. Some were the type to accomplish great deeds, and others only served as role models. This man was just bright enough for the latter.

That done, he watched as his three assistants, the only ones allowed to be armed in his presence, escorted the future martyr out of the building. A car would take him to the airport, he'd fly a circuitous route through increasingly more respectable countries until he reached Egypt, then Germany.

Shortly thereafter, an explosion would destroy a nightclub. A place filled with sexual music and rutting, filthy women, alcohol, drugs, and best of all, American tourists and soldiers. Bin Qasim would see to it that as many of them as necessary were blown up to force them out of the Islamic lands.

Perhaps he could arrange for a day-care center next. Any American who didn't grow up was a good American. Pondering that, he looked over the office, and focused on the pliers atop the toolbox. He'd been too distracted earlier to finish. Now, perhaps.

He rose, retrieved the pliers, and said to his guards, "I shall be some time. You may leave."

They nodded and filed out, grinning in amusement, but not in front of bin Qasim, for his temper was legendary.

Bin Qasim took the pliers with him into the back room, where the British woman reporter still waited, whimpering. He'd taught her her place, in fear and suppliant to God, then Man. Now to let her show her enthusiasm for that place.

"Sergeant Monroe, right face," came the voice on the radio. Sergeant First Class Kyle Monroe did so, and waited for further instructions. He knew what they'd be: the sniper trainee was clearly visible. But he was damned sure going to be letter-of-the-regulation fair to the student who was about to fail this exercise. The observer at the end of the range had to make the call, Kyle was only a marker for him.

But this kid was as obvious as a hooker in church.

Kyle sighed, feeling old again. He had fourteen years of service, and still felt physically capable and flexible. He hadn't slowed down when he hit thirty, the way everyone said happened. Inside he felt worn, though. It wasn't the years getting to him, but the mileage. But he had all his hair and none of it gray, a taut physique and clear eyes. After tours in Bosnia and the first Gulf, Ranger and Airborne Schools as well as Sniper, and a few miscellaneous radio courses, he felt that his physical condition was still decent and quite an accomplishment. He'd feel a hell of a lot better if he could lose the guilt over that event in Bosnia, which was something everyone said wasn't his fault. It felt that way to him, though. It didn't help that he had been an instructor here at the school since then. It was mere coincidence; they needed some of the best snipers to teach others, and everyone said he was that good. But he couldn't escape the timing. It felt like a punishment, no matter how much he really did like teaching the kids.

"Three meters," he was told, then, "left face," which he did, leaving him facing the boots of Corporal Samuel Merrick, clothed in a shredded burlap ghillie suit and hidden in deep weeds.

At least he imagined he was hidden in deep weeds. "Two meters forward and tell Merrick he's a corpse," was the next radio transmission.

"You got 'im," he confirmed for Staff Sergeant Dick Rogers, who was one of the "targets" the students were trying to "shoot."

"Stand up, Merrick, you're dead," Kyle said. Merrick sighed, heaving himself up as if a pile of weeds suddenly assumed human form. "Figure out what you did wrong?" he asked.

Merrick said, "The sun came out."

The boy was exasperating. "Sun came out, my ass. Relying on the light is luck. If you rely on luck here, you'll rely on luck in combat. Dead! Get me? Dead!"

Merrick looked slightly chagrined, but Kyle was still talking. Merrick likely wasn't cut out to be a sniper. He could shoot, he could hide, he could observe, but he just couldn't coordinate them with the patience required to be a true professional. He even took it lightly, wearing a grin.

"I'm not smiling, Merrick," Kyle said yet again. "Look there!"

The kid was a bit more attentive now. He turned to look behind him, where Kyle was pointing. Predictably, he let his heavy M-24 rifle— a highly modified Remington 700 in 7.62mm NATO—swing across his legs as he turned. It tangled with his right boot and his ghillie suit. He hopped, recovered, and stood.

"See that?" Kyle snapped, pointing at the tall growth of the range. "There's a very clear Corporal Merrick-shaped rut through the weeds there. Anyone can tell you crawled through here. And it's a *straight* line. Prey don't move in straight lines, only hunters. So what will anyone seeing this think?"

Without waiting for an answer, he continued, "Then, you shifted the branch you used as a rifle rest. And when you shot, you blew that stalk in two. See?"

Merrick looked, and finally gave evidence of remorse. That had been really stupid. Any one of the errors was bad. All of them together were inescapable. He'd screwed up.

Kyle's problem student nodded, turned, and headed for the trucks. He was done for the morning, and the loss of points wouldn't help his final class score.

Kyle wasn't sure if the kid needed a girlfriend, a thousand pushups, or just a couple of years to mature. He was all hyped on the glamour of being a sniper, and didn't want to hear about the slow, boring infiltrations. Those were in bad weather, bugs, dirt, and with the risk of being discovered and shot.

Kyle Monroe knew about all of that personally. It hit him again right then, that pain that wasn't fading. Bosnia. He and his spotter had been a bit too eager to advance on a target. End result, Sergeant First Class Jeremy Reardon dead, a Serb sniper's bullet through his head. The funeral had been closed casket, and Kyle really hadn't cared to discuss it with Reardon's pretty young wife and seven-year-old son, who was old enough to understand death, but not old enough to understand why.

He snapped back to reality. This time it was nausea, washing over him as he massaged the scar on his right arm. Other times it was fear, sweats, anger. And he'd be drinking tonight, fighting with himself over whether to not drink, drink enough to relax, or just burn brain cells with alcohol.

In the meantime, Captain Schorlin, the school commander, was over there watching, and the expression on his face indicated he wanted to talk. Kyle hitched at his load-carrying harness and headed in that direction. The other instructors and the French observer were looking at him, too, and he knew why. Normally, everyone snickered and laughed at inept movements, strange twists of fate, or sheer forgetfulness. There was enough stress in the class, and they tried to be relaxing when counseling. Kyle had been rather brusque.

Schorlin looked at him levelly. It wasn't unkind, just appraising. As Kyle approached, the blond-haired young man—he was only thirty—said, "I think you need to ease off just a bit on the kid, Kyle."

"He needs to grow up, sir," Kyle replied. "Or he'll wind up dead and taking people with him."

"We have time," the captain said, sounding relaxed and unperturbed. "And you know I won't let him graduate if he can't hack it."

"So I'm helping him with that."

"Yes," Schorlin agreed, "and making him think he can't hack it. At this point, we've gotten rid of the bad ones. He just needs encouragement and some sarcasm. Remember when you could be sarcastic without being mean?"

Kyle had to grin at that, though it was a sickly grin. "Yes, sir. So what's up?"

"We've got a meeting tomorrow. It might mean an assignment for you."

Kyle was immediately defensive. Were they trying to shuffle him off? "But I like it here, sir. Is something wrong?"

"Yes, but not with you. It's TDY only, I'm told, which is good, because we need you here. They want you to help with a problem elsewhere. But General Robash has the details. So be at the classroom at 0900. Look sharp. BDUs and beret," the captain said, pointing at Kyle's headgear, which, like his own, was a standard Battle Dress Uniform cap. It worked better in the field than the beret, and both men, despite being Ranger trained, took it as a point of honor not to wear the Monica, as it was deprecatingly called, unless they had to.

"Yes, sir," Kyle agreed, controlling the slight grimace he felt. He resented how the black beret he'd earned the hard way was now being worn by everyone and his brother . . . and sister. He realized it hadn't always been a Ranger symbol, but it had become one, and then it had been taken away and trivialized.

He turned his attention back to the broad terrain and work. There was a twitch of grass. It was Sergeant Brendt, moving too eagerly. From the radio came Sergeant Rogers's voice, "Sergeant Monroe, left face, ten meters." Rogers had spotted another one. Kyle sighed and went back to the task at hand.

It was a pleasant spring day, at least, though

the ground was damp, making it cold and squishy for the students. The undergrowth was thick and plentiful. Apart from daylight, it was the thickest concealment a sniper could ever reasonably hope for. If the students, all trained infantrymen, could get past the sharp eyes of the target/observers, they should be able to get past anyone. And "anyone" would be an enemy who was trying to kill them, not merely humiliate them.

For this exercise, Rogers and McMillan were seated at a desk in the bed of a truck, portraying driver and passenger. The students infiltrated the 1,000-meter range, trying to get under 800 meters from the targets and as much closer as necessary for a clear shot. Upon doing so, they would fire a blank and call the target. An instructor on the range, like Kyle, would report the shot, and the target would hold up a placard with a letter. The students would call off the letter, proving they had a clear view of the target through the scope, and the shot would be scored. They would then take a second shot. In the meantime, the targets were scanning with binoculars. If they caught sight of the students as they approached, or after they shot, indicating spoiled concealment, those students failed.

If the students had paid attention, they should easily be able to do it in this Southern pine forest, full of red clay, brush, rolling ground, and deadwood. If they couldn't do it here, there was no way they could do it in the desert or on open fields.

And right now, three of them were lined up about five meters apart, line abreast. So if one of them fired, it was likely that the spotters would catch all three of them. They were all infantry trained and should know better. But eagerness and carelessness brought them to this.

Then, there was Sergeant Favrot, who'd decided that 400 meters wasn't good enough for a shot. He was nearly to the 200-meter mark. He'd certainly get a clear shot from there, but he'd also be much easier to find. The point of being a sniper was to keep hidden and distant, getting as close as necessary, not as close as possible. Still, Favrot was good enough that he might pull it off. But he needed to be cautioned against excessive exuberance. They were here to shoot, not make records.

Kyle chewed an MRE for lunch, just as the students would when done. They'd have time for lunch between now and the afternoon shoot, which would be in a concrete building, one group sniping from it, and the other countersniping from outside. There was no time to drive off range, down long, rutted and washed-out roads, to the cantonment area of Fort Benning. But he knew he needed to eat, and wasn't in the mood for fast food or the chow hall, anyway. His lingering depression, anger, sadness about the Bosnian screwup he'd been involved in didn't encourage a good appetite. Neither did MREs for that matter, but he had one and chewed at it component by component. He washed it down with water from his CamelBak, the gallon capacity soft canteen he wore on his back, with a drinking tube running up the shoulder strap to his mouth. They were finally standard issue rather than just a nifty accessory, and he used it without even realizing it was there, which was the mark of good equipment.

After Favrot got in his shot, along with two others who'd pushed the time limit, the students climbed into the back of their truck and rolled off. Kyle followed behind in the stake truck, the jolting ride down gully-washed trails clearing his mind slightly.

The concrete training "house" used for the next exercise was also used by various units practicing assaults. Expended flash-bang grenades and blank rounds joined cobwebs and deliberately placed furniture and debris. While movie snipers would shoot from near a window, professionals, or those training to be, found contorted positions well back against inside walls, with several feet of space to absorb muzzle flash and dull some of the report of a shot.

Merrick picked a good spot, atop a sturdy table, out a curtain-shrouded window facing south. He could see through the sheer fabric *out* with his scope, but it would be near impossible for someone outside to see *in* to the comparatively dark room. His position was solid, his view clear, and took in the large drainage culvert that was an obvious hiding place for the infiltrating team. And being obvious, one of them would invariably take it.

The kid was shrewd when not in a rush. Kyle simply watched silently from the doorway to the adjoining room, where he could watch Favrot, calm and imperturbable, set up a low position through a loophole and across what would seem like a safe zone.

Just as when doing the shooting himself, the wait hypnotized him into calmness. He watched and waited for twenty minutes, until Merrick said, "Permission to shoot, Sergeant?"

"Stand by," he said. He grabbed his microphone and asked, "Rogers, Monroe, do we have permission to shoot?"

In moments, everyone confirmed readiness—hearing protection was necessary in the tight confines, against echoing high-decibel reports, and it was polite to warn the cadre and any students who didn't have plugs in yet. "Go ahead," he said to Merrick, who nodded and squeezed. The muzzle blast echoed tinnily around the concrete structure.

"Where?" Kyle asked. He passed Merrick's instructions on to Rogers, who walked to the culvert and retrieved a student who was probably disgusted. Kyle couldn't make out who he was from where he stood, but Merrick had done a creditable job. "Way to go, Sniper," he said in encouragement, a grin on his face.

"Roger that, Sergeant!" Merrick replied.

Two minutes later, another student bagged Merrick, who'd snuck a peak through the "curtain." Kyle sighed. Getting off a shot wasn't the end of the mission, and didn't make the area safe.

Outside, he waited for the end of the exercise. He wondered again about the possible TDY, both because it represented a pending upheaval, and because it took his mind off Merrick. He stared at nothing, face tight, until Rogers said, "Hey, Kyle, cheer up. You okay?"

"Yeah, just stuck in the past," he said. "And wondering about the future."

"Could be worse," Rogers said. "Could be raining."

As if on cue, the steady overcast dropped a few beads of rain on them.

"You jackass," Kyle said, smiling despite himself. Rogers just laughed aloud and walked back over to the mockup house, where half the students waited patiently for the other half to get within range and become visible.

The day ended eventually, and Kyle finished documenting the day's activities and logged off his computer. He wondered what the possible TDY—temporary duty—was about, and why a general was coming to see him. But Schorlin either didn't know or wasn't saying. So he climbed in his truck and joined the exodus toward the dorms, base housing, and off-base living. He drove without thinking, pulled up in front of his dorm, and parked his Chevy S-10.

Kyle had never been married, though he'd had a few girlfriends. Currently, however, he was single; Rebecca had gotten frustrated with his odd schedule and left the month before. She'd objected to a few other things as well, like his drinking to relax, drinking to forget. In fact, Kyle was pretty sure he was drinking too much to be healthy, and had been working on lowering his intake. Since she left, of course, he was drinking to forget her, too.

His mind focused on Merrick. If the kid would just slow down and not expose himself, he'd be great. As it was, he was heading for a violent screwup where people would die, just like that one in Bosnia.

Dammit, why did everything have to remind him of that flubbed mission and Jeremy's death? Kyle wondered as he grabbed a bottle of cheap bourbon from the cupboard. He poured three fingers and took it to the recliner with him. As a single NCO, he didn't bother with much furniture, just the recliner and the couch, both good for sprawling across. He had the TV on, but wasn't paying much attention. He sipped at the whiskey while staring into the glass. Screw up for two minutes, regret it forever.

It ran through his mind again. They'd been in good concealment, thick alpine scrub that was a sniper's dream. Then Kyle had decided to crawl out for a better view of the battlefield, because that same brush restricted vision to narrow apertures.

"I don't know that we should do tha——" Jeremy had said from beside him, the last word drowned out by a *Crack!* and his head exploding. Some Serbian sniper had seen movement in the brush, scoped them, and fired.

Then dirt fountained right under Kyle's face, up his nose, in his eyes, a *Crack!* and a soft, moist sound of the exploding soil interrupting his shock. He threw himself on hands and feet and scooted back behind a heavy bush, then farther to place an outcropping of weathered basalt between him and his opponent. Then he noticed the burning pain in his arm and the running blood.

The sadistic bastard had taken Jeremy's body apart with perfectly placed shots, while Kyle tried to call in helos for support and extraction. Three days of sneaking and his spotter's life wasted because he'd been too eager to grab a good shot.

It hadn't made him feel better that the Army had refused to place blame and dropped the investigation with no fault to him. He knew whose fault it was. So did the Reardon family. His assignment to the school was a step up for his career. It still felt like punishment sometimes.

It was then that his focus moved to the TV, which was showing a documentary on Bosnia. He punched at the remote until the screen went dead, and slugged back the burning liquor. He stood quickly and put the glass in the sink before he threw it, and decided to call it a night, dinner be damned.

2

KYLE WOKE GRITTY-EYED AND HATING IT. HE wanted to sleep in another two hours, but that wasn't going to happen. He'd never been a morning person, but fourteen years of service had conditioned him to rising early. Even that didn't make up for the night before and the lousy sleep.

But a general officer didn't want to hear excuses, so Kyle would just have to deal with it. He showered, shaved thoroughly, and put on his "dress" BDUs. They were starched and ironed, in violation of regs, because starch and heat defeated the anti-infrared treatment of the fabric and made it shiny and reflective. The pockets were stitched flat, in violation of regs, because stitched pockets were as useless as tits on a boar. Still, that's what the Army bureaucracy required to look "professional." It was one more way the pencil pushers forced style over substance. He felt ridiculous, but it was supposed to be impressive. He still had his old black Ranger beret, but instead would wear the new one, blocked to look pretty, that the Clinton administration had crammed down their throats to make everyone feel special, whether they were or not. He understood his predecessors had had similar complaints about Lyndon Johnson and SecDef McNamara's changes back in the 1960s. It was always the same. None of it helped his mood.

He arrived at 0600 and grabbed a cup of coffee. That in itself was an indication of how tired he felt. Caffeine caused shakes, which were bad for shooting, and he never touched it if he could avoid it. It was generic coffee, good enough for keeping people awake or scouring sinks and not much else.

Schorlin was already in his office with the door open. The office reflected the man. It was neat enough to use as a backdrop for press releases. Books were perfectly aligned on the shelves, desk dusted. His computer was on but idle, the screensaver showing a scope reticle over a black screen, the last image visible within the panning crosshairs. He had an I Love Me wall that was impressive. It started with Ranger school, covered West Point after that, direct commissioned, and wound up in Kuwait, Bosnia, and Afghanistan. There were certificates from the Marine and SEAL sniper schools, too, as well as foreign ones. Schorlin was the kind of officer Kyle respected, because he'd been there and done that. He was a pleasure to serve under.

Schorlin looked up and said, "Morning, Kyle. You look like hell."

"Morning, sir. I feel like hell." He threw a salute that was casual enough for their relationship, sharp enough to show he meant it and that he was ready for a general to arrive.

"Well, try to cheer up. The general will be here shortly."

"Yes, sir," he replied.

"How's that problem child of yours?" The question was conversational, but interested. Good commanders kept track of such details.

Merrick had done much better in the afternoon, patient and steady in the house. He'd scored a good kill. "He'll work out eventually, sir. But for now, the boy needs a serious ass-whuppin'. He could shoot for the Olympics. He can quote the book better than I can. He's got eyes like a cat. But he's too damned eager." Aggravating. That's what the boy was.

"Hmmph. Sound like anyone we know?"

Feeling sheepish, Kyle said, "Yes, sir. Me when I was that age."

Nodding slowly, he said, "So there's how you approach him."

"Yes, sir," Kyle agreed. He hadn't made the connection in those terms, though he had recognized the annoying attitude. He'd forgotten that it had taken him fourteen years to get where he was.

Right then, the phone rang. Schorlin grabbed the receiver and said, "Yes, Joe? Great, don't let him wait. We're ready." He hung up and said, "He's here."

Kyle nodded. It was unusual for a ranking officer to come to the soldier. Usually, the reverse was true. He wondered what was going on.

They stepped into the hallway and Kyle checked over his uniform. Good enough. Then they walked out the door, down the broad metal steps, and down the hill to the classroom.

The Sniper School's facilities were rather spartan. There was the office building, a maintenance building with a bay for cleaning and repair of the rifles, a basic barracks with racks and lockers and a small classroom, all inside a barbed-wire-topped chain-link fence. That was it, and it surprised the rare visitor with its spareness.

It was that classroom, a bare twenty by thirty feet, that was their destination. With the students on the range, it was very private. Kyle held the door for Schorlin, followed him in, pulled a chair off a desk and sat down.

"Relax, Kyle," Shorlin said. "No one's in trouble."

"I know that, sir," he said. "I'm just not a morning person." He winced at the fluorescent lights overhead.

Very shortly, booted steps arrived on the landing outside. Kyle rose to his feet with Schorlin, and awaited the general's appearance.

General Robash was alone, which was unusual for someone of his rank. He wore old but serviceable BDUs, and a standard BDU hat in lieu of the beret. He looked as if he were ready for the field. He was tall and broad, with a slight bulge in the midsection from too much office work. His presence preceded him as he paused at the door and knocked.

"Come in, sir, please," Schorlin said. "Welcome." He saluted and offered his hand.

"Thank you, Captain," Robash nodded. "This must be Sergeant Monroe. Good to meet you, Sergeant." He stuck a bear paw-sized hand over, and Kyle took it.

"Good to meet you, sir," Kyle replied. He saluted after they shook, not worrying about the breach of protocol if the general didn't. No doubt about it, General Robash was huge, and his demeanor even larger.

Schorlin asked, "Coffee, sir? It's not the best but it's fresh."

"No coffee, thank you. Too much already. That's why my eyes are brown, no matter what other rumors you may have heard." There were chuckles. "But let's step outside so I can smoke a cigar."

"Yes, sir," they both agreed, and followed him back through the door.

"Thank you," he nodded, as he drew one from a tube in his pocket. It passed under his nose for inspection as if it were on parade. A small, pearl-handled Case knife flashed from pocket to teeth to cigar, then closed and disappeared as the snipped tip bounced off the steel railing and onto the ground, and he used a badly scuffed Zippo lighter to breathe fire into it.

Through a rising cloud he said, "Good Dominican."

"Wish I smoked sometimes, sir," Schorlin said, eyeing the brown cylinder.

"No, you don't, but it's polite of you," Robash said. He stood easily. The cigar was an affectation. He wasn't an Academy grad, but maintaining that image was good for dealing with the network who were. Though like a lot of the younger ones, Captain Schorlin didn't smoke.

Robash spoke. "Well, officially I'm here to inquire about using some snipers in an upcoming field training exercise. We'll discuss that later. Right now, I need to impose on you."

Schorlin replied, "No imposition, sir. We're at your disposal. How can we help?"

The general smiled and said, "I need to talk to Sergeant Monroe for a few minutes. Privately."

It was obviously for show. Schorlin clearly knew what was going on, even if he hadn't officially been told. He saluted again and walked back to his office. That gave Kyle a slight chill. What kind of mission was this for, if deniability was an issue?

As soon as the captain was gone, Robash said, "At ease, relax, son. This is where I ask you if you can handle the TDY, and you impress me with your coldhearted expertise and gung-ho attitude. Then, when the BS is done, we'll talk for real. So start by telling my why you're wearing a stitched and ironed clownsuit."

Kyle was taken off guard by the attitude. "Ah, I was told to look neat, sir, so I wore a tailored uniform."

"That's not what you wear every day, then?" The general was an experienced cigar smoker, and puffed to keep it lit, then waved the cloud clear.

"No, sir," Kyle admitted.

"Good," the general blew another cloud of smoke as he spoke. "So don't waste any more time on that crap. The BDUs are supposed to be *used*. Class A's are for impressing generals. And this general isn't here for a beauty pageant. I need to know three things. Can you shoot?"

Nodding, he said, "Yes, sir. Well enough to teach here, at least." He was still snickering inside at the general's agreement with his perception of dress.

"That says a lot, and I knew that. Can you kill?"

"I have, sir," he agreed, a bit reluctantly.

"Not what I asked, son."

"It's my job, sir." He had a few reservations, but dammit, he was a soldier.

"Good. Will you bag an al Qaeda terrorist asshole for us?"

Kyle paused for just a second as that sank in. "Yes, sir!" he replied. His stomach was twitching in eagerness or nervousness or both, but that was an honest mission.

"Outstanding. You may know there've been a few mixups over in Afghanistan, and al Qaeda don't have the people they used to. Nevertheless, they're a real pain in the ass, and we're going proactive on them. The current number three man is a real sadistic piece of work, and we plan to use you to shut him up for good."

Kyle was startled. "Isn't assassination a CIA mission, sir? Or Delta?"

"Normally, yes," the general agreed. "This isn't normal. Delta is busy, and there's enough press and sympathizers watching them that they aren't as discreet as we'd like anymore. The CIA has only limited means, and this guy, Rafiq bin Qasim, is a paranoid freak who won't let anyone get close enough to do a proper job. So it's got to be a good, reliable shooter from a distance, who they won't know is in theater. You." He crushed the cigar against a raised boot, tossed it into the weeds, and opened the door.

Kyle hesitated for a moment, then preceded him in. "Why me, sir?" he asked.

"Why not you?" Robash asked, door closing behind him. "Airborne and Ranger qualified, two real world kills in a war zone, proven to be solid under fire. We've got most of our good shooters tied up in Iraq and Bosnia, and we've kinda let Afghanistan slide. We want this done quietly, and we need someone good, reliable, who can operate alone. You."

"Thanks, sir, I guess," Kyle replied. "Though

I lost my spotter on the last mission because we got eager. I got eager," he corrected.

The general lowered his voice slightly. "I know about that, son. It was a mistake. A bad one. But things like that happen, and you're aware of it and won't do it again."

"You're right about that, sir," he agreed, nodding. "I suppose I should take the mission. Though I would like a few more details before I jump aboard."

"Fair enough," Robash nodded. "Give me a second." He whipped out his phone and punched a couple of buttons. Whoever he wanted to talk to was on speed dial. "Sergeant Curtis, come on in."

A minute later, the person in question arrived at a brisk walk. Kyle had met him previously, the sniper community being small. Wade Curtis was a black man with coffee-colored skin and an expressive face built around deep, thoughtful eyes. His build was muscular but not overly large, and he matched Kyle's six feet in height. He had been an instructor when Kyle arrived, had left shortly afterward for the 10th Mountain Division. He was a staff sergeant, who'd also graduated Ranger School and had done a training stint with a British sniper section with the 42nd Royal Marine Commando. Despite that, though, he'd never actually been in combat. Still, he'd only been in the Army seven years, and there was a first time for everything.

"I believe you two have met," Robash said.

"Sir," they both replied at once. Kyle continued speaking as he rose to shake hands. "Staff Sergeant Curtis. Yeah, we've met at the club and on the range. Only for about a month last year. Been a while, Wade."

Wade shook hands back, firmly but with no macho-grip games. "Kyle," he nodded. "So, what are we going to do?"

Kyle looked over at the general as they both sat. He wasn't sure himself, and waited for enlightenment.

Robash nodded to both of them, took a deep draw on his cigar. "The mission is to go into the tribal area of Pakistan and take out bin Qasim. Obviously, that's the sticky point here. Not Afghanistan, but Pakistan. Technically, that's friendly territory. Actually, it's riddled with rats. Those rats have connections within the government, so anything we do officially they'll hear about. The plan is to give you orders to get over there, cash to operate, and only inform the Pakistanis if something goes wrong."

He leaned forward and continued, "Please note that distinction. This isn't a covert operation, exactly. We will be telling the Pakistanis, and we know Musharraf will be okay with it, as we hinted to him already without any specifics. So you can't bust up a lot of locals to do this, not innocent ones, anyway. It will be semiofficial afterward, even though it will likely stay SCI for a good long time, in case we decide to do it again."

Kyle thought for a few moments. Actually, that wasn't too bad. He wasn't expendable or deniable, he was simply going to be a secret weapon. He looked over at Wade, who was nodding appraisingly, his mouth and brow twisted in thought.

Kyle asked, "Why this way, sir?"

"Remember rumors back in ninety-one that we had a sniper placed to take out Saddam?" Robash waited for nods, then continued, "Those rumors are true. But the press got a leak and had to open their goddamned yaps about how it would be illegal to target a foreign head of state. So now we have the screwup before us. So for this one, we don't want any press and we don't want any leaks. As to why, same reason we've got the Special Operations guys running around doing what they were trained to do at long last. While we've got a leadership that will let us, we're going to hunt. We want to do it fast, the backlog's too much for the spooks, and there's always leaks. A couple of good Rangers who are also snipers is the prescription for this little disease, and one they won't see coming."

Cautiously, Kyle said, "Sounds worthwhile, sir. What kind of gear and backup?" He looked over at Wade.

Wade asked, "Or is there any?"

Through another puff of fumes, he replied, "Oh, there's gear. We'll be flying you out there civilianwise until you hit theater, then you'll take transports. You'll have Iridium phones, radios, orders to let you requisition stuff in theater and such. Use your government credit cards as needed. Your orders will be secret and just authorize you to ride along with no questions asked. You'll also have cash in U.S. dollars, Pakistani rupees, and afghanis. You'll take whatever gear you want, but it'll have to be stuff you can hump. Once on station, there'll be locals to meet you and help you find this jackass. You bag him, call in on the radio and we'll send air support and choppers. At that point, as long as the press doesn't know, we don't give a flying fuck who else does. Better if they do, in fact."

As they started to digest that, Robash asked, "What do you know about the border area of Afghanistan and Pakistan?"

Wade replied, "Damned little, sir."

"Me either," Kyle admitted.

"No problem," he nodded. "We've got people to take care of that. We'll get you briefed and up to speed. Can you leave in a week?"

The two looked at each other, considering. It wasn't a question to answer lightly. "Gear's not a problem," Kyle said.

Wade grimaced slightly and replied, "Training is going to be a bitch. We've got to be briefed, then you and I have to run at least one rehearsal if we're going to shoot together."

"That, and I need a refresher on radios. A week's tight."

"But doable?" Robash asked. "We've got a window we need to exploit."

"Doable, sir," Kyle agreed. He felt nervous about committing to such a deadline, but it didn't seem there was much choice.

Robash smiled. "Good! Once there, look as ratty as you can. Got to look the part. Don't bother with any more haircuts or shaves," he said, pointing at their closely cropped heads. "Though it's not as if you're going to look shaggy anyway. Still, we work with what we've got. Now, let's talk about training and prep. Hold one."

Robash drew the cell phone again from where it was clipped inside his BDU shirt, and thumbed buttons as he raised it. "Yes, we're ready," he said. He waited for a response. "Roger," he nodded, and disconnected. Turning back to the two snipers he said, "I took the liberty of bringing the personnel with me." They all chuckled, though there was a nervous tinge to it. He'd been ready, and wanted them overseas ASAP. This was a serious operation on a tight schedule, not an administrative deployment.

Twenty minutes later the two of them were ensconced in a briefing room manufactured on the spot. It wasn't hard. The classroom was set up to handle computer projection and had classroom seats, a dry-erase board and a phone. There were much cushier and more secure facilities on post proper, but, as Robash pointed out,

"There's going to be rumors either way. Fewer people will hear them here, and less significance attached to the event."

Time was short. For two solid days they would be educated as to terrain, the political situations in several regions and villages and the people they'd be dealing with, expected weapons, and languages.

The civilian language instructor came in first. He was portly but seemed to have good muscle tone underneath. He was roundfaced with graying hair, slightly balding, very alert and cheerful. He was lugging a laptop case and several books. "Sergeants," he said in greeting, holding out a hand. His grip was firm. "I'm Bill Gober. I'm here to tell you about the languages you'll encounter and give you some basics."

"Mostly Arabic, right?" Kyle asked, nodding.

Gober gave him a look that was faintly annoyed but mostly amused. "No, probably no one you meet will speak Arabic, except maybe some scripture from the Quran. The predominant language of the area is Pashto."

Kyle looked confused and said, "Never heard of it." Wade looked taken aback, too.

"Which is why I'm here," Gober smiled. "Pashto and Dari are the official languages of Afghanistan, and Western Panjabi and Urdu are very common, but there's about a dozen languages in the area. Even Farsi from Iran is not unusual. But we'll mostly concentrate on Pashto and its Pakistani variant, Pakhto. They're both very similar, almost interchangeable, and Dari isn't much different. I've got phrasebooks you can take, CD-ROMs you can study en route, and some audio to familiarize yourselves with the tonal qualities."

"Okay," Kyle agreed. "I'm not very good with languages, though."

Gober said, "Probably you are good enough, you've just not been shown the right way. It isn't hard to learn a few basic vocabulary words. Rather than perfect grammar and style, you need to hear threats when they're mentioned, or pick up key words. That's what we'll focus on. The hardest part is going to be learning the written language, as it's a variation of the Arabic alphabet, hard enough to read as is, and these languages aren't very close to Arabic."

They spent the entire morning and afternoon until two, munching takeout from the chow hall as they familiarized themselves with a hundred basic words. Gober had been correct; reading the street signs was going to be much harder than speaking. The entire language was curlicues and squirming lines and dots.

He gave them one easy-to-remember hint as to structure that had them laughing as he used a querulous voice. "Pashtuns the verb at the end of the sentence put. In this they like Yoda are. Silly it is; but likely you are, Yoda's speech patterns to remember, and remembering the whole point of this is. It in good health you should use and enjoy."

At three, Gober rose to depart. "It would be good to have a few more days to practice, but I'm told we have no time. Do make sure you spend a couple of hours a day at it, though."

Wade answered for them, "Will do, sir, and thanks."

There was one more thing piled on that afternoon: maps. Relief and political maps of the entire Afghan/Pakistani border area in question, with smaller scale maps for some of the towns and border crossings. "Ideally," they were told by yet another briefer, a Lieutenant Vargas, "you'll just drive across one of the existing crossings. There are some manned by U.S. forces that shouldn't pose a threat. However, if something causes suspicions or closes the border tighter, you'll have to infiltrate some distance away over the mountains."

"I can handle mountains," Kyle said. "Wade?"

"Climb, actually," Wade joked. "Been there. But I'd rather drive than hump those ridges. They look ugly."

"Can we get a practice run in? Hills, shooting?"

"You likely won't have time over there, and we really don't want to announce your presence," Vargas said.

"What about here? Out West somewhere? Nevada, say?" Wade suggested.

"That's possible," Vargas agreed. "We could fly you out West and hop up into the hills. Be a chance to practice a helo extraction, too, just in case. I'll talk to the general and set it up. But you're looking at a day, tops."

"We'll take it," Kyle said, wondering why the government always waited until the last minute, then began a panicky juggle of hurry-up-and-wait. These things really should be planned out. Idly, he wondered which Pentagon whiz kid had come up with this, then decided he probably didn't want to bother.

THEY CERTAINLY WERE GETTING EVERYTHING they asked for. Early the morning after next, they were aboard a flight from Benning to Nellis Air Force Base near Las Vegas. Their gear was crated and palletized with them. Once at Nellis, the sun barely up, they were urged aboard a USAF Pave Low helicopter, and taken out somewhere in the middle of nowhere. "We're going to use you as a search-and-extraction exercise," the master sergeant Pararescue Jumper told them. "I understand you're doing a mountain exercise? Shooting?"

"Something like that," Kyle agreed over the assorted turbine noise, blade beats, and wind. "We'll be most of the day."

"No problem," the PJ agreed. "You'll call for extraction, we'll come and get you. They briefed you on flares and smoke?"

"Sort of," Kyle agreed. "They gave us photocopies from the manual."

"Good enough. You practice your thing, we'll practice ours. Hopefully we'll get all the bugs ironed out. If not . . ."

"That's why we're training," Wade supplied.

"Yup."

Soon, they were flaring out over a relatively flat, high plateau. Wade and Kyle dropped out, turned in the whipping wind and grabbed their bulky gear, turned back and trotted away, low to avoid the downdraft.

Then they were alone. The bulky helo was away and disappearing fast into the cerulean sky.

"Well," said Wade, "the good news is, it's friendly territory and we have GPS and a computer. Not to mention cell phones."

"Right," said Kyle. "The bad news is, we have no idea where in hell we are, and it's as hot as hell already." It had to be ninety-five degrees if it were anything.

"At least it's dry," Wade said, looking for any shade. There was none to speak of.

"And dusty," added Kyle, as the wind wafted more grit in his eyes.

"And hot."

"I already said that."

"So I'll say it again."

"Yup. Let's find a place to start shooting. Then we can take a hike north, according to this map, and we'll be met about there," he pointed.

Wade looked and grimaced, "Ten kilometers? That's going to be a hell of a hike."

Kyle looked around at the bleak terrain. "Yup. But it'll be cool this evening. Or cooler. For now, let's just amble northerly for a good spot until it's too hot to bother."

The day went adequately. Both were trained for harsh climates, and apart from the heat it wasn't bad. Besides their rucks and full Camel-Baks, they had an M-107, the Army designation for the Barrett M-82 .50-caliber autoloading rifle. Kyle carried it, Wade the spotting scope, radio, and extraneous gear, along with an M-4 carbine with grenade launcher. He wouldn't use it here, but it was part of the equipment they'd deploy with, so he was carrying it to make the exercise more realistic. They made about three kilometers before they found a good place to shoot. By then, both were sweating, though their clothes were quite dry, the desert air evaporating the moisture as fast as they exuded it.

Looking around at their chosen position, Kyle said, "Think we've got about three thousand meters clear?" Kyle asked.

"I'd say so," his partner said. "That would suit me fine as a range to nail this guy. No reason to court counterfire from his buddies or those Russian howitzers they might have."

"Yeah, though getting more than a thousand accurately is a problem."

"I know that," Wade said. "Maybe we'll get lucky and we can nail some explosives near him. You're the one who insisted on the fifty."

"So spot me," Kyle said. "And we're taking this because it was suggested, because our target might be in an armored vehicle or behind cover." The Barrett was a huge piece of equipment, though it did have slightly better range and much better penetration than the 7.62mm M-24.

They each took ten shots, slowly and methodically. Precision shooting is as much science as art, and they recorded every shot and its impact for later review. The brass would go back with them. Not only was it good discipline for concealment, but the gunsmiths—"small-arms repairers"—liked to examine them for wear to ensure the weapons were performing to their utmost.

The weapon was already adjusted for good accuracy. Wade called, "Reference: upright rock. Base. Small boulder with yellow striations. One one five zero."

"Got it," Kyle said. He squeezed, and God kicked him in the shoulder.

A puff of dust erupted back from the left of the rock. "Again," he said, placed the reticle on center, squeezed, and fired.

"Both to the left, twenty inches," Wade said.

Kyle made two minor corrections to the scope. "And again," he said.

"Same target?"

"Sure." They had similar climatic conditions to what they could expect, so they'd keep shooting until they were happy.

Kyle's next shot chipped the boulder, the fragments spinning off into the air. The fourth missed to the left again. There were limits to the accuracy of the weapon, and Kyle thought they were reaching those limits. He could hit reliably with a .5 minute of angle weapon or better. The Barrett was only a 3 MOA weapon. But for armored targets or vehicles, it was what they needed. He would have preferred to take a 7.62mm M-24 as well, in case they could get a closer shot, but there were weight limitations. Three weapons cases would be a royal pain in the ass, as well as obvious. He'd made the decision, but he wasn't very happy with it.

"Slight adjustment to the right should do it," Wade said.

"Yeah," Kyle agreed, coming back to earth. A trickle of dust blew into his face as the wind eddied, and he spat drily.

Two more shots hit the small rock and reduced it to a pile of sharp-edged pieces of rubble. A .50-BMG round delivers better than 13,000 foot-pounds at the muzzle, more than twice that of most elephant guns and five times that of the 7.62 cartridge. It was better than a jackhammer for demolishing rock.

"We could tweak it more, but it's not going to get appreciably better."

"Agreed," Wade replied. "So take a few more, let me at it, and then let's get that other seven kilometers done."

By the end of forty minutes, twenty rounds had screamed down the barrel and delivered better than 200,000 foot-pounds of energy to what was now a sad-looking little splinter amid a pile of sand, sitting in front of a badly chipped boulder.

Seven kilometers isn't a bad hike. When lugging basic gear, an AN/PRC-119 radio, spotting scope, and a forty-eight-pound rifle, up and down stark, hard terrain, it's a serious workout. The snipers climbed and scrabbled up steep inclines, slid down others, passing the gear back and forth to keep it safe, and were abraded, dusty, and exhausted by the time they finished.

"Glad we brought the extra water," Kyle said, dousing his throat again. They both knew it was necessary to stay hydrated, and were drinking frequently. Besides, the more water in the body, the less there was to carry as gear.

"This should be about it," Wade said. They were on another plateau. He checked their position by GPS, then by compass and three peaks as landmarks. That done, he fired up the radio.

In short order, the Pave Low appeared as a large, intimidating insect to the southeast, and dropped in for a landing. They scurried in close, shoved the gear aboard, and clambered in.

"Good hike?" the PJ asked them.

"Good enough," Wade agreed. Kyle just grunted.

Yes, it had been a good hike and shoot. But how would it be in hostile territory, surrounded by witnesses and without close backup?

Kyle suspected the real mission was going to be quite a bit tougher. And he still had his own doubts to fight, too.

* * *

The next morning was their last before deploying. They were both short of sleep, after the grueling fifteen hours of flight and ten hours of climbing the day before. They'd snoozed on the planes each way, but were still groggy. The general was sympathetic, but didn't offer any slack. Nor did they expect it. Lack of sleep and food was the Army way, and they were both experienced with it.

"I've arranged cash," Robash told them. They were in the same classroom they were so familiar with. "And I brought a staff with me to take care of all this at once. I'd rather cut TDY orders for people to come to you, than have you shuffle around playing games." He nodded, and the staff sergeant in the corner came over.

He said, "Fifty thousand dollars, gentlemen. It's split into two packages of three currencies each. Sign here and count it. Please note that it's expendable, and spend what you need. We'd like it back if there's any left over, but don't sweat it."

Kyle was glad of that phrase, officially attached to the document. Many covert soldiers had later been busted for "embezzling" funds that had been issued to them. It seemed Robash was the straight shooter he'd shown himself to be already. They weren't going to get screwed over this. Of course, they still might die.

The money was ten thousand dollars worth each in Afghan and Pakistani currency and the balance in good American cash, useful almost anywhere on the planet. They each counted their half. "Try to keep the nonlocal stuff hidden," Kyle said to Wade, "and stash it in several places to minimize loss."

The finance sergeant left right after he checked their signatures. As soon as he was alone with them, the general resumed his brief, "Now, guys, let me give you your contacts. You can write this down, but lose it before you cross the border into Pakistan, and lose it well. You'll meet with General Kratman at Qandahar Airport and give him this letter." Robash handed them each a sheet, and they both stuck them in their increasingly bulging folders. "It authorizes you to take any routine equipment and charge it to the mission. Vehicles, ammo, small arms, anything reasonable. Though I'd think very hard before taking U.S. vehicles, as you'll stand out like a hooker at a Madison Avenue wedding. Kratman knows you're coming, but not what you're doing. My phone number is on all these documents. If there's any questions, call. If I'm not there, my XO and my civilian assistant are briefed on what to do, and can be reached by cell phone twenty-four seven. You're both on my call-through list. I'll bitch like hell if it's not important, but I'm here to support you on this mission. Use me if you need me."

"Yes, sir," Kyle and Wade agreed together. It certainly seemed as if he meant it, and that by itself was a huge morale boost. General Robash apparently knew what a lot of officers had never learned, that troops who feel they have support will do almost anything for their commander.

"Once in theater, you'll meet with a local tribal leader named Qalzai. He'll take you in and spot your target. He doesn't speak English, but he has a translator. He's very reliable on intel and anti-Taliban operations, so you're safe with him, but we have no idea who's in his unit. If you feel compromised, abort and exfiltrate, either on ground or by chopper. But get the hell out of there. We want you alive and our target dead, not the other way around."

"Right," Wade said. Kyle simply considered that. There was a hell of a lot of risk in this operation. But it was too late for second thoughts. They were just nerves anyway, he thought.

"The chain of command for this is Kyle, Wade. You're officially commanded by a colonel in the Pentagon, but I'm the Operations guy, so it's very odd, but very simple.

"Now, we go see Lieutenant Bergman for flight arrangements. From what I understand, you're going to be in the air a long time."

"Yes, sir," they agreed. That last wasn't unexpected; they were going halfway around the world.

"The last item," Robash said, "is that commo is going to be a bitch. I'm sorry guys, I tried, but there's no way to get the radios working properly. You'd need forty batteries for ten days, and there's no way to ensure you can recharge."

"Hell," Kyle said. It was the handicap of modern radios. They scrambled by shifting across 280,000 frequencies, but if they weren't powered in to the net from the beginning, they wouldn't be synchronized with the scramble code, which changed daily. They either needed a constant supply of charged batteries to maintain contact and scramble, or else any transmission would have to be in the clear. Neither was good. The batteries were three pounds each.

" 'Hell,' is correct," Robash said. "You'll have a one-nineteen for final call to the helo, because they can't handle Iridium phones. But you can call direct to the AWACS with the cell phone, and to me in an emergency. You've got a whole list of numbers for backup. But final extraction is going to require that you coordinate through the AWACS, then use the radio at the last minute. And be brief, because some of those Taliban bastards have radios and translators."

"Oh, lovely," Wade said.

"Yeah, it sucks to be you," Robash nodded. "But you have my thanks, and I want it to be a good mission."

By lunchtime, they had orders, more disks for the laptop, more documents to hand out en route, extra maps, and all the miscellany they'd need. With nothing else to do, they parted ways and headed back home to rest up and finalize personal gear.

The logistics experts at the transportation office would crate all their weapons and heavy equipment up in form-fitting expanding foam surrounded by wooden frames and sheathing, if it wasn't already packed in hard cases. Everything was receipted and accountable. It pained Kyle to hand over his personal stuff, and he was nervous in case anyone complained about his personal weapons. But no questions were asked and he accepted the receipts for file.

There was the M-107 Barrett .50 caliber, scoped and bipoded and with twenty rounds of match-grade ammo in a sealed pack. Its case fit tightly around the disassembled components, cradling them in foam. It probably wouldn't need to be resighted when they arrived in theater, as the scope was zeroed to the weapon and attached to a precision rail. They'd do a check when they could, of course. The scope was actually more important than the weapon; it could be transferred, and it could also gather intel. Everything that could be done to protect it was a good thing.

The M-4 carbine, a shortened M-16 with provisions for attachments, which Wade would carry most of the time, was in there, with its emergency folding sights flat and taped, and the Eotech Holosight encased. It was the backup weapon. It wasn't likely they'd use it beyond 100 meters, and the iron sights and the Eotech were good for 400. It had GGG Corporation's side-sling mounts at gas block and the rear of the receiver, so it would hang across the shooter's front, ready to deploy. Spare batteries for the Eotech were in a rubber plug in the pistol grip. Batteries were often more important than ammo in the modern army. It had an underslung M-203 grenade launcher for social engagements. It didn't seem like much, but it was likely they could get 5.56 ammo in country, and this was supposed to be a sniping mission. One shot, one kill, as the cliché went. It was Kyle's experience that it almost always took more than one shot, and sometimes a lot of suppressing fire, too. At least they would have a claymore and fragmentation grenades and smoke, once they drew them in theater.

In addition to his two pistols, Wade would have one, also. It was a standard issue M-9 Beretta 92F. "Standard GI everything, huh?" he'd asked.

His partner shrugged. "I like other stuff better. But issue stuff is easy to get parts for. And if it goes missing, Uncle Sam can weep, not me. I'd hate to lose that lovely piece of yours," he said, in reference to Kyle's Ed Brown custom .45.

"Me, too," Kyle said. "But it makes me feel safe," he joked. It should. The 1911-style frame had the mainspring housing contoured into a rounded, easy-to-conceal shape. The magazine well was welded and flared to make reloading easy. The expected palm-swelled thumb safety, Commander-style hammer, and deeply cut front strap let it sit low and securely in the hand. It had low profile, almost guttersnipe sights. The barrel was conical for a tight lockup. Then the mechanism was ramped, polished, and the ejection port flared. Outside, it was smoothed and phosphated with Pachmayr grips. It had cost two-thousand-and-nevermind dollars, but it was easy to find ammo for, accurate, reliable, and Kyle's best friend. It was going with him. He'd had it in Bosnia last . . . which wasn't something to dwell on.

His backup to that was a little nickeled Colt Mustang .380 that he could fit in a pocket. He never thought he'd use that on duty, but it was the ideal gun for the situation. It wasn't much of a distance weapon, but if it came down to that, things weren't good anyway, and it would reliably put out bullets.

Then it was home and a last night to prepare. If this had been a unit deployment, the unit would go out on a riotously fun drunk and decorate a bar or club. As it was supposed to be a TDY for an exercise, it was officially no big deal. So he'd sit at home, Wade in billeting, pondering the future and going through whatever rituals they wished to keep calm and thin the tension. Beer seemed the logical choice.

Kyle sorted through his personal gear and checked his list of what to take, making additions. Actually, there wasn't much debate. He'd take a couple of uniforms for blending in on military installations, one each three-color desert and woodland. His ID and the cash they were issuing him. They were shipping the weapons. A CD player would get lost or stolen or confiscated by some foreign security goon, so he didn't bother. There'd be no time to listen to music, anyway. He hated reading airport bestsellers, so he'd take a couple of cheap paperbacks to read while traveling. He was amused by the amount of action the characters in books could experience within the first hundred pages, and was glad that his own life was far less exciting. So it was down to underwear, socks, toiletries kit, and the essentials.

"The Essentials" evolved over time, but basically stayed the same. He had the large CamelBak for keeping hydrated, and he worshipped the man who'd invented it. He took his own small GPS to back up the one crated. He had the SOG Powerplier pocket tool he preferred to the issue Gerber, but had an old Gerber Predator BMF he'd carried for years. Sometimes, nine inches of steel was what you needed to do the job, whether that job was prying open a door, cutting a stretcher, or, theoretically, killing someone. He'd never been close enough to worry about that, but it could happen. Then he had the Sebertech pocket tool on his keychain and the Benchmade automatic with the four-inch Tanto blade in his pocket. He took an extra Lensatic compass for last-ditch escape. His sidearms were already crated. He had burlap and tan canvas sewn to a desert uniform to make a functional ghillie to blend-in in an arid mountain environment. He'd used the same ratty pair of gloves for shooting for fourteen years; everything one could do to make the conditions of every shoot predictable improved the odds of success. He had a calculator and measuring tape, and the M-22 binoculars. A laptop with ballistics information, language programs, and tech manuals. Parachute cord was always useful, whether lashing sticks, building a stretcher, or tying gear down. An empty sandbag that could be filled and turned into a rest was stuffed in. He carried extra triangular bandages to use as head covers or "do rags," as camouflage, slings and, well, bandages. A compact of makeup, in earthtones and greens was in there, rubber bands and a sewing kit for repairs and to improve camouflage, as well as a lighter and matches, and an eyepatch to let the off-eye muscles relax during long pauses, pencils, and an AA Maglight. Then there were the necessary chocolate chip cookies, Cajun beef jerky, a couple of six-packs of caffeine-free Coke and a box of shoestring potato snacks, which tasted almost as good as chips and wouldn't crush into powder when carried. All told, it was about thirty-five pounds, which was light enough to not be a hindrance, but packed enough tools and weapons to save his ass. He had permission for personal weapons this time, or more accurately, it wasn't an issue, this being a clandestine and deniable mission. Even had they forbidden it, though, he would have tried to smuggle the stuff through. You could never rely on dear old Uncle Sam to have what you needed, and a good soldier took his own supplements. The whole load when added to his issue gear would break 200 pounds.

Wade would have the M-49 spotter scope, AN/PVS-6 laser range finder, AN/PRC-119 radio set and blade antenna, night vision for both of them, a field surgical kit, a roll of 100 mph tape, a small toolkit, cleaning kits, and his own issue plus personal necessities like toothbrushes.

The guns were already loaded along with the issue gear, radios, and scopes. The rest packed, and set to go with him as luggage. All that was left was the waiting.

He could spend the night out, seeking entertainment or women, but he really wasn't in a sociable mood. He didn't want any emotional entanglements, and a bar quickie near base wasn't worth the effort. He could drink at home.

But he wouldn't, he decided. There just wasn't much point. And he wouldn't be drinking in Pakistan, so he should minimize the booze now. Heck, it would be good for him. He'd fallen into a rut of teach class, NCO club to be seen by the sergeant major for brownie points, then home to eat and drink. It had been a year. Time to get out of that cycle.

He crawled into bed and turned the light out. Eventually, he slept.

THE ALARM JARRED KYLE AWAKE AT 0330. Grumbling, he shut it off, got up and staggered to the bathroom. A hot shower helped him wake up, and as it might be his last for some time, he enjoyed it. He finished, left the door open to let humidity vent, and called for his ride. By the time he dressed, grabbed his bag and locked up, doing a final check on his list for anything he might have missed before tossing it in the trash and walking downstairs, the car was waiting for him. The driver, a cute female PFC, way too alert for such an early hour, opened the trunk for his bags and the door for him, then got in and waited for him to fasten his seatbelt. All by the book. Good. He wasn't up for socializing much. Wade was already in back, sprawled across the seat and with a flat cap over his face.

"Airport, correct, Sergeants?" she asked to confirm.

"Correct, soldier. Mind if I take a nap?" His question, like hers, was rhetorical. He wasn't going to nap, but he didn't want to talk.

"Go ahead, Sergeant," she agreed.

He lay back as far as the seat allowed and closed his eyes to think.

It was a good mission, and he'd agreed to it, so why was he so jittery? It wasn't just Jeremy, he tried to reassure himself. It was also that this thing seemed so haphazard and last minute. Actually, it very well might be Jeremy. That, and being in a country where he didn't know the language, alone with a spotter and no friendly fire support on the radio. Jitters did mean he was thinking and sane, he thought. If he wasn't worried about this, he'd be a fool.

So much for fairytale heroes.

The first leg of the flight was from Columbus aboard a small Army transport plane. It was a twin turboprop job, and the swaying of the wings as it landed at Atlanta's Hartsfield was disconcerting. They could see ahead through the cockpit, over the pilots' shoulders, and the horizon swung up and down as the little craft bobbled in the drafts.

Military personnel traveled in civilian clothes to keep a low profile, and they were already a bit unkempt after not shaving. Still, their bearing made them soldiers, and they both knew they'd have to work on appearances and body language. The idea was to be nondescript. How a tall, white male and a tall, black male who didn't speak the language were supposed to blend in in the Middle East and the 'stans was beyond Kyle, but he wasn't going to question anything else. It was obviously going to be a screwed-up mission. Then he tried to recall a mission that hadn't been screwed up. He couldn't recall one.

All their gear had been checked through ahead on transports with official paperwork to clear it through the DOD Courier Service. It would arrive still crated and undisturbed, they hoped. The two of them were flying like any other civilians, except they were using their military IDs and orders as passports. The orders identified them as "surveyors" from the Army Corps of Engineers going to Kuwait to do a construction survey at Camp Doha.

Kyle hadn't flown commercial since before the terrorist attacks. He knew security had been tightened, but had no idea how it was at the current time. He'd left everything except his keys in his checked bags, just to be sure.

"Final destination, sir?" the clerk at check-in asked him.

"Kuwait City," he said, because it was true enough for airline purposes, and "The ass-end of Asia to kill someone," just wouldn't be politically correct. She was too young and cute to freak out in that manner. Nor did Kyle need the probing that would certainly follow.

"Would you like to check your bags straight through?" she asked.

"Yes, please," he said. He'd been cautioned

to ask for that anyway. Otherwise, the bags would be held for customs in London first, which could take three days or more. Checked straight through, they'd only be inspected at destination.

That done, he took his small carry-on, which had a change of shirt, socks and underwear, toiletries, a notebook, and a garish scifi paperback with an exploding spaceship on the cover. What the heck, it looked like a good read. It was going to be a long flight.

He walked through the metal detector with no hassle. Considering that, he was a bit annoyed when some jackass came over with a wand and waved it over him. He remembered there'd been more threats, and an elevated security level.

"Raise your arms," the "Security Officer" said, then poked and prodded his pockets and belt before patting him down. Amateurs pat when searching. Professionals slide their hands to catch things. Nor did this punk kid check the small of his back or the collar of his jacket.

He sighed slightly and dealt with it. Americans were now being treated like criminals in jail, in case they might be Muslim terrorists. Certainly, that mother might have a bomb in her diaper bag. Better check the diaper, too, pal. That baby poop might be rigged to explode.

The annoying part was that the hassle was all for show. Kyle had seen the reports of testers smuggling guns and knives past the security at many major airports. This farce wasn't going to stop a determined terrorist, and was a pain for all concerned.

"May I check your bag, sir?" he was asked, as if he could say no. At least this guy looked competent. He was wiry and young, but had alert eyes.

"Sure," he agreed.

It was simple enough. A chemical pad was run over his bag, looking for reactions that would indicate drugs or explosives, he assumed. It made him nervous. Not because he had anything that would trigger it, but the whole atmosphere was one to cause paranoia in the honest person. A trained terrorist, of course, would blithely bull his way through, unconcerned.

While doing this, the man spoke to the kid with the wand, "Moore," he said, "don't worry about the small children and the old folks. They don't need to be kept standing around. And check ankles and wrists, too, okay?"

"Uh, yes, sir," the kid replied.

Kyle's bag was returned, and the man said, "Sorry for the hassle. I've got to check a quota per shift. It's late."

The sudden change in atmosphere was palpable. "No problem, sir," Kyle said, meaning it.

"No need to call me 'sir,' Sergeant," the supervisor said with a grin, as he handed Kyle's wallet and keys back from the conveyor belt. His military ID was in the clear front. "I worked for a living. Semper Fi."

The Marines. Marines had no trouble stomping on idiots. "Thanks, Marine. Rangers Lead the Way."

They all chuckled as Kyle and Wade headed for the jetway, except Moore, who looked confused. Everything went back to what seemed to pass as normal these days. Kyle heaved a sigh as Wade joined him and whispered, "You know, I thought we were the good guys. Nice to have the government agree."

"Yeah. Hell of a world, huh?"

There was still one more hassle. Along the jetway stood people in sports jackets and shirts with badges on neck cords. The badges read DEA and U.S. CUSTOMS. One of them waved at Kyle, the next at Wade. Sighing, Kyle went over.

"Can I see your passport, please, sir?" the man asked. Kyle handed over his ID card and orders. It took a moment for the man to track, then he smiled under his graying moustache as he asked, "Are you carrying more than ten thousand dollars in cash today?' "

Kyle smiled back. "Yeah, right."

"Have a good trip, sir," the man said as he handed the card and sheet back.

Kyle waited until he was in the plane to sigh. He was carrying $25,000 in three currencies. So was Wade. But it wasn't anyone's business but theirs right now. Certainly they could have explained it with a phone call, but it wasn't supposed to be an issue.

There were actually only about twenty people aboard the flight. Kyle didn't know if that was due to the economy, the "enhanced security," or the early hour of the flight. Maybe all. But it did mean that after takeoff he could loosen his collar, flop across six seats in the middle, and crash for a couple of hours. Wade did the same two rows back. The cloth seats were a bit rough, the gaps between them not comfortable, and a seat belt end jabbed Kyle in the kidney. Still, it was better than being stuck in tight quarters sitting upright.

The purser left them alone. The only noise intruding was the steady whining roar of the engines.

He woke much refreshed if a bit stiff over the Atlantic, and stretched as he sat up. The smells of food had woken him. He had the chicken, precut and cardboardy. Still, it was hot and it was lunch. He dug in. Wade moved up next to him and had the fish.

"Is there anything to drink?" Kyle asked as they were served. He wasn't going to get drunk, but one to take the edge off wasn't the same as drinking himself into depression.

"Certainly," the flight attendant replied. She was likely near forty, well tanned and slim with a few faint lines just forming around her eyes. Nicelooking lady, he decided. "We have a very nice red wine, and Budweiser, Heineken, or Sapporo."

"Better make it the Heineken," he said. "And thanks."

"You're welcome," she said, plunking two iced and sweat-beaded bottles down in front of him. Wade took the red wine. Kyle hated most wine and wasn't curious enough to try it to see if this was the exception. He expected to be charged for the beer; airlines always did. But nothing was said. Whatever had happened, it was a pleasant error or courtesy after—and before—many other less pleasant screwups.

Next to him, Wade said, "I'd offer to run through vocabulary, but they'd likely freak."

"Yeah," Kyle said. *They'd think we were terrorists.* He wasn't going to even think that word where it might be heard. Someone would panic. "So tell me about your career," he said. He wasn't sure he wanted to get friendly with another spotter. There was a loyalty issue, which was silly, because Jeremy was gone, and because he needed to be familiar with the man he was going to be working with. They needed to talk. Besides, there was nothing else to do for the next twenty hours . . . or for the month after that.

"Not much to tell," Wade admitted. "Grew up in the horrible ghettos of Bloomington, Illinois. My father's a doctor. You can imagine how rough a life that was."

Kyle laughed quietly. "Yeah, sounds rough. My old man's an engineer. So how the hell did we wind up here?"

"I wanted adventure and money for college," Wade said. "After I kept scoring expert, and went to a couple of unit competitions, they asked me if I wanted to crosstrain. So I did. Then I reenlisted and applied as an instructor. I figured it would be useful when I got to college."

"Never got to college," Kyle observed.

"Not yet," Wade admitted. "But I still plan to, eventually. And this is all useful for a degree in sociology."

"Sociology," Kyle mused. "From shoo . . . dealing with bad guys." The environment felt so hostile he didn't even want to say "shooting." What had America come to?

"Yeah," Wade said. "Ain't it a kicker? What about you?"

"Oh, I thought about college, but, really, I don't have the mindset. I learn by doing. The Army treats me decently, I guess, even if I do bitch up a storm—"

Wade cut in, " 'A bitching GI is a happy GI.' "

"About right," Kyle agreed. "So I'm still here. If I take retirement at a reasonable age, I guess I see if L.A. or some other city needs me for a special police team of some kind."

"Or coach the Olympic team," Wade suggested.

Kyle was silent for a moment. "You know, I hadn't thought of that, but it actually makes sense. Thanks."

"No problem."

They got back to the business of sipping beer, reading trash, watching movies, and running through things in their minds. International flights could be very long and tiresome. Kyle figured they'd learn to hate them on this trip. If he didn't already.

There was a four-hour layover in London, which was just long enough for a bite to eat and paperwork.

Heathrow was scary. Kyle hadn't realized things were so bad in Britain. First, the plane had to park far back, as there wasn't enough terminal space. They were picked up in a scissor-lifted mobile lounge that dropped as it rolled across the apron. From there, they shifted to a train at the terminal. Kyle couldn't help but notice that they walked unescorted from one to the other, and that it would take only a moment for someone in a coverall and coat to run through the unlocked door marked AUTHORISED PERSONNEL ONLY and ditch the coat.

That wasn't the only risk. Once they left the train, they were crowded up an escalator through a passage with faded, yellowed, and cracking walls. It didn't look like a modern, western airport. Then there was a delay at the top. There was only one metal detector. Nor did the staff have wands. Britain was proud of the fact that almost no one carried guns legally. But it meant that a dedicated terrorist could rush this point and be among crowds in seconds.

There was a delay caused by a man who appeared to be Indian or Pakistani. He walked through the detector and beeped. Apparently, he wasn't a regular flier, as he kept walking and had to be ushered back. The guards explained by pantomime that he should take off his watch and empty his pockets. Everyone else was made to wait.

Kyle thought at first that they were doing that for security reasons, to avoid distractions. But as it went on, he realized they were just incompetent. It took the man four passes through the machine, as he unloaded pounds of change, keys, a camera, a watch, some jewelry, and a handful of paper clips. He was still beeping, and they pulled him aside and had him spread his arms and legs. Then they gave him a cursory pat and let him go.

Kyle was very nervous as he approached, and their treatment didn't help. Even with his pockets empty, he beeped, likely his belt buckle. But the attendant merely took the trench coat he was carrying, hung it over a rail, gave him a quick pat, and then handed his coat back, unsearched.

Wade was waiting, and Kyle followed. As soon as he was sure they weren't being overheard, he said, "I could have hid a Beretta and two grenades in that and they wouldn't have noticed."

"Tell me about it."

Then they had to stand in line for customs, even though they were passing through. That took only a few minutes, but was marked by the large Middle Eastern family in front of them.

The five kids ranged from ten down to two years, and the mother was obviously tired as she took a seat some distance away. Then one of the older kids ran toward the restrooms. The father wandered off to talk to an official about something, and then suddenly, both middle kids, who were playing, ran off. That left a large pile of luggage unattended.

Anywhere in Europe, that is not done, and the crowd at once started backing away from the bags. Wade loudly said, "Whose bags are these?" and the two kids came rushing back to stand by them, wide-eyed, followed at once by the father. Perfectly innocent, but it was that type of atmosphere. Trust nothing.

With two hours wasted, breakfast was the only real option, even though it was evening by their clocks. They found a shop that looked clean and modern, with the typical turned wooden railing and vinyl booths, and grabbed seats.

Ten bucks for breakfast, after conversion. Ouch. And a thick accent on the waitress, who asked, "Worr I git fuh ye genlmin?"

British bacon was meaty, with bits of bone. That was good. The toast was better than American restaurant toast. The fried egg was barely cooked. Kyle thought about sending it back but decided to skip it and just not eat it. He'd been through Britain once before and recalled that was how they did it unless told otherwise. And there was that grilled tomato he wasn't sure if he liked or not. The potatoes were cold and greasy, so he left them.

At that, it might be the last civilized meal for some time, or ever. He left a fair tip as they departed.

"What now? Duty-free or departure lounge?" Wade asked.

"Lounge," Kyle decided. "Better to be early."

"Right."

Kuwait Airlines, however, ran a tight operation. They had their own metal detectors, and wands, and staff searching people professionally. Wade said, "Excuse me," and headed for the restroom, so Kyle held his place as the line advanced.

Wade returned in time to squeeze past the large family from earlier. They were scanned, their kit bags opened and inspected right down to Kyle's paperbacks and Wade's CD player. Then they were searched thoroughly enough. Kyle wondered about asking the guy for a date, just as a joke. But the procedure made him feel much more secure. If you were going to have a security point, then by God have a security point.

The KA desk staff were Aer Lingus contractors from Ireland. Kyle slid up to an attractive redheaded young lady in a green smock, who smiled and said, "Pahsspoht, please, sah?"

He extended his military ID card and the orders that would take him to Kuwait. "That's foine, sah," she agreed with a smile, and in moments he was waved through. He took a seat near the jetway, and leaned back.

Wade joined him, and as he lowered his bag said, "Well, that was close."

"What?" Kyle asked.

Leaning in close, Wade whispered conspiratorially, "I had one of those Cold Steel nylon-bladed Tantos. Just in case. But that checkpoint made me take a detour and drop it deeply in a trash can, wrapped in paper towels."

"Jesus, man," Kyle replied, grinning slightly. "All those searches and no one noticed?" He was bothered that Wade had brought it, and, bothered that no one had found it.

"Who checks a man's tie?" Wade asked with a smile as he flipped the end of it.

He was right, Kyle thought. One could tuck a slim item in there and it would be unnoticed.

The lounge wasn't crowded, but quickly became so. Based on their headdresses, many of the passengers could be Muslims or Sikhs, and Indian women in richly brocaded silk saris were numerous. Kyle wasn't familiar enough with their caste marks to place them. Judging from some of the nomadic-looking bunch, they could expect camels, goats, and sheep in the back. Not really, perhaps, but there was a huge spectrum of culture and societal levels represented.

Shortly it was standing room only. "Where are they all coming from?" he asked quietly.

"Well," Wade drawled, "it occurs to me that if you're flying from Europe to the Far East, there's only three main routes. Through Russia, through Iraq, which is almost impossible and inadvisable, or through the emirates or Kuwait."

Kyle nodded. That made sense. So this flight was going to be seven hours with their tall frames crammed into airline seats and elbow to elbow with other passengers. The flight from Atlanta seemed a wistful dream.

Shortly, they were boarding. "Well, this is *nice,*" he commented.

"Very," Wade agreed. Kuwait Airlines was state owned, and like everything else with the Kuwaiti stamp, was brand new, gleaming, and perfectly maintained. The Boeing 777 still smelled of the factory. Every seat had its own personal LCD TV screen on the chairback in front, and pillows on the seatbacks. They were both nodding as they stowed their carry-on bags and sat. They couldn't know that they'd shortly come to loathe those screens.

The standard preflight safety briefing started even as the last passengers were being helped to their seats, and moments later, a tug shoved the plane free. "That's fast," Wade muttered and Kyle nodded. Apparently, the pilot was in a hurry to keep his slot. The briefing was in English, Arabic, and some Indian dialect. Kyle didn't hear anything resembling Farsi, Dari, or Pashto.

In short order they were airborne and winging southeast. The default on the screen in front of him showed the plane's direction, velocity, and expected arrival time on a continental map, then on a regional map, then flashed to a screen with the direction of Mecca. He knew Mecca was important to Islam, but this drove it home with a dozer blade. It was vital to the devout Muslim to know where Mecca was five times a day for prayer, and at other times for reassurance. More so than Jerusalem or Rome, that one city was crucial to how a large number of people lived. It would be smart, he thought, to study more of Islam. He'd just exhausted most of his knowledge of the faith. He had a feeling it could be important knowledge in the future.

He was wiped out from the trip already. It was noon local time, 6 P.M. by his internal clock, and he'd been up since 0330. It was already a full day. It would be almost twenty-four hours by his clock by the time they arrived. Not wanting to watch prerecorded TV or a fluffy movie, he turned off his screen and reclined against the pillow, hoping to nap.

That's when he started hating the screens. His neighbor was elbow to elbow with him, and his screen was still on. He couldn't see the flatscreen well at an angle, but it *was* on and it was annoying. It flashed and moved against its dark background. Farther over was another. The other way, Wade's was off, but the next one was on. He had four screens within ten feet of him. And he couldn't shut them off.

Growling silently, he closed his eyes and pretended TV didn't exist. But that left him with his own images. Those weren't pleasant.

5

HE AWOKE AS THEY DESCENDED INTO Kuwait City. Wade nudged him, he stirred and pulled his seat upright, and responded to his partner's, "Look at the map," with a grunt.

He flipped the screen on and stared. Yes, that was interesting. He nodded.

Kuwait Airport's main runway ran north-south. It was so close to Iraq that landing from the north was all but impossible, so all flights approached and departed from the south, contorting their routes along the border. That had to be a pain. Perhaps that would change shortly, if Iraq could be turned around.

They landed and cleared the plane into a new terminal, all white and chrome and huge hanging billboards. The ads were similar, except that the American Express Card display bore the name ABDUL ALI MUHAMMAD, whoever that might be, and the gorgeous women staring back from the banners were covered to the necks. Still, their elegant arms and piercing eyes were sexy, and being used to push product. Some things never changed.

The security were Kuwaiti soldiers with rifles. If they weren't oppressive, they weren't smiling, either. Doors that led to secure areas had lights that blinked when they were unlatched. The customs and passports people were more soldiers, behind bulletproof glass. And they were too helpful.

A sign above the booth warned travelers in a dozen languages to HAVE YOUR PASSPORT AND VISA READY. Kyle slid his military ID card and orders under the window when he reached the front.

With only a moment's glance, the moustached sergeant replied in rough English, "Ah, military. Gohead, gohead," and waved him on. Kyle wanted to ask a question or two, but the man's attention was already on Wade and saying, "Yes, yes, you, too. Gohead. Welcome."

There was such a thing as too much courtesy, Kyle reflected. They'd been helped so thoroughly they didn't know what to do next.

"Baggage claim," Wade pointed, and Kyle followed him over that way. Yes, folks, we're a tall white guy and a tall black guy with short hair and good muscle tone, picking up duffel bags and flight bags. Nothing suspicious here.

A hungry-looking porter eyed their bags and his cart, but Wade shook a negative and they shouldered their loads. "Got to be someone here who speaks English," Kyle mused aloud.

"As long as we don't use those other languages yet," Wade joked in caution.

But the soldier at the door just smiled and waved them through. It was dark, and warm and dry, the air flowing over them as the door opened.

"Welcome to Kuwait, what the hell do we do now?" Kyle muttered. "Either someone's waiting for us, or we call that number on a pay phone . . . where the hell *is* a pay phone?" He looked around the spotless pickup loop, but saw nothing resembling a phone. Would they have to make a scene just to be found?

Moments later, an olive-colored Chevy Suburban rolled up in front of them. An obvious American stood up from the driver's step and said, "Al Jaber Air Base?"

In relief, Kyle replied, "Yes, that's us."

"Then please come around here," the man waved. He was blond, in civilian clothes, and had a Midwest accent, and it was *good* to hear that accent.

"Tech Sergeant Henderson," he introduced himself, holding out an ID card.

Kyle examined it, nodded, and carefully drew his own. "Sergeant First Class Monroe."

As soon as Wade identified himself, Henderson nodded and said, "Sounds good. Load your gear in the back, and climb in. I'll inspect the vehicle." He popped the hatch.

Henderson walked around, eyeballed all the wheel wells and the bumpers for potential bombs, nodded, and got back in. It was a formality, as he'd not left the vehicle, but a necessary habit in the Middle East. Kyle and Wade slammed the back and climbed in, Wade riding shotgun. Kyle let him so he could stretch across the back.

The trip to al Jaber was at near eighty mph. Every so often, the vehicle would hit eighty-one and the dash would whine, a warning sound to indicate excessive speed. It didn't stop, either. "Yeah, it's annoying," Henderson said. "But that's how they cut down on speeding." As he spoke, a Mercedes coupe whipped past them doing at least a hundred.

The freeway was as modern as anything else, and brilliantly lit. Signs warned in Arabic and English that CARS MAY MERGE AT ANY TIME by driving straight in off the desert, and that SPEEDING CAUSES DEATH. The locals seemed unworried about either. A car merged from the sand, bouncing lightly straight onto the freeway, and Henderson slid over a half lane. "Sorry, but this is how they drive here."

"No worse than L.A. or Chicago," Wade assured him. "Hell, I'll bet some of them even have AKs." They all chuckled.

"What are those tents?" Wade asked. "Part of the oil facilities?"

"Those are houses," Henderson said.

"Houses?"

"Yup."

Kyle had wondered, too, and looked them over. Each was a compound of tents about the

size of GP mediums, on concrete slabs with generators, air conditioners, and fluorescent lights.
Chevys were preferred, and Suburbans abounded.
Considering the temperature never got much below fifty degrees Fahrenheit, it was a cheap and
practical way to live.

They turned off the freeway onto a well-paved
road that had sand drifting across it like snow
during a Great Plains winter. It was a familiar but
strange sight. The road here was dark, but the
windshield was clear as soon as Henderson
turned on the wipers to clear dust. No crushed
bugs, no water spots, just dust. It was pervasive.
Arabian sand is in reality very fine clay, desiccated to powder.

They drove past a camel-racing club that took
a few minutes and jokes to explain, then off the
major road onto a narrower, potholed one, then
through three perimeters of guards, the first
merely a warning to civilians to stay away, the
inner ones increasingly stiffer, until the inner-
most was USAF Security Forces.

"No photos, no cameras out of your luggage,"
Henderson warned them. He spoke to the sergeant at the gate, exchanging passwords buried
in the talk, though not very hard to spot. The
military was so predictable, Kyle thought. All
their IDs and orders were checked, the vehicle
exterior inspected. "Has the vehicle been out of
your control?"

Henderson replied, "I haven't left it at all."
Then they were waved through.

"So where are we taking you? Billeting office?" Henderson asked.

"That's a hell of a good question. We're supposed to board a cee-one-forty-one here."

"So let's call Ops and find out."

Twenty minutes later, they were in a large Quonset-type hut near the runway proper. It was one of the Air Force's nifty modular things, with actual windows that were covered by solid panels against light leakage or bomb damage or both, air conditioning, and proper lights. Although there were lots of curious stares, no one asked who these guys were and what they were doing. They did collect a couple of sly, casual nods, though, after they changed into uniform. They'd change out again after leaving the base, but the idea was to appear nondescript to the U.S. forces en route. Apparently though, everyone had figured out they were doing something clandestine.

They were provided cots, and dossed out to nap for an hour. Better to rest here, under bright lights and with generators roaring in the background, occasional aircraft up close as A-10s, F-16s and Kuwaiti F-18s flew patrol over Iraq, than aboard a plane, vibrating them slowly insane.

Kyle was just getting comfortable, his mind a warm haze, when his shoulder was shaken. "Sergeant Monroe, Sergeant Curtis, flight's here."

"Roger," Kyle groaned. He stretched, ignored the dead-mouse taste in his mouth and sat up.

Well, he'd gotten fifteen minutes of snooze, which was better than nothing.

They wore their ID in pouches on the left arm. Everyone on base had to have visible ID, and the guards weren't shy about asking for it. They were IDed again as they ascended the ramp. They were both very familiar with cargo aircraft and lashed themselves in on the troop benches, backs against the webbing. As it appeared there was plenty of room, they propped their feet up on their duffels and, after inserting earplugs, thought about sleeping further. Whether or not the thought became reality would depend on several factors.

The flight was for three pallets of unidentified gear and the two of them. The loadmaster was briefly friendly, then left them alone.

It was 900 miles to Qandahar Air Base, Afghanistan, as the crow flies. Detouring around Iran made it 1,200 miles. For more than two hours they tried to sleep, existing in a precarious fugue state between unconsciousness and awareness, joints stiffening and aching, ears ringing despite the hearing protection, from the engine noise and frame vibration. A trip to the latrine at the front that was basically a porta-potty and small sink were the only chance to stretch and unwind, though the loadmaster did let them walk a couple of laps once they were at altitude. It was cold even with their Goretex on, and even the bitter, rancid Air Force coffee was welcome against the chill.

Kyle remembered a brief stay at an Air Force training site when he'd first enlisted. The coffee came from a machine in paper cups emblazoned, THANK YOU FOR USING UNLEADED GASOLINE. The quality was what one might expect. It seemed some things didn't change. Heck, this might be that same coffee, recycled.

They arrived near dawn, and there was no welcoming committee. They walked stiffly down the ramp and looked around in the gray half-light.

Qandahar Air Base was also Qandahar Airport, which had obviously been modern in the recent past. It had a huge, arching, terminal, all white concrete and broad, darkened glass. But a closer look showed it to be chipped and peeling. There was no real firefight damage, but it had clearly seen better days.

They were expected, sort of. They identified themselves and were greeted with "Oh, right," and then shuffled off into a corner for the sin of violating "the process." They were patient, and it was only fifteen minutes before a specialist with a Humvee arrived to take them into garrison proper.

Once outside the flight line and terminal area, literally thousands of troops were billeted in tent cities and transportable barracks. It was a logistical marvel, Kyle thought, that they'd moved so much stuff halfway around the world and set it all up in the middle of nowhere.

Ten minutes later they were reporting in to General Kratman. He didn't look thrilled.

"So," he said, swigging coffee as he spoke, "I'm supposed to extend support to you two gentlemen, to do something I can't be told of, somewhere I can't be told of. You aren't in my chain of command, or even an attached unit, you're just sort of tourists packing personal weapons, looking scruffy and with two crates I'm not supposed to look at. And they tell me you're Army, not CIA." He was lean, healthy, and had an I-take-no-crap presence.

Kyle didn't need to be polite, but it seemed a good idea to not ruffle feathers. "We are Army, sir. And this is secret, but nothing to be ashamed of or illegal. It's just low profile. If I could tell you, I would."

"All well and good, Sergeant," Kratman replied. "But I've got an orderly operation here, and I don't like rumors. A squad of Delta came through here a couple of months back, and basically helped themselves to anything not nailed down. I don't mind support, but I'll be damned if it's charged against my operation. My troops need that stuff, too, which is why we brought it. So tell me what I do need to know and make it quick."

"Sir, we're departing the post with the predeployed gear and some extraneous equipment such as MREs, in civilian clothes. We will accomplish our mission. There may be calls for support from above, if we run into trouble. After accomplishing said mission, we may depart through here or another route. We don't intend to interrupt your operation. It's just a staging area."

After a few more minutes of talk, Kyle being the solid, reliable NCO, Kratman was mollified somewhat. "Fair enough. You do your mission, I'll give you what I'm supposed to. Nothing more. I don't need my command or my ass getting entangled in stuff I'm not authorized to do myself. So list what you need and I'll see it's delivered. You'll be clearing post when?"

"Daylight tomorrow, sir."

"Good. Hopefully this will all make sense in the end. Staff Sergeant Morrow at the end of the hall will get you bedded down and fed, and see to any gear you need. And gentlemen," he ended with a pause.

"Yes, sir?" Kyle asked.

"Good hunting, whatever the hell it is." An almost-grin appeared on his face.

"Thank you, sir." Kyle grinned despite himself as they turned and left. He could understand a commander in this hole being a bastard about equipment, and the man was no-nonsense enough to make exceptions when needed. But he did need to see a reason.

Once they'd paid their respects, plugged into the chain of command, and grabbed a bite, they sought out their gear. If all went as planned, it was supposed to have been waiting for them. A couple of inquiries got them where they needed to go, and they approached a warehouse that was functional and solid if stark. As they were climbing the steps up to the door, a First Sergeant opened it briskly and exited. Flipping his hat on his head, he looked them up and down. "Gentlemen, is there some reason you aren't shaved?" he asked.

"Mission orders, First Sergeant," Kyle said at once. "We'll be out of uniform very shortly and off post right afterwards."

"Ah," the grizzled old NCO replied. He smiled faintly. "Good luck, then."

"Thanks, First Sergeant," they chorused. His question had been professional and his response appreciated, but the sooner they stopped getting such interest, the happier Kyle would be. Once in civvies, everyone would just assume they were Delta or CIA—or manufacturer's reps for some of the deployed equipment—and stop hassling them.

Inside, the blocky building was unpainted, as it had been outside, but not bleached by sunlight. The office area was neatly kept and all papers were stacked. The computers were tactical models and in use. Wade murmured, "At least they're organized. Hopefully everything's here."

"It better be," Kyle replied, "or we're not going."

A specialist arrived at a run. "Sorry, Sergeants, we're short on manpower. Can I help you?"

"SFC Kyle Monroe," he said as introduction. "Here to pick up transported equipment and some additional gear."

"Yes, Sergeant," the specialist nodded. "What are you needing, and do you already have the documents executed? Or do you need some?"

"You do have a crate for us, I hope?" Kyle asked. He felt queasy, and it wasn't just over his personal weapons. That Barrett was his baby.

"Oh, yeah," the specialist agreed. "Big, long thing. Heavy, too. Almost took Jacko's toe off when we dropped it."

Kyle was cringing, even if it didn't show much on his face. Wade spoke up and said, "Well, Specialist, I hope it *did* land on his toe, because the contents are far more valuable than a soldier's foot."

"Oh, it wasn't damaged," the kid said hastily. "It had one of those shock cartridges on it that would break if it dropped more than three feet. It never did."

"Good," Kyle said. "Still, that's a *maximum* allowable drop, not something to be attempted."

The specialist realized he'd better shut up and get to it before he admitted anything else. They were taken through tunnels of boxes at once, to where the crate lay near a receiving door. Wrecking bar in hand, he pried the top loose. "Here you go," he said. He started reaching in before Wade said, "That's good, soldier. We'll take it from here if you don't mind."

"Sure thing, Sergeant," he agreed with a nod. "But I have to observe the contents to ensure it's all accounted for."

"No problem," Kyle grinned back. The kid was going to have an orgasm when he saw this haul.

Getting the stuff out was a bitch, though. The kid—Leo Darcy was his name—had to pry all four sides off. Then he helped them, carefully, under their direction, to cut away chunks of foam with a knife. He was warned that a scratch would cost him his testicles. "Doesn't seem worth it," he commented. "What's in here, anyway?"

"You'll find out," Wade said. "Then you'll keep your mouth shut."

As the contours were revealed, the kid almost drooled. "Jesus H. Christ! What are you guys going to do? Bag the Taliban's head goon?"

Well, thought Kyle as he gritted his teeth, it was rather obvious why two lone snipers were here in country with a crated .50-caliber sniper rifle. "That's really something we and you aren't going to discuss with anyone, okay?"

"Sorry, Sergeant," Darcy admitted. "I'm cleared, and I won't say anything. But whatever you're shooting with *that*," he said, pointing, "is going to be a shoe."

"Shoe?" Wade asked, beating Kyle.

"S, H, U," the kid said. "Severely Hurting Unit."

Chuckling, Wade nodded, "That they will be. Now don't mention it again."

"Mention what? All I do is open boring old crates of crap all day."

"Very good."

Shortly, the gear was all uncrated, cleared of dust and staticky packing foam. Everything appeared to be in good shape.

It only took a few minutes to fill out the appropriate documents for the shipment. "We need a few other things, too, Specialist Darcy," Kyle said. "Ammunition, grenades, claymores, batteries, usual stuff like that."

"Not a problem," Darcy replied. "Sergeant Korkowski's the armorer, and he's not here, but I can do the paperwork and he should be back at 1800. I'll need to see orders authorizing you, though."

"No problem," Kyle said, pulling out a spare copy of his blanket letter. "Here." He handed it over.

Darcy looked surprised, and a bit disturbed. "Holy crap, Sergeant, I've never seen one of these!" He gave the letter another quick read and said, "Okay, when do you want it by?"

"We can come back tonight, as long as the stuff is ready."

"Okay," Darcy agreed. "It'll be waiting for you right after chow."

"Thanks," Kyle said.

In a few minutes, they were back outside, festooned with radios, GPS, sidearms, rifles, and loaded rucks. "We need a vehicle," Kyle said. The load was staggering.

"I think we need to fire a few rounds in this terrain to help break us in," Wade said.

Kyle thought for a moment and replied, "That's a damned good idea. We've got a day, we've got the weapons, they need to be checked out anyway, so let's find a mountain."

It wasn't quite as easy as that. The motor sergeant was reluctant to sign out a vehicle, especially to just two soldiers. He wanted to see orders for an operation first. "It's not safe, gentlemen. And I can't lose vehicles on someone's word. I'd be paying for the damned thing."

Kyle agreed, angry. He reassured himself that the motor sergeant likely hated paperwork as much as he did. Still, it was aggravating.

"What now?" Wade asked.

"I suppose we find a patrol and tag along," Kyle offered.

That wasn't easy, either, although patrols were leaving all the time. A number of them were aboard choppers. Those in vehicles were going a considerable distance for several days. Some were in tracks. None were suited to the task in question.

"I've got an idea," Wade said. "Going to cost us some ammo."

"Fair enough," Kyle agreed. "Lead on."

Nodding, Wade reached out and took the Barrett from Kyle. "Watch this," he said. He led the way down a dusty street between tents. It was classic Army architecture and hadn't changed in centuries, barring minor variations in tentage.

"All we've got to do," Wade said, "is offer a bribe."

In a few minutes, they found a platoon that had returned from a patrol and was cleaning weapons. It was obviously a day-after affair, and they were stripped to T-shirt or skin in the warm sun. Jokes flew as they scrubbed their encrusted weapons industriously. One or two noticed the Barrett's blocky case and nudged each other. They had to be wondering what it was.

Wade's target was the lieutenant. "Sir, we've got a problem. Perhaps you can help."

"Perhaps I can," the fresh-faced kid replied. "Who are you gentlemen?"

Introductions were made, the bare bones explained, and the bribe offered. "If you can find us a few guys to throw a patrol together, we'll let you shoot a few."

Suddenly, fatigue and aches were forgotten. To fire a monstrous M-107 .50-caliber sniper's rifle, the troops would forego sleep and eat another MRE or two. There was no shortage of volunteers.

The lieutenant snapped, "Quiet," and was obeyed. He might have been young, but he was competent enough to be respected, and that said a lot. Turning back, grinning now, he said, "That sounds like a blast. I can get a squad or two together, but transport could be a problem."

"I've got that," Kyle said. The general wasn't

going to like it. In fact, Kyle was making a career of pissing off high-ranking officers here, but it was all legal and kinda fun.

Twenty minutes later, a squad of infantry, the lieutenant, and the two snipers rolled out the crude gate. The rest consoled themselves with smuggled beer and pictures of women.

"So where do you sergeants want to go?" the lieutenant, Daniels, asked.

Wade said, "Anywhere safe, with lots of room and a good clear field of fire for a thousand meters or so."

Snickering, Daniels said, "Well, there's nowhere really safe, but this is the least unsafe area. And we can just go south to a mined and abandoned village and shoot at the buildings."

"Sounds good. Can one of your guys hold the target for us?" Wade suggested, holding up an apple he'd snagged at the chow hall. To the lieutenant's look of confusion and consternation he said, "I'm joking."

"Right. Sniper humor?"

"Dunno," Wade said. "My humor." Kyle snickered. It was good to be joking with a spotter again. The school had made him morose.

On a flat stretch of desert hardpan overlooking a collection of crumbling walls that could be called a town only by the most generous of definitions, Kyle and Wade set up as fast as they could, treating it as a timed range exercise. Behind a very slight lip, Kyle scraped a groove for the bipod, dropped the bipod down into the depression, flopped down behind the rifle and pulled off the scope caps. He drew a ten-round magazine, loaded two rounds, inserted it and worked the bolt. Wade already had his scope out, M-4 laid aside in easy reach. As Kyle worked the action Wade called the target.

"Reference: tall building, large gray stone construction under peak at forty degrees left. Target, yellow protruding ledge, eight seven zero."

Kyle wasn't sure it was 870 meters, but he'd trust Wade. "Sighted," he said, and squeezed the trigger.

The world exploded. The Barrett went "*Blam!*", the stock shoved back against his shoulder, and dust blew up from the gale out the sides of the muzzle brake. There were exclamations of "*Yes!*" from some of the spectators. They loved their M-16s, but the Barrett was a better hung weapon than most of them would ever handle.

"Up twenty," Wade said.

"Correcting," Kyle said, then fired again. Another kick to the guts came with the shot.

Wade studied the impact. "Looks good. Let's try a closer one, then a farther one."

"Right." Kyle extracted the magazine and loaded two more rounds.

Wade located another target. "Reference: patch of green, right of peak and under overhang. Target: lone tree between two large rocks, four six zero."

"Sighted." *Wham!*

"Good shot. Reference: roof peak. Target: bare patch underneath and right, lone broken concrete chunk near right, one two seven zero."

It took a moment, even with the resolving power of the scope, then he found it. "Sighted." Kyle eased the muzzle a few hairs, let the reticle align, controlled his breathing and grip, and squeezed.

As soon as the trigger broke past the notch he knew it was a good shot. The shove and the bang and the face full of dust were just treats. "I got it," he said. It was over a second later before dust kicked up at the rock, and three seconds later, while everyone was silent, before a faint, echoing, anticlimactic crack came back.

The troops were both eager and hesitant. None of them approached, but they all clearly craved to. Kyle cleared and safed the weapon, extracted the magazine and handed it with two rounds to Lieutenant Daniels. "Want to give it a try, sir?"

"Thanks, Sergeant," he replied, looking like a Boy Scout at his first day on the range.

Daniels slipped easily down behind the Barrett. He still had a young man's flexibility and eagerness. He had enough familiarity with weapons and had watched carefully, so he had no trouble sliding the magazine in, cycling the action, and preparing to fire. Wade read him off a target, he squeezed and *Blam!* "HOO*ooly*

Shit!" he grinned, looking up from the massive recoil.

"Give it another one," Kyle encouraged.

After that, there was no hesitation. The entire squad lined up to take their two shots. Kyle noted one with particularly good technique. "You shoot expert, soldier?" he asked.

"Three years in a row, Sergeant," he replied.

"Good. If you can learn good scouting and concealment, you could do this."

"Really?" the young man asked. He looked positively elated.

"Really. Call the school and ask about class schedules. Tell them SFC Kyle Monroe referred you."

"Will do, Sergeant Monroe, and thanks!"

"No problem, soldier. We always need more shooters."

It wasn't long before they were heading back in, jolting over the uneven ground. It seemed as if, thrills done, the drivers wanted back on post as fast as they could manage. "Don't bump my scope," Kyle said.

"Sorry, Sergeant," their driver, the same one who'd shot so well, said, and slowed. They were just taking a curve in the road and Kyle was shoved against the door. The cased rifle on the hump between the seats slammed into his shoulder, twisted and fell and banged his knee as the other end almost bashed Wade in the head.

"Oh, sonofabitch," he said, exasperated.

The driver said, "Ah, hell, is everything okay?"

"Yeah," Wade said. "Everything's cased and we'll heal." He untangled the rifle.

"Good," was the reply, but he did slow a bit more.

"Are we expecting to get shot at?" Kyle asked.

"Er . . . no, just to not miss chow," the young man replied.

"I'll make sure we get fed," Kyle promised.

"Okay. Understood, Sergeant."

6

BIN QASIM SAT BEFORE THE COMPUTER AND checked for messages. It was brilliant and poetic the way it was done. One of the billions of pornographic websites the Satanic Westerners loved had pictures modified with encoded dots. He downloaded the images in question and ran them through for decoding. It was obscene the things the Godless enjoyed. Two scrawny, half-fed women, their loins shaved, licked perversely at each other. Somehow, this abomination was considered exciting.

But of the billions of sites, it was statistically impossible for the security forces to find this one, deduce the algorithm for the code, and crack it. Even then, it was a positional notation of numbers that had to be fed through a proper matrix of the Arabic alphabet to make sense, and code words were used. No code was unbeatable, but this was very secure. And very ironic to make their technology a weapon to be used against them. Especially when it generated some tens of thousands of dollars a month.

While the program worked on the series of images of *Jana and Laurie, the Teen Sweatbox Lesbians,* bin Qasim pondered other issues.

The newspaper woman was becoming jaded. No longer was she reacting with terrified eagerness. She knew what he expected, and it seemed she no longer really cared. It was always that way. They learned fear and obedience, then they learned contempt, then they had to be dispensed with, like a dog that would no longer follow commands.

Still, he considered, that meant he could strangle her, slowly. That would elicit a response. She'd quiver and gasp and thrash around, and that would be exciting. He understood, he thought, why Western men liked responsive women. But allowing them to join the world of men was a dangerous way to get a thrill. Far better this way.

Yes, she'd gasp and moan and her muscles would tighten under him. It was time for that final thrill before he moved on. And he'd be relocating his headquarters within a day or two anyway. There was no need for excess baggage.

The system was done. Turning his attention back, he opened a window. The information there made him smile. Another revolting club was about to feel the wrath of Allah, if not through Osama, his chosen instrument, then through bin Qasim, his messenger until the grace of God returned Osama to them from hiding. From bin Qasim the progression led to a lesser courier, to the man who would plant the bomb. Thus did Allah light the way for dozens of the Faithful to fulfill His commands.

He typed a reply that would be uploaded later that evening, with a "new" series of images. The photographer through whose camera eye these disgusting pictures were captured had no idea of how useful he was being. Nor would he be killed. His sins were, for now, of use. It would be just to gouge out his eyes, but punishment often waited for Allah, as was proper. Only certain actions in the mundane world were justifiable. Lesser evils would have to wait, and patience was one of the virtues.

Bin Qasim had been patient. Now he would take that bitch by the throat and enjoy the justice he would deliver. It was a small justice, but it gave him pleasure, and if Allah was thereby served, that pleasure was not a sin.

So far, so good, Kyle thought the next afternoon. Of course, all this, with stuffy bureaucrats, paperwork, jet lag, and crowding had been really minor compared to the leg ahead of them. Any deployment was like that, on the way in and the way out. The closer one got to the objective or home, the worse the trip became.

But they had all their gear prepped and ready, a TEMPER tent to themselves to rest in, the weapons sighted in and cleaned, then stuffed into soft cases wrapped in rags. If they could only get some rest, they'd be good to go at 0400.

Kyle had a problem, however. He could never sleep well the first night anywhere. Or, right before a major move. So more fatigue was in the cards for him, despite the nap he'd caught in the stuffy heat of the day. He sighed and lay still, comfortable enough in borrowed blankets on an issue bed frame, and focused on a spot on the side of the tent, hoping to zone himself asleep.

It didn't work, but somehow he got an hour or two of honest rest anyway.

They were up at 0400, and out the gate at 0600, chauffered by two MPs in civvies, one with an M-4 and the other with a pistol. They rode in a civilian Suburban rather than a CUCV, so they could pass as press or other foreign visitors, as long as no one took a good look inside the vehicle. The troops on gate control had been warned to expect them, and made no comments, only nodded.

Then they were in the streets of Qandahar, stomachs full of butterflies. Kyle was regretting the oily coffee he'd had to warm him and wake him.

It was a city that was alive. Dirty it might be, with culture ranging from medieval barbarous to twenty-first-century hi-tech, from donkey-drawn carts with produce, textiles, and livestock, to the occasional cell phone and computer. But it was unique and interesting. The wandering armed men, burqa-clad women and rag-clothed children clashed with business people in Western-style suits or fined jellabas with kaffiyehs, turbans, or local hats. Persians, Indians, Afghans, Tajiks, South Africans, Pakistanis, Indonesians, Chinese, and almost every other culture were represented in some degree. Despite the early hour, a respectable portion of the populace was awake and about.

The driver sought the designated meeting place, weaving through tight, narrow streets that had been built with no thought for automobiles. They squeezed past a truck that looked to be seventy years old, with green plywood framing the cab and bed. It was stacked fifteen feet high with goods. It was well they had a Suburban, because a Humvee wouldn't have fit. In fact, a smaller Toyota would have been large for these routes, and less conspicuous. The roads were what an American urbanite might call alleys, like those behind 1920s houses for garage or delivery access, except that shacks and buildings with raised wooden porches butted right up to them, with barely enough sidewalk for vendors. Merchants and foot traffic spilled right out into the street. Everything was a dun, dusty color.

Finally, the driver stopped. "Okay, we're here. Now what?"

"We wait," Kyle said. They were supposed to meet their local escort and guide, and be driven over the border quietly. It had all been arranged ahead of time, and by messages he was assured had been received. He'd feel better if he knew who had sent them, and what method had actually been used. Phone? Radio? Messenger snail?

"Okay. But can you help keep an eye out? I'd like to still have all four hubcaps when I return."

"Sure." Heck with the hubcaps, Kyle thought. They'd be lucky to hang on to their boots. Children were scraping at the doors, holding up food, jewelry, trinkets, even spare car parts. He'd forgotten what it was like in the third world. Bosnia had been much the same, as had Egypt during that training mission.

He was startled from his musing by loud honking from behind. The horn was flat and wheezed, but it was obviously intended to get their attention. Then the vehicle with it, a shabby old Toyota that might be twenty-five years old, pulled around them, close enough that Kyle expected sparks.

Sergeant Fleming, the driver, carefully rolled down the window to the gestures from the passenger, and a torrent of Pashto came through. There were four men in the crew cab, and three more in the bed. In the Suburban, the specialist riding shotgun was clutching at his M-4 and looking very nervous.

"Hold on!" Fleming said, gesturing.

Kyle in back tapped his partner on the shoulder and said, "Wade, let me over," and began to scramble in the tight confines. The web gear they were wearing didn't help. Wade squirmed underneath, Kyle on top, and they managed to swap

THE SCOPE OF JUSTICE | 95

places. He got the window down and said, *"Ta tarjumen larey?"* Do you have a translator? What was wrong here?

In response he heard a long but slow and enunciated phrase in Pashto and caught only "translator," "dead," "soon" and "sorry." He thought he heard "Taliban" in there, too.

"Great," he said to Wade. "Do we still want to go?" The irregularity was not reassuring. Frankly, he wasn't convinced it was a good idea. So far, the whole thing seemed cobbled together.

"I think we should," Wade said. "It's not tripping my ohshit meter yet. But let's keep an eye out for other irregularities."

"Yeah." Kyle thought about calling in on the Iridium, but there wasn't much anyone would be able to tell him. He'd have to make the decision.

Suppressing a mental image of things going to hell and them getting shot, Kyle indicated the gear in back with his thumb, and pointed at the back of the other truck. Grinning wide teeth through his beard, the driver pointed forward, indicating they should follow. His teeth were dirty but intact. He probably didn't get a lot of sugar here, but he likely didn't have a toothbrush, either.

Fleming followed the truck into an alley, whereupon the passenger in the bed indicated they should reverse in. Fleming nodded and pulled them around, while the specialist riding shotgun kept a firm grip on his weapon and scanned every face he saw.

But there were no incidents as Wade clambered into the back cargo area, climbed through the back window and dragged the fabric-wrapped rifle case and two old battered rucksacks behind him, with Kyle bringing up the rear. Kyle relaxed his grip on the little Colt in his pocket, and hopped over the side of the bed to get in the empty front passenger seat.

"*Sta noom tse day?*" he asked. What's your name?

"Qalzai," was the answer. Good. That was who he had been told to meet. At least the names matched. Now he just hoped they hadn't been compromised. Though it could still be a Taliban setup to kidnap or murder them. Kyle was flushed, and his pulse was likely over 100 beats a minute.

"Okay," he shouted back to the MPs. "Follow us until we're out of town, and I guess we find a new translator as we go." He was still prickly. He wanted a translator.

"Are you sure you'll find one, sir?" Fleming asked. He hadn't been introduced to Kyle until that morning, and to him, any American in this region in civilian garb was a "sir." Delta, CIA, whatever, they were above his level.

"No, but it's likely. We all want the same thing, so I expect some cooperation." Kyle just wished he felt as confident as he sounded.

"Very well, sir." It was clear the driver wasn't very happy with the idea.

Turning back to Qalzai, Kyle said, *"Lar,"* and hoped it meant "go." Whether it did or not, his meaning was clear and Qalzai grinned, nodded, and slipped the clutch.

The ancient vehicle's gears ground and caught and they pulled away quickly. The Army driver followed at a reasonable distance as they wove through the streets. While it was clear Qalzai wasn't trying to lose them, he was cheerfully and carelessly buzzing along.

"Um, ah," Kyle said as he fumbled for the right phrase. Dammit, he needed to calm down. He was dwelling on the past again, not paying attention. He was a shaking bundle of nerves.

Wade spoke from the back, *"Mehrabani waka pa karar kooz sha,"* straight from the phrase book by rote. Please slow down.

With a quizzical look, Qalzai eased off the gas.

In a few minutes, they were at the edge of town, the shacks looking more and more bedraggled until there were none left. The ground was reminiscent of western Texas—slightly rolling, scrubby and fertile enough for a few hardy crops. The shacks were gone, Kyle noted, but occasional wide tents with sloping sides were visible here and there. To the south were the hills they'd have to cross.

With all the formalities taken care of, they waved a clear signal to the MPs that everything was as it should be. At least, they hoped so. Kyle felt suddenly very alone.

Shortly, they pulled over to the roadside.

"What's happening?" Kyle asked, suspicious at once.

"We're cool," Wade said. "Clothes."

"Ah. Good," Kyle agreed with relief. From behind him came a local "chappan" jacket in bright cotton, a hat and head cloth, and a rough shirt for later. He got out, swapped jackets, climbed back in, and they were off once again in their Central Asian Plateau limousine. He was reassured. If they hadn't been shot and dumped here, it was likely as it should be. But he was still nervous.

Trying to get names, Kyle turned toward the truck's bed and introduced himself. "I am Kyle," he said, thumbing his chest.

Qalzai chattered and pointed while Kyle and Wade wished he'd keep his hands on the wheel and eyes on the road, though there wasn't much to hit on this plateau. Except boulders. Herds of goats. Maybe the occasional unexploded Russian bomb or land mine or Taliban artillery shell. But from the gestures and a few snatched words, they gathered the gist. Behind Qalzai was his son, Khushal, twenty something and not yet aged beneath his beard. Behind Kyle was a nephew, Shamsuddin, who looked about fifteen and skinny, though not naïve. In back now with Wade were Ustad, Mirza, Qalendar, Bait, and Ajmal. They were all cousins or nephews of Qalzai, and varied from Ajmal who also looked like a teenager, through Bait, about thirty, who had leering, weird eyes, to Mirza who was about forty, though well worn for his age. They were all skinny, leathery, and with ragged hair. Their garb was boots, trousers, coats, and wool hats. Mirza's coat was an old Soviet armor NCO's overcoat.

With nothing else to do, and hoping to improve relations, Kyle pointed at the coat, back through the glassless rear window and over Shamsuddin's shoulder. "Coat?" he asked, indicating his own jacket.

It worked. Mirza launched into a long story that almost certainly started with the Pashto equivalent of "No shit, there I was, thought I was gonna die . . ." He talked loudly, to be heard over the vehicle noise, for a good fifteen minutes, to chuckles and jeers from his fellows, while Kyle and Wade picked up local intonation and rhythm for the language, and got an ear on phonemes. As to vocabulary, they only caught about one word in ten or fifteen, but that was enough to confirm that he'd fought the Soviets as a boy and was quite proud of his trophy. And the story was a familiar social interaction to Kyle. It helped calm him down.

The road across the plateau was fairly decent by local standards. It was dirt, but marked with rocks periodically, and signs put up by some residue of government long ago. Most of the signs had been salvaged as building materials long ago. Debris was mostly cleared to the sides, and picked through for anything useful. They rumbled along to war stories from Mirza and Qalzai, punctuated by grinding gears, occasional backfires, and a clatter from the rusted exhaust.

Kyle learned to loathe the vehicle in short order. Sure, it had character, with its chipped and faded paint, exposed and crumbling foam in the seats, the hole rusted in the floorboard, and the missing roof, replaced by a sheet of tough canvas attached to the pillars.

But then there were the ticking valves and the cylinder that kept missing, the carburetor that backfired whenever the engine revs changed substantially, grinding gears, and howling differential. The combination made conversation impossible. That "tough canvas" over the cab was full of pinholes worn by age and flapped and snapped in the wind. And there was a spot on the seat worn to bare metal, which kept jabbing Kyle in the spine and right kidney, even through his jacket and load vest underneath it. They jounced over a potholed strip that could only charitably be called a road and every bump and shimmy caused him to be stabbed again.

And that shimmy . . . he could swear a motor mount was broken, and perhaps an axle mount, too. He was just glad they were not yet riding the edge of those mountains. This was a hell of a way to travel. He almost wished for a horse, though he'd only ever ridden nags at fairs or on his uncle's neighbor's farm.

It was a long trip, even as short a distance as it officially was, less than 200 miles. Besides the worn vehicle, there were detours around flocks, holes, burned or broken vehicles. Those last were quickly stripped of anything useable, and were mere hulks. It seemed as if any car parts were quickly scavenged, and it didn't take long for even engines to be pulled. He'd seen a couple of truck beds used as wagons, too. The materials were too valuable to waste.

He wondered how much money he could make by opening an auto parts store.

They ate on the road, cold goat and rice and beans. It was mostly bland under a sauce that provided heat but little flavor. Goat was close to lamb, of course, but stringier. Still, it seemed sanitary enough, and was nutritious if boring. Water was from their own CamelBaks, and they'd filter everything they came across. While it was supposed to be a short mission, Kyle didn't crave screaming diarrhea while he tried to take a shot. There were at least three rivers on the route, and they'd crossed the Tarnak and Argestan Ruds already.

The trip was dusty. It had started chilly in the morning, was warm at midday, and quickly cooled again. The local clothes were stale and smelled of dried sweat, but kept him warm. The hat and head cloth were actually quite comfortable and practical, and would mask his features. He hoped no one noticed Wade. Height might be overlooked, but black skin was very out of place here. On the other hand, Wade was a good sergeant, a great shot, and very steady and reliable. It was an Army thing that Kyle wasn't going to dig into. He was quite sure Wade had his own musings on the subject.

They passed through several small villages, drawing gasoline from 1950s-style pumps, from rusty gravity-flow tanks set on scaffoldings and from cans they carried in the bed. It seemed precarious, especially as the gas gauge didn't work. None of the instruments worked, in fact, but their host was cheerful and unconcerned. He acted as a tour guide, pointing at sights and waving and gesticulating. Kyle nodded back, made "yeah" sounds now and then and tried to feign interest in little huts, rocky ridges, and bends in the road. He couldn't tell if the stories were "we fought a great battle here" or "here's where my youngest boy's son was born" or "best breakfast in the country, until they got shot up." Still, he tried to be polite.

By later afternoon it was chill as they rose higher into the Toba Kakar Range toward the border, then turned to follow it east along a very crude track that could only charitably be called a "road." They wished to avoid the refugee camps at Chaman, and to the west was lifeless desert. Toward the mountains was their best route. Traffic was almost nonexistent and what there was was animal drawn.

The road had been built in the 1970s, as a

U.N. project. The U.S. had built a modern, two-lane road around half the perimeter of Afghanistan. It had been a good road in its time, but thirty years of weather, wear, and abandonment had reduced it to rubble. It was a pity. To the north and east, the Soviets had outdone themselves and built a modern, multilane highway. Everyone had wondered why, until their tanks had rolled in by that route a few years later.

Kyle mused until they pulled off into a draw that paralleled the road, apparently in search of shelter.

A canvas tarp was stretched out from poles set into crudely welded rings in the truck's bed, and stretched out with thin nylon twine and metal stakes forged from rebar. They were done in time for sunset, and prayers were chanted, everyone facing southwest toward Mecca. After that, Shamsuddin and Mirza lay down in the truck bed, across fuel cans and spare tires and went straight to sleep. Bait and Ustad, mean and worn-looking, walked off a few feet with their AKs and lit up cigarettes while they stood watch. Wade commented, "Think we should tell them how badly that screws up their night vision?"

"Nah," Kyle replied. "We're taking turns on watch. I don't trust anyone with our package," he said, referring to the cloth-wrapped, cased Barrett.

"No problem. Four hours?"

Kyle nodded, "Yup. I got some bad z's in the cab. How about you?"

Wade smiled, teeth white in startling comparison to the locals. "That's the most comfortable bed full of sharp metal, spares, guns, rotten boots, slimy muck, gas cans, trash, and assorted crap I've ever slept in."

"Well, good. I'll swap off with you tomorrow."

"Don't worry about it," Wade said, shaking his head. "I'd be cramped as hell in that tiny cab. The honor is all yours."

"Right. Goodnight, then," Kyle said, pulling a thin GI blanket from his ruck and using it and his poncho as bedding.

"Sweet dreams, don't let the bedbugs bite."

Kyle did sleep well. He didn't realize how comfortable he was until Wade woke him at 0200.

"Rise and shine," he heard, and shook himself awake. It was chill out, and he realized he'd been clutching the poncho liner around himself. It was like camping again, as it had been when he was fourteen. Only that had been his uncle's farm and this was a range of mountains where unfriendly strangers would try to kill him.

"I'm up," he said, standing, stretching, and taking the M-4. He made a quick and automatic chamber inspection. "What's up?" he asked.

"Just you and our two teenage chaperones," Wade said, indicating the two boys on watch. "Though they seem reliable and not too nervous."

"Good," Kyle said. "Not nervous is good."

"Right," Wade agreed. "See you in four hours." He had his own poncho in the truck with his gear, but it made more sense to just swap off as they had weapons. Less packing was less time wasted. He lay down and was snoring before Kyle had walked out to the patrol point manned by the two locals.

"*Assalam u alaikum,*" he said in Pashto. Peace be unto you, the local equivalent of "Good evening."

One of them replied, "*Wa alaikum u ssalam.*" And upon you peace.

"*Saba hawa tsanga da?*" he asked. What will the weather be like?

"*Rokhana,*" he heard. Cloudy. Then a bunch of what was gibberish.

"*Ze ne pohigam, wobakha,*" he said. I don't understand, sorry. They shrugged back and all three resumed silence. He'd used what little Pashto he had to stay in practice. It wasn't enough, even with a laptop and phrase books. There was no time for that while shooting. So they'd still need an interpreter to get anything done. But hopefully they'd find one soon.

The teens were quiet. They stayed still and didn't fidget, and didn't smoke at the post, taking turns to go back behind the truck and shielding their eyes. Decent discipline, for what were essentially militia. Kyle was reassured. At least they weren't bumbling amateurs, even if they were largely illiterate tribespeople.

It was a good watch, which is to say a boring one. Absolutely nothing happened before 0600. No animals stumbled across them, no one attacked, no stray rocks dislodged and fell. Nothing created any disturbance. Kyle was relieved to see dusk grow from gray to purplish blue overhead.

They drove as soon as everyone was awake and prayers said. Breakfast was bread and a few precious cans of soup, heated over the engine during a few moments' rest an hour later. Kyle and Wade settled for MRE spaghetti, also heated against the block.

Looking over, Kyle asked, "Got enough hot sauce there?"

Wade grinned and finished emptying the tiny bottle. "I carry extras. Always useful. Makes the stuff edible, at least."

"Yeah, they're pretty bland," he agreed. "But some of the new ones are decent."

They dug in with spoons, stirring to mix the hot and cold areas of the packets into something resembling warm food. It wasn't really breakfasty food, but it was familiar and nourishing. "You did bring extra toilet paper, I hope."

"Four rolls," Wade agreed. "Dunno what they use here. Leaves, sand—"

"Skidmarks," Kyle suggested.

"Thank you," Wade said. "That goes so well with spaghetti."

"You're welcome," Kyle replied, smiling. He reflected it was a good thing he wasn't a coffee addict. Coffee here was almost nonexistent, thin and bitter, the imported Arab beans not the best.

Of course, heating it on the engine didn't improve the flavor. Though likely some of the glop that passed as engine oil would. Some of the men were grumbling about not having any tea, but they'd have to wait until lunch.

While they stood around the opened hood, their escorts jabbered back and forth. A couple smoked unfiltered cigarettes down to bare stubs, which they saved for reuse later. Unlike Western cigarettes, they came in bundles, not packs, and were slightly conical rolls. Kyle had wondered at first if they were joints, but they did smell like tobacco. The smoke was fragrant. "Indian," Wade said. Kyle took his word for it. He sucked down a few cupfuls from his Camel-Bak to stay hydrated. They had spare canteens along, but would still have to find a well or river soon.

Then they were back on the road as the shadows shrank and the few brave drops of dew lost their battle with the arid environment. A dry wash was to their right and south, weathered and old. Farther west, it became a stream.

Shifting in the seat, Kyle tried to get comfortable in some fashion, back at an angle against the seat, feet toward the drive hump, elbow on the window ledge. It didn't work, though he could have been much more uncomfortable, he thought. The bench seat was far enough forward for Qalzai, who might be five feet six. Kyle broke six feet and was much longer limbed. He wondered how Wade was managing in the back, crammed in with junk and five militiamen. Plus their very expensive and very precious rifle.

Ahead, he could see what was the peak of this particular ridge of the mountain range. There were likely others beyond it. Wade had been right; it was much like Nevada, only more lawless and desolate.

He didn't realize that he managed to doze. His body had adapted to the inevitable, head on hand, and the steady bouncing had a hypnotic effect. That combined with the warmth, the very short sleep plus the fatigue of the trip zoned him into a nap.

He was still out when the rickety old vehicle braked and stopped. "What's going on?" Kyle asked, shaking himself awake. They were alongside a vehicle that was coming the other way, and Kyle was disturbed that he'd been asleep. If it had been a threat . . .

But it didn't appear to be. Qalzai spoke to the other driver. They rapid-fired words at each other, loudly and with furrowed brows. Gestures passed back and forth as both troops grasped at pistols, just in case. Kyle opened up the laptop, keeping it in the footwell for now. He had a feeling the dictionary was going to be useful.

As the other vehicle drove off with waves all around, Qalzai spoke to his son. Kyle handed him the laptop, and the boy brightened. A computer was a neat thing to him, and after a quick explanation, he scrolled through the words on screen and said haltingly, "Border ahead. Guarded American Marine soldiers."

"Oh," Kyle said. It was the smartest thing he could think of to say.

Wade asked, "Bypass it?"

"No," Kyle said. "We've got ID, we'll go through. Let me handle it." He turned back to Khushal and said, "Approach slowly and let me talk." He used his hands a lot to get the point across.

"You're the boss," Wade agreed, sounding unsure.

As they reached the peak of the rutted pass, the road split. To the left was the road to Ghazluna, which they wanted to avoid. Not only was it a visible area, but there were solid border patrols. Instead, they curved off to the right and south. Ahead could be seen a checkpoint, clearly guarded by Marines in Humvees mounting M-19s and M-240s, and a Pakistani detachment with an M113 APC. Apparently, something was expected to cross the line that the Marines wanted to take a look at. But they'd be easier to deal with than Pakistani guards in a populous town, with no U.S. presence, had they taken the other route.

One of the armored and helmeted figures waved them forward, palm flat to indicate they should slow and stop. Qalzai eased the grinding clutch in and crept up. Everyone had his hands visible. The tracking guns helped keep everyone's attention.

As they stopped, the M-4-armed Marine spoke in halting Pashto. Kyle drew back the cloth over his face and said, "I'm American, Marine. So's my assistant."

"Who are you, sir?" the kid asked. He might be twenty-two at most, but he spoke the language, was dusty and dry and had eyes too wise for that age. He might be surprised but he wasn't impressed. Across from him was another youngster with an SAW.

"Army. Intel. Monroe, SFC, and Curtis, Staff. Here's our orders and our ID," he replied, handing forward the documents as Wade uncovered his own face. His dark skin actually helped here, as further identification. There were almost no blacks in Afghanistan, and almost certainly none who weren't American or French. "We need to talk to your commander."

The Marine read over the orders a bit haltingly, strange acronyms giving him pause. But they were clearly U.S. Army orders, and the accompanying letter said to extend any requested facilities or equipment to the two soldiers identified. "Gunny Reagan is in charge. Come with me, but leave the weapons, please."

"Can do," Kyle agreed, and climbed out the back slowly. Wade would stay to guard the gear.

Gunny Reagan was obvious. He had a slight grizzled look, a demeanor that bespoke confidence and command. This was a man who wouldn't need to raise his voice. He extended a hand for the orders, and said, "Gunnery Sergeant Reagan, and you are?"

"Kyle Monroe, SFC, U.S. Army. Pleased to meet you."

"What's the deal?"

" 'Fraid I can't say, Gunny. Sergeant Curtis and I are cleared to cross the border, and we may or may not be back this way. In the meantime, I need to ask that you and your men forget I was ever here."

Reagan nodded that he heard the statement, but not that he agreed. He looked over the letter, flipped back to the orders again, scanned them, and said, "Then let me call in this code here and see what I'm told." He looked at Kyle for any evasiveness.

"Go right ahead," Kyle agreed. He didn't blame the man. Documents could be forged easily enough, and the two could be reporters, spies, drug dealers, sympathizers, or anything else. even antiwar nutcases wanting to make headlines. The Marine strode briskly over to the nearest Humvee, climbed in the passenger side but left a leg dangling, and reached for a radio.

It could be a few minutes, with relays through various air and ground stations, so Kyle dropped into parade rest and waited. It was a comfortable enough position and it wasn't likely to make anyone nervous. He was glad of the cloth over his head in the hot sun. He hoped no one lost a file and left him with the Marines. It would be embarrassing.

Shortly, Reagan came back. He handed over the dusty sheets and the ID and said, "Forget what?" There was a perfectly rehearsed confused look on his face. He gave a thin, tight-lipped smile, extended his hand to shake and said, "Good hunting, whoever the hell you are and whatever the hell you're doing."

"Semper Fi, Gunny," Kyle grinned back.

"Semper Fi. No problem. Good day." He turned and said, loud enough to be heard but not shouting, "Let this vehicle pass." One of the troops repeated it in Pakhto to the Pakistani squad. The two and their guides were scrutinized curiously, but they weren't hassled with further questions.

They resumed their jolting, dusty progress. The only good thing, apart from the few minutes of respite, was that the gunny's call had confirmed their whereabouts for the chain of command and made the next call-in less urgent. Still, Wade dialed in and reported their position. Things got lost in passage, and it was better to contact directly. "We're good," he said as he disconnected. "Spoke to his exec."

Kyle had thought downhill would be less nerve-wracking. He'd forgotten that the truck's brakes were as bad as the rest of it. They squealed and slipped and pulled to the right, while Qalzai ground the gears to torque-brake against the engine, and pulled on the hand brake, too. Hopefully, it wouldn't be necessary to use feet. Once, when they met a car coming the other way, also overloaded with gear, they seemed to hang in empty space. Kyle held tightly to the door handle, clutched at the seat and said nothing. Somehow, the thought of a roll down the mountain was less appealing than that of being shot. He reminded himself that Qalzai had done this before, likely for his entire life, and that it should be safe. While he did so, the wheels slipped for just a moment on a slope that was a bare hairsbreadth from the cliff.

Kyle was only too glad when they hit a wide spot with rock on both sides, and took a break. He had to pee very badly, and Wade did, too.

They continued up and down sharp ridges and escarpments, the road cut at steep angles and worn. The wind and the weight of vehicles and even the centuries of animal hooves and human feet had worn things down. Many of the routes had never been intended to take motorized vehicles, and had been damaged further. Sometimes, the truck would scrape one side or the other on rocks as they negotiated a narrow stretch. Qalzai could be heard to mutter what could only be curses.

That was scary, Kyle, thought. If the local guide was worried, he probably should be, too. He began to wish they'd simply parachuted in where they needed to go.

But they were stuck with this, and it had only been two days so far. Two long, aching, sweaty, gritty nerve-wracking days.

It was dusky by then, making the descent even more interesting. Kyle heaved a sigh of relief, as did Wade, when Qalzai leveled them out at the bottom of the slope. They stopped again for the night on this local plateau. It gave them good visibility against incoming trouble, but less protection against wind. As dark fell fast and hard, Qalzai pulled them off into the scrub and picked a spot where they should be slightly hidden. They were behind a slight rise that would also give them the tactical advantage if attacked.

"We shouldn't be at risk," Wade said. "Pakistan is friendly territory and a civilized nation."

"Do you really believe that?" Kyle asked. The two were standing back as the Pashtun pitched the canvas tarp.

"No, but I sound convincing, don't I?" Wade grinned.

"Yeah," Kyle said. "Keep that thing loaded and a sharp eye out."

"Right," Wade agreed with a nod. He was still smiling, but serious underneath.

The night chilled rapidly. Ustad and Qalendar unpacked a salted haunch of goat, which they roasted over a small, smoky fire of scrub stalks. Along with beans and rice, it made an adequate meal. The beans and rice were so much cardboard to the Americans, but the goat had a rich aroma and the salted flavor was welcome, if a bit strong. It was stringy, chewy meat, too. Still, it was meat, and the smoke from the fire added to their hunger, even if it was a bit astringent and harsh. Kyle had brought a box of rations, and decided he'd break them out within the next day or two, to boost morale and pull favors, though the idea of pulling favors with MREs was hysterical.

Once done eating, Kyle slipped down into his poncho liner and blanket, ruck as a pillow, and was soon in that warm state between dreams.

Then a shot crashed nearby.

He kicked off the covers automatically as he snatched for his .45. Wade was already dropping down behind him, safety coming off the M-4 with a *snick*. Kyle's heart was thudding as his body temperature soared and sweat beaded on his skin. He wished for something heavier than a pistol, but the Barrett was too heavy and there was only one M-4. None of the locals had a spare AK, or if they did, now was not the time to be asking.

"What happened?" he asked Wade. He was shaking. The shot had his nerves fried.

"I dunno," Wade said. There was yelling, and another shot as everyone else finished scrambling out and for cover.

Recalling what had happened so far, Kyle asked, "Were both shots outgoing?"

Wade hesitated, and said, "Yes."

"Okay. So let's not do anything sudden."

"Agreed."

Qalzai was yelling out at one of the others, who was yelling back. Then he went out into the dark, shouting as he did so.

"Who's out there?" Kyle asked.

"Er . . ." Wade said, "Ajmal and Qalendar."

Shortly, Qalzai returned with Qalendar. Qalzai held both rifles. His face was a cross between amused and disgusted.

"What was it?" Kyle asked.

Qalzai said something that was hard to comprehend, but included "fighting" and "sick." Turning to Wade, Kyle said, "Near as I can tell, the man suffers from PTSD." He could see that. He had some of it himself. And right now, it was very near the surface.

Wade said, "Post traum—well, I guess that's understandable."

"Yup. And we're not in any danger. So why don't I take over on watch and you sleep?"

"Sleep? After that?" Wade replied. "Funny. But I can hold your hand and sing you a lullaby until you calm down."

They both laughed nervously. It had been terrifying for a few moments there.

"We're both staying up, I assume?" Kyle asked.

Wade nodded, "Yeah, for now. Hell, we don't need sleep anyway."

It was cold, near freezing, with frost and hoarfrost and gelatinous dew clinging to every patch of green amidst a sinking, swirling mist that was starting to settle.

"If we'd had this fog when we woke up, I think I would have crapped my pants. This is *creepy*," Wade said.

"Tell me about it," Kyle agreed. "Isn't it amazing how a mission so simple on paper can turn to shit at every stage?" Their mission was very simple in theory: go in, meet up with locals, find target, eliminate target, withdraw. He still doubted it would go that smoothly.

"The Army way. Has been since at least the Romans."

"Yeah," Kyle replied, his nod unseen in the dark. "Want me to get out NVGs or warm up something with an MRE heater?"

"Save the goggles," Wade advised. "But yeah, something warm. Cocoa? Coffee?"

"Sure. How about a blend of both with extra creamer to create a nice Italian mocha latte?"

Wade grimaced at the thought. "You can really be a sick son of a bitch, you know that?" They both chuckled and he said, "Just cocoa, thanks."

The MRE heater was a calcium carbide grid in a plastic bag. Adding water made it churn out hydrogen bubbles and lots of heat. There were also ways to use them as small incendiaries, but Kyle hoped mightily they wouldn't get that far down the drain on this mission, no matter what went wrong. He dropped one plastic heater package each into their canteen cups, risking minor contamination and bitterness, which got the water boiling. He decided cocoa did sound preferable to coffee, and doctored his with extra sugar. Wade kept up a small patrol area, with the rise, the truck, and a rock dome as cover, while Ajmal and Shamsuddin watched the heaters in amazement. Their whispered conversation was unintelligible, but they were obviously awed by the technology. They knew of radios and small arms, artillery and aircraft, even chemlights. But there were many very basic military items they'd never encountered.

7

KYLE AND WADE WERE BOTH STILL GRITTY-eyed and exhausted when dawn turned to a boiling oil sunrise oozing over the ranges. They hoped to reach their destination today and start the mission proper. Aching and stiff, still chilled from the night, they crawled back into the truck.

Qalzai turned the heater on, and it worked after a fashion. The fan had long since burned out, but motion created positive airflow. With the windows closed and the broken back glass wide open, all they succeeded in doing was drawing hot air past the boots and up their legs, but that helped immensely. Kyle shivered in his Goretex parka and pants and Nomex gloves, and wondered how Wade was managing in back. The day was warming slowly.

Amazingly, he did manage to sleep, head lolling forward. He awoke like that around eight, and had an excruciatingly stiff neck to go with the acid stomach and headache. Sighing, he drank water, that being all that was currently available. He longed for the one thing he couldn't have: bacon and eggs.

Qalzai said little, but he did mention "*Da sahar chai*" and "*rasturan*." Breakfast tea something restaurant. Kyle agreed and nodded.

They splashed across a shallow ford of the Pishin Lora River. What was here might have been a road and proper crossing at some point. Now it was just a wide spot with flat rocks. The vehicle tilted and swayed at a steep angle, but they were across soon enough.

Their first destination became visible as they cleared a rise beyond the bank. Berishtiya was a sizeable town, which surprised Kyle, it being located in the ass-end of nowhere. It was likely a center for what passed as trade and government out here. "Not even a McDogfood's," he quipped to Wade, who chuckled. They could see all of it easily from here. It was all block and bleached tin roofs packed in closely.

Wade leaned close and whispered, "Not even a bar or whorehouse. No wonder some of these guys are mean." They both stifled laughs from that.

Khushal was giving them an odd look as Kyle turned back around. "Just a joke about the terrain," he said, figuring to be vague. "It's similar to some of our Western desert." Then it took ten minutes to use the laptop to assemble the sentences into something understandable. By then they were near the town.

"I think America is green?" Khushal asked, looking quizzical.

"Oh, no," Wade cut in. "Desert, mountain, arctic cold to the north, wet forests, plains, swamps, some of everything. We just don't have time to visit a lot of it."

Kyle added, "And we don't often fight in the mountains. More often in the woods or cities." They picked out enough words to get the points across.

Khushal studied the screen and nodded. "All mountains here. Pretty, yes?"

"Sure are," Kyle agreed. *If you dig bleak, cold, and lifeless.* But he wasn't going to insult a man who was his host, brave enough to fight the bloodthirsty freaks who were not anxious to relinquish this land, and who was necessary to keep him alive.

Berishtiya was in a high valley. There actually was quite a bit of greenery there, compared to the stark cliffs. Flocks and herds of sheep and goats munched here and there, and they had to slow to get through them. The roads were dirt mostly, though there was one section that had been paved sometime in the last century, and some graveled areas.

Traffic wasn't heavy, but the streets were as narrow as they'd learned to expect. Donkey-drawn carts, VWs, rattly old Mercedes cars, and unknown Indian cars fought for space, drivers cheerfully shouting and waving fists at each other, demanding Allah bless or curse the obstacles in front of them, depending on mood.

Among the shanties and shacks were a few better buildings. Some appeared to be civic centers. There were nicer houses, in that they had land, block walls with pierced concrete, and stone walls around courtyards, sheds, or garages and balconies. One had a worn fountain or pool, now dry and choked with dust. The mayor and chief of police lived here, Kyle surmised. Or perhaps some local warlord or black marketer. He didn't need to know and wasn't going to ask.

Small shops were scattered, and small was the operative word. Some of them might be a hundred square feet, a ten-foot hut with an awning, open in front. Some were more spacious. Kyle didn't understand that. With all the empty room they had, why not make use of the space?

Then his thoughts were distracted by the smells of food.

They pulled up near a clutch of small buildings with a courtyard. A fire was going in a brick stove, and pots were crowded on the surface, with other things in the oven area. Two women in long dresses and veils were bustling about tending the food, and several children, better fed than their northern neighbors, scurried about, helping and hindering and being chastised.

Qalzai and Khushal hugged another man and swapped greetings, then laughed loudly. Shortly, they were all hunkered down around a low table, drinking at hot, sweet tea and tearing at bread, with jam and goat milk to spread and dip. It wasn't the most appetizing breakfast the Americans had seen, but they managed.

Kyle grabbed the laptop from his coat—he'd been carrying it alongside everywhere, figuring it was harder to replace than a rifle, and easier to steal. He opened it up and grabbed the dictionary program, so they could communicate more.

At once, he was surrounded by a mob of children, who were highly impressed and very excited. They'd likely never seen anything like it, heard only stories, and here was a screen with images on it. They were delighted.

Kyle swore, and heard Wade mutter, too. The last thing they needed was publicity. While it wasn't an obvious connection from computer to assassin, it was certainly a hint of visitors from the West, and that combined with a shot or two would be serious intel for their target, the Pakistani authorities, or anyone.

He closed it at once, shooed the children away, and Qalzai said what was clearly, "You children go play and leave the adults alone."

"Phrasebook for now," Kyle said to Wade.

"Apparently our best choice," Wade nodded.

After eating, they sat back as the men pulled out a tall vaselike ceramic container with a narrow neck.

"That can't be what—" Kyle started to say as Wade said, "Hashish pipe."

"Oh, great," Kyle said.

"Typical here," Wade said. "Hash has been

used in Central Asia for at least three thousand years. Just smile and ignore it. If they make a stink, fake a hit."

"I'm sure the Army will love this in the after-action review," Kyle said.

But the man charitably offered to share, and simply smiled when Kyle and Wade declined. The others each had a few good lungfuls, and seemed to mellow out. It didn't appear to be an addictive habit for them, merely a social thing like a drink. But Kyle hoped they didn't plan on driving again soon.

He was relieved when Qalzai said, "We stay here," or something close to it, with, "Friends help." So they were waiting for allies, or spies or something. Fair enough, as long as it wasn't too long a wait. Kyle and Wade both knew they were nervous, and kept eyeing each other, waiting for one of them to express their distrust. It wasn't that their guides were unreliable, it was that the locals were well networked and they weren't. The word would get out sooner or later, and that would make their stalk and shoot much more problematical. Best to do it quickly, shoot and scoot, before anyone had any suspicions. But if they needed more intel, they'd have to wait.

They spent all day in the compound. At least it felt like a compound. Wade explained the reason it felt that way.

"The home is all-important. So the buildings look in on the courtyard. It's part of why they're so clannish and have so little nationalism. Comes from early times, and was reinforced when Alexander stormed through here; they built to provide defensive walls. And since then . . ."

"Since then they've been at each other's throats in some fashion," Kyle offered.

"Yes," Wade said. "Mongols, Moghuls, the Afghan empire, the Kazakhs, the British, the Soviets, always someone."

"Wonderful," Kyle groused.

"They're a very proud people," Wade said. "Unfortunately, they're stuck in the Middle Ages."

"I wondered," Kyle said. "They seem to have bright cotton fabrics, lots of horses, all stuff that would have made them rich five hundred years ago."

"It did," Wade nodded. "But they haven't changed much since. And the Taliban influence took them back even further. The burqa used to be a mark of a high-class lady who didn't need to show her face. Now it's a prison."

"So let's get our shot and leave them in peace," Kyle said.

"Suits me."

They passed the day reviewing manuals mentally, looking over maps, practicing the language, handling gear and discussing it, talking tactics, and swapping war stories. Lunch was brought to them by a very pretty young girl, perhaps ten, in bright diamond-patterned cloth with a scarf over her chestnut hair. She smiled and blushed and gave them a flat bowl of mutton and lentil pies. "*Sta na shukria*," Kyle said. She giggled and left.

The only odd part of the day was the constant prayers. Five times a day, everyone bowed to the southwest where Mecca was and prayed.

"That's a lot of time used up," Kyle said.

"And keeps them subservient. The nutcases make use of that."

"Yeah. Remember the plane flight and the map?"

"Exactly," Wade said.

Kyle leaned close and spoke softly, "Do you notice anything odd about Bait?"

"You mean that he's always watching us and has beady eyes?" Wade replied.

"So it's not just me."

"No, I see it, too. I think he's the real contact here."

"So why isn't he open about it?" Kyle asked.

"Dunno. Bears watching though. Or he could just be curious."

"Could be," Kyle admitted. He didn't believe it. The man looked at them every time he passed by. Either he'd never seen Americans before, or he wanted something.

Or maybe he was just eager to have the shot taken. Perhaps he'd lost family in the war? Many had.

Kyle and Wade were busy enough reviewing maps and texts, and Qalzai and his men returned around dinnertime. They couldn't converse much. Khushal gave them what he could. They would rise early, and then would travel again and work on the shot. That seemed reasonable, and they nodded agreement.

As it grew dusky, the sun leaving violet streaks over the plains to the west, they rolled out their bedding, set their gear for easy access, and tried to sleep.

The hut they were in was crude but weather-proof. The blocks were tight against wind and the corrugated sheet-metal roof kept potential elements at bay. The floor was earth, but packed hard enough from years of use to be almost concrete. There was a faint smell of goat. Still, they decided to swap off on watch, cradling the loaded M-4. Kyle paced quietly, far back from the lone window, occasionally sneaking a peek through a chink in the back door. That way were mountains and nothing else. Out front was the courtyard, plunged in deep shadows with little going on, except the occasional person walking through to the latrine out back. An occasional passing vehicle overheard outside—he counted only three in four hours, and one of those a donkey-drawn cart—was the limit of activity. He scratched at his scraggly, growing beard. It was one more minor annoyance that wouldn't go away.

When he swapped off with Wade at 0200, he was drained from the tension, and managed to sleep easily.

Still tired and aching, they cleaned up with baby wipes and headed out. Qalendar nodded from across the small compound where the others were, and soon Qalzai and Khushal joined them. Qalendar stayed behind and the four walked into town. Kyle was nervous as hell about leaving the weapon unattended, and said so to Wade.

"Yes, but we've got to show some trust. Besides, I've got the bolt and the ammo," he said.

"Yes," Kyle said. "But I signed for the damned thing. This is very nonreg."

"So it is," Wade agreed. "So's the whole mission. But if we make a point of always leaving one of us by the truck, everyone will figure out in a hurry that there is something there of interest to the Americans. Guarding the truck is good. Only us guarding the truck is bad."

"You're right," Kyle admitted. "But I still don't like it."

"Neither do I," Wade said. "I've got to keep the radio with me. That's even more accountable than the rifle."

"True." The encryption hardware for SINC-GARS was something any foreign government would pay a fortune for. It wasn't excessively large, but had to be carried at all times. Wade had a small, nondescript canvas bag to tote it in.

Dawn had brought activity, and the townspeople were bustling with their day's activities. There were cries from peddlers, occasional curses from teamsters wrestling carts or trucks through the narrow accesses, and smells of animals and food.

"Very Middle Ages," Kyle commented.

"Except for the Mercedes diesels, yes," Wade replied with a wry smile.

"I dunno. Looking at the shape that sucker is in," Kyle said as he pointed at one such, "I could believe it's five hundred years old."

"Nah, not more than two hundred. It still has unrusted sections."

"That's due to the dry climate," Kyle replied. This was fun.

"You win," Wade conceded.

Indicating with a tilt of his head, Kyle said, "Those hills are just as impressive from this side."

Wade said, "Yeah. Greener than Nevada, about like northern New Mexico. Or maybe parts of the Arizona desert, but more bush and less cactus."

"What's that sound?" Kyle asked.

"Hold on," Wade said, and cocked an ear. It was a repetitive, rhythmic droning. "I think that's a classroom."

As they walked the noise grew, and became discernible as a chant of children. It did sound like a classroom, not a mosque.

Wade said, "Yup, right in there," and pointed with a head tilt. They'd both become very good at not waving fingers around in just a very few days.

Through the open door they could see the stereotypical schoolmarm, except dressed in a full dress and with her head covered. Like many in the region, she wasn't subtle. Her dress was purple with a shawl of checked blue and yellow, and her sleeves were embroidered as well. She was scribbling squiggly phrases on a blackboard and coaching young children through them.

"That's a good sign, in this area," Wade said.

"Yup. Best chance to end the paranoid theory that the Religion of Peace has to blow up every other group on earth."

"It's weird," Wade said. "Since we got in theater, everyone has been kind, generous, decent. No one has mentioned you being white or me being black. We're Americans, we're not Muslim and they know it, and no one treats us badly because of it."

"Yeah, it only takes a few assholes to make an entire nation look bad. Like this scum we're going to bag."

"Or Congress," Wade added.

Kyle laughed, deeply but quietly. "We aren't supposed to think seditious thoughts like that, my friend."

"What sedition? I'm talking treason."

"As long as it's just talk," Kyle said.

"Oh, sure. I'll trust the political process. But I'm sure you agree there's a few honorable members of Congress who'd look better as a billboard ad for the benefits of life insurance."

"Yeah, and if we all did that to our own tastes, we'd have no Congress left."

"I don't see what your problem is," Wade replied, deadpan.

This time they both laughed.

They found an actual restaurant, and had scrambled eggs for breakfast with fresh flat bread. The tea was strong and very sweet. It was better than coffee, Kyle thought. Tasted lighter and cleaner, had caffeine but it wasn't the kind that gave shakes nearly as much. He remembered in time not to insult the staff by leaving a tip—it implied that they weren't paid enough. He did pay for all of them, and Qalzai hugged his thanks.

Back out on the street, the day was in full swing. There were numerous and varied people running around, some locals, some obviously transported refugees from Afghanistan. They were identifiable by the scrawny children. There was a boy of possibly five who might manage twenty pounds. Sad. And propaganda aside, the blame for that was purely on the Taliban for not letting the nation advance out of the Dark Ages. There simply wasn't enough food, distribution, or education to operate. Reading scripture was a good thing, in Kyle's view. Reading nothing but scripture, and doing nothing but read it, was a waste of life.

Back at the farm, while the men went out with their local cousin to ask questions, Kyle and Wade slept in shifts all afternoon, catching up from the draining travel. It was comfortably warm in the hut, if dusty. The little farmstead had a well and cistern that gave enough pressure to shower with under a bronze head well encrusted with scale and green with verdigris. But there was real soap, and they got clean. The women and children washed their clothes and kept them fed.

They used the well to fill up the five-gallon can they'd brought for the purpose. Once done, they siphoned the water through a filter and decanted it to their CamelBaks and canteens, then refilled the can for later use. They weren't about to risk untreated water here, even after typhoid shots. If necessary, they had water treatment tablets, but those didn't improve the taste any. Filtered was their choice.

The men all returned in time for dinner, and curried chicken over rice was served. They'd smelled it all day.

"You know," Wade said, "if these people opened a restaurant in New Orleans, they'd have people flocking."

"Yeah, it's good," Kyle agreed, throat worn rough from cumin and eyes watering. Holy crap, but it was hot. He'd had south-Texas ass-burner chili that didn't come close. But Wade was packing it away with ease. Kyle consoled himself with the thought that it would come out as corrosive as it went in, and Wade wouldn't be so calm then.

But he did thank their hostess, Noora, and her daughters. He'd seen the scrawny old chickens they had to work with, yet the meat in the dish was tender and juicy. They had to have been stewing it for a week to get it that soft. And under the heat it had been tasty, far more so than the beans and rice they'd boiled or had cold en route.

That evening, they went out for another walk. The town rose up from the valley floor to the hillside where they were. Everything was dun and brown under pale green and straw growth. The buildings were amazingly like Southwestern adobe buildings. Form followed function, Kyle guessed. They were roofed in tile, sheet metal, or occasionally wood.

The streets weren't in a grid, but wandered around. Between rickshas, carts, wagons, horses, donkeys, occasional Bactrian camels and pedestrians, even the late evening quiet kept them alert.

Something made Kyle stop for just a moment. He cocked his head and listened. "What was that?" he asked.

"I didn't hear anything," Wade said.

"Wait," Kyle said.

Wade nodded silently.

"There it is again," Kyle whispered. It was a hissing crack followed by a muffled, whimpering cry.

"Down the alley. Watch it and stay clear," Wade warned.

They stepped past the dark tunnel carefully, peering into the darkness. Then the noise came again. Suddenly, the shadows resolved as an image, and Kyle flinched.

He wasn't sure exactly what was going on, but

he did know that hitting a woman was unacceptable to him, and, as far as he knew, unacceptable
to Muslims. As far as flogging and kicking and
punching and ripping at her robe was concerned,
he wasn't going to stand for it no matter the local
customs. He sized up the terrain quickly. It had
trash cans, piled crates and pallets, some cardboard boxes, and a heap of something. There
was enough room to maneuver, and it looked
clear enough otherwise.

He slipped down the alley quietly but with
haste, grabbed a good position behind the short,
little asshole, and went to town.

Kyle knew how to "fight like a man." He also
knew it was usually a good way to lose, and that
this punk didn't deserve it. His first punch
slammed the man in the kidney enough to make
him stagger and cry out. He smashed his boot
toe into an ankle, then spun the figure around
and caught him a stiff hook up into the guts.

His victim dry-heaved and his eyes bugged
out. Kyle took that as a sign, and pasted his left
fist into the right eye, knowing it would bruise
his knuckles and not caring. He followed with a
right across the jaw, and a symbolic kick to the
groin. He had near eight inches on the man,
probably fifty pounds, and was in top shape. The
snaggle-toothed little cretin tumbled back and
struck his head on the wall and collapsed unconscious, broken and bleeding in the dust and grit.

"*Tsanga ye?*" he asked to the shifting form on
the ground. How are you feeling? "*Ye doctor*

larem?" He knew it was atrociously ungrammatical, but it was the best he could do.

A woman's voice replied. He caught "okay," "Allah" and "You (something) good." Then she continued in accented but clear English, "Are you English?"

Wade hissed behind him, "Dude, this isn't our fight!" and he laid a restraining arm back.

"We speak English," he said. It wasn't as if they could really deny it, but there was no need to admit a home country. There were Aussies and Brits here, not to mention a lot of Indian and South African traders who spoke English. It wasn't much of a cover, but it wasn't an admission.

"Thank you," she said simply. "I am grateful to you."

"What was that about?" he asked. He got a look at her now. Her face was red over the right eye, and would swell. Her lip was cut slightly, and had an ebon drop clinging. Other than that she was disheveled and dirty. Her attacker was still unconscious, though he wiggled slightly and moaned, so was obviously alive. That was Kyle's only concern.

"I am a schoolteacher," she said. "Some of the more . . . conservateef immigrants and refugees object to me teaching modern things. I've been harassed before, but never attacked." He recognized her then. It was the woman they'd seen in class the day before.

"Do you need a doctor?" he asked. She was rising now, and he gave her a hand up.

"I have only bruises," she said. "Besides, most doctors won't touch a woman, and I have no man to allow it."

It took a moment for that to sink in. If she wasn't married or a daughter of someone, it would be hard for her to do anything. The Taliban-imposed customs required permission from a man, and without that she was not human, not to be dealt with. Kyle got angry all over again. The Taliban were officially gone, but their stink remained. Even across the border in Pakistan.

"We can find you a doctor," he insisted. He wasn't sure where, but he'd find one if he had to jam a pistol up someone's nose.

"Really, I am okay," she said. "I am bruised and sore, nothing else."

A scheme began to form in Kyle's brain. "Do you speak other languages?" he asked.

"Yes," she agreed. "Hindustani, Pashto, Dari, and French. I went to college in France. Before the Taliban I was a professor of economics. Now all I can do is teach children, but I will do that no matter the beatings. They must be taught!"

The shock was getting to her at last. She was babbling and shaking. That was actually a good sign.

"We need a translator. Could you help us?" he asked.

Wade was covering the mouth of the alley, but overheard. "Oh, no way!" he hissed. "You're going to get us killed!"

"But it's perfect!" Kyle argued. "As a local woman, no one will notice her. And with a woman along, we're less obviously an aggressive force. She can help us get set up, then we can give her some money or something to help with the school."

"Translate?" she asked. "Don't you have a translator?"

Kyle agreed that it was an odd situation. "He died, apparently, before we got here, and our company couldn't find another one in time."

"I see," she said, slightly frostily. "An odd company that is so eager to do things that it can't wait for a translator." She sounded amused but disconcerted.

"Very odd," he agreed. "Will you do it?"

"For how long?" she asked. "I'll need to let the parents know, and find someone to teach, and someone to protect them. You'll need to pay for that."

"We can pay, we're on an expense account," he said. He wasn't sure how much she had in mind, but it couldn't be much in American money.

"Very well," she said. "I am Nasima."

"I'm Kyle Monroe," he said. He was about to stick out his hand to take hers, but realized she hadn't offered it. Instead, she bowed very slightly, eyes cast down. Right. No touching of women at all.

"Wade Curtis," Wade said, and she bowed to him, too.

"Can you meet us at the inn tomorrow morning at nine?" Kyle asked. "And we'll head out from there." He gave her the name and street.

"I can," she said. "Don't mention me in public, though. Modesty is essential, especially with my position."

"Sure, we try to be sensitive to local customs," he agreed. "Can we help you home?" he asked.

"Thank you, but no," she said firmly. "I must not be seen with men unless properly escorted. Especially now. I will see you tomorrow, Kyle and Wade."

"*Shpa dey pe khair,*" he said.

"Goodnight to you, too, dudes," she said, smiling. The effect was spoiled by the blood on her lip.

After she left, Wade said, "I think it's a mistake."

"Wade, we need a translator. She's available," Kyle said.

"I'm sure if we ask around we can find a man who won't be so obvious, and who won't bother the locals. How did we meet her? Oh, yes, she was being beaten by a man for the crime of existing." The sarcasm was clear in his voice.

"So we'll cover for her. It doesn't seem to be a big deal in the cities, it's just the hicks who are the problem."

"Yes," Wade said, "and it's those hicks we have to deal with."

"Well, for now, she's who we have."

8

THE ARGUMENT WAS IN REMISSION, THOUGH not gone the next morning. They walked across the street for breakfast, not sure if she'd actually be there. She might have decided to simply avoid them.

But Nasima was there, and cleaner than the night before. Her dress was vertical stripes of black and purple, with a black-edged head scarf printed in geometric reds and yellows. Whatever the requirements of dress here, they didn't let themselves be drab. Her black hair was clean and hung over her shoulders past the cloth, and she rose to meet them, bowing slightly.

They nodded back and sat. With her was a man, fiftyish and lean. His hair was largely gray, bald on top, and all of it kept short, including his beard and moustache. "This is Kamgar," she said. "He owns the school."

"*Assalam u alaikum,*" Kyle said with a nod.

"*Wa alaikum u ssalam,*" he replied with a broad, friendly grin.

"I will need money," she said, "and you must pay Kamgar, or some of these people will think I am a prostitute."

"Right," Kyle said. "How much?"

"Five hundred American dollars," she said. "Or afghanis or rupees to equal it." She looked ready to defend the demand.

Considering the standard of living here, it was a high rate, but reasonable for professional consulting, Kyle decided, especially in light of the risk involved. And hell, Uncle Sam could afford it.

"Sure," he said, and waved his hands a bit. "But let us pretend to make small talk first. Can I get you some breakfast?" he asked in English, pointing at food and making an open-armed gesture to the table.

Kamgar agreed, grinning comfortably. Everyone was as they said they were, and they all relaxed. Kyle was still glad to be armed. There was no way to know who people were around here, with assorted tribes, the war with India to the east, Afghan refugees, black market dealers . . .

Shortly, they had all eaten, cash had been exchanged, Allah praised, and a letter provided introducing Nasima as the servant of the school's owner, working for the two Americans and an honorable Muslima. She should be treated as a lady and given leeway to speak for the foreign guests. It seemed professional enough and clear for the local customs, and everyone was happy. It didn't quite seem like Kyle was renting a mule.

They walked back across the street to the hotel, Nasima following. She was short, Kyle realized, maybe five feet two. A slip of a woman by Western standards, maybe a hundred pounds. More of the poor diet, he presumed. But it hadn't affected her mind, if she had a PhD in economics from a Western university, nor her looks. She was a gorgeous combination of Indian, Caucasian, and Persian with a hint of Chinese. Her almond eyes were deep and mesmerizing.

Khushal was waiting for them. "He's one of our party, and watches our gear," Kyle said.

"I understand," she said. At once, she introduced herself and chattered away. Khushal looked confused, then a bit disturbed. He replied slowly.

"He says he's glad for a translator. But I feel he's not thrilled with the idea. His father is in charge?"

"Well, that depends," Kyle said. "I'm in charge, he's the local guide for our project. I do take his advice."

"I see. By the way, what is your project here?" she asked.

"It's a military mission," he said. He'd decided he had to tell her that much. "We're looking for some specific information for a study."

"I understand," she said. It was clear she

wasn't going to leave it at that, but would for the time being.

A few minutes later, there was a familiar knock at the door. Wade nodded, Khushal opened it, and Qalzai came in with Bait, his assistant. At once, they spoke. Qalzai looked up at Nasima, at Kyle and Wade, and started to speak.

He made it clear he wasn't happy with a woman along. Nasima translated easily for him. "He says I'm a woman and have no place in the battles of men."

"Well, tell him if he can find us a good English speaker, I'll leave you behind, but I'm not doing this mission unless I've got someone who can help us," Kyle replied. What was the problem? It seemed to be more than the gender issue. They seemed uncomfortable that he was showing initiative.

Nasima turned back and rapid-fired Pashto at Qalzai. She held her body so as to indicate she was the poor, meek feminine underling he expected, but there was steel in her voice. She'd play the local game to get the job done and teach her kids, but it was only a game to her. Kyle was developing a lot of respect for this young lady. There was no way in hell he'd play the slave for these people, or for anyone else.

He realized that she'd have a much easier life in one of the larger cities, which were much more modern and Westernized, and that she liked where she was and what she was doing.

His musing was interrupted when Nasima turned back and said, "He says I can come along until the last part of the mission and then must stay behind, and that you are responsible for me. The word he used isn't 'father' or 'husband' but more like 'keeper.'"

"Isn't that so thoughtful and modern of him?" Kyle muttered. "Agreed," he said. "So let's stock up on food and supplies and get to it."

"Very well. Kyle?" she asked, "what is it we are to do?" She'd already asked, but he'd clearly been evasive.

"Oh, I'm leaving that one to you, boss," Wade said, chuckling nervously.

Feeling a flush of embarrassment, Kyle said, "First, we're going to find someone."

"And then?" she asked, looking curious and distrustful.

"And then I'm going to shoot him," he said. He realized he had some defiance in his voice. What about it, lady?

She paused for only a moment. "Very well. So long as I know."

They were saddled back up within the hour, and rolling west. Nasima sat in back on one of the spare tires. The others introduced themselves, gave her nods of acknowledgment that were a mix of surly, friendly, and gallant, and then kept quiet.

The hills would continue through the area around Quetta, a sizeable town, where they hoped to get some intel. They'd avoid the town proper and hit the outskirts. There was no need to court official notice by the government.

It was very disturbing, Kyle thought, that Qalzai was their only source of information. They had nothing current from American sources. Who had ultimately planned this mission, and what were they basing it on?

Sighing, he leaned back in the cramped seat and tried to relax. Hopefully, it would all make sense afterward.

He wasn't really asleep, more just zoned, when he heard what was obviously a curse from Qalzai, then from the others.

"What?" he asked.

Qalzai steered the truck off the rocky road in a hurry, shouted something, of which the soldiers caught, "*Lar!*" Quickly. There wasn't really anywhere to hide, the hills steep and straight, the growth low. Kyle moved for what concealment there was, trying not to jump to frightening conclusions.

They were urged out, and Shamsuddin, Mirza, and Ajmal joined them. All their gear was tossed over the side, everyone gathered up an armful, and they ran for cover in the rocky terrain. As soon as they were clear, Qalzai took off, tires spinning on the shingly surface. Nasima was with him.

"What the hell?" Kyle asked.

"I think," Wade said, "I saw the edge of a tank over the next ridge. Might be a convoy."

"Ah, hell," Kyle said. "Last thing we need."

He could hear a rumbling and the clank of road wheels. The occasional revving diesel confirmed that it was a line of military vehicles.

Mirza was saying what was obviously "Quiet!" as they ducked low behind rock.

Kyle looked around. Wade had the .50 and the M-4 in addition to his ruck. Kyle had his ruck and someone's old Russian rig and an AK. Shamsuddin had Kyle's briefcase and laptop. Ajmal was invisible behind a pile of valises and bags. It appeared everything threatening was accounted for.

They sat there silently, not daring to speak, while the convoy rattled past. Qalzai and Khushal had driven on, with Bait, Qalendar, and the others. And Naslma. Kyle assumed they intended to return after the convoy was gone, but still felt very lonely all of a sudden.

The convoy was a tank, a couple of M-113s, four cargo haulers, and two jeeplike technical vehicles. The troops were professional, but bored, and apparently hadn't seen fit to stop Qalzai. Of course, finding two Americans along would likely have changed that.

Once it had passed, they all sat facing each other, waiting quietly until the valve clatter of the truck returned, and Qalzai's voice called out. They rose, trooped down the hill lugging their gear, and clambered back aboard.

They rumbled along in the cramped vehicle for several more hours. It was near dark when they could see the glow of a city ahead. It wasn't bright, but it was definitely civilization. It was something familiar to Kyle and Wade, and helped them relax.

Quetta was large enough to have modern conveniences, including hotels. It also had an Army base. They detoured wide around it, with a glimpse of a perfect turquoise lake in the middle of desert mountains to the east. Once clear around to the west of the city, they sought a smaller town, Bemana'abad.

While small, it was modern enough. There were modern signs, paved roads, and some light industry. There was working electricity and lights, and quite a few more cars, though most were old and rattly and animal power was still very common. Small stores were scattered along the street as they headed in, mixed with houses and small industrial shops. There was a major marketplace, with gorgeous tile work in blue over the arches and columns of obvious Islamic architecture. The blue was lapis lazuli, which was native to the area and not many other places. Street vendors pushed their way through the evening crowds. As they drove through, Kyle thought longingly about a proper shower and clean clothes. But they had to blend in, so he killed the idea.

"Let's spend some money for good will," Kyle decided on impulse. "Qalzai, *ghuaram kheh otel.*" Nice hotel. He flashed the corners of a handful of rupees, keeping it low and discreet. "Was that correct?" he asked Nasima.

"Ah, hoo. Sta na shukria!" Qalzai said, all grins. The rest of them lit up, too.

"No," said Nasima, "but I understood your intention. Money translates universally."

They were a sight. While remote, Bemana'abad was a town, it had a government and business. They were hillbillies in Des Moines, and looked very out of place. And weapons were not encouraged here. Still, they made it inside, Kyle paid for two to a room, with a room at the end for Nasima, and they headed down a long bricked walk to their lodgings.

The water was cold, but clean, the heater lacking the capacity for a large crowd. There was a lamp in the room. No TV, of course, but there was a radio, all in languages the two didn't speak. The facilities were shared with the entire hallway, and were typically Eastern. But the mattresses were clean and modern, and Kyle and Wade were both able to stretch out, sleep unfettered, and their only sop to security was to sleep with loaded pistols and the M-4 between them, there being only one bed. "Just don't grip that trigger late at night," Kyle joked.

"It won't be the trigger I grip, trust me," Wade replied. But he pointed the muzzles at the foot of the bed, rather than the head, just in case.

The next morning they were all much refreshed. Khushal sat down with them at the laptop, while Qalzai stood behind them. Nasima arrived, and they left the door open for reasons of "modesty."

Nasima looked furtively around to make sure no one was in the hallway, moved in close and said quietly, her eye on Khushal's back, "The man whose name in English is what you use to fish is an Afghan, not Pakistani. He moved here a few years ago."

"Okay?" Wade prompted while looking at the computer. "Hell," he said. "Not working." He examined the case, which had a huge ding. As it had been in a nylon carrying case during the rush out of the truck, it had been one hell of a smack.

Kyle sighed and jiggled the battery. He tried the external power. Rebooting, sliding drives out and back. "Near as I can tell, the hard drive is damaged," he said. "No way to get that fixed here."

"Or rather," Wade said, "there might be, but not quickly, and it would make it *very* obvious that two Americans are here, and all the data on the disk would be unsecure while a tech looked at it."

"Right. So we can't fix it here. Dammit, must have been when we bailed out of the truck. Was it that rough a landing?"

"Oh, yes. We hit the ground pretty hard," Wade said.

"Hell. So we smash the drive and dispose of the pieces . . . okay, Nasima, what about that man?" Fish with Bait. Right. And she didn't want to say his name where it might be overheard.

"I don't trust him," she said. "He's not part of

the clan, and he's very condescending, even by local standards."

"That's disturbing," Wade said, while doing another check of the laptop, just in case. "We'll keep it in mind. Anything specific?"

"No," she said. "But I have a feeling he's not right. I know it sounds silly."

"Not at all," Kyle said. "We work that way, too. Thanks for the input."

"You are most welcome, and do be careful," she said.

They tried to hash out what details they could. They were waiting here for more info, apparently, no more than a day, then they would go west again. They had an approximate area for their target, and Qalzai was sure that was the right place.

"Well," said Kyle, "it's only money, we might as well stay right here until we hear more. We can afford it."

"Sure," Wade said. "I think we might have been a bit obvious when we showed up, but staying won't hurt anything, and might give the impression we're U.N. types or reporters. Next time, let's bring cameras to use as cover."

"Good idea," Kyle agreed. He thought for a moment and said, "Very good idea, actually. We should suggest that."

"Let's suggest they send an entire squad, or better intel, or just bomb the hell out of somewhere instead," Wade said.

"True," Kyle nodded. They were discreet, certainly. But he wasn't sure how effective they could be. And two men alone in hostile territory was still bringing back memories he didn't want.

"Whatever," he said finally. "Let's get Khushal to sit the gear, and take a look around. We need to get acclimated, and not just be trained monkeys for these guys." Dammit, he wanted more intel. Nasima was helpful, but it still felt as if he was a hireling to the locals, not a soldier with an independent command.

"There is that," Wade agreed. "Okay, let's do it."

Khushal was agreeable, and they promised to bring him back a Coca-Cola. He might be a militia fighter, but he was also a teenager, and travel into this part of the country was an adventure to him. He had a small camera he'd bought earlier that day, and intended to record the mission. Both Qalzai and Kyle had cautioned him not to take photos of any of their people or gear, only of the surrounding areas.

The two men dressed in cleaned clothes, had Khushal help them wrap their lungees and drop the tails across their faces, and headed out into the nightlife of Baluchistan Province.

The city had a liveliness to it. Even late at night with the vendors gone, there were tea houses open, and restaurants. Parties here and there celebrated weddings or births, some buildings decorated with colored lights like those for Christmas trees.

It was becoming familiar. That brought its own dangers, of course. Familiarity breeds contempt, and there were hundreds of cultural cues the two of them would miss. Much like tourists learn to feel safe in New York, London, or Havana, only to be caught by a mugger or gang by missing obvious local hints. Still, the look around helped them acclimate further. They were trained enough to stay cautious.

Kyle decided he'd never acclimate to the beard. It was still itching. Sighing, he scratched at it as they walked.

9

THE NEXT MORNING, BAIT AND QALZAI
knocked on their door early, excited. Soon,
the entire clan was gathered around. Nasima arrived at a run, in a long skirt and sweater in dark
brown. Practical for the terrain. "They say we
are ready," she said. "We head northeast again,
very close to the border, and into lower hills. The
man we seek is in a village there."

"Sounds good," Kyle said. "Wade, call and tell
them."

"Right," Wade nodded. He dialed a number
and reported in, location, destination, current
conditions.

They loaded up the truck again, and rolled out.
They did, in fact, look like yokels, even in this
small town. It was obvious to all that they were
poor farm folk on some kind of errand. Good,
Kyle thought. Better to be thought hicks than
killers. There'd been a lot of creepy and scary
happenings so far, but no real pucker factor.

He hoped it stayed that way.

The ride took all that day. On the plus side, they'd bought a cooler in town, and filled it with fresh food, including apples, bananas—imported at some expense—and sandwiches rolled in the local bread. Everyone was much happier, and grinned at their guests as crumbs fell from their beards.

"They say you can join their missions anytime," Nasima said, "if you arrange the hotels and food."

"Tell them they're welcome, and we're glad to be able to do them a small favor for all the help they're giving us," he said.

After the meal, they resumed the aching, bouncing ride. It was near dark when they stopped and pulled behind some concealing scrub. At once, the men emptied out the cab and laid cloths over the windows.

"I will sleep here," Nasima said. "They're being polite."

"No problem," Kyle agreed. It did make sense socially. He just hoped they didn't need to leave in a hurry, with gear left piled in the bed to fall out. "Can you ask Qalzai for a mission update?"

"Yes," she said, and turned and chattered. Qalzai deferred to Bait, who seemed to leer. He had odd expressions, sneers, snarls, and leers, that didn't match his pleasant demeanor. Or pleasant enough to the Americans. Nasima apparently wasn't finding him so. But she turned back and said, "We're in the area. We will look for him tomorrow," she said.

"Got it, and thanks. Wade, call up and update them. We'll let them know after we get the kill."

"On it," he said, whipping out the phone. He was through and back off in moments.

As they prepared a sleeping area, the air chilling quickly in the dark, Wade asked, "What I want to know is why they need us? They're brave enough, have the weapons and intel. Why can't they wax this jerk?"

"I dunno," Kyle replied, pondering. "Maybe Uncle Sam wants the credit. Maybe they're afraid of some feud. Or maybe they can't get close enough for a good shot. It is unusual, though."

" 'Ours not to reason why,' " Wade said.

"Right. Time to sleep."

They were up before dawn, and patrolling on foot. Tired from little sleep, weighted under their rucks, the two men cursed silently as they followed the locals into the "lower" hills. Kyle and Wade were trained and experienced, but these people moved like mountain goats. In short order, they were wheezing and huffing.

"I'm going to cheat," Kyle said to Wade. Turning to Nasima, he said, "Call a break. We need to report in."

Everyone squatted down to wait, while Wade took his own sweet time about making the call, and reported to the AWACS on station that they were commencing their recon of the target. After that, he faked it for a few moments, asking about Yankee scores to a dead phone. Nasima grinned but didn't say anything, and after catching their breath, they stood to continue.

Their breath steamed out in front, as if puffed from locomotives. It was dark, in the forties, and while they had lots of experience hiking, it was harder in local garb over terrain that was so unfamiliar.

They broke at sunrise, and brewed tea over a small British trioxane stove that might have been fifty years old. Kyle and Wade were glad of it, and wrapped their hands around their canteen cups. It was tasty tea, with sugar and some undefined spice. Cardamom, perhaps. Qalendar was a gourmet. It refreshed and revived them, and a few nibbles of sweetened bread helped immensely.

Then they were back to it, as the sun bled over the hills and dripped down on them. Ghostly wisps of mist arose from the dew, and burned off as the temperature rose.

Bait led out in front, looking for signs of patrols and other threats. Qalzai brought up the rear. Nasima and the snipers were safely ensconced in the middle, which did relieve some of the worries, of loose rocks, discovery, and other threats.

They scrambled up and down slopes, across old, wind-weathered sheets of rock, and past jutting shards. As the sun rose, it became warm enough for them to unbutton their coats. Then it got warm and sweaty. The wool and cotton breathed, but still insulated. That was fine when it was near freezing, but not above fifty degrees while exercising hard.

Straps cut into their shoulders, adding aches to the mix. The rigs were comfortable certainly, but seventy pounds plus each was a staggering load. They were glad to have left the extraneous gear at the truck.

"Doing okay, buddy?" Kyle asked between breaths.

"Passable. You?" he replied.

"Yeah." It was all the reply Kyle could manage.

They ate dried goat en route, and Kyle passed around the last three MREs. He still wasn't keen about sharing germs with this crowd—they all dug their spoons into the same package—as none of them had bathed recently, and didn't seem worried about it in general. But they were all in the same unit, so it was good for morale. The dried fruit and gorilla cookies went over well, and the coffee was shared at lunch. They were all hunkered in a small ravine against discovery. Though if they were sighted, it was crap for a defensive position. Bait walked off during lunch, waving as he did so. They finished without him, and the men lit cigarettes.

Bait returned within the hour and conferred with Qalzai. Nasima translated from Qalzai, "The man we want is in this camp. We'll have to wait for a good time to get a shot."

"Excellent," Kyle said, a feeling in his stomach like that of a giant rat scrabbling. This was what they'd come for. So why did it seem so problematic?

Probably because there hadn't been any problems.

It still could be a setup, to embarrass America, or to put them in a bad political position. Kyle realized he should have asked more questions Stateside—how had this mission come about, and who had set it up?

"He says he'll take you up there in time for the shot," Nasima said, interrupting his thoughts.

"Tell him I need to reconnoiter the area first, so we know what our escape routes look like."

They argued over a plan. Kyle found it annoying. While these men were more local to the area than he, he was the professional. They didn't seem to grasp that a good escape was dependent upon knowing the local map, surface, and features. They actively fought against preparation, saying they were worried about discovery. Kyle told them that was the point of having Wade and him along; concealment was what they did. It took nearly an hour to get the point across. Apparently, the local method of fighting was to take cover, throw as much lead as possible until one side or the other quit, and leave. Their bravery and dedication were excellent. They weren't strong on tactics or discipline.

Luckily it was a warm day, over sixty degrees. Considering the altitude of nearly a half mile, and the fall season, it was a blessing. Of course, it was also of use to their target. Kyle preferred cold, wet weather, mist, and calm air. But you worked with what you had.

While the debate took place, Wade slipped off to make a map anyway. Khushal went with him, grinning. Kyle saw it from the corner of his eye, and smiled inwardly. The man was a pro who needed only a hint. It was a pleasure to work with him.

But Kyle also needed that information himself, first hand. Finally, he got them to agree that they had to do it his way. He opened the case and assembled the Barrett while he spoke, hoping the sight of the massive rifle would encourage them.

Nasima argued his point while he turned to Wade and discussed their observations. They picked three routes down the mountain they felt they could handle. "We'll each take a different one up," Wade said. "You on one, me on another, Qalzai on a third. According to the map," he shuffled through the sheaf of them until he found the one they wanted, "there's a saddle right about there," he pointed up the slope, "that should give us a good position."

Grumbling, they split into three pairs, Kyle and Khushal, Wade and Mirza, Qalzai and Bait. Qalzai could read well enough to follow a map, and had a watch. They each tightened gear, dumped excess equipment, and prepared to ascend the rough slope, Kyle lugging the long mass of the Barrett in its tough bag. Nasima returned to the truck with the rest.

Kyle contented himself during the rough scramble with the thought that the mission was about to reach completion. Shortly, they'd be overlooking a camp and Kyle would take his shot. They'd extract quickly from a good range, find a place to recross the border, or call a chopper and be done with it.

The mission couldn't be this easy, he thought. On second thought, the terrain was anything but easy. They constantly slipped on dust-covered shelves. They were sweating and panting. It was dry, and the sun cooked moisture out of them as sweat and the wind sucked it off their skin. It kept them cool now that they'd removed their coats, but greased them with dust and parched their throats.

He was having second thoughts the whole way. Good thoughts, then bad. He took several slow, measured breaths to refresh himself. This was a bitch of a climb.

A big part of it was the scrubby terrain. Almost any other terrain like it would have tree roots and such he could grip. Here, it was scrub with very shallow, thready roots, and rock. He was glad they'd split up, and he hoped the others had an easier time. They'd need a fast descent against incoming fire.

When he finally reached the saddle and peeked over, he could see Wade already there. Or rather, he couldn't. Wade was a shapeless lump of dun and dusty burlap in his ghillie suit. Kyle crawled out farther and saw Qalzai's element, too. He was last. That was fine, that meant the other routes were easier. He started dragging his own camouflage out.

Wade said, "We'll take my route down. Easy descent with a gully and lots of grip."

"Glad to hear it," Kyle said, panting. He sucked down some more water.

"No problem. And I found a spot to shoot."

"Even better," Kyle agreed. "Show me."

Wade had found a fine location. It was just below the military crest, in a dip between two rocks, and had a panoramic view out across the plain. The sun was to their left, so there'd be no reflection off a scope. All in all, it looked good.

And two thousand meters away, in a long, lazy arc, was the camp they sought.

"That is a long-ass shot," Kyle commented. At that range, he'd be shooting a two-meter circle. Getting the human body in that two-meter circle was going to take several quick, precise shots and some luck. Otherwise, they'd have to extract and do it again.

"Will be," Wade said. "Are you up to it?"

"I think so," he said, squinting and taking in the whole scene. "Good weapon, good rest, plenty of time. But we've got to get him to hold still long enough, or in a vehicle I can nail."

"Right, so let's set up our exfiltration."

The two looked back along Wade's route. "If we're going down there, we've got good cover. But we'll need supporting fire in case of disasters."

"I see a spot," Kyle said.

Qalzai was quietly jabbering away. Wade shook his head, "I don't think he understands the concept still."

Growling in frustration, though under his breath so their host wouldn't be offended, Kyle turned with what he hoped was an eager look on his face.

"We aren't just going to blaze away," he told Qalzai. "*Delta intazar?*" he said, trying to say "wait." "*Ghuarum arama loya tiga.*" That was as close as he could get. *I'm looking for a quiet rock.*

As they started reconnoitering the area, Qalzai seemed to understand. He pointed out several well-hidden areas. Though that wasn't quite what the two snipers wanted. Qalzai looked confused as they seemed to retreat slightly from the area, along the route they'd be departing.

"There," Wade said. "Easy to reach and solid cover."

"Good," Kyle said. "And we can keep it under fire from there."

"Right. Now to explain to our host. Any ideas?"

"I think so," Kyle said. He turned to Qalzai and indicated several areas in turn. "*Yau negdey loya tiga. Yau porta korner. Dua pe manz ke.*" One at the rock, one above the bend, and two inside the cut in the cliff. It was amazing, he reflected, how much one could convey with fewer than fifty words.

He couldn't remember the phrase he wanted, and the closest in the ratty, dog-eared phrase book in his pocket was, "*Lutfan lag saber waka.*" Please wait a while. We need to be patient.

Qalzai seemed to be with the program now, and indicated the lower positions to the three men. He would take the nearest. Bait was apparently unhappy at being at the bottom. He wanted to see. Sighing, Kyle relented. "I think he's got some kind of grudge," he said to Wade.

"Seems like."

They snuggled close to the rocks and looked through binoculars and scopes. Bait had an old Russian pair that had seen better days, but whose optics were still good, even with a scratch or two. Kyle used the Schmidt binoculars, Wade had the spotting scope.

They waited in the sun for six hours, watching and learning. Kyle and Wade switched off on the scope to gather intel. They kept a log of comings and goings and drew a map. They estimated weather and atmospheric pressure, calculated what trajectory the bullet would describe, and what the sight picture should look like.

The camp was all men, so it was a militia operation. The tents were arranged in a box around a central area. That central area had a review stand. All the men were armed with AKs, and there were a few RPK machine guns, rocket-propelled grenades, and a mortar in evidence. Wade thought he saw what might be a recoilless rifle stashed under an awning. The vehicles were pickups, four-wheel drive, and two of them mounted machine guns, Russian 12.7mm heavies. The men moved around in such a way as to suggest they planned to move within the day. There was no immediate activity, but the vehicles were being checked, and some packing was taking place.

"So we wait more," Kyle said. "If they plan to move, they'll rally around the vehicles at some point. And if he sits and has to wait for a driver, even better." That would be an ideal shot, in fact.

Or what was happening now. The men pulled the trucks back from the cleared area, and gathered on foot. That left one truck with a clear bed. They formed a rough semicircle around it, and one man climbed up to stand erect and address them.

"That's him, he says," Wade confirmed.

"The tall guy in the blue turban with the brown coat?" Kyle asked. He wanted to be sure. The man didn't look a lot like the photos he'd been shown, but at this range, clothes and a beard change could easily mask features. He was clear enough in the scope, just small and distant.

There was another exchange and Kyle heard, "Yes, man, shoot," among it.

"Dammit, are we really sure?" he asked. He didn't like this at all. Something seemed wrong. He kept his eye to his scope and his stance easy and ready to shoot. If this was the wrong guy, they'd have a fight for nothing, possibly screw things up worse than they already were. If it was the right guy and he didn't shoot, they might not get another.

"Yes, do it," Wade said. "They're sure that's him and I showed them through the scope."

"Okay," Kyle said. He sighed, got as comfortable as he could, and zoned into his shooting trance. You had to trust the other guys to know their job, even if you thought they were idiots. If for no other reason than you couldn't do their job for them. He steadied down, aligned the reticle and calculated lead by eye. Breathe . . . squeeze . . . *Blam!*

Flight time was over a second, sound would take three seconds. There was time to take several shots, and Kyle did. In an instant, he had the reticle aligned again and shot dead center of mass on his target, then again, align and shoot, then three more rounds through the space filled by his body just to make sure. As he squeezed that last one, the first round hit.

Even at that range, the .50 packed more punch than most cartridges intended for cape buffalo or elephant. On a human figure it was overkill. The second round that hit the torso and the one that caught a waving wrist were redundant. He was blown into three pieces, all hanging together by bits of flesh, and collapsed in a gory heap.

His followers, troops, cheerleaders, whatever the hell they were, wasted no time in reacting.

They scattered, ducked, and began spraying with their AKs in seconds. One of them ran over, took a look at the shattered body, and squinted uphill. He yelled something undiscernible, but it was clearly something about large-caliber weapon and the ridge. "Right, let's move!" Kyle said. He'd seen enough. Kill was good, reaction was fast. It was time to leave posthaste.

The Barrett was a bitch to lug. Kyle took it, banging his knee hard as he hefted it and singeing hair off the back of his hand. He stuffed it into the long drag case, not worrying about any possible heat damage. Wade grabbed the scope. As they passed Qalzai, and Bait, the two fell in behind them. They passed Khushal and Mirza, who brought up the rear.

The locals were in hot pursuit, though. While they were well out of range still, that didn't stop fire from the Russian machine guns from ricocheting past them. Then someone opened up with one of the recoilless rifles. It was loud, potent, and blew chips from the hill.

Luckily, they were heading down fast, and the fire was well above them. But if anyone made it through a cut in the ridge, they'd have superior position to shoot down at them. Kyle felt an itch between his shoulders that he knew was psychosomatic. He was scared even if he didn't want to admit it aloud. Inside, however, he knew he was terrified. Bosnia all over again. The itch became a tickle, then an empty, exposed feeling all over. He slipped and the rifle landed atop him, knocking his breath out. He swore, stood carefully, despite a burning sensation in his thigh from sliding in gravel, and continued, breathing deeply and deliberately to avoid doing it from panic.

The run downhill was a roller-coaster ride without the roller coaster. As they hit the cut that would take them down, a mortar shell exploded behind them. The explosion rocked them with a *bang!* and threw rock around, the shockwave tugging at their breath.

Kyle swore as a rain of stinging pebbles came down, accompanied by a cloud of dust. The rifle was long and clunky and didn't fit well between the walls of the crevice they were descending. It was straight, but straight is a relative term when speaking of fissures in cliffs.

But he made it. They skidded and skittered over the sandy surface, suffering contusions and abrasions. Kyle skinned a knuckle and swore, banged his head and swore again. Then they were on a spreading slope and running fast, digging their feet in as brakes.

It would have been good, Kyle thought, to have had vehicles closer. But this would have to do. It was to be a high-speed sneak and exfiltrate across rough terrain.

The fire stopped for the time being, but would resume as soon as their pursuers hit the high ground. It would be wise to use that time to get away. Not hidden; knowing they were there would cause a search that would lead to discovery. This wasn't a fight they could win standing up, it was a fight to run from. They'd already made their kill.

For ten minutes, they scrabbled across the ground in the failing light. Dark would be good, though they couldn't assume the enemy didn't have night vision as well. Heedless of throats chilled by drafts of air, burning lungs, and aching guts, they pushed on. Any distance now was a good thing; there was little cover and no support to rally.

Then the enemy cleared the ridge and were shooting at them.

The fire was grossly inaccurate, but there was a sufficient volume of it. While beyond effective range, it was shot from a clear, elevated position. Kyle had thought himself worn out and unable to go faster, but suddenly found a burst of energy he hadn't expected. Incoming fire does that to a person, he thought, as a round cracked off a rock ten meters away. He was glad at that moment that Nasima wasn't along. Small and untrained, she'd be a liability and none too safe. He wondered why he was thinking about that now, as he grasped another ledge and swung over and generally down. He was still half exposed, but it would help.

He saw movement, realized they were bunching up and making an inviting target for an area effect weapon. He was about to say so when Wade shouted, *"Shindel!"*, scatter, which was not in the phrase book, but had been on the CD-

ROM of useful military phrases. Glancing around, the others fanned out and staggered their line.

Ahead, they could see the sharp bluff that led back to the road. They were safe, as long as they could make it there. Again urging speed into his burning thighs, Kyle swallowed between breaths, the spit cold and hard in his throat after the extreme effort.

They took the ledge far too fast. Wade was just ahead of him and slipped, grazing an elbow and abrading through his shirt. Blood seeped through whitened, raw skin, but he cursed a single word and kept on. Kyle slowed for that spot, and avoided injury with the exception of a toe jammed inside his boot. It was uncomfortable, but not really painful, especially in light of the dings to knuckles and knees, the strained shoulders and rasping throat he already had.

Shortly, they were tumbling to the ground, leaping into the back of the trucks, and Qalzai and Khushal were gassing the engines. They took off amidst roostertails of dust, heedless of the obvious sign they were leaving. Kyle yelled, *"Wro wro!"*, slow, and they did, but the panic had done its damage. It would be obvious where they'd started from.

The only thing to do now was to get onto a road and drive fast, far, and out of range. Then they could call in for extraction.

They were done.

"How was the shoot?" Kyle asked. He knew, but wanted another opinion.

"Clean, fast, and solid," Wade said. "A bit high, likely due to the reduced atmospheric pressure at this altitude."

"Yeah, I thought about dropping the aim a minute or so."

"It was fine. Clean kill. So scratch one asshole and let's get out of here."

"Yeah," Kyle agreed. Over. Done. No one hurt. Yet.

Despite the immediate fire, there was little pursuit. They drove insanely for fifteen minutes, but there was no visible threat after that.

"We should go as far as we can before stopping," Kyle said. "Tell them, Nasima." He was again glad she'd stayed behind, because he knew he would have worried about her.

"Okay," she said, and relayed the message.

Qalzai agreed, and they drove, while Mirza capped off a few bursts at their increasingly distant pursuers. Or maybe he was doing it in defiance, like ceremonial fireworks.

After another ten minutes, Wade said, "Relax, Kyle."

"Huh? Oh," he said, realizing he was still white-knuckling the cab and holding his breath. He let out a sigh. "We got away with it."

"Yeah, done," Wade said. He seemed elated, but was as ragged as Kyle. They swapped glances, and began sorting gear and packing their camouflage away.

* * *

They stopped for the night in yet another small farm that was linked by blood somehow to Qalzai's family. This one had an outer wall that had once been sections of building, and an inner courtyard that had once been a smaller house. It was on a dark green-mottled hillside with scattered sheep, and the oddest-looking goats Kyle had ever seen. Their asses stuck out about a foot past the hind legs, like the tailcone on a plane. He wasn't sure if it was a genetic trait, or a medical condition, but he decided he wouldn't eat goat here.

He needn't have been concerned. As they arrived, greeted by dozens of people he wouldn't remember, amid cheers and shouts and soon dancing and instruments, he was handed a bowl of curried lentils and rice. It was tasty enough, with fat, crisp lentils in a sauce with some vegetables, and rice pilaf underneath. Though he longed for meat, he avoided the goat. They were served naan bread to dip into the bowls, and served Coca-Cola, goat's milk, and tea. He passed on the milk, decided a Coke was in order, even if it did have caffeine.

Some man started to ask a question. It seemed to be a standard, "So, how was the mission?" inquiry, with a big curious grin breaking his beard. Qalzai made surreptitious shushing motions, laid an arm over his shoulder, and led him away, waving an arm and talking.

They got some odd looks, and Kyle chalked it

up to them being foreign. But eventually, he decided the stares were more than that. They weren't threatening, but they were not just curious. And some of the grins looked familiar. He'd seen them in high school when someone had staged an elaborate prank.

He might be overreacting, though, he thought. He'd be ready in case of some local ritual or hazing, but he'd be cautious. It would be bad manners to respond to a local jape with gunfire.

"I think they're planning something amusing and degrading to the naïve Americans," he said to Wade.

"Yeah, I noticed," Wade replied. His hand was in his coat, obviously near his Beretta. "I won't do anything brash, but I'm ready in case of an issue."

They all gathered in the main room, which was roomy enough at twenty feet across, but cramped with so many men jammed in. But the conversation was not elated. There was satisfaction, certainly, and some grins, but the atmosphere definitely made Kyle think they were about to be set up for an elaborate practical joke.

Nasima had been banished to the kitchen with the women and girls. She slipped through the door and gave Kyle a look that seemed to ask for help, while asking him to keep quiet. Wade caught it, too.

"I don't like what I'm feeling, Kyle," Wade

said softly, big grin plastered across his face as camouflage. "We got that son of a bitch. How's it feel?" He made a big show of high-fiving Kyle.

"And now all we have to do is get out. Soon," he continued. He was still grinning, and emphasized his meaning with a nod.

"Sounds good," Kyle said. "Creepy, yeah."

Nasima came through then, and served them, Khushal and Qalzai with curried chicken, tender and richly sauced, with rice. Under Kyle's platter was a note on a tiny slip of paper. It said, in block letters, NOW WE SHOULD LEAVE.

That did it, Kyle decided. If two trained troops and a local all felt nervous, something was up.

Except there was no way *to* leave that wasn't obviously a bug out. They'd have to play this for a few more hours, and sneak out by night.

As they lay down in a guest room, they were glad to see an outside door. They'd be through that when things quieted. "I'm on first watch," Wade said.

"Asshole," Kyle replied. "As if I can sleep now."

"I know the feeling," Wade said as he turned out the light. Both men were fully dressed and had their hands on their pistols under their coats.

The house quieted bit by bit, but it was past 1 A.M. before the last of the clan settled down. And the women would be up around five, to shoo the boys out to herd and milk and to start cooking. There wasn't much of an aperture there.

There was a scuffling at the door. Kyle clutched for his pistol.

"Who's there?" Wade asked in a whisper.

Nasima was speaking very softly. "It is I. We have to leave at once," she said.

"What? Why?" Kyle asked, nodding to Wade to open the door.

She came in, heedless of any customs of propriety. "There's no time to explain now. We must be out of sight by dawn, and I'll explain as we go, but there is danger for you both."

Kyle hated situations like this. Still, he did trust Nasima and his own instincts, and if there was a threat, they should get moving. It had to do with Qalzai and Bait, and he figured they were safer off alone with her as translator than with those others and no translator. "Grab your gear, Wade," he said, above a whisper but not much. "We'll do as she says."

"Understood," Wade agreed. He had his ruck in seconds; it was already packed, and the three of them started walking. Kyle carefully maneuvered the cased Barrett through the door, and they were off into the dark. They eased through the courtyard, and Kyle was glad that dogs weren't common. They bumped brick or stone twice, but didn't make any major noises.

As they slipped out the gate, Nasima said, "It is good we are near a town, so we can find a place to hide."

"Right," Kyle agreed. "Now, what's going on?"

She looked at him and said, "Kyle, the man you shot was not who you thought it was."

"What? How do you know?" he protested. She didn't even know who he had been shooting at, as far as he was aware.

"Because I heard Qalzai talk about settling a grudge. It's a man he's been fighting with for twenty years."

"Okay, so it's an old grudge, so what?" he said, but her comment was setting off alarms in his brain.

"Kyle, he shouldn't have known him in that case. The Taliban haven't been around that long, and al Qaeda even less," Wade said.

"Yes," Nasima nodded. "He said you'd done well for him, and he was glad to have American money. He doesn't know where your target is, and doesn't care. That kill was for him."

"You mean we're in the middle of a hillbilly feud here?" he asked. Things were spinning, and he shook his head to clear it. Dammit, they should have had more intel.

"If I understand your idiom, yes. Tribespeople killing each other over old hatreds," she said.

"Ah, shit. Sorry," he apologized to her.

"It's okay, I'm familiar with the term. Also *merde, scheisse*, and a few others." There was a twinkle in her eye as she swore in multiple languages. "And it fits," she said.

"Okay, so we get hid and figure out what

we're going to do. Though under the circumstances," Kyle said, hating what he was thinking, "we better abort the mission and have them try something else."

"Right," Wade said. "But first, we have to get out of this area and into another town. Any ideas?"

"Nasima," Kyle said, "We have money. Is there a discreet way to get a ride?"

She thought for a moment. "There are always vehicles that will carry people. But the word will be told. There's no way to stop people from talking."

"So we need to be on the first vehicle anywhere, and hope the rumors are behind us," he said.

"That is correct," she said. "But there are few vehicles this late."

"Hell, I'll buy one if I have to," he said. But he knew that wasn't a practical idea in the middle of the night.

"So we keep walking and grab what we can," Wade said. "If we need to, you can pass off as a local better than I can," he held up his coffee-toned hand as emphasis, "and I can stay hid while you get us space."

"We should avoid a public bus," Nasima said. "Do you want to go to Quetta? Or somewhere else?"

"Right now," Wade said, "we just need somewhere quiet, so we can call and report in. Then we can call for a helicopter if we have to."

"Very well," she said. "And what of me?"

"We give you a ride home," he said. He wasn't sure of Army policy, but he wasn't going to take "no" for an answer. They owed her.

"Thank you," she said, sounding honestly relieved. Well, with the way the government dicked everyone around, including him, he couldn't blame her.

10

THE NIGHTCLUB WAS LIKE MANY OTHERS IN Germany. This being Oktoberfest, it was packed with revelers, even if they weren't celebrating in traditional fashion. Dancing and drinking and fumbling gropes were still ongoing at 2 A.M. local. A number of American airmen from Rhein-Main Air Base were mixed among the crowd, and a platoon of soldiers fresh from Iraq were taking a couple of days to unwind while the military sorted out travel arrangements. Rough German industrial music shook the structure, low guttural voices amplified to almost painful levels. It was unfamiliar to some, but to the soldiers it was definitely Western and definitely a sign of civilization. That in itself made it good. Add a few pitchers of rich German beer and tall, blond women in tight leather and spandex, and they loved it.

Where the bomb had been planted was a mystery that would take days to solve. Its size was easy to estimate. It had been fifty kilograms of Semtex, somewhere toward the rear of the building, behind the steel cage and grated floor that served as a DJ booth. At 2:01:06, it detonated. The stylish metal cage, the grating, chunks of speaker magnet, cabinet, and grille all served as shrapnel. Not that they were necessary. The blast was sufficient, and contained by the walls for a mere fraction of a second, it propagated forward into the open dance floor.

Seventy-nine people were pulped or crushed to death by the explosion. Two hundred and six others would bear scars from minor scratches to missing limbs or shattered faces. It was headline news on the Web and TV within minutes.

Kyle, Wade and Nasima were still walking at dawn. There wasn't much else they could do. Luckily, all three were used to hoofing it, and their spirits were adequate. Though all three were nervous at every little sound in the desert.

"If we can get back to Hicheri, I know the area," Nasima said. "We can get transport anywhere. But how can you cross the border?"

"We have papers," Kyle said. As long as he could hang on to them. They were now rolled in a metal tube in his ruck, and he wasn't putting it down. The briefcase could go, so could the weapons. But the radio, phones, and the papers were their link to home.

"Okay," she said. "Then we will try to ride with a truck."

Kyle broke out one of his hoarded MREs and the tub of shoestring potatoes. They shared them around, including the freeze-dried fruit salad and crackers. It wasn't much for the gourmet, but it was calories and filling.

They lucked out shortly when a truck came by.

It was a truck like none Kyle had ever seen.

The bed had canvas over arched metal bows, like a military carryall, but they were high-peaked and arched. Another bow angled forward half over the cab, jutting up like the peak on a Nazi cap. There was no hood, and the engine stuck out in greasy mechanical contrast to the rest. For the rest of it was painted in lime green and garish geometric art.

"Pakistani hippies?" Wade asked.

"Hippies?" Nasima replied, confused. "Oh, no. Just as with the bright colors of clothes, people are proud of their vehicles." She waved an arm and the driver slowed.

It took her less than a minute, while Wade held his lungee over his face and squinted. She turned and said, "He agrees to carry us for fifty rupees."

Fifty rupees. Less than a dollar. Kyle would have paid a thousand times that to put distance between them and their former allies. "Done," he said.

They were ushered into the back, which was covered with plywood and had a plywood door with a brass knob set into it. The wood had faded from green to a contrasting black and straw as the wood aged. Inside was obviously someone's store. There was a narrow walkway, perhaps eighteen inches wide, and the rest was bundles and bureaus of assorted stuff—textiles, spice jars, hardware, and more they couldn't see. Wade scurried in first with the rifle case and his ruck, then Kyle with the rest of their gear. Nasima came in last, thanking the driver and paying him. The door was closed, leaving them in virtual darkness, the weak dawn entering through a window eight inches square.

Kyle squatted with his arms around his knees. "Well, it's cramped, but private," he said as the gears clashed and jolted them forward.

"He will get us to the next town," Nasima said. "From there, we can find some way to Hicheri."

"I don't suppose we can rent a car?" Kyle asked. He'd feel much safer with the minimal privacy of doors and a roof over their foreign features.

"No," she said. "But it may be possible to buy one. How much money do you have?"

Kyle tried to look at Wade over his shoulder, realized it was impossible, and said, "Almost forty-nine thousand dollars in afghanis, rupees, and dollars."

"Forty—!" she started. Then, "I think I should have asked for more money as your translator."

"Nasima, you can have whatever's left when we leave. It's an asset we're supposed to use,"

Kyle said, trying not to sound desperate. He didn't want her feeling put upon.

"That's generous of you," she said, "but not necessary. I will work for my pay. It was an honest price." Her smile was faintly visible in the growing half-light. "But we should be able to buy a car with that easily. Perhaps with far less." She chuckled.

It was a disconcerting ride, jolted and bounced in the dark, hanging on around bends as the old truck swayed. The springs were shot, and the shocks of course, and the differential howled. It reminded Kyle of the duct tape and baling wire monster of a pickup he'd had in high school, except that this was a twenty-foot Mercedes that was likely older than he was.

The light improved, their hunger increased, and the bouncing and squatting didn't help bladder pressure. It was late morning before they arrived back in Bemana'abad. It wasn't too soon to suit them. The weather was mild, but under the dark, musty canvas of the truck, it had been stifling and sweaty.

They nodded to the driver and started walking, following Nasima's lead. Eyes turned and followed them.

The problems were obvious. Either Kyle or Wade alone could have managed to have stayed discreet. But they were both very tall, well-built, and had obvious American weapons. To avoid that, they'd wrapped them, but it was still clear they had large hardware. The natives noticed them.

It wasn't the curious glances that were bothersome. Those were to be expected. But some of the looks were puzzled, mean, or offended as people deduced who they were. Clearly, the word had got out about their shoot. Not one person in twenty belonged to the tribe in question, but they'd talk. Eventually, the word would get back.

"Nasima," Kyle said softly, "we need to become better hidden, or get out of here fast."

"Yes," she agreed. "So let us find a vehicle. There's a merchant over that way. I assume the first one will do?"

"As long as the car works, yes," Kyle said. "Wade, how good a mechanic are you? I'm used to big American cars, not the little foreign ones."

"I know enough to spot a lemon," he said.

"Good."

Nasima asked, "Lemon?" and looked quizzical.

"Slang for a sour, bitter, lousy car," Kyle said.

"Ah."

It wasn't much of a lot, being simply a cleared and graded corner with weeds poking lazily through the dust and a shed as an office. It contained several vehicles ranging from three years old to ancient. Rust wasn't bad in the dry climate, but all were abraded and bleached to some extent.

Nasima swept up and engaged the dealer in rapid-fire Pashto. They smiled and gestured and occasionally he'd nod his balding head. Kyle and Wade smiled as they exchanged glances, and sidled up on an old Toyota. It looked like a Camry.

The cars were actually cheaper than the trucks, and it took some thinking to figure out why. The farmers needed trucks. Only urbanites would have cars, but they'd prefer a newer one. Anyone buying basic transport would get a truck or van first. But this would be fine for their needs, and when Wade popped the hood, it was obviously worn but functional. There was a dent on the right-rear corner, which was hardly surprising the way people drove here. "Chaotic" was the politest word for it.

The dealer would know who they were anyway, so they spoke in English. Wade started the engine with the provided key, revved it, and listened. "Smooth enough," he said. "Let's haggle over the body, the nonworking air conditioning, and the clutch."

Nasima bargained for them. She was animated, pushy, and seemed quite confident. The man feigned disgust at her offers and jabbered back. It took only a few minutes before she turned back and said, "One thousand dollars, and I suggest another two hundred to keep him silent about us."

"Done," Kyle said. He peeled out rupees and passed them over. A few minutes took care of title in Nasima's name, and they filled the trunk with gear and piled in. The wrapped weapons went with them.

"Who's driving?" Kyle asked.

"I am," Nasima said. "When we get out into the country, you might need to take over. But for now, I know the way."

"Got it," he agreed.

It was frightening driving through town. They were almost used to the insanity of the drivers by now, but the additional risk of being recognized caused them to keep glancing about. "Where are we going?" Kyle asked.

"Hicheri," she reminded him.

Once on the road, Kyle punched for General Robash on his phone. This was important enough that he wanted to talk directly.

"Robash here," was the answer on the first ring.

"Kyle here," he said. "General, I hate like hell to say this, but we've failed. We're heading out." The admission was nauseating, painful. He hoped it wouldn't be taken too hard back home.

"What happened, son? Talk to me," Robash said.

"Sir, our so-called allies were playing us as patsies. We assassinated some other local gang leader for them. They're very happy. The other tribe is not. The word is out, and we're being watched."

"Shit," Robash said.

"Yes, sir. We've secured transport and a translator, and are heading for the border. Do you have any specific orders for us?"

"Stand by," was the reply. Kyle waited, looking nervously out the windows as Nasima took them swiftly out of town. He listened to nothing as Robash did something, with the expensive line open.

Shortly, he was back on. "Status report, please."

"Sir," Kyle said, "we are uninjured, all equipment except the laptop accounted for—it's broken—in control of the situation, and with transport and a translator. We have broken contact with our former allies, whom I judge to be uninterested or potentially hostile at this point. We have over forty thousand in cash left, and are heading for a safe zone before retreating across the border. Several local tribes are seeking us, and I judge the risk to be moderate at this time."

"Right," Robash said. "We need you to stay if you can. Is there any reason not to?"

Kyle thought furiously. "Other than the local search, I guess we're still clean. But we're known now, and our target is likely to get word."

"There is that," Robash said. "But we've had a car bombing, three hundred casualties in a club in Germany and several other threats. As we tighten the noose on these assholes, they're getting desperate. We can't get another team in anytime soon, and they'll be watching. It's good that you're making noises of retreating; we want them to think that. But if you can regroup and push on, you're still the best shot we've got at doing this."

"If you tell me to do it, sir, we'll do it," he said. He turned his head and Wade nodded. "There's risk, but I understand your point." A nightclub. Lovely. Likely one he'd been in less than two years ago, too, if it was in Germany.

"I'm asking, not ordering," Robash said. "You're the man on the spot. Tell me you need out, we'll do it. Tell me you can push on, and you'll make a lot of people very happy."

"We'll do it," Kyle agreed, though he wasn't one of those who'd be happy. And "request" aside, it was an order. He'd have to justify bailing. He could, but it stuck in his craw, and Robash had to know that. It was polite railroading, but still . . . "There's risk, but we'll do it. But I'm not sure how to find him now. Suggestions?"

"Not yet," Robash said. "I'll get you intel as fast as I can. You get hidden and rest for a day or two. And thank you both. You're handling a bitch of a situation in first-class fashion."

"Thank you, sir," Kyle said. The compliment was honest. Other commanders might have complained, or been overly understanding. Robash was competently aware and let his people do their jobs.

"Roger that. We'll get you intel, you bag this dirtball, snipers."

"Will do, sir. Out."

"Out."

Turning to Wade he grinned and said, "We're fucked." He wasn't worried about offending Nasima anymore. The lady was tough.

"That bad?" Wade asked.

"I guess not," Kyle said. "Looking at it logically, we had allies we couldn't trust. We now have one ally we can, and familiarity with the area. But we have no intel on this guy at all."

Nasima asked, "Who is the man you're looking for?"

Swapping quick glances, Wade nodded and Kyle said, "Rafiq bin Qasim, one of al Qaeda's best people." There wasn't any reason not to tell her now.

She looked surprised for only a moment, then recovered. "He shouldn't be hard to find," she said. "He's bound to have local allies, and word always gets out among the tribes."

"Okay," Kyle said. "Then who do we ask? Lost and found?"

"First we get to Hicheri," she said. "Then we look."

"Okay," he said. "You keep driving, I'll think."

"Don't hurt your head," she said, smiling. He chuckled.

For several minutes, he said nothing, eyes closed, head back, letting his brain digest all the data. And also to ignore Nasima's driving, which was fast enough over the rough road that he wished for a helmet against bumps.

The biggest problem was the lack of intel. The biggest risk was that of discovery. The former required local sources, which Nasima might help them find. Nothing more to be done about that. The latter required better disguise.

Sitting up, he said, "One of the problems is that lovely piece of hardware." He indicated the trunk with a finger.

"The Barrett?" Wade asked.

"Yep. It's big, clunky, and obvious. Can't hide it. I'll bet everyone within a hundred miles knows about it and is scanning with binocs. And really, we're not going to need a thousand-meter-plus kill. Eight hundred, even as little as three hundred will do it. We need a weapon better suited to the environment."

"You aren't thinking what I think you are, Kyle?" Wade asked. He looked a bit wide-eyed and disturbed.

"Oh, I'm not going to sell it," Kyle grinned at him. "I do plan to stash it somewhere. We've got enough cash to buy whatever we need."

"You're going to buy an M-24 Sniper Weapon System in the ass-end of Pakistan?" Wade asked, incredulous.

Chuckling, Kyle said, "I probably could. But that would be obvious, too. I'm sure we can find a Mauser though. Or even a Dragunov."

Nasima was still driving, quietly. She'd heard everything, but hadn't offered any comment. "Rifles are available on the street where the metalsmiths are. I can show you," she said. They started bouncing over a rough spot in the road, and she jolted with the motion of the wheels and steering.

"Great," Kyle said. "I'll tell you what I need and you can buy it."

"I wouldn't know what to get, or how to bargain," she said. "I know weapons when I see them, everyone does. But not enough to talk about them."

"But, Nasima," he said, "We're obvious. You're a local."

"I suppose," she replied. She was clearly unhappy with the idea.

Kyle spoke to reassure her. "Fair enough," he said. "We'll try another approach."

"Like what?" Wade asked.

"I'm not sure," Kyle admitted. "But let's stash this sucker first. I'll think about it meantime. What I'll do is pull the bolt. Nothing they can do with it then. We'll keep that, and find somewhere to hide the rest of it."

"Makes sense," Wade nodded, though his tone made it clear he wasn't happy parting with the massive weapon. A lone M-4 and pistols against artillery, machine guns, and Kalashnikovs was not an appealing state of affairs.

"I know of a cave," Nasima said. "It's remote and very narrow."

"Sounds good," Kyle said. "Nearby?"

"Not far from Hicheri. We played there when I was small. Since I came back from Afghanistan, I haven't seen anyone go near the area."

"Sounds good," Kyle said. At the rate she was driving, it was less than an hour before they reached it. With all the convoluted routes, they'd come within twenty miles of where their failed shot had been, and were now heading back roughly toward Quetta.

No, Kyle decided, the shot hadn't failed. The shot had been good. The intel had failed, and that wasn't his fault.

11

THREE HOURS LATER, HE WASN'T SO SURE about the hiding place. With the Barrett disassembled, he and Wade each carrying half, it was still an awkward climb through jagged outcroppings. The path was up a fissure between two large massifs, and was well-hidden from town or the plateau, but it wasn't a pleasant walk in the park.

"It's just up here," Nasima said, indicating to their right. "Come."

Tired and sore, they followed her. It was a bit disconcerting to have the slim woman radiate so much energy as they lagged behind. Kyle kept reminding himself that she was familiar with the terrain. It did make a difference.

Shortly, they were gathered around a long crack. "Here," she announced.

"Very nice," Wade said, looking at the convoluted opening. He shone his Xenon flashlight inside, and decided it was deep enough for their purposes, as well as being out of sight. "Just one problem," he said.

Kyle finished the thought. "Neither of us will fit in there," he said. It might be fifteen inches wide and there was no section long enough for legs or torsos for a six-foot male.

"It is smaller than I remember," Nasima admitted. "I think I can still squeeze in, though."

"Great, if you can," Kyle said.

"Okay," she said. For a moment she stared at him, considering. Then she said, "That means you'll have to turn around."

"Huh?" he asked, confused.

She blushed red and said, "I'll need to pull up my skirt and squirm in. It's not proper for a man to watch."

Of course. Muslim doctrine demanded she not show anything except her face and hands. "Oh, no problem," Kyle said. "Sorry, it's just that we're not used to these things. Here's the components," he said, unlimbering the filthy burlap package from his shoulder. Wade dropped his alongside. "We'll move down about ten meters and just keep an ear out for emergencies, okay?"

"Excellent!" she beamed. She sat there, legs folded demurely under herself, until they moved away.

Behind them were scrabbling noises. "Dammit, I want to look when I hear sounds like that," Kyle said.

Wade snickered. "And you want a glimpse of leg, too."

Kyle punched his shoulder and said, "Yeah, she's cute, what about it? I'm not going to piss off our only reliable guide to get a gawk at something I can't have anyway. No fraternization."

"Right," Wade said. "Let's hope she's done soon, and that none of the kids come out here hacking around."

Kyle gazed over the terrain. "Not a lot here to indicate activity. I'd say it's pretty dead."

"Yeah," Wade agreed. "Kids these days. No matter where you go, they're more urban, less adventurous, and listening to industrial music."

"Hey! I listen to rock on occasion," Kyle said.

"Great, old man. You must be a huge hit with the over-eighty crowd."

They joked quietly until the scrabbling sounds stopped, and listened carefully, ears twitching for signs, eyes alert for movement.

"Thank you, gentlemen," her voice said. "It's hidden, and I appreciate your modesty."

They turned. Her skirt was dusty and scraped, with a puckered pull of thread over her left hip. "We'll have to give you some money for more clothes. This is wearing out your wardrobe," Kyle said.

"I'll be fine," she said. "Besides, there are no clothing stores nearby and there's little selection in the marketplace."

"Speaking of which," Kyle said, "we need to get more local garb, and shift to another village where we can hide better. And where we can buy a rifle."

She thought for a few moments. "If we can leave tonight, I know where there is a road east. It will take us where we can find a rifle and allies. And we need allies."

"Let's leave now," he said.

Nasima drove again. Kyle was getting used to her Eastern style. It involved no philosophy or mysticism, it was simply based on being mean and rude to other drivers and pedestrians, and barreling along as fast as possible.

After so many direction changes, Kyle wasn't entirely sure where they were. He was glad they had a GPS receiver, because he was sure they'd be needing it before this played out. In the meantime, they were approaching another town, and even from the outskirts it was obviously full of small industry. The rust stains and metallic stenches said as much.

By now, they were less obvious. Between two weeks' worth of beard and dirt and sun they looked like any other peasants, so long as they were seen from ten feet away and kept their short hair hidden. Wade's facial features were still problematic, but a lungee and a stiff coat fixed that. His skin tone was unremarkable. The people here varied from tan to near-black in the sun, skin leathery and stiff on all but the very young. Like Nasima.

She'd been right about the town. He could see various children working at buffing wheels and using files on metal, and glimpses through curtained doorways showed revolvers, shotguns, even a few AKs. Whatever they might need should be available here. Quality would be debatable, but they could do some work themselves and pay for other aspects.

It was amazing, Kyle thought, how a few hours' travel and the disposal of the Barrett had made them invisible again. The lawlessness and lack of proper TV or Web gave them a camouflage reminiscent of the Old West. As long as rumors didn't catch up in a hurry, or any rumors were garbled by the time they got here, they'd be okay.

First a rifle, then intel. He really had no idea how to accomplish that second requirement.

They parked the car in a sunny, dusty street. The dust was pervasive, just like that in Arabia, and covered everything. It was worse here, as the road was mere dirt, gullied and with stones protruding from some ancient rain.

The stores they wandered past were a bewildering mix. There were restaurants, textiles, dry goods, a video arcade with twenty-year-old games from the U.S. and a handful of Russian machines, a dealer of plastic cases, and gun shops. Lots of gun shops.

Wade picked the store that seemed quietest, pointed, and they slipped through the translucent fabric. The walls were lined with rows and stacks of rifles of all kinds. A clutch of pistols sat atop a shelf behind the counter. The shopkeeper nodded. He and his son both were dressed lightly in cotton, neatly bearded and kempt, and carried AKs. There were likely other weapons handy. At least, Kyle would have weapons handy if he ran the place, so he assumed they did, too.

They all nodded and bowed, and Nasima handled greetings and small talk. Wade watched the door as Kyle sought the left side of the store, which seemed to have many grimy, dirt-encrusted examples. The son watched him firmly but not threateningly as he examined the merchandise. There were many old Mausers, some Russian Moisin-Nagants, some Indian-made Enfield #4s, a scattering of odd things like a Swedish Ljungman and a Parker-Hale .22 that had seen far better decades. There was a lot to sort through.

Then he stopped short. That looked like . . .

It was. A Short Magazine Lee-Enfield. World War I British surplus. Only this one had been worked over quite a bit. He picked it up and examined it.

The muzzle-length Mannlicher stock had been shortened to a reasonable modern length, and the stock cap that held the bayonet mount removed. It had been refinished and phosphated instead of blued. The length of pull was a bit short for a man of his stature, of course, but that could be fixed. Then he saw the stamp on the left side of the receiver. PROPERTY US GOVERNMENT.

It clicked in his mind. During the '80s, lots of these, cheap, familiar to the locals and easy to procure, had been cut down and packaged for the mujahideen. The SMLE or "Smelly" was a reliable, accurate weapon, almost as good as a 98K Mauser, and easy to maintain. With a bit of work it would make, as others had before, a fine shooting rifle.

"*Da pe tso dai?*" he asked. How much?

"*Zer rupee,*" the man replied confidently. Kyle figured for a moment. One thousand Pakistani rupees was sixteen bucks American. It was cheap, and ridiculously within his budget.

But it would be out of place not to haggle, and he couldn't have stories of a stranger tossing money around freely. "*Penza sawa,*" he countered. Five hundred rupees, eight bucks.

The man looked offended but clearly wasn't, and stuck to his price. Kyle pointed out the "defective" stock, how short it was, the grunge and dust, no bayonet mount. He didn't speak the language well enough, but didn't need to. All he had to do was point, shake his head, look grossly put upon and disgusted. Twice he put it down and walked toward the door, and each time the man countered with a slightly lower price. Kyle would turn back and they'd start again.

It took ten minutes, with much grumbling and complaining, gesticulating and shaking of heads, but finally they settled at twelve dollars, 750 rupees, with sixty rounds of match-grade ammunition included, twelve stripper clips to hold it, the rifle to be adjusted to his specifications, and a sling added, along with an abused but functional

Dragunov bipod and better sights. He'd have to settle for iron sights, but they'd be good ones. The ammo made him suspicious. It sounded too good to be true.

"You bargain well," Nasima acknowledged.

"Lots of flea market trips as a kid," he replied. She looked confused at the term and he added, "I'll explain later."

Haggling done, he sought to explain the modifications he wanted made.

"What do you seek?" the man asked. He didn't seem bothered at Nasima translating. That was typical. As a woman helping a man, she was in her place. Besides, he was being paid.

Or possibly he was modern-minded enough not to care. Kyle decided he was being too harsh in his assumptions. So far, almost everyone had been very hospitable. Even Qalzai's people, while they screwed him over, had been polite and helpful. There was no reason to impute bad thoughts to everyone.

With a bit of conversation and a few gestures for technical matters, Kyle got his point across. "Ah, yes," the man said. "Ah, yes," when he understood the nature of the changes. "Ah, yes." It might be the only English he spoke, though Kyle wasn't going to assume so, and would watch what he said around him.

Kyle stayed on site while Nasima and Wade went to shop for food, more clothes, and assorted accessories. He watched and advised with a few basic words and hand signs as the smith cut off the remaining barrel band. He then dismounted the weapon and carefully placed the stock in a vise, padding the jaws with leather. He gestured for Kyle, who used a scribe and straightedge to carefully mark how he wanted it cut, then held up his hands to indicate it should be hollowed in a semicircle along those lines.

What he was trying to do was relieve most of the pressure of the stock against the barrel, free floating it. This would allow the barrel to oscillate with a harmonic resonance as it fired, rather than shaking the stock. It also prevented warped wood from humidity changes from affecting the barrel, and left a small air gap to reduce the effect of bangs and strikes against the barrel. A small amount of pressure at the front of the stock would make things stable and consistent.

Kyle almost jumped in shock when the craftsman grabbed a chisel and mallet and banged along the lines indicated. He was sure the stock was ruined from the rapid, careless striking. He held still, not screaming, jumping or reacting, trying to think of a polite way to address the issue. He'd be needing one of the Mausers now.

At a wave, he stepped closer to look at the damage, and paused. In actuality, it was a job almost as neat as a precision machine could do.

It came to him that this man was a craftsman in the old style. He'd be lost in a modern machine shop, but with a handful of files, a drill, and chisels, he could do any of the same precision work, it would just take longer. Though "longer" was in comparison to machine tools only. His work so far was faster than Kyle would dare try with a chisel.

Impressed, Kyle nodded agreement, and indicated that the foremost part of the stock should be left proud so as to support the barrel. The grimace the man gave him indicated he was well aware of that fact, and the arrogant foreigner should stand back and let him work. He selected a large riffler rasp from his rack and commenced to shave out long, paper-thin strips of the old beechwood.

Kyle simply watched. The man's hands were sure, his eyes squinty and clear. Stroke by stroke the well-aged wood was scraped and cut into a more modern shape. It took about an hour, which was surprisingly fast.

How to indicate fiberglass bedding? He sought a piece of plastic, found a Stanley chisel with a translucent handle, and indicated it and the inside of the stock.

At first, the old man thought he wanted him to use the chisel. Then after a few moments, the idea caught on and he limped over to a cabinet. He pulled out a can that contained a popular American brand of fiberglass resin for autobody repairs.

With that, he created a slurry of shredded fiberglass cloth and resin, pressed it down into the cut and smoothed it out. He used a rubber glove that had likely been used for a thousand other fiberglass jobs, crusty and crackly over much of its surface.

It took only a couple of hours to complete, including a wooden cheek piece shaved to fit and pinned in place with wooden dowels as a Monte Carlo-style stock, and another piece screwed in place on the butt to lengthen it to fit Kyle's long frame. It was a good three inches longer than the short British stock. Careful pegging and filing filled out the grip to something Kyle might hold more easily.

Wade and Nasima returned with meat-stuffed pies. The filling was mutton. Though if Kyle hadn't known, he wouldn't have asked. He'd learned to eat what he was given, enjoy it or reject it and not ask about pedigree or breed. But Muslims were strict on eating only mutton, goat, or beef as far as mammals went, and there were few streams here to fish from. He bit at the pie, and gave the spare one to their host, who hugged them graciously and plowed in as the fiberglass finished setting. Once he'd munched his meal, he returned to delicate filing and hammering on the bolt mechanism. After that, he drilled the rear of the receiver for a proper sight assembly. He actually had a small drill press that looked fifty years old and held a standard hand drill, but it cut straight holes, which he threaded by hand.

"That is one ugly-looking bastard son of a left-handed, red-headed stepchild," Wade said, eying the stock critically.

"Ain't it, though?" Kyle agreed, beaming. Yes, it was ugly, its soft old lines surgically altered to rakish angles and now converted to butchered curves. But it was purely functional. It should, if everything had been done correctly, and to Kyle's eye it had, shoot every time he squeezed the trigger, and put every bullet within a couple of minutes of arc of where he aimed.

After the glass bed had set, the smith smoothed it down with files and a metal scraper with better curves than a French stripper. There was no sandpaper in evidence anywhere; all finish work was scraped patiently to a fine, smooth surface.

Meanwhile, the trigger had been reshaped and the bolt reworked. Once reassembled and set into the stock, the man presented it to Kyle for examination. He wore a confident smile.

Kyle hefted it, liking the balance. The bipod had been screwed to the forestock and added just enough weight that it should help hold the muzzle down. The stock was long and tall enough for his arm and neck, the grip swelled to fit his large hand. He raised it, worked the bolt and safety, though he wasn't likely to use the latter much. Still, it was a good test of function. He drew the trigger, which still had a long, creepy draw, but was crisp at letoff and not mushy.

He nodded satisfaction. The man had done a fine job.

"Ammunition," he reminded the smith, and the man nodded. He spoke to his son, who slipped into the back. After a patient three minutes, Kyle asked Nasima, "Do we know what's taking so long?"

She spoke, the smith spoke back, and she said, "The match ammunition is hidden at the back of the safe. It will be here shortly."

"Okay," he agreed. But it was another five minutes before the son returned. He handed over a paper wrap that contained the rounds, and another that held the clips.

Kyle examined the rounds carefully. The case markings varied, and he wasn't very familiar with British ammo. This batch was stamped A 79 7.7R 1M3Z. 1979, 7.7mm rimmed? That seemed likely, but the rest meant nothing. But the cases were very even in shape and length, had faint turning marks on the necks, and the bullets were in nice condition. He had no idea where "match-grade" ammo came from out here, but he'd seen all kinds of stuff, including a titanium Taurus .357 that couldn't reasonably be here. He shrugged inwardly and decided to take them. A dozen tight, springy stripper clips let him load sixty rounds for easy feeding. One could carry extra magazines for the Smelly, but typically, the magazine was left in place and ammo fed from strippers into the top. The clips were phosphate finished and looked recent, though they were worn from use.

With that accomplished, they paid the man in rupees, thanked him profusely, and accepted both a modern sleeve for the rifle and a burlap wrap to hide that. Then it was back outside and into the car. It was time to test-fire the weapon.

They drove out of town and found a quiet area with rolling fields. On a broad, stalky-green area about 200 meters from the road, Kyle found a boulder, and propped two smaller rocks on it as targets. "Spot me," he told Wade.

"Of course," Wade replied. He uncased the spotting scope and got comfortable on the ground.

Kyle dropped prone, extended the bipod and set its length, checked the sling and stock in case he needed to shoot from rest, and did a full check of the weapon. His life would depend on it. "Good enough" wasn't good enough.

It snugged comfortably up against his cheek, and the bolt and safety worked very smoothly. He loaded one round. With curly green stuff against his face, he eased lower and closer. The Zen of rifle. It was a joke of his. Become one with the weapon. Be the bullet.

The trigger pull was still long, but steady. It fired crisply, and recoiled more than he expected. The .303 was a respectable round, and this wasn't a heavy rifle. The "*Boom!*" rolled out and echoed pleasantly.

He missed, throwing up chips from the boulder.

Wade was on it, though, and said, "Five inches low, three inches right."

"Stand by," Kyle replied. The original sights had been a midmounted tangential ramp and a post in front. They were adequate for battle, but not for precision. The new rear sight was mounted to the receiver ring and was click adjustable. It wasn't any brand Kyle recognized, but it ought to work well enough.

He clicked up and left, said, "Ready," and loaded one round. Consistency was essential to a good sight-in.

As that shot echoed and more chips flew, Wade said, "Barely low, one inch right."

"Stand by," he said. He corrected again, leaned in, and fired.

The rock shattered in bits.

"Second target," he said. One round.

That rock joined its neighbor in igneous heaven.

"Good enough. Your turn."

"Suits me," Wade said. He might have to take the shot, and they might wind up mixing weapons. He needed familiarity, too.

There was one small piece of the second target left. Wade flopped down, eased in, loaded, squeezed, and shot. The now-pebble jumped high into the air and disappeared. "Damn, sliced," Wade quipped.

"I'm happy," Kyle said.

Nasima had been silent. Now she said, "I am impressed."

"Thanks," Kyle said. "But we're trained for much farther than that."

"Yeah, do we want to resight for farther?" Wade asked.

"Adjust the vertical. Zero for three hundred."

Wade nodded, and whipped out a calculator and notepad. "Assuming one eighty grains and twenty-four sixty at the muzzle with a two hundred *yard* zero, which is the figures I have here, plus two point five inches at one hundred, sixteen point eight inches low at three hundred. Zero at three hundred."

"Right," Kyle agreed. The projectile would hit high on a closer shot, rapidly drop after three hundred, but would be within a human silhouette for the entire flight. After 350 yards, he'd need to aim higher, on the head or above it, for a center of mass shot.

They discussed some finer points of trajectory for a few minutes, and potential deflection from wind. "It should do the job," Kyle said.

"Hope so," Wade said. "Because I don't think this is 'match' ammo." He held up a round and indicated with his finger. "That turning on the throat was done with emery paper. The rim is a bit beat. And the shoulders are not fire-formed." That last referred to fitting cases to a chamber by shooting them, forcing them to shape. "Looks like standard ball."

"Ah, hell," Kyle said.

"Go back and complain?"

"Nah," Kyle said. "It should be consistent enough, if it's standard ball. The work was good. We don't want a scene. Let him keep the extra buck fifty."

"Sure, though it makes me itch," Wade said. "Bet that what took so long was the emery cloth and polishing?"

"No bet," Kyle replied with a shake of his head. "Now, we're using iron sights on this. I've got the scope from the Barrett to use for intel and spotting, but you're going to have to do most of the spotting for me with your scope."

"Roger that," Wade nodded.

"Are we done here, then?" Nasima asked. She'd been quiet through the technical discussion, but appeared impressed.

"Yes," Kyle said. "What now?"

"Now we try to find your target," she said.

"I'm dying to find out how," Wade said.

"We ask questions," she said. "The key element is to ask the correct questions of the correct people."

He knew that much. "I guess we're in your hands," he said. Because he had no idea where to start.

"I have an idea," she said.

They returned to the car, hid the weapons carefully in the trunk and climbed back in. Nasima started the engine and pulled back onto the road.

Shortly, she pulled over. Hopping out lightly, she asked something of a woman on the street. A pointed finger and directions were returned.

From there, they drove across town and sat waiting near a mosque. It was a stunning piece of architecture, and the two Americans gaped like tourists. Even in this backwater, the mosque had arches, minarets, rich blue tiles, and other exquisite decorations. Lunch came from a passing vendor with a rickety wooden cart, and Nasima disappeared inside for nearly an hour while the men sweated in the sun. She emerged, they climbed in the car, and off they went again.

They crossed town three or four times, Nasima stopping to ask questions. They circled a good piece of the outskirts and then headed west again, up into the hills.

"We're seeking a small village nearby," she said, "where three tribes have been fighting. One is known to have been involved with the Taliban during their reign. We will seek one of the others and ask of their enemies."

"Good, just ask carefully," Kyle said.

She turned and gave him a look that would freeze a blowtorch. "I have some experience avoiding trouble, Kyle." Her tone made it clear she didn't like being patronized.

"Right, sorry, nerves," he said.

"It is okay," she said, and softened slightly.

"How will we find the final information?" Wade asked. "I'd think we don't want to ask about it at all."

"And we won't," she nodded. "We'll see who is afraid, and hasn't been warring recently, or who is deferring to the others. The Taliban are bullies. Others avoid them."

They stopped at another ultramodern petrol station in a tiny town that was a scattering of huts. The station was the most modern building they'd seen all day, and was a local hangout of sorts. The Americans stayed in the car, Nasima went in. When she returned, she was smiling.

"I have another lead," she said.

"Oh?" Kyle prompted.

"I asked about safe routes for driving. I was told where to avoid, and why."

"Ah," he said. Yes, that was a classic way of doing it, and it wouldn't have worked if he'd tried it. Nasima was very useful to them. They'd gotten far more than their money's worth from her already.

It was evening when they rolled up into the hills proper. At dusk, they stopped at a convenient farm, paid a few rupees, and were bedded down in two rooms. Nasima had cautioned them against trying to leave the rooms and associate, and they stayed quiet. It wasn't easy, though.

"Dammit, Wade, I want to know what's going on!" Kyle fumed in a whisper. "She drives us around, asks questions . . . what happens when someone associates her with two strangers, and those two strangers with a dead leader in the area?" They sat in a room lit by a single candle, with bare dun walls and a packed earth floor. They'd rolled out ponchos and rucks as bedding.

"Chill," Wade said. "We're better off this way. We'll have more warning of any trouble, and we have transport we control."

"Yeah," Kyle said. "I had the illusion of control before. Now I have control, but it's limited, and through a young woman who doesn't know military matters."

"Not formally, no. But she does have a knack for intel. I think it's inbred here. So many factions and relations that you have to learn diplomatic ways of gathering data before you even greet someone at a party, in case you piss someone off."

"True," Kyle considered, sitting on his ruck. It sank under him, despite its fullness. "And I suppose I'd better sleep. Long day again tomorrow."

"Yeah, I've got watch. See you in four hours."

"Right," Kyle said. But sleep wasn't easy with ghostly enemies haunting his dreams, prepared to knock down the doors and shoot him . . . and under all that was an image of Wade, being shot by a sniper, screaming in agony. Then everything shifted and Nasima was the target. His mind was recalling old hurts with new friends and confusing the images.

It was a long time before he slept, and it was restless when it came.

12

SO, BIN QASIM THOUGHT, THERE WERE AMER-icans in country. Or more accurately, more Americans in country. The CIA was getting tricky. This pair had not come to his attention through the usual sources. His informants in the Pakistani Inter-Services Intelligence had not mentioned them. He would have to caution them against contempt. The Americans were not to be underestimated. Their money and arrogance could not stand against faith, but it was still a threat, which is why jihad was necessary.

Whoever they were, the illiterate savages of the border were keeping them busy. Faithful, those tribes, if stupid. But it was their place. All who worshipped Allah were assured of the rewards of faith, but Allah chose which gifts to bestow upon His people.

It was also possible they were SEALs or Delta, those annoying thorns in his side. Or perhaps Marines or Air Force. The Americans had a bureaucratic mindset that caused every service to duplicate efforts, including commandos. That maze of paperwork often kept data hidden for months, even years. Of course, that same morass had kept the September 11th attack hidden at their end, so perhaps he shouldn't curse the inefficiency. It was also a blessing that he'd just moved his headquarters. Darting through the ground like an animal was undignified, but it was one of the many sacrifices he'd had to make for Allah's will, and he bore the burden stoically.

Either way, military or CIA, ISI should know. Pakistan had one security apparatus. It simplified working with them. So someone needed a reminder of his human failings, and urged to dig deeper. Perhaps Shujjat's daughter would serve to guarantee his future loyalty. And if he proved unreliable, she might be most entertaining.

Bin Qasim smiled as he picked up the phone.

After a breakfast Kyle didn't remember, blearyeyed and nauseous with fatigue, they rolled again. Nasima had asked more gently probing questions the night before. It was reasonable for a traveler to ask about threats, and the local people were friendly and liked to chat. He did vaguely remember the herder and his wife talking about the tribes, how they had shifted over the years from bolt rifles and shotguns to captured Soviet and surplus Pakistani military weapons. The farmer had a well-worn Russian side-by-side shotgun in the corner that he had pointed to.

"All I have, all I need," he'd said. Kyle had picked up enough vocabulary to grasp the statement. The man was in his fifties, gray and lean, and seemed wistful and reminiscent.

They thanked the man and his wife, who had accepted Nasima's story that the men were mercenaries looking to set up a smuggling route. The government was a remote concept out here, and smuggling not regarded as a sin, only a crime on paper. It wasn't the safest story, but it was the best available to explain two foreign men toting rifles and radios.

They were on the road again, with curried rice and vegetables wrapped in bread for lunch. Kyle had left a little more money, offering it as a gift, not as pay. These were a very proud people, and he didn't want to offend them. Given better access to modern technology, he saw them becoming a major power in the world. They had far more independence and self-reliance than say, the French.

"So what now?" he asked Nasima.

"We know who we are to talk to," she said. "Though it's difficult."

"Difficult how?" Kyle asked.

"One of the leaders mentioned is named 'Qalzai,'" she said. Their stunned looks must have been visible even with her eyes on the road, because she said, "Yes, it is the same man. He is not involved with the Taliban, but he will not be friendly to you. I'm told he is trying to avoid them, and has paid several bribes of weapons."

"Oh, great," Kyle said. "That's all we need. So he did know, but wasn't going to queer a deal he already had. And by using us to gap his local enemy, he was trying to avoid more trouble. That fucking weasel!"

"About right," Wade said. "And I assume that by now, everyone has heard of us?"

"Yes," Nasima said. "I'm also in danger. They are told of a woman translator. So from now on, one of you must lie down in back and not be seen."

"At least," Wade agreed.

"Then there's the other tribe, under a man named Gul," she said.

"What about them?" Kyle asked.

"They were under a man named Rahman, who was shot only three days ago," she said.

After that sank in, amid fifteen seconds of silence, Kyle said, "Wade, how would you feel about bugging out right now? We're not that far from the border here."

"Tempting, my friend," he said. "Nasima, what do we do? Is there any way we can find out what we need safely?"

"Safely? Where the Taliban and al Qaeda are concerned?" she asked. "There is no safe in this."

"Not anymore," Kyle agreed. "What do we do, then? Pull out? Go elsewhere for allies?"

"We must meet with them," Nasima said.

"*What?*" Kyle asked. "You've got to be kidding!"

"No," she said, shaking her head. "Carefully,

of course, but we must meet and explain, so they stop the rewards for you."

"Nasima, they aren't going to drop it with an apology, believe me."

"Believe you?" she asked, voice rising. "Who has lived here? Who speaks the languages? Who has traveled the world and learned the language of the other? What makes you an expert on the ways of my people?" She was panting when done, and clearly annoyed.

For a moment, Kyle said nothing. Everything in his experience said she had to be wrong. Yet, he understood intellectually that this was a different culture with different rules.

"Okay, Nasima," he said, "I'll listen to your expertise. And I'm sorry."

It was her turn to stare for a moment. Clearly, she'd expected him to argue more.

"Very well," she said. "And I shall explain my reasoning."

"Please," he said. "It's outside my experience."

Taking a deep breath, she began to lecture. "Nearly all these tribes have fought each other at one time or another. They shift sides and allegiances as Americans change musical tastes. Bitter enemies today might be allies tomorrow, and change sides in the middle of battle."

"Okay," Kyle said. "But I don't find that reassuring." He could see finding new allies who would also want him to settle a score. He felt like a cross between a mercenary and a charitable organization.

"Maybe not," she said, "but it is the way. That is why prisoners are so hard for your army. One group captures others, and a brother of a cousin of a stepson reminds one of an obligation, and gets his group set free, or offers to change sides if the loot looks good."

"Right," Wade nodded. "I've heard of that. You think we can exploit it?"

Taking a deep breath, she said, "I don't know. But we must try. You can't accomplish your mission otherwise."

"True," Kyle said. There was something else he needed to ask, and he hoped it wouldn't make her angry.

"So tell me," he said, "why are you helping us? We appreciate it, but what's in it for you?" The right phrase came to mind and he said, "I know it's not about money."

"No," she said, eyes glazed. "It's about my job as a professor, gone because I'm a woman. It's about other women treated as dogs, run over in traffic, dead from lack of proper medical care. It's about children blown up by land mines, because cards or games to teach them what to avoid are 'gambling tools' or 'distractions from the Holy Quran' or 'American Satanist capitalist attacks on our purity.' It's about our homeland, torn apart by tribes, armies, terrorists, religious extremists, and the Russians. The Taliban and al Qaeda are creating trouble where there was more than enough already, and turning families against each other. People are poor and starving already, now they are weeping with hopelessness. The people you hunt are demons, and if I can help you kill them, I will."

Both men sat silently for some time. Nasima was literate, well spoken, controlled, and mature and had the deadly poise of a coiled viper. Small and feminine she might be, but she was sharp-witted and determined. No amount of religious fervor would shake her foundation beliefs.

"Good," Kyle said at last. "So tell us what to do?"

"First," she said, studying her hands on the wheel, "we must find someone who will carry a message to them."

Another tiny village was ahead. Kyle was slightly smaller than Wade. Only slightly. So he agreed to be locked in the trunk, so long as he was armed. He could breathe well enough through a gap in the rear deck. Wade lay down in the rear footwell, covered with rubbish and an old cloth they found. That left Nasima to ask questions like a local, while they sweated from heat and fear.

Had I known all this when the job was offered, Kyle thought, I would have laughed and asked for a discharge. But he knew he wouldn't have. Men like him were soldiers because of the constant trouble. They'd be bored to drink by doing nothing.

With sudden clarity, Kyle realized that his assignment to the Sniper School, good as it was, was the wrong task for him at that time. What he'd needed was to be tossed back in, like this, to recover his nerve and work through the pain.

The door opened and slammed, the engine started, and as the car pulled back onto the road, he heard Nasima mutter something. Wade said, "Okay," and there was no further response, so he concluded that he should just wait.

"I have found where Gul is," she said loudly enough to be heard. The gap through the rear deck meant it was clear, just distant. The only muffling was from engine noise and the rattling exhaust under Kyle.

"Excellent," Kyle said. "I hope."

"Yes, it's good news," she said. "But the meeting is going to be tense and awkward. I'll translate, and you'll have to take my advice." She seemed nervous about that.

"Nasima, we'll do exactly as you say in this area. You're the expert," Kyle said.

"Good," she said, and there was a slight sigh. Egos here could create trouble, and Kyle and Wade knew that. Kyle regretted his earlier condescension to her, but it seemed best to simply ignore it rather than dwell on it. He'd offended her, and that disturbed him on a professional level, and on a social level below that where he really shouldn't go.

"You should not carry rifles," she said as she pulled over. Kyle gratefully squeezed out of the trunk and squeezed back into the rear seat, as Wade slipped up front. Chinese fire drill done,

Nasima resumed driving. They'd have to hide again when they stopped, but for now, the fresh air was welcome.

"Yeah, that would seem to be provocative," Kyle said, thankful for the interruption. "I'd like to have a pistol, though. Just in case."

"Okay," she said. "But don't handle it or draw it. Just keep it inside your coat."

"Agreed," he said, as did Wade. No doubt, he'd carry his Beretta.

"So where are we going?" he asked.

"Another farm," she said. "The people we want to see are there now."

"Now," he repeated. "Well, I suppose there's no need to delay."

"You are nervous," she said.

"No," he said. "There are people who want us dead. People who betrayed us and now realize we're a threat and want us dead. Not to mention other people we've offended who are likely to want us dead. Not nervous at all," he said.

" 'Terrified' is, I believe, the word we're looking for," Wade said.

"Terrified," Kyle admitted. And his pulse, respiration, and body temperature agreed. Facing a threat across the battlefield was bad enough. Walking into the home of someone who had every legal and moral right to execute them for murder was an entirely new level of pucker factor.

It was less than an hour, while they sweated and worried and discussed their negotiations with Nasima, before they drove off the road onto a worn but maintained track on a low slope. Goats covered the area, cropping at what low greenery there was. They appeared well fed. Whoever this Gul was, he was considerably better off than Qalzai's bunch. He even had a Mercedes, ten years old but in good repair, parked outside the broad house.

A teenage boy watched their approach, and Nasima waved. He returned the gesture, but wasn't smiling. It was simply an exchange that acknowledged their arrival wasn't clandestine, but a public entrance. Nasima drove up near him and got out. She said, "You should stand against the car so you can be seen as not a threat." They nodded and stretched.

The pending meeting was enough to cause near panic, and both men kept glancing at each other as they surreptitiously checked their pistols. Rifles they'd agreed would be obvious, of little use in close quarters, and could be perceived as a threat. But both wanted to be armed.

"What do we do if they tell us to disarm?" Kyle asked.

Wade pondered, and said, "I say we do it. It's not as if we could do more than take a couple with us if they want us dead, and I don't see them waiting for us to get that close if they plan to."

"Right," Kyle agreed. "So why are we bothering at all?"

"Because there might be an impulsive idiot," Wade said.

"And it makes us feel five percent better."

"That, too."

Kyle didn't know what it felt like to face a firing squad, but this had to be close. And very well might be doing so.

Nasima returned a few minutes later. They climbed in and let her chauffeur them, hoping she was as competent as she was confident.

The house was spacious enough; Gul was definitely more prosperous than Qalzai. The trucks were newer, and there were several of them. Two Nissans were behind the Mercedes. The courtyard had tall plants arranged, and was neatly paved. The gateway actually had a gate, of wrought iron. The pattern of it was interesting, but they were through too fast to decipher it. Inside, the wind was the barest zephyr with a faint smell of flowers. It wouldn't have helped cool them, even if they weren't terrified and sweating, hearts palpitating all the way up their throats. Brave men can face death. But only fools are fearless.

The men within did not look friendly. Kyle was glad he had his pistol, but equally sure it was only a reassurance, and wouldn't matter squat if it came to a fight. They were crammed into a small common room with chrome chairs, like those from a 1950s American diner.

Nasima introduced the Americans. She never got a chance to introduce the locals.

The headman, Gul, stormed at her, while pointing at them. He didn't shout, but the deadliness came through his voice just by inflection.

There was fury, hatred, murder there. She spoke back, when he stopped for breath, in slow, measured tones. Then he'd rage some more. Kyle felt partly that he should step in and take the blame, and partly that he should stay the hell out of it. He might just get them all killed. And for now, the men were waiting for Gul, and Gul was still talking with Nasima . . .

Realistically, Kyle couldn't blame him. If someone had shot one of his friends from 2,000 meters, he'd be pissed as all hell, too. Still, that wasn't reassuring.

He noticed, however, that Nasima was getting in longer and longer phrases. Her exotic features were calm and unafraid, and she seemed to be holding his attention. *No wonder she can handle forty kids,* he thought. She had the poise of a master actor.

It took about a half hour, during which time he and Wade sat motionless and aged ten years, before the two were speaking in conversational tones. Kyle no longer felt naked and vulnerable, but he still let his fingers brush his little Colt. Things weren't good, but at least they weren't ugly.

He realized how far things had progressed when Nasima interrupted his musing. "Kyle," she said, "now is the time to apologize."

He stepped forward nervously in the small room, and stood before the short, wiry man. "Gul," he said, "*Wobakha*. I'm sorry about the shot." Nasima translated as he spoke. "He wasn't the man we were sent to shoot, and we have no quarrel with you. Our quarrel is with others, and with those who set us up to attack you. They're cowards, afraid to fight their own battles, but we won't fight for them. I just wish we'd known sooner."

Nasima's translation ended, and Gul replied. "I accept it as honest," she said for him. "Though I am angered in my heart, raging. Your truth doesn't change the event. But fighting you will not help us, and won't bring to justice the ones who were behind it. I forgive you."

"*Sta na shukria,*" Kyle said. "I will have my government make compensation, if it will help a family in need." He'd phrased that carefully. An offer of a bribe wouldn't go over well. But it was possible, even likely, someone had been widowed or orphaned.

"The family is in need," Gul agreed, "and it would help much if you provided compensation."

Kyle nodded to Gul and quickly flicked his eyes to Nasima. "How much should I offer?" he asked.

She replied at once, "Offer him five hundred dollars worth of rupees. I will tell him it is a personal gift from you, because you haven't spoken to your government yet. That will make it seem more of a sacrifice on your part."

He nodded and drew two stacks of money from his pocket. They'd been counted into wads before the trip, for easy bookkeeping. That way, he didn't have to flash any more than that.

Thirty thousand rupees. Five hundred dollars. That was a fair price for a human life out here. Part of him wondered what twenty million in the right place would do.

Likely screw things to hell, he thought. Money didn't solve problems. But it did occasionally make things easier.

Gul accepted the money gravely, then handed it back to another with what were obviously instructions on where to take it. As his assistant nodded and scurried away, Gul turned back to Kyle and said, "That is thoughtful and gracious of you," was the reply. "An honest man fixes his mistakes. Let us eat and talk."

And only then did Kyle take his hand off his pistol. An offer to eat was an important aspect of hospitality, and that meant they were safe. For now.

So they sat and smoked—Kyle and Wade faked it—and ate lamb with noodles and a ton of cumin. Between tobacco fumes, spicy aromas, and body heat, the air was quite thick. To clear the tears, they drank water and imported grape juice. Gul laughed at their discomfort, then had less incendiary dishes brought. It seemed he accepted them on some level, at least.

Kyle decided he'd run a gauntlet of paddles, tar and feathers, if it would ingratiate them to these people and not get them killed. The hot food was hardly a real test.

When he thought that, he was afraid their new

hosts might see it that way, and devise something *really* rough.

It didn't seem as if their hosts had warmed to them. But they were at least now distant professionals who could collaborate, much like another tribe or faction. No one was about to shoot them, Kyle was sure, and honor was a significant factor here. With that in mind, he relaxed just a little, and looked at Wade.

"So far, so good," he said.

"We hope," Wade replied.

Nasima came over and sat with them. "Welcome back," Wade said. "And thanks."

"Yeah, you've saved our behinds. Again," Kyle admitted. If they'd had her along from the start . . . Part of him wondered if the CIA could use her. If they'd sought someone like her in the first place, this mission would have been a lot smoother. Trust the bureaucrats to act before thinking.

Another part wanted to get done and leave her in peace. She was a fine lady, dammit, and didn't deserve all this crap.

"We are all saved, for the time being," she said. "I am in the odd position of sitting in a man's meeting, from their view. I am needed as a translator, and to tell them about you. So if things seem a little strained, that's part of it."

"I'd be surprised if there weren't many more straining things," Kyle said.

"No," Nasima replied, shaking her head vigorously. "Changing alliances are the way, here. They are sad still, but you have acted honorably. They might be stiff, but that is their own discomfort, not any fear of you. Our situation is much improved," she explained.

"Good," Kyle said, believing her intellectually. He just wished his stomach would relax. He was still in fight-or-flee reflex mode. "When are we going to discuss the situation?"

"Soon," she said. "We can't impose on hospitality for long without a reason."

"Will they be receptive?" he asked.

"I think so," she said. "There's little love for the others here, and I've not heard anything that would suggest it with this tribe. Remember, these are working people. They have to do more than worry about religion. Religion is very important, but civil life also has its needs. Those are subordinate to God's, but they still exist. If they are offered something worthwhile, they are less inclined to stray. America is a place they only hear about, it's not real, so there's no strong urge to fight it."

"More money?" Kyle asked.

"Properly offered, yes," she said. "It must never appear as a bribe, but as a gift or contract."

That was fine, Kyle thought. Buying their way out bothered him morally, but they had the cash, and if that's how things were done here . . .

After they were done eating, and the cigarettes and pipes were puffing out smoke, Nasima prompted Kyle. "Now would be a good time to talk," she said.

Nodding, Kyle took a deep breath and said, "Gul, we're grateful for your hospitality. It's been a tough time for us all lately. Now I need to ask for your help with a task."

"What do you need?" Gul asked back, blowing smoke from his nostrils. It ringed his head as it eddied and rose, giving him a sinister look despite his almost smile.

"We are sent to hunt a man," Kyle said. He wasn't ready to throw a name out yet; he needed to feel his way. "We need help finding him and getting to him. The people we dealt with turned out to be less than honorable and clumsy, too. But from what I have seen of your people, you could help us. I want to persuade you to do so."

"Americans need our help?" Gul replied through Nasima. "That's a change from the past." He didn't sound unfriendly, but he did sound a bit put upon. The irony in his voice was clear.

"America has always needed your help," Kyle said. "You live here, and know more about this region than we ever can. Any soldier knows this. Our politicians just think they know everything."

"Much like ours," Gul replied with a grin a foot wide. He chuckled. "Who is this man, and why do you seek him?" he continued, serious again.

"His name is Rafiq bin Qasim, and he's an enemy of our people," Kyle said. And again, he was glad for the .45 under his coat. A wave of tension swept across the room. It was palpable, almost physical as it silenced everyone.

"Mr. Qasim is well respected by some," Gul said, waving his hand to calm those nearest him. "He provides money for the poor and helps with those wounded in our battles."

"Be careful, Kyle," Nasima added.

"Oh, I will be," he said. Facing Gul, holding his eyes, he said, "In some ways, he may be well respected. But that is an act. He wants to use your people as a shield, because he knows we won't bomb him that way. In the meantime, he was part of the attack against our people."

"I have heard of that," Gul said. "They crashed planes into your greatest buildings."

"Those weren't just our buildings," Kyle said. "There were embassies in them. Also offices for the poor. Very few soldiers were attacked, because these people are too cowardly to fight real warriors. They now hide among other women and children, afraid to come out. There's only the two of us," he indicated himself and Wade, "but they still won't fight like men."

That seemed to have some effect. "Coward" was a grievous insult here, and while the Americans were not held in high regard, the two snipers versus bin Qasim and his personal army were a David to Goliath. They could call him afraid, and only by meeting them would he be able to prove his courage.

The faces around them were full of conflict. People don't like having their values challenged, nor being taken advantage of, and the suggestion of both was causing turmoil and debate. At the same time, there was no doubt that al Qaeda was being generous in the region to maintain diplomacy. The Taliban were loved by some, loathed by others, but feared and respected as Islamic warriors with a mission.

Wade caught Kyle's eye. He had something to contribute, and Kyle nodded. The man knew his history and politics, and Kyle was glad to have the backup. Wade had been an excellent choice for the mission.

"The people they attacked were innocents," Wade said. "They were women and children, tourists and workmen, merchants and diplomats. The Quran says that such people should be left out of war. Some of the victims were American and Eastern Muslims. This was not an attack on our government, it was an attack against children."

Kyle took over again, "If they want a fight, we're here for them. I've already told you how sorry we are for our mistake. Imagine if we'd sent a plane to bomb the village. We pick our targets with care, because we don't want to hurt the innocent. These, Nasima, please find a word for 'scum,' preferably involving pigs in a crude fashion, want only to create trouble. They seek a martyrdom."

Gul had been listening calmly, with nods and gestures to prompt them on. He spoke at last. "What if they seek a martyrdom? It is their right, even duty."

"Gul, if they want to meet Allah, we are here to provide the travel arrangements," Wade said. "But it is not just they who will suffer. We've had people in America speak out against all of Islam. We know you are respectable, and Nasima, and the Kuwaitis we met on the way—" they hadn't really met any, but a global view couldn't hurt—"but our people at home don't. All they know is that they were attacked by men who claimed to speak for Allah. If you help with this, it will be a favor to our innocents, and let you . . . show the true face of your God to these corrupt idolaters. If everyone unites against them, they'll go away. Then we can devote our efforts to peace and farming."

Gul was nodding more often. "I think he sees the logic of our position," Wade said.

"Right," Kyle said. "Do you think they agree enough to help us?"

Nasima spoke again, her poise very submissive, almost begging. The exchange went back and forth for several minutes.

"Dude, we're still waaay up the creek here," Wade said.

"Don't I know it. And that bodyguard type looks nervous, so let's stop talking." Kyle didn't point at the man in the corner, arms crossed, who was a knotty giant by local standards.

Neither Kyle nor Wade said anything. Nasima talked on and finally turned back.

"He says he doesn't want a fight with America. But he also doesn't want a fight with the Taliban or other tribes."

"So tell him we don't want a fight, either. We haven't done anything over here since we sent weapons to the mujahideen, and we will leave as soon as we get rid of al Qaeda, because they are hurting our people at home," Kyle said. This wasn't easy, trusting to a translated phrase to carry the proper logic and emotion for the diplomacy he wasn't trained for anyway.

Nasima spoke again. He wondered how she did it. If this screwed up, she'd be killed out of hand, or worse. Kyle had an oath and a mission here, what did she have?

He thought and decided she had her own country to protect. And by getting rid of the Taliban influence, even on this side of the border, she had a better chance at a life. Probably her motives were better than his.

Nasima interrupted his thoughts. "He says that America didn't do anything to stop the Taliban from taking power, and forgot his people after the Russians were gone."

"Dammit, I was afraid he'd see it like that," Wade said.

"So you phrase our arguments. It's your field," Kyle suggested.

"I'll try," Wade sighed. "We don't make policy for our government. Our leaders are as fragmented and childish as the tribes here are."

She looked wide-eyed at him. "But that's insulting—"

"Yes, I know, but tell him that," Wade said. "Then tell him we came here because it's easier to talk to leaders here, who can clearly see their own interests, than to our leaders, who are interested only in money."

Kyle saw where Wade was taking it and nodded. That might be a better approach. Let the locals think they could do things the U.S. government could, which was true enough, and that they'd be heroes out of it, even if only they would know.

Nasima got both phrases out in a hurry, even if she seemed to protest a bit. *Don't blame me, I'm just telling you what the Yankee said to say.*

But Gul nodded very slightly, and turned his lined face back to Kyle. Nasima translated his reply as, "I am a man of my word. I feel sorry for you if your leaders are not."

Wade said, "Tell him we're sorry, too, and wish our government had done more. The people here are kind, generous, and we've made many friends. We're sorry Qalzai lied as he did, and we'll try to see that something is done. But that's not our mission. Our only mission, our jihad, is against al Qaeda and only al Qaeda. We have to do it, and we're going to do it."

As soon as she finished speaking he added, "But we'd like his help, because he is more trustworthy than our former allies, and knowledgeable of the area. We can't buy that kind of ally; we can only gain one through trust and faith."

Still thinking as he went, he said, "And if he'll

do it, he'll have our gratitude, and will sooner see the day when all his enemies leave him alone to live in his own land." He motioned at his pocket. Nasima nodded, and he drew out another packet, containing almost $2,000 in rupees. "How do we offer it properly?"

"I'll tell him it is a gift with which to buy weapons and equipment."

"Not peaceful stuff?" Kyle asked. He didn't really care; he knew where it would go. It just seemed an odd way to offer it.

"That would imply he cannot take care of his people alone," she said. "But if it's offered as foreign aid for defense, so to speak, it's diplomacy, not charity."

"Right," he agreed.

Gul nodded at this, and accepted the money coolly. He didn't even bother to count it. Clearly, the money couldn't be perceived as a bribe. His reply was slow and measured. "You flatter him, he says. But it's honest and restrained flattery, and there's logic to what you say. He'll help you find your man. But in exchange, he expects that you will fight for him if he finds Qalzai."

"In a second," Kyle agreed. "As long as our first priority is our target. We'll nail Qalzai if we see him, or afterwards if there's time, but our mission is first. As Wade says, it's our jihad."

Nasima said to him, "I think you actually understand jihad, rather than it being merely a phrase to you."

"Damn straight," Kyle said. "We'll haunt him as ghosts if we have to. But I'd prefer a good, clean shot."

After another exchange, Gul started laughing. Nasima said, "I told him everything, including your last phrase. He says you are a hill man at heart."

It was late by the time everyone had agreed to work together. They were shown to rooms, Nasima with an eldest daughter, Kyle and Wade to a room along the outside wall.

They slept adequately. The beds were comfortable, with real mattresses. The room was lighted and heated, if small. And it had a poured concrete floor. All in all, it was about equivalent to a military barracks or cheap rustic motel. The facility wasn't the problem. The pending fight and the prickliness of new allies was what was still a worry.

They had tea and naan again for breakfast, with jam and butter. It was tasty, but Kyle agreed with Wade's comment that, "I can't wait to get back Stateside for bacon and eggs."

"Yeah, but they're better than MREs or T-packs."

"True," Wade said. "I'll stop the bitching."

THEY WERE ON THE ROAD AGAIN AT ONCE, IN three pickups. These, however, were in much better shape than the last one. They were dusty and faded, obvious working trucks, but everything worked and there were no sharp metal bits poking through the seats. Rested enough, with food and a full CamelBak of water, weapons, ammo, translator, and reliable (hopefully) allies, it seemed as if it was a real mission at last.

Just before noon, they turned off the road and angled uphill. It was a jolting ride, but the drivers were familiar with the area and experienced in the techniques needed. They'd done this a time or two.

Just how long had these feuds been going on? Kyle wondered. They were less urgent and intense than the Middle East or the Balkans, but they were remembered for just as long. A strange life, plotting and scheming and never being at peace. And there were people who insisted America was militant and violent. He smirked. A few of those whiners needed to spend a week here.

Or Bosnia. There were too many similarities, and he didn't want to go back there yet again. Dammit, the past was the past. And this future might not be too long, so he'd have to pay attention.

Shortly, they got out and started slogging on foot again. Gul had confirmed that the cell phones could call his farm, and at the suggestion, Kyle had taken another risk and given one of the two to Gul's burly bodyguard, herder, and deputy, Pir, who was far more perceptive than he looked. Nasima wrote out directions for using the phone, and he seemed familiar with them. So the vehicles could catch up later, when they were needed for extraction. For now, they'd move quietly.

The walking was a bitch. Kyle had a sore spot on his left foot he felt sure was a small stress fracture. It wasn't debilitating, but it was annoying. They were definitely getting their route marches in. He didn't think the Army would waive PT for the year, though. Pity.

"I wonder how much of a problem it's going to be to find this weasel?" he asked aloud.

"I don't think finding him is the problem," Wade said. "I think it's more that no one wants to screw with this guy."

"Yeah," Kyle agreed. "If he'll blow up children and torture women for fun, who wants to piss him off and see him when he's *really* mad?"

"Exactly. But that means we can hope it's not that hard of an infiltration."

"Except for that part about two Americans and a translator," Wade said. "I think he knows we're here."

"Yeah, it sucks to be us," Kyle said, "but I don't think a squad would be less noticeable."

"Right, he'd be gone. We're along because we won't scare him. Until it's too late, that is."

"That's the plan," Kyle chuckled. "I bet he crapped his pants after that shot I took."

"He should," Wade said. "He's only big and bad because we haven't found him yet."

"That's the idea. Keep in mind how cool we are, how efficient, and eventually we might believe it."

"Well, us and our allies," Wade said.

Gul had been good to his word. His tribe was also better equipped than Qalzai's had been. They had newer, cleaner weapons, including AK-74s in 5.45mm and even one AK-100. They clearly had better sources of intel and materiel. In that light, Kyle had reason to be thankful.

After jabbering around a map, Gul and his next deputy Nasrulah, who had no teeth and a bald head, pointed out a likely area. "We'll go here," he said, "and then over this way. We'll find them."

It was reassuring to the Americans to see a map. It was even a standard 1:50,000 military map. They brought out their own, newer copy and took a look at the area. They were trained professionals, and the contours on the map formed into peaks they could see in their minds. It would improve their navigation on the ground.

"You know," Wade said, slipping on another loose rock, "if I'd thought it was going to be this much of a pain, I wouldn't have been so eager. To hell with the enemies, this terrain sucks."

" 'A bitching GI is a happy GI,' " Kyle replied with mirth.

"Screw that," Wade said, though he smiled, too. "I'd say it could be worse, but I won't, because I can think of fifty or a hundred ways it could be a lot worse."

"We could be on an alien planet, tracking down some strange artifact . . ." Kyle said.

"Or just rain and incoming fire. That seems a lot more likely and real," Wade said.

The poor excuse for a road dove into a deep cut in the hills. Wind whipped occasional dust devils down it. It was foreboding, even though silent and empty.

At least it seemed empty. A burst of fire boiled sand from the rutted track in front. Everyone scattered for cover.

"Son of a bitch!" Wade gasped as he dropped down between Kyle and Gul behind a boulder to one side.

"Hey, you're the wiseass who mentioned incoming fire," Kyle said. Frankly, he was getting sick of it himself. He just wanted to take this shot, drop this freak, and get home. The universe seemed to be conspiring against him.

"Right, so what do we do now?"

"Nasima?" Kyle called after the next burst. She looked over from behind another rock, keeping low. "Tell them I want them to shoot where Wade shoots his tracers."

"Tracers?" she asked.

"Bullets that light up."

"Ah, yes," she said, and told Gul, because of course, she couldn't give orders, only he could, and she could only relay the request.

Luckily, Gul nodded agreement with a grin.

"Right, Wade, you light 'em up, they pour out the fire, I'll spot for you and hit anything that needs precision."

"You got it," Wade replied. He had already swapped out his magazine for one of straight tracers. He pushed the button to light up the Eotech sight and hunkered down around the little carbine.

It was noisy, Kyle thought. He hadn't expected this much fire from as few people as he could see. It took a few seconds before he figured out what was happening.

Their fire discipline, to put it mildly, sucked rocks. They were great at pouring out long bursts of automatic fire that did little but waste ammo and make noise. Some of the more experienced ones stayed on semi and banged off rapid fire groups that were likely yards across. Only two or three of the group were worth a damn.

Kyle reflected that that was often true in American units, too. But in an American, or any, actual military unit, there'd be an instructor to train the panicky kids out of that. Some of these guys had been shooting like this for forty years, and he wasn't sure how they'd lived that long, considering the real battles they must have been in.

Unless, of course, the people they fought against were equally bad shots.

Still, there was enough metal in the air that something was bound to hit sooner or later. A quick, decisive action would end this before that happened, or before their allies ran out of ammo.

Kyle sighted what looked like a vintage Russian RPK, from the snout protruding between two clumps of bedrock and the muzzle flash. Whoever it was was spraying with abandon. "Wade! Reference: twelve o'clock high. RPK."

"Sighted," Wade said. "Nasima, have them fire on my tracer!" He squeezed off a short burst that came close to doing the job itself.

This was a game to the locals. As the streaks appeared, they enthusiastically turned their weapons on target and actually *aimed,* at least as far as the start of their fire. Enough bullets hit to carve the outcroppings down some, and there were several dings against the weapon itself. Its fire stopped. Whether or not there was a casualty behind it was unclear. Either way, the incoming fire declined.

Kyle had already scanned and found a competent marksman. He called to Wade, who ended the problem by himself, his tracer round cracking center of mass as the man slipped from behind a boulder to shoot, and dropping him. Nevertheless, their friends poured out a sufficient volume to reduce the corpse to hamburger. That was of great psychological effect, as the incoming fire tapered off another order of magnitude.

But someone over there was shouting orders, and the copper-clad hornets picked up once again. One of their own allies had been hit and was screaming. Chips flew above Kyle and he decided it was time to duck. He pulled in close to the earth, shimmied forward just enough to get a peek, and sought a target.

Yes, there was Qalzai, that sneering, conceited jackass. It wasn't a good idea to mix business and pleasure, but in this case, Kyle would make an exception. There were rounds cracking close to him now, but he ignored them. He eased the SMLE forward, clicked off the safety, and sighted carefully. The range wasn't great, perhaps 100 meters, and that was an easy range for this weapon. As long as there was no sudden movement.

Qalzai ducked and shifted, to yell at another of his men. Kyle sighed, avoided letting it get to him, and resighted. It was only a matter of a second, though in battle, seconds of action could decide the issue. But calm and professionalism would win. He breathed, squeezed, and felt the sharp kick against his shoulder.

Qalzai came apart in a mess, half his face blown off. Better yet, from a tactical point of view, he wasn't quite dead yet. He screamed and thrashed and provided all kinds of gratuitous special effects to dissuade his buddies, who were now not firing, but running. They left their wounded and even some of their gear in their haste to retreat. Kyle wondered at the effect he'd had with that one shot, until he realized Wade had accounted for two others. That was five down out of twenty or thirty, a respectable casualty count and more than these people liked to see in thirty seconds of feuding.

Most of the kills had been by Kyle and Wade, or at least under their direction. That left far fewer wounded than could be expected. Kyle destressed with a long drink of water, ignoring the grit and slime in it for the cooling, cleaning wetness it provided. He tried to ignore the screams of the wounded, which were punctuated by cracks of fire as several were put out of their misery.

He and Wade at once administered first aid to their side's casualties. One man had a vicious wound to his shoulder, the bone nicked and fragments scattered through the flesh. He bandaged it as best he could and tied the arm in place. One man was dead, a bullet through the lung leaving a pool of blood two yards across. Wade had bandaged up a man with an excruciating shot to the hand, and three minor wounds where people had crashed into rocks.

While they were finishing, the patrol Gul had led up returned with loot, including the damaged RPK. Considering the local craftspeople, it was likely to be operational again within a few days. Gul was grinning a yard of teeth. Nasima translated his raucous comments. "He says you shoot with Allah, destroying the enemies. And he congratulates you on Qalzai. He doesn't say so, but you've proved yourself to him."

"*Sta na shukria*," Kyle said in thanks.

Several bodies besides Qalzai's were brought down. Mirza was one of them, and Kyle felt saddened by it. He'd been a good man. It was likely his only fault was in teaming up with Qalzai. Khushal had gotten away, apparently, or had not been involved.

"No Khushal. Good. He's a good kid," Wade said. They'd both been thinking it.

"Yeah," Kyle agreed. "And there's Bait," he said, pointing at another corpse. "I guess it wasn't a bad day."

"Glad to hear it, but we better hurry," Wade said. "We need to be well clear before dark."

Nasima nodded, repeated it, and Gul shouted orders. In moments, everyone had formed back up, the bodies left behind with some hasty dirt and rocks thrown over them. "They will bury them better later," Nasima said. "We are moving for safety. But it's not right to leave any Muslim exposed to carrion birds and wild dogs."

Kyle frankly didn't give a damn about Qalzai and Bait, but it would make sense tactically to have them better covered. Although it wasn't likely to happen before this mission played out. "That's decent," he said diplomatically, taking another pull of water and falling into line.

14

BIN QASIM WAS VERY HAPPY. THE NIGHT-club blast had been perfect. Better yet, the soldier of God had not died in the explosion, but had been captured by the German authorities. Since decadent Westerners would never execute an enemy, except for the Americans, and even they did it so rarely and after such a long time that it was meaningless, he could be ransomed in exchange for reporters or diplomats. Perhaps Allah would smile and some of them would be women, who could learn of God's hierarchy from bin Qasim first.

Or, the bomber could be shot in custody, by another soldier, of course, and turned into a martyr, creating greater fear. Already, southern France's Muslim population had managed to close many of the clubs, and impose decent standards of dress upon women. If Germany could be brought along next, the new wave of Islam could sweep the world.

And if America could not be persuaded, why, then she could be raped like the whore she was.

The phone rang then, line number three. He picked up the receiver quickly but carefully.

"Yes?" he said.

"We are on our way," a voice whispered. "There has been a fight. The Diversion Unit was hurt badly, but inflicted three casualties. Here's our coordinates," the informer said. There was a pause as he switched to text messaging, followed by a string of numbers on the display.

"Thank you. Call when they are within five kilometers."

"Go with Allah," was the last comment before the line went dead.

Bin Qasim marked the map. That was a convenient location, but he'd wait a while. When they were closer, he'd spring the trap. When they were too close to escape.

Grinning, he shut down the computer and turned to matters of the soul.

After which, those American snipers would be turned into a sign from God.

It was Wade who suddenly said, "What the hell?"

They were moving along a shelf that protruded from the hillside. Wade had casually leaned against the wall to adjust his ruck, and seen something . . .

"Does that man have a radio?" he asked aloud.

There was instant reaction to the tone of his voice, and Kyle turned. Sure enough, there was a short, shaggy man with what looked like a radio or cell phone just disappearing into his pocket. The expression on his face was of utter surprise, though a quick storm of other emotions rolled across. He clearly was embarrassed.

Nasima said something that included *"Telepone,"* the word borrowed from English, and in seconds the man was surrounded and pinned to the wall. One of Gul's close henchmen held up the device. It was, in fact, an Iridium phone, similar to that the snipers carried.

There was shouting, curses, and accusations. Gul and Kyle both had to yell for silence. That left the man, Sidiq, standing surrounded by a semicircle of bewildered, angry people. He was relieved of his weapons in short order, but not without a struggle. He was pushed down, acquiring a bruise on the cheek along the way. Again Gul had to shout for order. This time, silence and calm prevailed.

"I can't think of a valid reason for this clown to have a cell phone. Can you?" Kyle asked, voice quivering with rage.

"No," Wade said. "Nasima?"

She was already speaking to Gul, and it was clear that he was not happy. Not only was this a threat to him, but it was a threat to his guests. The two together amounted to a major sin against propriety, the tribe, and what nationalism there was.

"How much did he talk? Do we need to abort?" Kyle asked. He hated like hell the idea that they might have to bug out, but if someone was waiting for them, it would be suicide to continue.

"I am asking," Nasima assured him, her tone snappish. Kyle breathed slowly and mentally backed off. He kept trying to run every detail himself, and he simply wasn't qualified for some of this. *Let the other guy handle his own MOS*, he thought. *Or woman in this case.* There was too much to do, and too much he didn't know, for him to throw his weight around.

Sidiq was defensive and outraged at the accusations. But when Gul asked him point blank, "Who did you call? Three numbers here. Who?" he didn't have a good answer. He shut up entirely.

While in an American court the Fifth Amendment would protect him against self-incrimination, this was neither court nor America. It was a battlefield, and they had to know what was going on, and act on that information quickly.

Gul punched Sidiq, a heavy, straight smash to his face that knocked him back against the rock. He staggered, eyes unfocused and head lolling.

When he recovered, with a shake of the head that threw drops of blood from his nose, his attitude had changed. He started ranting something about Allah. Kyle didn't need a translation to know he was justifying himself, but when Sidiq faced him, he spoke in English anyway.

"It is a holy honor to die for Allah," he said. His eyes had that look of the true believer. The nutcase who will endorse hatred, killing, socialism, or other religious idiocies, no matter how illogical or how often proved wrong, just because he believes.

Kyle had had enough. "An honor indeed," he said. He wasn't opposed to torture for information in this case, but it would take time they didn't have. He snagged a grenade from his harness, flipped the pin out with his left thumb, and stuffed it down the coarse shirt of the little troll. He gave him a heartfelt knee to the balls, driving his leg to his own waist, a good foot above the skinny little runt's crotch, then drove his heel into the man's chest. Sidiq grunted, "Guhhhhh!" with a terrified look on his face as he bounced over the precipice and down. Precisely at the three-second mark, a horrendous *Boom!* indicated that his body was splattered over the cliff face. "Bon fucking voyage. Say hi to Allah for me," Kyle said.

There was a slim chance someone might hear the boom, identify it, and come after them, but there were so many little engagements, uses of grenades for mining, celebrations, stray land mines, and fire for God only knew what else that he wasn't worried. And didn't care. He'd been a traitor, and he was dead. And with bin Qasim knowing their location anyway, it couldn't really hurt.

And, he reflected, killing the little bastard made him feel quite a bit better.

That done, fury and fear fighting inside, he drew out his own phone and called in.

On the second ring, it was answered.

"Gilpin." Gilpin was Robash's civilian assistant. His voice was deep, and he likely bellowed in person.

"Mr. Gilpin, Sergeant Monroe. I have a problem," he said.

"What do you need?"

"We've got a local infiltrator with an Iridium phone, who likely called our target. Can we check the numbers called and track the physical location of the receiving party?"

"Stand by, Sergeant," Gilpin replied. "Can you give me the ID from the phone that called, hold on air, and I'll get a rep to talk to me?"

"Sure," Kyle agreed. He read off the serial number, and the phone's ID from memory. "Holding," he said.

Kyle spent the pause twitching and fidgeting. It was only two minutes, then Gilpin was back. "Sergeant Monroe, the number belongs to a geologic survey company based out of Kazakhstan. The call was received within two hundred miles of your location. That's as accurate as they can say unless the user attaches a GPS option."

"I don't think the user is going to do that," he observed wryly.

"Neither do I. Sorry I can't be of more help on that."

"Oh, that helps," Kyle said. "It was definitely in theater, therefore it's a threat. One of our allies had a cell phone and was calling out."

"Understood. What do you plan to do?"

"I'm not aborting yet, if that's what you're asking. We'll take a different route in," he said. He probably should abort, but it had become a point of honor. He and Wade were going to get this rat bastard.

"Understood. We'll be here if you need us."

"Thanks. Kyle out." He disconnected. "Well," he said to Wade and Nasima, "that's that. They know we're coming. What do we do?"

"Hide in a hurry, and either evac or at least clear the area," Wade said.

Nasima spoke to Gul, who said, "If we get higher, we will have better position and visibility."

That was true, Kyle thought, and there wasn't much in the way of air support here. "Sounds good," he said. "Quietly and quickly."

The terrain wasn't that hard to climb; it had plenty of texture. Still, they were at altitude, and the air was thin. Adding huge rucks to the equation made it an athletic event. Gul's people helped carry some of the gear, but even so, it was crushing. The safest technique was to slither over the rocks, using hands and feet. Dust and sweat turned to mud on their skin, and they were all soon abraded and scraped.

They rested every hour, sipping water slowly and chewing at boring rations. As soon as their parched throats were comfortable, they were climbing again. The locals, Kyle thought, moved like mountain goats. Even Nasima was ahead of him, bouncing easily. He actually had caught a glimpse of ankle, and her muscle tone was rather attractive. Sighing, he pushed on.

They were still safe at sunset, and it seemed there'd be no more interruptions. Wade had suggested, and Kyle had agreed, that they should bite the bullet and travel around the village to another site. There was no need to risk setting up where their traitor had known they would be. Gul nodded at the suggestion, said, "Very wise," and led them widely around.

They pushed on in the dark until progress was impossible. The Americans had night vision, and Gul had an old Russian set that was twenty years old. But the rest had eyes only, and even with a half-moon, it was too dark for safe footing. They unrolled blankets and snuggled against the hillside, under a slight overhang that cut the wind. It did nothing about noise, and whistling whines announced gusts all night. Any audible approach would also be apparent, of course. Sometimes, the best shelter was in the open.

Under blankets, wool chapan coats and shirts, with their lungees wrapped down around their faces, it wasn't chill, but cool. It couldn't be above forty-five degrees outside, and the windbreak and clothes stopped them from getting hypothermia but not much else. But they'd trained for worse, and the locals seemed used to it. Or maybe it was just the lack of central heating most of them had.

Gul posted sentries, using his night vision and

one of the American sets. Kyle felt as if he were loaning out his car to a teenager. But the young man took only a few minutes of fiddling to decipher the controls, and slipped off like a ghost. He seemed to know what he was about, so Kyle tried to concentrate on sleeping.

Oddly enough, he did. Exhaustion put him under, but there was something that lowered his suspicions. With Nasima along, and the effort Gul had made toward communicating, planning and tactics, it *felt* right. No yokels, these; they were competent guerillas.

They awoke at dawn, breath misting in the frigid air. There was some frost, and Kyle ached all over. He had blisters on his cold, stinging toes, chafing around his boot tops and on his shoulders, and a crick in his neck. His mouth tasted horrible.

There was no tea, but he brushed his teeth as they started walking again at once, out from the ledge they'd sheltered under and up the slope. A swig of water to rinse with made him feel five percent closer to human, and he shifted his gear around as he marched, trying to find the most comfortable arrangement. He forced himself not to favor his right foot, that being the worst-blistered one, because he could injure himself worse with bad posture.

"Man, you look as ugly as I feel," Wade said to him, catching up alongside as they crawled over a steep slab.

"Same to you, pal," he snapped back. "Enjoying that great fresh air and the huge paycheck that comes with it?"

"Oh, absolutely. I feel like singing," Wade said.

"You do and I'll shoot you first," he replied. "I didn't think you could get a hangover without drinking."

"Altitude," Wade said.

"Yeah, I know. Doesn't mean I like it, just because I understand it."

The verbal sparring stopped as one of Gul's men slipped back and extended his arm. He held the night vision goggles, cased and secure. *"Sta na shukria,"* Kyle said as he took them. It was more natural to him now than "thank you."

The terrain wasn't all uphill. They spent as much time angling obliquely across slopes down. That was sometimes worse, with slippery dirt over loose, scaly rock underneath.

Kyle estimated their progress at perhaps one mile per hour, with the rough ground and slope. Some areas were smooth and green, lush with growth from rain caught by the hillsides. Other areas were chaotic jumbles of bedrock. It certainly never got boring, he thought, as they clambered over a sharp, jutting point and lowered themselves.

Nasima was panting, but gamely hanging on. She'd started with youthful energy and flexibility, but in the long term, the veterans could push beyond the fatigue barrier. Even sheened in sweat with stringy hair escaping her hijab, she was striking. Kyle wondered again why she stayed here. With her drive, she could be very successful in the West.

Still, home was home. He'd do well here, with an American pension. He couldn't see himself doing so.

"Are you okay?" he asked her at a break.

"I am," she said. "Though my shoes are too stiff. But I will manage." She drank water from her canteen, a typical camping-style one slung over her shoulder, and then greeted Gul as he approached. She translated effortlessly as they chatted.

"We are in the area," Gul said. "I expect they are in the village over that next ridge," he pointed. "It's about seven kilometers, and we'll have height. What do you want to do?"

Wade spoke first. "We need to reconnoiter the area, and find a good route down and on. We'll have to get within about five hundred meters."

"Next time, I suggest the mortar," Gul said with mirth.

"Wouldn't we like to," Kyle said. "Or just spot for an Air Force jet. But we have to be discreet, and we have to avoid casualties. The press will cause trouble."

"Perhaps you should use the reporters for target practice," he said.

"We had that exact conversation," Wade said, "only with politicians."

They all laughed.

Gul continued, "We are on the far side from the road. We'll need to sneak around and across.

If you can call, our drivers can be waiting to pick us up."

"Right. Where?" he asked. It wouldn't do to have vehicles close enough to take fire from direct-fire weapons and give away their position. They looked at the map and selected a location. The ridge they'd be on tapered off to the west, and a road hooked around from the south. It was about two kilometers away from the target, and would be concealed until pursuing elements cleared the ridge by going either over or around.

"Looks good. But if I were this guy, and knew we were coming, I'd have patrols all over these ridges," Wade said.

"Assume so," Kyle nodded. "So we can't have the vehicles show up until after the shot. We can do that with the phones easily enough."

"And meantime?"

"Meantime," Kyle said, "we need very good hilljacks to find where those patrols go."

Gul grinned, "I have three men who are perfect. They will tell you who made their shoes."

"I'll settle for the shoe size," Kyle said. "I hope they won't be disappointed."

Gul whistled up three of his men. All looked to be on the older side, though with their living conditions, that could be late twenties. They nodded, and slipped off in three directions; along the ridge, down behind it to the road to the south, and back to the east where they'd come from.

Gul said, "We'll want the trucks on the road,

and traveling, not parked. No one will attach significance to them."

"Of course," he continued after a pause, "that little bastard Sidiq may have given them the license numbers."

"Risk we take," Kyle said. "But if they aren't close by, it shouldn't hurt us."

"True. Let's rest while the scouts search."

So they did, and Kyle actually got a precious hour of sleep. Wade woke him and they switched off. Nasima could translate, she couldn't make tactical decisions. One of them had to be awake for that.

After they were both awake, they fidgeted. Nothing would speed up the process, and Gul's patrols had binoculars but not radios. They'd report back in person when they had something substantial, and not before.

15

AFTER A LUNCH OF BEANS AND RICE WITH vegetables, heated over a trioxane stove, Gul asked, "How do we approach this?" His scouts had come back and drawn a map of the area. The al Qaeda patrols were marked.

"It's not that hard, really, at least on paper," Kyle said. "We find a good spot for a shot, set up support, take the shot, and run. Once we're done, we can call support aircraft. We just have to hold out long enough to get a chopper in. Hopefully no more than an hour or two. If we run fast . . ." he tapered off.

"Running is not dishonorable when a task has been done, or to save soldiers for a better fight," Gul said. "How do we arrange supporting fire?"

That was an excellent question. The discussion was important, but Kyle was groggy and wanted a nap. He'd settle for sitting still while they talked tactics.

It was decided to make the shots in the evening. They'd be to the southeast of the target, which would give them shadows and illumination. There was a risk of reflection from the scopes, but long shrouds and careful use of fabric should avoid that. The sun wouldn't quite be in their eyes, but they might get some glare.

On the other hand, it would be much harder for them to be pursued at night, it would avoid another night camping, and would let them use NVG and then aircraft for overwhelming effect. There were no ideal conditions. But this was a good compromise.

With an improving grasp of the language and Nasima's assistance, it was a much easier infiltration. They moved up the ridge before dinnertime, flitting from bush to boulder. They kept below the military crest until they found a good site, and made a quick, surreptitious recon over the peak.

Yes, there was a village. And it had signs of being more than that. First, there was a twenty-meter radio mast. Also two surplus Pakistani army technical vehicles, guards at the door of one house, and patrols on Suzuki dirt bikes. "Looks like it," Wade said.

"Yeah," Kyle agreed. This was much more military than the last encounter, and the radio antenna was the key item. Almost everyone around here was armed tactically. But communication implied a strategic mind. And that slight arch behind the house was . . . yes, a satellite dish. "This be the place, I think," he said.

Gul eagerly took his directions, dispersing his men in groups of two and three to provide cover fire. Once Kyle or Wade took the shot, they were going to pour automatic-weapons fire and RPGs into the camp, then run.

"I'll wait here," Nasima said.

"The hell you will," Kyle replied. "We need our translator alive. I'll motion if I need you. Get down the hill where you're shadowed from stray shots."

"Yes, Kyle," she sighed, clearly not happy at being pushed aside again.

"Not sure if she's just eager to see the climax of all this, trying to be one of the guys, or afraid to be down there alone," Wade said.

"Dunno," Kyle said quietly. "I do know I don't want a civilian this close. And she's got a real life I'd hate to see wasted. I know it's cold, but I couldn't care less if two or three of these guys buy it."

"Yeah," Wade said. "She's got presence, a way of grabbing you. And she's a babe."

"I hadn't noticed," Kyle lied. Yes, she was stunning. He couldn't know her genetic mix was Pashto, Moghul, Turk, and Hazara. He did know she was exotically beautiful, and her temper, wit, and keen mind made her that much more exciting. And as a local, a Muslim, and a civilian support specialist, she might as well be on the moon for his chances of approaching her. So he wasn't going to go there. Anymore. He reached into his ruck and drew out his ghillie. He wanted the best concealment he could get.

" 'Hadn't noticed,' " Wade said with a snort. "If you say so." He reached for his suit, too.

"What's our range?" Kyle asked, ignoring the comment.

"About eight hundred meters."

"Not close enough," he said. The SMLE could reach that far . . . but it would be a high-arcing trajectory, and not reliable. Especially with the bogus "match" ammo he had. As near as he could tell, it was standard ball. Still, the smith had done an honest job on the rifle. And there wasn't anything he could do about it now. "Can we get closer?"

A brief exchange yielded the answer, "Five hundred meters. No closer." That was a very respectable range for the SMLE, but doable. It had been a mistake to bring the Barrett in the first place. It wasn't a weapon for extreme precision. It was a weapon for busting armor and vehicles. An infiltration with support was how it should have been played all along.

Next time, he'd tell them he wanted a weapons platoon.

"Three hundred," Kyle said as he donned the shapeless tan ghillie. There was nothing without risk. He'd prefer to simply call an air strike at this point, but that wasn't possible in putatively friendly territory with so many undefined people around. He wasn't going to call them "innocent," but he would give them the benefit of the doubt because his orders said so.

Gul sighed in exasperation as he answered, "Yes."

So they sought an approach down the rocks. It would need to allow them a swift retreat, heavy cover, good concealment, and a clear field of fire. The criteria were tough. Luckily, the ridge was long and geologically recent. There would be an appropriate place somewhere, they just had to find it.

It only took twenty minutes. While Gul and his boys might not be professionally trained, they were experienced enough to be patient and calm. One of the teenagers whistled softly for attention, and grinned a mouth of teeth as he pointed.

"Good enough," Kyle commented. It was. Bedrock with enough texture for traction lay down the hill, with tumbled slabs over it, slowly weathering away after their collapse from a vertical peak above.

He and Wade, with Gul and the teen moved forward. Kyle would rather have had another experienced troop, but it was the kid's right as the finder to be along. Still, he seemed reliable. Above and behind them, the other six hugged the ridge, prepared to fire and under orders to do so only if incoming fire threatened the snipers. That left one driving each vehicle, and one each on the guns in case of pursuit.

The sun was angling down, shadows lazily falling across the landscape as they snuck down. "We might get darkness for cover, too."

"Excellent," Wade said. "Though I don't think we've got the only night vision."

"I bet we use it better," Kyle said. It was arrogant, he knew, but really, most of these guys weren't that well trained. Cunning, sneaky, intelligent, sure. But not trained and schooled. Education was key.

Education, patience, logistics, communications, adaptation . . . even on a mission with only two troops, he reflected, battle was a complex skill that took massive support. "An Army of One" might be a great PR tool for recruiting, but this mission depended on two snipers, their knowledge, local support, a chunk of cash, a radio, a computer, an orbiting aircraft, satellite intel, CIA-gathered intel, several transport aircraft, and four military installations. Two generals, their staffs, an infantry lieutenant, a whole chain of supply clerks, and several pilots and mechanics had put them here.

He shook himself back to the present, though the mental drift was good, as it meant he was in the mindset to do his job. One couldn't have a wandering mind if scared or overwhelmed, so he was calm. All he had to do was keep a focus on the operation, and zoom in where needed.

He found a good position, in shadow from the falling sun, framed by rocks and wide enough to pan across the entire village. Wade was right next to him.

"I'd call this three hundred and fifty-five meters to the near edge," Wade said, "three hundred and ninety to the antenna."

"Right. Far side?" Kyle asked.

"Eight hundred meters. But we're waiting for him to get near the radio, right?"

"I figure he's in there now. Hence the guards."

"Good bet," Wade agreed.

Next came the waiting. They stared in turns, taking time to rest their eyes. Sweat rolled down them, and the rock underneath was cool, then chill. As the shadows lengthened and swallowed them entirely, the temperature dropped. That left them dusty and sticky, then wishing for more clothes. The wool itched and scratched, as did Kyle's two-week beard. He might be less noticeable, but he was not comfortable.

But he'd been less so before, and this was the crux of the mission. He put it aside, and nibbled crackers from his ruck, letting the crumbs and the plastic packaging stay inside. No need to leave any traces. The weapon was placed, sighted, loaded, and safed. All he needed was a few seconds.

Wade jerked suddenly.

"What?" Kyle asked, but no answer was needed. Wade pulled out a vibrating cell phone. It was the one Sidiq had carried.

"What the hell do we do?" Wade asked, staring at the phone as if it were a grenade.

"Don't answer it," Kyle said. "It's bad, but answering it would be worse. If they don't know what's happening—"

"They might think he's surrounded and can't answer," Wade finished.

"Right. Still, it's a Bad Thing."

Everyone had clustered around, and was staring. "Let's not bunch up, folks," he said. He made shooing motions and the gaggle dispersed.

Wade said, "There's no number given. They're blocking."

"I think we're pretty sure who it is. Let's let him stew a while."

"Sure," Wade said.

The phone buzzed again at once. After that, nothing. Whoever was calling had apparently decided there wasn't going to be an answer.

"This just keeps getting more and more succulent," Kyle said. "Emphasis on the suck."

"Well, we can't turn around now."

"No," Kyle said, "But I'd really rather call an air strike. Why'd this bastard have to be in Pakistan? Just over the border, we could blow him to Mars and be done with it."

" 'Ours not to reason why. Ours but to punch holes at long range,' " Wade said.

"Yeah. Enough chatter out of me. Back to the task," Kyle said.

It was more than an hour before anything of further interest happened. Meantime, men wandered around, joked, swapped off on guard. Several vehicles drove by on the road, and were watched suspiciously from both sides. Yes, these guys were hiding something.

There was a smell of stewed goat and burning

grain under the oily fire smoke. Kyle lay low on the rock, chin on arm, and cautiously twitched his toes in his boots to keep circulation going. He was too well trained to make large movements, but he needed to shift a little or his body would fall asleep from inaction.

"There," Wade said, interrupting his musing. At once, he leaned over the rifle, wrapped around it and eased up into a shooting position. Then he waited.

"What?" he asked.

"Someone opened the door, and one of the guards nodded. Not sure what's next, but it's the first action we've seen all day."

"Right," he agreed. "Tuck a dollar in my G-string." But he stayed on the weapon, waiting. With his left hand, he raised his scope and took a look.

Wade chuckled. "We'll see."

But the action was followed by more. A few minutes later, the door opened again. A figure came out and strode away. His face was in shadow, and Kyle cursed, begging for light to identify his target by. The dusk was making it a bitch to use available light or night vision. If need be, they'd stay here a day, two, a week, however long it took. But patience and eagerness are not opposites. Kyle could be patient, but he was eager.

Then the figure turned and the orange sun caught him in profile.

It was a repeat of that first shot days before,

only with, Kyle hoped, reliable allies. *This* face in his scope was quite similar to the provided photo. "Good," Kyle said. He put down the scope and leaned over the SMLE.

"That is him," Wade confirmed. "Three seven zero meters."

"Got it," Kyle said, and squeezed. The trigger pull on the venerable rifle was long and slow, but even. Patience was called for even here, as he held the reticle firmly on the man's chin, expecting the shot to take him high in the chest. Squeeze, squeeze, and then it broke.

It was a crisp, clean letoff, the rifle boomed and kicked, and the short stock had his hand close enough that he banged his nose with his thumb.

"Hit," Wade said. "Breastbone. I call him dead."

"Good," Kyle said, calmly cycling the bolt, lowering his aim and putting one through the brain to make sure. *Bang!* "So do I. Let's move."

Bin Qasim wasn't happy. Sidiq had reported on the Americans' location, but had not reported back. His phone was intact, but he was not answering. It could be that he was too close to report or reply, but in that case, he should be faking an injury and slipping off. Once they were within five kilometers, he could easily direct artillery and roving patrols to them.

It was also possible Sidiq wasn't smart enough

to handle the situation. That was a common problem. Many of the smartest had died in the attack upon America, Allah praise their names. Many others with an intellectual bent were too . . . detached, reluctant for operations. Bin Qasim would call them cowards, but as he needed them, he tried not to think it too loudly.

None of the patrols had found any sign of the Americans or their traitorous peasant allies. They had likely been lost and slowed by the mountains. He couldn't rely on that, though. He needed concrete intelligence about his enemy soon.

Additional patrols were going out in an inner perimeter. It wouldn't do to appear nervous or afraid; there were two of his own people who might jump at an opening and do something stupid and criminal. But he did need the patrols.

It was time to send out another update. The lesser soldiers were often competent, but lacked the fire of the warrior of Allah. They needed to talk to a real leader in order to maintain their courage. Which was fine; it was why Allah, all glory to him, had placed people like bin Qasim on this earth.

After that, he would see about planning another relocation. The Americans were constantly biting at him, hordes of insects against the power of Allah, but even insects could be dangerous in number. Faithless, vile, but nonetheless a threat.

He looked up at the door of the communications center to see the guard snap to attention.

Then excruciating pain tore the breath from his lungs as a 180-grain .303 bullet smashed through his ribs, his heart, and out the back. He staggered, stepped, and saw the shocked look on the guard's face.

"Help me," he uttered, but it was silent, no air behind it. He knew he was on his knees but not how he'd got there, his memory fading. Then he was prone, nose and lips battered by the impact, but that pain paling in comparison to the mule kick to his chest. He breathed a choking mouthful of dust, and the cough that followed felt like the fires of hell.

He died too quickly to feel the shot that pulped his skull like a melon.

16

KYLE AND WADE WERE ON THEIR KNEES, then their feet. Kyle slung the rifle, grabbed his ruck, and waited in a crouch. Wade stuffed the scope into his pack, scurried back, and took a defensive position. "Move," he said, and Kyle crawled back past him. Then Wade. Then Kyle. Gul gave them a triumphant grin and a raised fist as they passed his position.

The thrill didn't last long. It was less than ten seconds before massive fire came their way— 14.5mm Russian, or perhaps Chinese. Either way, it was heavy, aimed with skill and vengeance, and lethal.

Splashes of splinters came off the rocks around them, and for a moment, Kyle lost it. He saw a repeat of Bosnia, saw Wade dead, saw fire blowing around him and himself bound for hell with the next burst.

Then Wade grabbed his arm and pulled him, and he was back to normal. "Come on!" Wade shouted. "We've got cover fire, let's move!" Then he lobbed a 40mm down into the square before retreating again. It was extreme range, but it couldn't hurt, and might keep people's heads down.

They ducked and crawled. The fire was heavy, but other than the one machine gun, it wasn't very well aimed.

It struck Kyle just like that. *These assholes can't shoot for shit!* It applied to both the enemy and his allies. They were enamored of long, raking bursts, but only the most experienced were using their fire wisely. To the untrained, automatic fire is better because it puts more lead out. But one crucial lesson in training is to see how widely a burst disperses after the first three rounds. A few minutes of angle leads to missing by yards, and that's what was happening.

Still, it wasn't fun to retreat while bullets lashed the hills around them. There were interspersed ear-shattering bangs from something larger, perhaps a recoilless rifle or grenade launcher. Hell, it might even be a small mortar. There was no telling what those jerks were firing, and the growing grayness, smoke, and dust made it impossible to look.

Nor did Kyle particularly care. He wanted out of there, and now.

He had no idea how they made it up to the ridge, but then they were over it and heading down. As they ran, he peeled off the ghillie. It had served its purpose, and was a hindrance now. He dropped it behind a rock.

At least the trip was easier than it had been with Qalzai's morons. The terrain was better, and the troops knew how to retrograde. They were shouting, joking, cursing while they burned through three or four magazines each in the growing dusk. *Give them this, they've got plenty of ammo,* Kyle thought. Wade wasn't firing at all; there were no targets. But he kept dodging past Kyle, low and fast, taking a position and covering him. No doubt, the man was professional. It might be his first time in a war zone, but he wasn't panicking, wasn't wasting fire, and wasn't freezing. Kyle couldn't have asked for a better spotter.

The slope of the hill was relatively gradual. They went down fast, but that meant the enemy would, too. There was no time to slack off. Every second of distance would improve their safety, and Kyle relished the pending ride in the trucks almost as little as he did the incoming fire. It was going to be brutal. But at least they'd bagged the right guy, and the Army's part of the mission was done.

Surviving and extracting was nice for the troop, useful for the Army, but secondary to the mission. If he died now, the Army would give him a medal and a nice funeral, and that would be all. The men and women of the Army would do everything they could to keep him alive on the way out so he could be used again, but the Army as an entity was done for the time being.

Not that it mattered. Wits were what were going to keep them alive for the time being.

The trucks were waiting, their tailgunners watching the rocks and panning back and forth. They weren't firing yet, and looked disappointed at the lack of targets. The drivers were waving and shouting.

Then they were skidding out on the scree slope at the bottom of the hill, and making a mad dash for the vehicles. At any moment, their pursuers might reach the peak and have a beautiful view straight down. It wasn't reassuring. The armor value of these vehicles wasn't enough to stop a BB gun, much less a 7.62 Russian round or any support weapon.

They leapt into the bed of the lead truck, Nasima clutching at their free hands while they tried not to crack her skull with the rifles. She shouted, *"Penza! Shpag!"* as they tumbled in. Gul was next, and she called, *"Owa!"*

Bodycount, Kyle realized. Then, *"Ata!"* as the last man came aboard. Five, six, seven, eight. Plus four on the trucks, plus Nasima. All accounted for. While Kyle was sorting that out in his mind, the driver nailed it.

He banged his head against the bed, falling on the rifle painfully. He stayed still for a few seconds, though the truck's motion continued as it turned.

Once oriented, he rolled and twisted carefully among the feet and weapons, until he was on his back. The bouncing ride was banging his head repeatedly and painfully against the bed, and he tilted up quickly, then heaved himself to a sitting position.

He was just in time for the incoming fire from al Qaeda.

At this distance, with those troops, small-arms fire was of negligible import. However, someone had an RPG on the ridge, with a beautiful field of fire down at them, and someone else had a heavy machine gun mounted on a vehicle. A quick glance, in fact, showed three of them. It also showed the RPG round incoming in a blur, the setting sun a boiling halo behind it.

Luckily, it missed. The explosion was in the dirt to the right front of the vehicle, which meant they drove right through the debris cloud. The explosion was horrendous, even from thirty meters away, slapping at them and beating them. Dust and dirt choked the air, particles got in their eyes, and a few chunks of rock crashed down. One scratched Kyle as it crashed into the bed of the truck. Wade cursed as a smaller piece hit him, dislodging his hat. Luckily, the thick wool cushioned the strike. There were curses in Pashto, and several bangs as rocks pelted metal or glass.

But they were through that one. The driver braked hard, the truck nosed down and stopped, and the gunner aimed a burst up that way. The range was about 500 meters, but Kyle took advantage of the bare few seconds to snug up the rifle, wrap his arm through the sling, aim and squeeze. He had just fired when the truck started rolling again, the recoil merging into the forward momentum as if he'd moved it all by himself.

His shot was good enough; the RPG gunner staggered and dropped his weapon. His assistant scampered back from the cover he'd taken from the fire and scooped up the launcher. But by then Kyle's crew were moving fast and the threat was greatly diminished.

The incoming fire from the machine guns, however, was getting closer. The men fired long raking bursts, but they had plenty of ammo and were walking the bursts closer. Even with the truck's evasive maneuvers, they were going to hit sooner or later.

Then three more vehicles pulled into the chase.

"This is not good!" Kyle said. He leaned over the back to try a shot on the fly, hoping to damage a vehicle or driver enough to reduce the threat. Wade leaned next to him and started rapid firing, the shots synched to the vertical movement of the oncoming truck. It wasn't made easier by the setting sun in their eyes.

One of them hit a radiator, and fluid sprayed. That vehicle wouldn't be in this chase for long, but it was still driving at present. Also, when it stopped, it would be a stable platform to shoot from as soon as the gunner figured it out.

"Nasima, have us stop again!" Kyle yelled. He knew the word *"wadrega,"* but not enough grammar to get anything substantial across. "I can hit better if we stop for five seconds," he added.

She shouted, the driver stopped hard again, leaning Kyle and Wade backward. "Get the gunner," Kyle said. It had nothing to do with penetration. Contrary to folklore, 5.56mm rounds will handily punch through vehicle glass and metal. It did have to do with Wade being able to put out more fire against the gunners who could move easily, while Kyle would have only one shot against a driver who couldn't dodge in the seat.

Wade said, "Gunner," in confirmation, and they both settled down as the vehicle stopped. Kyle let the sights settle over the driver, squeezed, and watched a hole punch clean through the windshield. One. Above that, three rounds from Wade ripped through the gunner, tearing him and his clothes to shreds. Kyle cycled the bolt with his thumb, slipped it back in, and swung across at a second vehicle, just coming around the first. It was a larger, heavier truck, likely a Mercedes cargo hauler, but it still had a driver behind glass, and his snap shot was adequate, cracking the windshield as it entered at an oblique angle. He'd at least wounded whoever was in there, and Wade blew the second gunner's head open a moment later. Then Wade leaned back and fired a grenade. It was extreme range, but the explosion couldn't hurt and would make the enemy think twice.

Then they were moving again, the truck weaving and evading. It was that moment that the al Qaeda troops concluded they could use the same trick. They stopped, and the machinegun muzzles pointed dangerously.

"Duck!" Kyle said, gathering Nasima close and dropping flat in the bed. Wade was alongside in seconds, and their own gunner poured out a burst, empty cartridge cases and belt links bouncing and stinging over them. Gul had climbed through the missing back window into the passenger seat, and was shouting orders while he fired.

At least, Kyle thought, we don't have any break in fire. Moving or stopped, we're shooting constantly.

But they were outnumbered, and the pursuit was dogged. Kyle fought a moment's panic. They were still alive, no mistakes had been made, and if they got shot, it would be because of the disparity of forces, not because of any errors he'd made.

A sharp bend in the road put solid ridge between them and pursuit for a moment, and shadow almost at once. Kyle heaved a sigh and then realized he'd been holding his breath. He inhaled deeply and said, "Sit up." He checked himself over for injuries, then glanced over at Wade and Nasima. She was panting, but appeared unhurt, though disheveled and scared. She certainly put out heat, too, he thought. It had to be the exertion, because he'd felt the heat off her in waves. Wade was sweating and panting as he replaced his partial magazine for a full one. That reminded Kyle to slip another five rounds into the SMLE, thumbing them hard and tossing the clip. He had limited ammunition anyway; there was no need to worry about a fifty-cent metal spring.

"We need to split up," Gul said. "We can attack them from the trucks if they dismount. Nasima should go with you. She will be safer."

"Is it that bad?" Kyle shouted back.

Nasima nodded even before she translated Gul's reply. "Yes. They will pursue us until they completely lose us or destroy us. They won't be discouraged by casualties. If they chase us, you are safer, if they stop to dismount, we can attack them. You'll have less pursuit, and so will we."

"Okay," Kyle nodded. "You're taking a hel . . . a major risk," he said, wanting not to even get close to religion. He didn't know the way the colloquialism would translate. "We appreciate it."

"It is an honor," Gul said. "You have shot well, and perhaps we can get rid of the rest of these dogs soon."

"I'm not thrilled at the prospect, I have to admit," Kyle said.

"I'd feel safer with you than chased by those thugs, Kyle," Nasima said.

Gul made one last comment and she translated it. "Gul says he hopes we can meet again some day, and extends the hospitality of his village to you or any relatives. That's a gesture of friendship, like a diplomatic offer."

"Sounds like it," Kyle said. Turning to Gul, he said, *"Sta na shukria, de kuday pe aman, assalam u alaikum."* He finished by hugging Gul and shaking with both hands.

"Out at the curve ahead," Gul said. He snatched a ragged map from his old Russian pack. "It's here," he said, pointing at the approaching bend. The road turned back out from the ridgeline, and they'd be visible again.

"Right," Kyle said. "How?" Were they going to roll or stop?

"We'll stop for Nasima for a moment. We'll drop any other gear as we drive off."

It was a measure of trust and respect that Kyle didn't think Gul would take the opportunity to abscond with the equipment.

"Good," he said. "Wade, carry the prick," meaning the PRC-119. Because trust aside, no SINCGARS encrypted radio equipment was left out of U.S. control. "We'll head for that outcropping and up from there."

"Got it," Wade said, shouldering his ruck. He clutched the SMLE and got ready to bail. Kyle grabbed the M-4, which he'd use for any needed cover fire, and his ruck could be dropped.

It was seconds only before the curve came up, and at a signal from Gul, the truck skidded with a roar as the driver slammed the brakes. Nasima was lifted out quickly but gently by Gul and a man whose name Kyle had never gotten. Kyle was out the back and ready to shoot from a low crouch. Wade dropped over the side to his knees and stood. They sprinted off as the driver peeled out, throwing up dust to add concealment, Kyle detouring five feet to grab his dusty, tumbled pack. Kyle again noted the professionalism of these people as he shrugged into it. Give them some proper training in fire discipline and radio, good support and equipment, and they'd be a very competent force. The Special Forces should look into it. He made a mental note. He followed the others up the hill, and dove behind a rise as soon as he saw movement to his left.

Then Gul and his people were manning the machine guns on the racks in their vehicles. They were off in a noisy clatter of gravel on undercarriage and with much banging of metal.

But the pursuit knew they had split forces. While the fire from Gul's crew was plentiful, the maniacal idiots weren't being deterred. One truck stopped and spilled out men, then another.

"Shit, they've got radios!" Kyle said, seeing an old Russian rig.

"So we run and call the helos," Wade said.

While the al Qaeda troops were bent on pursuit, they had to pause against the fire from Gul's crew. One of his people fired an RPG round that took out a truck in a bright flash and bang. Taking the better part of valor, Kyle motioned for them to move low and fast up the hill, providing overwatch positions as they went.

"I feel like a rabbit," he muttered as he passed Wade on one movement. He dropped the M-4 in front of him.

"So find a hole," Wade quipped back, voice low. There was fire down below, close enough to be a sharp reminder. He passed the SMLE over.

Kyle found a hole. There was a crevice in a rock that gave him excellent cover and field of view. He took it, and Wade and Nasima hopped behind the outcropping it was split from. Then he scampered farther up and slid behind a scraggly bush that wouldn't stop a fart but would at least break up his silhouette. That let Wade and Nasima dart to a flat ledge and move back. Lying there, they were out of sight and protected.

"I think we may have lost them in the confusion," Kyle whispered. He crawled past and took a position in a gully anyway. He was panting for breath already. He was still carrying about a hundred pounds of gear, and while he'd trained for it, it wasn't a walk in the park.

"No, they are definitely split and definitely following us," Wade said. There was movement down below, and occasional pot shots.

"Oh, that's great," Kyle said, and threw out a string of creative obscenities he hoped Nasima didn't understand. It was bound to be considered sinful to a Muslim, he thought, entirely outside her experience, most likely, and he had no idea what she'd think of him for it. But dammit, it summed up his feelings.

"Yeah, well, if we can break a crest, you can call," Wade said.

"Right," Kyle said, patting his pocket where the cell phone was.

Where the phone wasn't.

As Wade ran past, then Nasima, he clutched at all his pockets. No phone. He swore again, stood, and dodged. As he passed them, he said, "Unless it's in my ruck, we don't have a phone."

"That falls under the heading of 'sucks ass,' " Wade said to his back, as he slid behind more rock.

"Let's get over the crest and look," Kyle said. "But I'm sure it was in this coat pocket, and isn't. Must be on the road down there."

"Might as well be on Mars," Wade said.

"Yeah." It was true. There was no way they'd ever get down there. Damn, damn, damn.

"Well, we've got the radio. As long as the battery is good, we can call in clear," Wade said.

"We were going to have to do that anyway. But they've got a radio, too." Dammit, they needed that phone! It was the only reliable way to contact their support.

"Yeah. Sucks all around."

"I don't understand," Nasima said as she slid in with Kyle.

"The radio encrypts the signal," he said. "But we're out of the net and not encrypted. We'll have to transmit in clear. That means they can hear us and possibly find us with theirs."

"Oh," she said.

Wade was in cover, and Kyle and Nasima skidded out and up. They were near a saddle, now, and could be over shortly. That would give them some time to seek better position. "Looks like a valley with a bend to northwest. Heading that way gets us closer to the border, and gives us tactical position."

"Good," Kyle said.

Nasima said, "I have an idea."

"Yes?" Kyle prompted as they moved again.

"Once you make contact, do you have anyone who speaks French?"

"That's not a bad idea," he said, seeing where she was going. "Likely." And it was unlikely that any of the enemy spoke French. "But I don't know if we'll be transmitting long enough for that to matter. They know who we are. Any transmission helps them."

Suddenly, with a quick glimpse for trouble, they were over the saddle. The pursuers were temporarily stymied, but they'd likely have backup soon.

Kyle was surprised at how dark it had gotten. His eyes had adapted to the dusk, but it was now rather dark indeed. That was of use, as they had night vision. The al Qaeda might also, but would have the harder job of finding people who wanted to stay out of sight. The hunters had to move. The prey didn't.

Meanwhile, it was time to get backup. "Wade, get the battery in now."

"Suits me," he replied. "Means I get to drop my ruck." He unshouldered it, opened the compartment and pulled out the radio. He opened up the compartment and set the battery. He slipped the blade antenna in place and fastened it. "Here goes," he said.

He warmed it, set the frequency, and keyed the handset. "Bossman, this is Roadkill, over."

Nothing.

"Bossman, this is Roadkill, over."

There was still no reply. "I don't think we're in range," Wade said. "They're rather far north. Even at this altitude, we have mountains in the way. Have to catch them as they come over the horizon, or else get someone to relay."

"Right," Kyle agreed. "Meantime, we walk. It's only about forty kilometers to the border anyway." Only. The terrain wasn't inviting. He looked around at the steep shadows.

"I'm not sure this group will recognize that line," Wade said.

"I'm sure they won't. But it gets us closer to our people, away from them, and it gives us fresh air and exercise."

"All in all, I think I'd rather sit on the couch and watch football," Wade said.

"You do that," Kyle said, smiling.

In moments, they were up and moving again. The only support they had at the moment was position and distance. It was time to make the best of both.

For now, they moved on. It was slow going in the increasing darkness, but while they had the advantage, they'd take it.

"Wade, let's go to night vision. We can guide Nasima."

"Roger that," Wade agreed. They'd barely touched the NVGs. They had batteries to last a hundred hours.

"Going to be cold tonight," Wade said as he snugged his on his forehead.

"Yeah. Exercise will keep us warm. That's what they taught me in basic."

"Funneee," Wade said.

"I am tired and hungry," Nasima said. "And I need a toilet."

"Er . . . behind the rock, if that's okay. We'll wait here. I have a few nibbles." He tried to think what else he might have.

"So do I," Wade said. "Though I doubt any of it is halal."

"Under the circumstances, I think Allah will forgive me for eating unclean food. As long as it's not pork."

"Spaghetti with beef."

"That will be fine. Thank you. One moment." She slipped behind the rock to take care of business.

"Have we even bothered with GPS yet?" Kyle asked. It was a change of subject, and it was something he wasn't recalling.

"No," Wade said. "As far as maps and routing go, we've been fine so far. The batteries are good. Holler if we need them."

"If . . . when we get hold of support, we will need it. I want to give them a good grid from which to start a search if we lose the radio." There was no reason to actually lose the radio. But the batteries could fail. It might get shot. There could be other issues. After everything that had gone wrong so far, he was not optimistic.

"Yeah. This mission isn't getting any better."

Nasima came back. "Thank you," she said.

"No problem. It's not my rock," Kyle said. "Wade, quick break?"

"Yeah, in turns. Cover me."

Kyle had been about to say, "Try not to get it shot off," but decided not to. Nasima was at once very tough and easily embarrassed. He would keep the innuendos to a minimum.

Shortly, they were trudging again. Nasima seemed happy with the spaghetti, loaded with Tabasco. Wade had an extra entrée he was sucking from the pack, and Kyle stuck to a couple of strips of his hoarded jerky and a handful of cookie crumbs. Anything that lightened their load now was a good thing. Though there was little they could abandon, and nothing they dared leave to be found.

The terrain was easy to handle when moving

at a comfortable walk. It required some care when placing feet, but there were plenty of things to grasp for support. They moved downhill steadily, hoping not to have al Qaeda hop over the ridgeline and start shooting. For all they knew, they'd been observed, and artillery was about to start dropping on their heads. The technology gap between the U.S. and al Qaeda and the Taliban was substantial. But the gap between them and the two snipers was just as vast, and didn't depend on technology, but brute force.

After hours of moving obliquely down into the valley, Kyle said, "It's after oh one hundred. Let's find a place to hole up for a couple of hours."

"You think that's wise?" Wade asked.

"No, but I think it's necessary. We need a break. And Nasima isn't complaining, but I think she's about dead. Nasima?"

"Yes, Kyle," she said. "I am too tired to go much farther."

"Two hours?" Wade asked.

"Three. Ninety minutes for each of us. A solid nap, then back to it."

"Okay. There's a depression there. It won't be visible from behind us."

"Good enough," Kyle agreed. He was so tired, he wouldn't even notice the cold. It was promising to be in the thirties again. Forties, if they were lucky. It wasn't that cold to people dressed and active, but the ground would suck heat out of people holding still. He wished now he still had the ghillie.

"My turn to sleep first this time," Wade said.

"Sure," Kyle agreed. He needed some time to think, anyway. About that damned phone. They could have been back on base by now. Should have been.

Maybe the enemy would assume so, and leave them alone. Though he wasn't betting anything on that, either.

Nasima and Wade wrapped in blankets and dropped down. Kyle stayed standing, because he was afraid of falling asleep otherwise. It had been a wise decision to rest, he thought. He could barely avoid hallucinations as it was.

He was sure of that when he looked at his watch. It was ninety-seven minutes since they'd called time to rest. He'd passed the time and not even been aware of it, it was just a hazy blur behind him.

"Wade," he whispered as he shook Wade's shoulder.

"Yo," Wade said, waking fast. "Got it." He stood, took the weapon and stepped out. "Anything?"

"Nothing," Kyle said. He dropped down, grabbed the blanket and rolled up. Nasima was very cute and very young-looking hunched down in her blanket. He started to move a rock that was jabbing him, and was asleep before he got hold of it.

17

HE WOKE QUICKLY WHEN WADE SHOOK HIM, and realized he was somewhat refreshed. "We'll need more breaks," he said, "but they can wait until we have distance."

"I know that," Wade said.

"Sorry," he said, waking fully. "Thoughts coming straight out."

"Well, we haven't slept much the last month. Why start now?"

"Very Army thinking. You should get a job at the Pentagon," Kyle said.

Nasima woke easily enough, but still had huge bags under her eyes. "I can walk," she said. "Let's go."

They were in the valley proper soon, and turned northeast, heading for the rocks ahead. "This morning is when I bet on trouble," Kyle said. "They have a radio, know our approximate distance and direction, and can look for all the signs we left behind in the dark. Then they'll call more people in from other directions. We're only a few kilometers from the village."

"Do you have to be so optimistic?" Wade said.

"Sorry. But that's how I see it," he replied.

"Yeah, me, too," Wade said.

"If I were to guess, I'd say the same," Nasima said. "It's not the first time they've stalked an enemy."

"So we all agree we need to get up that hill," he pointed at the stark cliffs ahead, "so we can call for help and have good shooting position."

The climb up wasn't easier than the previous one, though they did have more time and less immediate threats. But they were underfed and exhausted. Wade's CamelBak was empty, Kyle's rapidly getting so. Nasima wasn't drinking enough, and he had to force her to pay attention to hydration.

During their second break, Wade said, "That's it."

"Nasties?" Kyle asked.

"Yup. Movement on the hill." He rummaged for his spotting scope, and swung it up for a glance. Kyle eased slowly down behind the boulder he'd been resting against, to avoid silhouetting.

"Yes," Wade said. "I count six, with radio, rifles, and an RPK. Also, movement on the southeast, would be coming just about straight from that village. Unknown number."

"Great. Makes me wish we'd stayed on the vehicles."

"I don't think it would matter," Wade said. "They aren't going to back off until superior force kicks their asses. We'd have the same problem somewhere else."

Nasima said, "It would be worse in a town where we don't know who is trustworthy."

"I suppose," Kyle said. "I don't have to like it. We need elevation quickly, and a position to shoot. Try the radio, just in case."

Wade nodded, reached into his ruck and twiddled controls. He made two more calls. "Nothing," he said. "Higher is all I can suggest."

"So let's get higher fast."

It was none too soon. As they rose, dust burst from the hillside in a fountain, accompanied by a bang. It was two hundred meters away, but it wouldn't be the only shot.

"Mortar!" Wade said.

"Yeah, move!" Kyle added, digging in. He grasped Nasima by the hand and pulled fast. He doubted this bunch could adjust fire quickly. Lateral movement was what they needed; anyone could get distance right from adjusting elevation incrementally.

"Eighty-two-millimeter Russian or Chinese?" Wade asked.

"Yeah," Kyle said. "Everyone makes them now."

"Haven't they heard of gun control?" Wade quipped.

"Likely not, or they would have hit us," Kyle said, as a second round dropped farther uphill. It wasn't far below their elevation now. "Next round will be to our right," Kyle said. "What's the spacing on the shots?"

"That was about twenty seconds."

"Okay, so now's the time to start moving left!"

They dug in, turned, and headed back, angling uphill as they did so. The threat assessment, of course, assumed that this bunch could figure out how to adjust the mortar properly. It was possible they'd get directions reversed and drop one right on them. But that wouldn't hurt at all, so Kyle didn't think about it. Nasima was gasping next to him, because they were moving at a near sprint. Her legs weren't long enough for this.

Kyle suddenly remembered Bosnia. It didn't affect him anymore. It had just been a screwup, as this was a screwup, and there was nothing to be done about it afterward. He almost smiled at the sudden burden lifting from his mind.

Another round cracked rock. It was still distant enough not to worry about, but any incoming fire is bothersome. There are vets who can glibly watch it and not panic, but Kyle wasn't that experienced. He also hoped like hell he never got that much experience.

"Let's keep heading west," he said. That was to their left. "If we get past the curve of that hill, they'll have to come looking. Go lower!"

"Lower!" Wade agreed. The recent impacts had been about the line they were on now. Anything that forced the crew to adjust their mortar reduced their probability of hitting.

It was less than a kilometer to where they'd be out of visual range of the enemy. That kilometer was across rough ground, however, and would have been a serious race even without all their gear. As it was, Nasima was choking, and Kyle had a hideous cramp in his guts that blended with the pain in his lungs.

Worse yet, the crew had seen what they intended, and were concentrating fire at the edge of their visibility. Three rounds had landed in a vertical line ahead of them.

"We'll have to time it and dodge through," Kyle said.

"Expect them to lob a couple just past that line as we do," Wade said.

"Agreed. Wait for the next one . . ." Kyle said as they turned straight uphill, wanting to be moving anywhere rather than be holding still.

Just below them was an enormous bang. They should almost be used to it by now, Kyle thought.

"Now!" he said, and they turned left and downhill. It was a dizzying, slipping, skipping route, threatening to tumble them and break a leg at any moment.

It worked. The next round exploded far uphill, and none of them fell.

"Uphill now!" Kyle said. They were out of view, and needed to get into heavy cover fast.

It felt like a marathon. Kyle regretted not being twenty-two again, because it had been a bastard of a movement under fire.

"I think we have about ten minutes before they get a view over this way," Wade said. His face was purple.

"About right," Kyle panted, nearly sick. Nasima was dry-heaving on her knees. "Rest a moment," he said, "then sip water. Are you okay?"

"Uh huh," she gasped between heaves, nodding her head and letting it loll.

"We're going to take a position and shoot. Any comment?" Kyle asked.

"Sounds good," Wade said. "If we're hidden, we can try for the crew or the weapon as they get here, then take them as they advance uphill."

"Yes. You think ten of them?"

"Or more," Wade said. "I saw ten. I'm sure there were others."

"Okay, uphill while we can. We've got about five hundred meters to the top. Can you make it, Nasima?"

"I won't stay here," she said. "I'll walk."

They took the climb in slow, steady steps. Kyle placed his hands on his thighs and pushed with every step, using the extra leverage to help take the load. His gear balanced well, and wasn't hard to carry, but it was damned heavy, and that manifested itself worse when moving quickly or in awkward terrain.

"Once up there, we try the radio again."

"Okay," Wade said. "Got to work sooner or later."

"Yes," Kyle said, though he wasn't sure about that. Its range in these conditions was likely about 100 miles. They were about that from Qandahar. But the AWACS was operating more to the north. The other option was to try several frequencies and hope to find another unit, like that one along the border.

Otherwise, they'd have to walk out or fight it out. Neither option offered good odds. They were down to dregs of water.

Then they were at the crest of the hill, and over. It was a jagged, rocky top, and Kyle smiled. It had cover, concealment, and a good, clear field of fire. A quick glimpse showed the valley below in a clear panorama.

"Well, this is one bright spot," he said. He took a look around for the best sniping points. He had a choice of several.

"I'll take a good position there. You offset to the right in that notch, and call shots. When they get close enough for me to handle on the fly, you pick off a few in front, then at the rear to slow them, then anyone who tries to flank us. And pour out fire while I reload." He again touched the loaded five-round clips in his pocket, wishing for more than eight of them. That and ten rounds in the weapon were all he had. Plus two loose ones.

"Got it," Wade said, squinting through the harsh, reflected light at the depths of shadow where Kyle had pointed. It was a short climb, perhaps five meters from their present position. Yet it looked foreboding in these cliffs. He made it up in seconds, leaned back to make room for his ruck, and pulled the radio out again.

"What about me?" Nasima asked.

Kyle looked at her quizzically.

"I can shoot a pistol. They might get close. Show me one," she said.

He gulped, said "Okay," to stall for time and rearranged his thoughts. She was a goddamned civilian! But she was in the middle of the fight. The best thing she could do was duck. On the other hand, more fire going out would keep people's heads down while he and Wade dropped a few. She was here; she might as well help.

He reached into his waistband and drew the Colt Mustang .380. Start her small and work up as needed. He held it flat in his palm and pointed at the controls. "Magazine release. Safety. Trigger. Hammer. Slide. Slide release. Draw the slide, watch it chamber a round. It will lock back when empty, press the slide release to close it and rechamber from the fresh magazine. It holds five rounds. I have only two spare magazines."

She took it, cycled it with only a little fumbling, ejected and replaced the magazine, and nodded. "Only close range or subversive fire?" she asked.

"Suppressive fire," he corrected. "Yes."

She nodded. "How do you say? 'Let's do it'?"

"Let's do it," he agreed. Wade echoed him. "And take care of the pistol. I can't get another . . . and take care of yourself."

She nodded and smiled. "I shall duck like a mouse."

Kyle crept up the rill and pointed out a good spot for her. It was separated from his position slightly, had lots of rocks to echo the shots and confuse an observer, and a good field of fire at an angle to his, should anyone get close. It also put rock between her fire and him. He'd seen enough Afghan "veterans" shoot to be leery of them as allies, terrified of a half-trained woman raised in this culture. She might be able to hit the broad side of a hill, if it held still. But even unaimed fire would be a help. The enemy wouldn't know it was unaimed, and wouldn't expect her. Also, if they saw her, they'd be confused and reluctant to shoot. It might last only a second, but he could kill two or three if they held still for that long.

Hopefully, she wouldn't get her head blown off in the process. He'd seen that, too. The thought of it happening to a cute young lady schoolteacher whom he liked wasn't something he wanted to dwell on.

He crawled up near Wade with only a few dings, and then tried to get comfortable on cold, sharp stone. Kyle was under a slight arch, his head and shoulders filling it and making it look like solid, shadowed rock from a distance. He'd be hard to hit at this angle, but could see adequately, though he wished for a better view to the right. He also wished the points stabbing him in the belly, hip, and crotch weren't there, but they came with the territory.

"No luck on the radio," Wade said. "I tried for other units, too. Nothing. We're going to have to get closer."

"Okay," Kyle said. "It sucks, but it's all we can do."

Nasima scrabbled up the slope to his right in her lousy shoes and goofy robe, making him wonder again at this pathetic waste of a region. He couldn't see, but could track her progress by skittering rocks, scraping sounds of flesh on basalt, and occasional invocations to Allah in Pashto. She needed jeans and sneakers at the very least. The VC women had had jeans and sneakers. So had the Bosnians.

After that, it was back to waiting. Still, it gave them time to catch their breath, sip a few precious drops of water to clear dust and phlegm, and cool from the burning endorphins. It really was an addictive high, Kyle thought. Or maybe that was just the adrenaline from being shot at so often.

"Hell," Wade said.

"What?" Kyle hissed back.

"Even more than we thought. I'm guessing at thirty. Entire platoon."

"Wonderful." No matter how well they shot, there were limits to the odds. There were also limits to ammunition.

"Yeah. And I think I see some on the hill across."

"They're too far to worry about," Kyle said. It was a kilometer or more across the valley. No small arms were going to make it that far. Unless, of course, they had another mortar. "They'll come down or go away."

"Or have a mortar, or spot for one," Wade echoed Kyle's thoughts.

"We can run."

"Sure. We've been doing that a lot," Wade agreed.

"Well, for now we shoot. Tell me when."

"Will do," Wade whispered.

"Are you okay back there, Nasima?" he asked.

"Yes," she said in a hoarse whisper. "What should I do?"

"Just stay there unless they get up the hill. You'll know from the cussing and shooting," he said.

"But Kyle, you've been cussing and shooting for days."

He had to chuckle. "Yes, but this will be worse."

"Worse language than you used last night? I'm impressed. One hopes you haven't done most of those things."

"Yeah. The Army wouldn't like it," he said.

"Nor would the goat, I suspect."

Wade was chuckling now, too.

"Right, let's keep quiet," he said. It was the best retort he could think of, and it was a good idea, too.

For minutes they sat, physical stress draining while mental stress built. There was nothing right about this part of the mission. It was a Giant Mongolian Clusterfuck, as the slang went.

He wondered how far they could walk if they had to. They might manage two days, if they dumped a lot of gear. That would get them close enough that even the border posts should be within range.

If they weren't, then they were going to have to find water. There wasn't much green this way. The prospects weren't good. They were less good back toward Pakistan, as they'd be running a hostile gauntlet.

Kyle didn't feel like a superhuman killer in a movie. He felt like a man alone and scared. It was one thing to shoot and be shot at, when you knew you had support, medics, radios, and food and water. It was totally different to imagine dying in the middle of a desiccated desert and never be heard of again.

Wade's whispered voice disturbed his thoughts. "Got 'em, Kyle."

"Right," he agreed, and hunched to shoot. He checked again the venerable rifle, flexed his hands to get more familiar with it, and got a good cheek weld. Shooting was a relaxing task, especially now. It was something he could do to improve the odds.

Wade called him his first victim. "Reference: Directly below the tallest spire ahead of you, left of the notch. Target: one asshole. Two hundred fifty."

Kyle had to smile at the ID. There. He was creeping along the cliff at the edge of the trail. Should he fire now, or wait for more targets? Now would bag one bad guy of thirty or so. Waiting might get three or four before they scattered, but would have them closer and more of a threat. "Got him sighted. Others?" he asked.

"Nothing."

So take the shot. He shifted just slightly, eased the rifle over until the man's turban was just above the post, took a breath and relaxed his mouth, then squeezed the trigger.

And squeezed. And squeezed. God, it was so creepy. Whole wars had been fought with this thing. It really was accurate. But the trigger sucked. Would it creep forev—

Bang! The shot took him totally by surprise. The recoil still wasn't bad, but he was wedged in tight and banged his skull on sharp points. Lacking room to shake his head, he squinted and grimaced, waiting for the flashes in front of his eyes to stop as he cycled the bolt automatically. Through his ringing ears he heard Wade say, "Hit! Right through the goddamned nose! Scanning . . ."

He resumed his sight picture, then glanced above the peep to see what was happening below. Someone somewhere was shooting at something, but it wasn't at him. No fire discipline and absolute panic. Should we duck out now? he wondered. No, better thin the herd a bit more first.

Wade called, "Reference and target: behind the first at one hundred sixty meters. Flush to cliff."

"Can't see him," he replied.

"Want me to take the shot?" Wade asked.

"Is he advancing?"

"Not right now," Wade said.

"Wait."

"Roger."

There were suddenly five figures down there, and he didn't need a spotter to see them. They shot as they ran, mostly suppressive, but with a few shots aimed in the general direction of Kyle's position. One of them pinged nearby, scattering dust. But Kyle was well hidden and they obviously hadn't marked him. He squeezed off another round that gapped the first one under his breastbone, eyes bugging wide as he tumbled. A second shot caught one in the hip and the man behind him in the foot. Nice! Then the other two dodged as the third shot smacked into rock. Kyle swore and closed the bolt, took several breaths to catch up and calmed down for more waiting.

He hadn't banged his head on these shots, but had been flinching to avoid it. He'd shot okay anyway, but he should have been able to get off at least one more round in that time. Damn.

"Wade, shoot anything you see," he said. "I think it's about time to mov—"

A flurry of shots came in, including some automatic fire. Dust kicked up in his face and he shimmied back in a hurry, tearing cloth and skin on the lip as he did so. He was about to clutch at the empties he was leaving, then decided they didn't matter. They weren't any use as intel and the enemy knew who he was and where. They could stay on that mountain as a memorial for the bodies below, who would either be carried off or eaten by buzzards. Hell, maybe some archeologist a hundred years from now would find them and annotate the incident, if it was ever publicly admitted.

"Nasima!" he called. "Let's go!" Then he swore at himself. He'd just used her name where they could hear. Damn. Maybe they hadn't heard over the din of fire and the distance, but it was a bad thing, anyway.

Fire started coming from the right.

He yelped and rolled behind a boulder, slid down the slope, belly exposed as his shirt peeled up, and gratefully took several gouges rather than a bullet.

"Seven, about forty meters, just below the crest," Wade said. Damn, but the man had sharp eyes. Any movement at all was a cue to him.

Another fusillade came in, but Wade rapped off a few bursts in response, along with a canister from the grenade launcher. There was no chance of hitting anything at that range, in this terrain, on autofire, but it did make the enemy duck. The canister load might have done something, but it certainly let the enemy know the Americans still had teeth. There was no comparable Russian weapon.

Kyle shot and worked the bolt three times to voice his own opinion, and Nasima fired three times. She was about twenty meters away and running toward Kyle in a fashion to do credit to a sprinter. "I'm behind you," Wade said.

Good: All three together for best fire effect. Bad: All three together as one target. Worse: Seven bad guys at point-blank range, and more on the way. Dust and chips of stone flew, bullets ricocheted in cracks and whines, and Kyle raised the Lee-Enfield and shot three times. He nailed one, winged a second, and missed with the third. Wade was firing on semi as fast as he could pull the trigger and got two more. Nasima fired twice, the Colt running dry.

Someone had to be ready before Wade ran dry. That someone was Sergeant First Class Kyle Monroe. He had perhaps a second. The Ed Brown .45 came out of its holster, familiar and snug in his grip. He drew it, raised it, and then immediately had to shove it at a tribesman standing over him, shoving an AK at him in a parallel motion.

He yanked the trigger, let his arm ride the recoil rather than try to shoot center of mass again. The muzzle caught under the chin of the thoroughly surprised and pop-eyed native, then Kyle shot again. The man's head exploded out the back in red mist, his cheeks and throat jiggling like Jell-O as the hydrostatic shock tore through them.

Kyle looked around frantically to locate the rest. Wade had gotten another, and Nasima had somehow managed to reload while some idiot had tried to grab her. He lay in front of her, neat holes in chest and face. Kyle's first thought was that the stupid SOB planned to either capture her or rape her in the middle of a firefight. Either way, he'd gotten dead, and that was fine.

Everyone was panting for breath. The lone survivor, who Kyle had wounded in the side of his belly, was moaning away. Nasima jumped across two rocks as if they were stepping stones, pointed the little pistol at his head and said a phrase he recognized, "Go with Allah," as she pulled the trigger. She looked green and nauseous as she turned back around. Part of that might be due to a wound in her head, oozing through her scarf.

"Are you all right?" he asked.

"It is a rock chip," she said. "I'll be okay." It didn't look okay; it was a dark, spreading stain.

Wade had reloaded, and Kyle followed suit, topping the Enfield with a fresh clip. He couldn't find the one he'd dropped, but wasn't keeping track anymore.

"Let's move," he ordered, forcing his body to ignore the stings, dings, and chunks of bruised and torn flesh. They needed to get farther away in a hurry. He detoured to snag an AK from the nearest body. There was only the magazine in the weapon, and a quick check showed it to hold five rounds. By then, they were a hundred yards away and still running. It didn't seem worth it to lug the weight for five rounds, so he stripped it and scattered the bolt group as they ran. At least no one else would use it.

"Nine dead, two wounded," he said as they scrambled up and down the hill, glancing behind for signs of pursuit. "But I'm down to thirty-two rounds of three oh three and my pistol. Wade?"

"Five mags left. We'll be fine, boss. Nice shooting." Turning, he spoke to Nasima, "And you, too, young lady."

Nasima blushed and looked shocked, embarrassed, and ill. "I only got one. And I used seven shots." She was examining the magazines.

Kyle said, "With that pistol, that's about right. It's backup only." He turned to his partner and said, "Wade?"

"What?"

Kyle made a pistol shape with his hand and held it up.

Wade caught on and said, "Oh, no!"

"Wade, you've got the M-4. It's plenty of firepower. I have a bolt and a pistol to save me from reloading in a hurry. Take the Mustang if you want, but let her have something worth using."

Sighing, Wade said, "Oh, all right! I suppose it makes sense. Now, or when we stop?"

"Better be as we travel."

"Right. Oh, Nasima!"

Wade handed her his Beretta and showed her the differences between the pistols as they moved, she nimbly like a goat, he more like a lumbering bear. She nodded and said, "I have no belt for a holster. I'll just carry it."

"Fine," Kyle said from ahead. "I'll loan you a belt when we stop. Will the spare magazines fit in that little pouch of yours?"

"Oh, yes," she said. "But I can't reach them quickly."

"If we get attacked, grab one and hold on to it. Then take cover. We'll do the shooting, you just defend yourself or make noise if we tell you to, okay?" he said.

"You are the expert in this field," she smiled. "I will obey."

"Touché," he said, and smiled, with a hint of blush. "So let's walk."

It was already well past noon. They'd had a busy morning, Kyle reflected. They were all still alive and unwounded, and the longer that was the case, the better. But there was no telling how many people were closing in on them, and it was becoming beyond imperative to make radio contact.

They stopped every hour for Wade to try a call. The second time, he announced, "I have static!"

"Good!" Kyle said. "Anything else?"

"No, but stand by," he said, and clutched the handset. "Any U.S. military unit, this is Roadkill, say again Roadkill. Contact Bossman. Inform Bossman we are three zero kilometers north of previous grid. Request Bossman contact us. Critical. Over." He ran through the spiel twice more. If anyone could hear them, they might get the backup they needed soon. "That's all I can do," Wade said.

"No sweat," Kyle said, trying to sound nonchalant. "It's better. It will keep getting better. Let's move." He wasn't sure it would, but he had to encourage his tiny command.

"Right," Wade said.

"As we must," Nasima said, trying to sound cheerful. She looked as if she'd been through a washing machine.

The distance between breaks got smaller, as they tired. They were in a fugue state beyond exhaustion, and kept going only because they had to.

"We haven't had any immediate pursuit," Wade said.

"No," Kyle said. "But I'm betting on a hot reception in Afghanistan. They've got a very good idea of our route, and roads to get there."

"Yeah. Once we get there, it's plateau, too. Nowhere for good cover," Wade said and indicated the map. "We're here," he said, pointing out the grid he'd taken from the GPS module.

"Right," Kyle said. The terrain ahead turned to rolling hills, a bit like the moors of Scotland or the high plains of Wyoming. It was warmer and dryer, though, with tough, stalky grass in clumps amid the rocks. They'd driven through a bit of it on the way here. Crappy terrain for a fight.

Around them, everything was still a dun color. Long rills of the mountains trailed off onto the southern Afghan plateau ahead. "We stay with the hills," he said. *And hope to get in radio range Real Soon Now.*

Three hours later, the sun was dropping quickly. "We need to find a cave if we can, or a hollow if not. And it's going to be chill again," Kyle said. The clear skies and unprotected heights meant any warmth was radiated away or blown off. It wasn't going to be really cold, but it would be cool enough by contrast to make things unpleasant and potentially dangerous.

"I'll look," Wade said, moving ahead. He was getting more sure of his footing as they traveled, but was favoring his left leg. Likely from some injury or other. Kyle would ask him when they stopped, but he'd likely deny being hurt.

They'd better check each other for injuries and not pretend, Kyle thought. That "rock chip" was soaking Nasima's scarf with a dark stain. Head wounds were bloody, and needed treatment. But when he mentioned it again, she said, "It's not necessary."

"Nasima," he said, "it needs to be bandaged. Really. You've got to let me do it." It had bled a lot, and could still have shrapnel in it, or worse, damage to the skull. Even if it were only a slice, it needed to be cleaned and dressed.

They'd been following one of the ridges, and it seemed to still have a feature or two they could use. Up on one granite cliff, there were pockets that could be caves, or at least overhangs to hold air still and reduce convected cooling. They trudged wearily up, slipping and tripping.

It was fully dark when they reached the pocketed area. The holes gaped like huge mouths, dark and foreboding. There was an instinctive fear of the black maws, but also a tactical one. Kyle's nerves were naked wires as he eased up to the first, the muzzle of the SMLE preceding him by a few inches. He held it close, not wishing to have it snatched or deflected by some waiting threat. Not even his NVGs showed him much inside other than a hole. It was that dark.

He used his Maglight with a red filter to take a better look. That was insufficient illumination to give their position away to an observer, but enough for the goggles to see the confines of the mountain. It was a cave a few meters deep, and not even bats were present. It was still eerie and tense, but with the goggles he could see well enough to know intellectually there were no threats present. Now if only he could persuade his quivering guts of that.

He stepped back out carefully, fearful of making a disturbance of rockfall. It was possible, even likely, they'd be surrounded by dawn, and have to stay hidden for some time. Or shoot their way out.

Or, he reminded himself, die a messy death. One RPG round into that cave would mince them to sausage.

Wade was waiting, muzzle down but ready. They nodded at each other, not a prearranged signal, but merely an acknowledgment that they were both okay. Kyle stepped down slowly, each foot in place before he moved further.

He crouched back with them. "It's safe, tight, and not too large," he said. "Let's get in and shelter. Nasima, I'm going to look at your head. It needs treatment."

Her face worked, mouth twisting. "Wade," she turned and said, "I must be rude. Will you stay outside?"

"Huh? Sure," he agreed. "Someone needs to be on watch anyway."

Kyle suddenly got it. For her to take her scarf off was a major breach of the modesty protocol. Even when hurt, she had an issue with it. Like an American woman taking off her pants or exposing her breasts. And it was just her head. He just couldn't understand it.

She led the way inside, and sat down facing him. Taking a deep breath, she unfastened and unwound her scarf as he held up a blanket. He needed lots of light for this, but couldn't risk it being seen. With the blanket tossed over his ruck and a protruding rock, they had a tent of sorts to shield the glare. He held his Maglight out, shaded with his hands for now.

Underneath, she was much prettier, her head and hair framing her face. That hair fell in wavy cascades down below her shoulders or longer, and was a lustrous blue-black in color. It would likely be even shinier cleaned of dirt and sweat and the dark, oily sheen of blood above her right ear.

It was as bad as Kyle had expected. He could see white edges to the wound. He might have to suture, and scalp wounds hurt like hell. But before that . . . "I'll have to cut away some of your hair," he said, feeling ill. It was gorgeous hair in contrast to an ugly wound. She was a tough young woman, and there was an electric tension to the moment that was disturbing and exciting.

She nodded slightly, then winced. "Yes, I thought so," she said.

"Hold the flashlight," he said.

She took it from him and held it still. "Where?" she said. He reached over and adjusted her arm and the beam and felt that tension again.

It was lust, plain and simple. She was pretty, young, self-assured. In this foreign wasteland, she was the only link to his world, by speaking his language, and they were both under a lot of stress. Add in not having been laid in weeks, and it was easy to explain.

He shook it off and continued. "Tilt your head to the left," he said, and she did. Carefully taking a small handful of hair, he raised it and held it clear of the scalp. "Hold still," he said.

The blade on his SOG Powerplier hadn't been abused and was razor sharp. He placed his hand against the back of her head for balance and moved the blade carefully in close. It sliced the strands off in a single pass as she winced only a little. He selected a few more and sliced, some more and sliced, and cleared the area around the wound down to a half inch or so.

The edges were raw and he'd have to do quite a bit. It was a small, triangular wound, but it was ugly and stale, blood congealing in shiny globs. "I need to shave it," he said. "This will hurt."

She nodded and clenched her teeth as he leaned in again. The blade was sharp enough, but the scraped off strands stuck to the bloody mass around them. Her breath came in hisses and her chest heaved. The light wavered as she gripped it tightly. Kyle barely noticed. He was intent on doing this safely and perfectly, and forgot the trouble he was having.

Leaning back and releasing a breath, he reached for his canteen. "Here," he said as he handed her a soaked bandage. "Pat it clean and away from the wound."

She nodded and took it. Gently she stroked it to the surface. Her hair looked odd now, with a wedge cut above her right ear. Her scalp was pale, then inflamed, then red as it got closer to the hole. And suturing was not an option in the field. The edges of the flesh were curled under and too wide to stitch.

"Can't suture," he told her. "But it's not bleeding badly anymore. I'll need to sterilize it though."

She nodded through what was already a wince, tears forming at the thought of the pain that was to come. She kept her eyes averted as he splashed merthiolate into a wadded bandage and closed the bottle. Then he raised it.

Her wince became a whine became a whimper and then a suppressed cry. Blood-tinged liquid ran from under the bandage, and she trembled. Head wounds are horribly painful, and this was traumatized, bruised, abraded, and now tortured with chemicals. Then she was crying, mouth open, keening to keep the noise down and let out the pain.

He caught her as she passed out from the agony. That wasn't unexpected. Kyle had had a thrown rock split his scalp in school, and could remember what he thought was terrible pain as two nurses held him down to clean it. This had to be excruciating. "Superficial" does not mean "painless."

Her head was in his lap and he reached over for the light, plucking it from her limp fingers. He stared into the wound. There didn't appear to be any damage to the bone, but it was going to hurt like unholy hell for weeks. There was no grit, the hair was mostly gone, and it would be fine until she could get into town. But there'd be a nasty scar there forever.

She stirred, and her eyes fluttered. Her first mutter was in Pashto, then she said, "I was passed out?"

"Yes," he said. "But you're okay now. It's clean at least."

She nodded just barely and said, "Help me up, please."

His arms were under her shoulders, and he lifted. In a moment, they were face to face, eyes reflecting the reflected glimmer of the flashlight from the rocks, and their lips were perhaps two inches apart.

Kyle knew he shouldn't. It was tactically, medically, morally, and politically insane. But those liquid eyes were drawing him and he leaned forward just a fraction, and she did, too.

Then she pulled away.

They stared for a second, eyes locked, and her hand was caressing his arm. "I can't," she said, and stopped stroking, too, as she averted her eyes. "I'm sorry you have been excited by me. But I am Muslim and unmarried and I can't. It would be a sin I could never repent."

Closing his eyes for a moment, Kyle said, "And I can't. Don't apologize, because it's not your fault. I shouldn't have even thought of it, because this is a mission." At the same time, her strength in her faith made her that much more unreachable and that much more of a prize. Jesus, it was a nightmare. He shuffled back to give her more space. And to get away from the attraction.

He pulled out a dressing, laid it carefully over the wound as she offered her head. He wrapped it and tied it securely but gently. "Is that okay?" he asked.

"Yes," she agreed. "And it feels much better, now that the burning is gone. And I thank you."

"I wish I could do more," he said, meaning it on several levels. Dammit. "I'd better go take a turn on watch," he said. "Do you need a clean covering?" he asked.

"I have another scarf," she said. "Are we done?"

"Yes," he agreed. In seconds, her scarf covered her head. It was as if it were a shield, and he felt the frustration retreat just a bit. He shut off the light and reached for the red filter again. He gathered up the trash and her ruined scarf and stuffed it into a pocket.

"I'm going to dig out all the remaining food we have," he said. "You eat what you need to, we'll finish it off."

"That's not fair to you," she said. "You're bigger."

"That means I can lose more mass and keep going," he said. "You're injured, we may need you yet, and even if not, I'm not leaving you for those animals."

"Thank you," she said. He could almost see her smile in the dark.

With the red filter in place, he dug through his ruck and turned up two more sticks of jerky wrapped in plastic, a handful of hard candies, one small bag of airline peanuts, and a stale apple. There was a packet of MRE peanut butter, but nothing to spread it on. It would have to be sucked out. It didn't appeal to him; the stuff tasted like cardboard. But it was protein and calories and they needed it.

It would be even worse with no water to wash it down. "Dig in," he said. "I'll leave the light on for you." She wouldn't get the joke, though.

As he found his way cautiously to the cave lip, he pondered the spookiness of that cultural issue, and how it could affect him, an unbeliever.

"How'd it go?" Wade asked as he came out.

"Messy and painful," he said. Then he realized he meant that another way, too.

"Going to be okay?"

"Yeah, it'll scar, but it's sterile and bandaged."

Wade chuckled and replied, "I meant you, jackass."

Kyle paused for a moment, flushed in embarrassment, then realized it was an honest question. "I'll be okay."

"Good. Let me know if you need to talk."

"Thanks," Kyle said. Wade was a hell of a decent man. "I think we just did. Go get some sleep. We're going to share whatever food is left now. Let me have the carbine."

"Sure," Wade said, unslinging it and passing it over. "Nothing so far. It's dark and still, and unless someone has infrared, we should be fine."

Wade slipped inside. Kyle had nothing to do but wait, worry, and watch. He decided now might be a good time for another attempt at the radio. He set it up on a ledge, set the frequency for the AWACS and hoped. "Bossman, this is Roadkill, over," he said, wishing he'd picked a different call sign. It had seemed amusing a lifetime ago. Was it three weeks?

Nothing. He set a frequency the Army should be using at the borders. "Any U.S. military unit, this is Roadkill. Urgently need relay to Bossman, over."

Nothing. There had to be units within one hundred miles now. Though if they were encrypted, they wouldn't really be looking for him on a single frequency. But the only way to plug into the encryption algorithm was to have another set do it remotely.

He'd try again around 0200, he decided. Or have Wade do it. If they couldn't get a good signal then with the nighttime atmospheric effects, it wasn't going to happen. But dammit, they had to be close! It was frustrating.

Carefully, he shut it off and disconnected the battery. The nominal eight hours in that battery was likely down to seven, minus any loss from not being used for two weeks.

That left him nothing to do but look at the sky. It was the prettiest sight he'd ever seen.

Stars by the millions, a sliver of moon that set quickly . . . and a moving light far overhead and to the south that had to be a satellite. A Satcom unit would have been great, he thought, but too bulky for this.

All those bright pinpoints made him feel even smaller and more insignificant. Just the thing while being chased by half the world's terrorists in the ass-end of nowhere.

About two, there was rustling and whispers from inside the cave. Wade came back out. "Your turn," he said. "We should pull out early."

"Right. How is she?" Kyle asked.

"That's one brave but crazy lady," Wade said, sounding bewildered.

"Oh?" Kyle prompted. What now?

Wade said, "She wanted to stand watch. Said it wasn't fair that she sleep so much."

"Dammit, she needs the sleep, and to be still, and she's not trained with the weapons!" Kyle said.

"Easy, pal. You think I let her?" Wade replied. "She's sulking but agreed with me. I fed her some more Motrin. Now go sleep."

"Right. Sorry. Long night. Check the radio. Thanks," Kyle muttered, handed over the M-4, then turned and felt his way into the cave. There was a dim glow from the Maglight, left on for his convenience. They'd left him the peanut butter. As he grimaced at that, he noticed a dried fruit component from the MREs and half a pack of chicken with noodles. There were four Oreo cookies, too. It was no banquet, but it would let him sleep more easily and last another day.

After eating, he turned the light off again, curled up in his blanket, and leaned against a naturally perfect hollow that was quite comfortable.

18

WADE WOKE HIM BEFORE DAWN. "LET'S move." It was just a voice in the dark, with a presence behind it he could just see against the stars.

"Right," he agreed. "Nasima?" he called softly, afraid of touching her.

"I'm awake," she said. "Can you step outside and wait?"

"Sure," he agreed. He and Wade went outside and relieved themselves into a depression between two rocks. Hopefully, no one would see the puddle, and it would dry quickly. Obviously, Nasima was doing the same in the cave in the dark. But it was one of those things not discussed between men and women here.

"We're ready," Kyle called as soon as he was done. In moments, she rustled out from the black mouth in the rock.

"My head is throbbing, but better," she said. "I'm ready to travel."

Wade nodded. "I think I should take point, Kyle, with you in back. Nasima, stay between us. Even if we get attacked, don't shoot until we're down on lower ground. We might dodge suddenly."

"I understand," she said. She sounded quite calm.

"Makes sense," Kyle agreed. Wade had more experience in the mountains, having just come from 10th Mountain Division.

The climb was tiring but not dangerous. They were careful of their footing, and slow at first. Twilight is hard to see in, but by scanning the eyes one can get a good image of the area, better than with the focal point of the eye.

Then the sky was gray. It hadn't happened suddenly, but it had reached a level discernible to the brain. Shapes began to resolve themselves as boulders, protrusions. Spiky spiderlike terrors became bushes.

The rest and food had done them a world of good, Kyle thought. They were moving more easily, and were alert and awake. It turned to proper dawn, crisp and cool with a hint of dew. All he needed now was bacon and eggs. How did these people survive without bacon and eggs for breakfast now and then?

By sunrise, the ground was flattening out. That was good, in that they could make better speed, but bad in that they were exposed to fire from behind.

"We just keep slogging," Kyle said. "Nothing else to do. And if we get far enough away, they may give up."

Nasima said, "They won't give up. But we may find territory they don't like, or a place you can call for help from."

"I figure we should be in range now. So if we can get a bit farther north and find a high spot, we should be able to reach the E-three. Assuming there's still an E-three up there. Of course, it could be on the far part of its orbit." An AWACS plane, usually an E-3 Sentry, was constantly circling or "in orbit" above the region, to provide command and control. They were primarily intended for aircraft control, but could be reached by radio from the ground, if the radio were in range and line of sight. The mountains were making that impossible at the moment.

"Right. Well, we work with what we've got."

Nasima said, "This is not good."

At once, Kyle asked, "What?"

"Listen," she said.

He did. Wade did also, and kept very quiet; his feet on the soil were barely audible. There was a faint sound that was familiar and disturbing.

"Dogs?" he asked.

"Wild dogs," Nasima confirmed. "Following us. They attack travelers in packs."

"Ah, hell. How many in a pack?" he asked, dreading her answer.

"Twenty to fifty. Mongrels, large but not well fed. They take goats, even cows, and people if they find them. Very dangerous outside towns."

"Right, and a dead giveaway to our pursuers," Kyle warned.

"Will they stop if shot at?" Wade asked.

"Yes," said Nasima. "Or if hit with rocks. But it takes several wounded before they understand."

"Rocks are good," Wade said. "But I've also got canister loads and HE." Kyle snickered, Nasima looked confused, until he patted the grenade launcher and the high-explosive shells slung from his belt.

"Ah," she said. "Yes, but very loud."

Kyle said, "I think we should save the grenades. At least until they're up close. For now, let's run. The dogs might get bored, at least."

"Dogs, al Qaeda assholes, what's the difference?" Wade said.

They all laughed at that, and broke into a brisk jog. The men could have gone considerably faster, but they weren't going to leave Nasima behind.

"We would be on flat ground by now, of course," Kyle said. "Oh, the hell with running. If we have to fight them now, let's get it over with!" He dug in his heels and stopped. "We're on open ground anyway, so why get tired?"

"It appeals to my sense of valor," Wade said. "But part of me wants to haul ass."

Nasima said nothing. She just looked scared.

"Keep walking," Kyle said, checking the loads on the SMLE and his Ed Brown.

He wasn't going to run, but there was no reason not to be at a fast walk. They needed distance anyway.

"Grab a couple of good rocks each as we go," he said, and reached down to scoop up a heavy chunk of something. "If we can cripple a couple fast, they may leave." He stuck the rock in a pocket of his coat, and watched for more.

The parade of canines drew closer, and the noise grew. If they could just persuade the dogs to bark away while they moved, it would be excellent cover, and their pads would obliterate any tracks the humans were making. Somehow, Kyle didn't think they'd listen to his plan. But at least the noise told them where the pack was. There was no need to look over their shoulders to gauge the distance. They did anyway, however.

"I will *not* ask what else can go wrong, I will *not* ask what else can go wrong," Wade chanted. Kyle had to agree. Armed pursuit. Phone lost. Radio not working. Ammo low. Food and water gone. Chased by dogs. Feet blistered to pulp. Beard tangled and itching and with a sweat rash underneath.

At least, he reflected, they had good maps and GPS, so they'd know exactly where they were going to die. It was a melodramatic thought, but it fit his mood.

Ahead was another valley. It seemed to be an ancient riverbed, or maybe a seasonal wash. Farther on, it deepened to cliffs. Eventually, it would all lead down to the rivers on the edge of the Afghan plains.

"I hate to suggest the low ground for cover," Kyle said, "but terrain features of any kind are what we need. It's too flat up here."

"May as well," Wade said. "Nothing else has gone by the book."

They were almost to the rills of the valley wall when the dogs caught up to them. They were well inside rifle range, even inside pistol range, and Kyle itched to take a shot. He didn't dare make that much noise unless they had to. He was pretty sure they'd have to, though.

The mutts were spreading out, closing in, and slowing. That meant they were doing a quick assessment of their prey before attacking. Kyle had never seen such ugly, scrawny, vile-looking dogs in his life. No wonder no one thought of them as pets.

"That's close enough," Kyle said, reaching into his pocket. "Hit 'em."

It was good, he reflected, that he'd never been a dog lover. His first fast pitch smashed one of the mutts in the jaw, throwing strings of gooey drool and blood back over its shoulders. Nasima wasn't much of a thrower, but the dogs were skittering back from where her stones landed. Likely she'd never had much practice playing ball.

Wade, however, was doing brilliantly. Kyle recalled him playing for a local softball league, and the man had a snap to his wrist that was devastating. Three rocks landed smack, smack, smack, on a snout, causing one to roll on the ground in anguish, on a forehead between the eyes, braining the beast, and into a foreleg, shattering the knee. At that moment, Kyle nailed a second one hard in the ribs.

But the dogs were close now, and he could smell them. Their barking and yipping was a cacophony from all sides. He snatched at his pistol and started shooting. One dog was snapping at his leg, trying to nerve itself to close in. He kicked at it, aimed and shot, yanking his foot back just in time. He'd panicked and almost blown his own toes off.

The shot shattered the rear of the skull and upper spine. Wade pinged one with the .380, which had more than enough muzzle energy to drop it. Nasima was rapid firing, but seemed to have gotten two with five shots as Kyle literally blew the brains out of another. The skull shattered like a watermelon did when he went shooting back on his uncle's farm, and red, wet contents splashed.

Then the remaining dogs were retreating at a sprint, tails low and ears folded. In seconds, they were bounding back the way they'd come.

Which was where the men on horses were. They were galloping like a posse in a bad cowboy movie, only they brandished AKs.

"Kyle, we need to get into that valley now," Wade said. His voice was surprisingly calm.

"Amen, brother. Nasima, let's go. Hold your fire again. We'll need a lot of it when they get close, and the pistol doesn't have enough range for this."

"I understand," she said.

This time they sprinted, and it seemed wrong to Kyle to run from these scum when they hadn't from dogs. As far as he was concerned, the dogs were a far cleaner breed.

Kyle realized he should have expected horses. There were enough of them, and they were the best vehicle for this terrain if there was no road. He recalled a game played with a beheaded goat, which resembled polo. That summed up the mind-set of the people they were facing.

Then the first incoming fire of the day slashed past them.

He didn't need to tell anyone to duck; it was a technique they all had down by now. They scurried downslope to the valley, and rose gradually to a crawl, then upright. Then they were below line of sight, and could run.

"Want to take a few shots as they clear the horizon?" Wade asked.

"No, I want to get into those rocks so they have to dismount," he said. He also didn't want to shoot the horses, though he would if he had to.

"First time I've seen horses with the assholes on top," Wade said.

"Good. I hope you plan to shoot like you crack jokes."

"Count on it," Wade assured him.

They plunged down into the ravine, cut, whatever it was, and scanned around for any good shooting positions. The ideal location would offer height, view, solid cover, and concealment. Right now, Kyle just wanted a tree or a rock. His back felt naked and exposed, and he was panting in fear. Would the first warning of them catching up be a bullet through his spine?

The ground dropped away. Grass grew in tufts, forcing its way between unyielding rocks. With little water for erosion, it was rough, raw terrain. It was the first good news of the day.

"Let's get up on that ridge," Wade said.

"Yeah, I see it, too," Kyle agreed. It wound its way along a strata break in the ground, with lots of hard cover and a view down lower. Any pursuit would have to be single file along it. Under the circumstances, it was the best terrain they'd find, and it was available now, so there was no need to push their luck hoping for better.

"Give me ten seconds," Wade said. He had the radio out and was setting it up.

"Okay, but hurry the hell up!" Kyle said back, panicky. Yes, they needed it, but now was not a good time. On the other hand, there wasn't likely to be a good time.

It was back in his ruck in seconds, warmed and ready. Wade grabbed the handset and called. "Bossman, this is Roadkill, over."

He started walking again, M-4 cradled low

and sweeping for threats. Kyle brought up the rear, and tried to keep the pace. The urge to back along was powerful.

Wade unslung his ersatz radio pack long enough to change frequencies. "Any U.S. military unit, this is Roadkill, urgently need relay to Bossman."

Wade paused, and Kyle came up short. What was the problem?

Then Wade said, "Roger, Bouncer Five, this is Roadkill. Relay to Bossman. We are thirty kilometers north of our last grid. Urgently need contact, over." They had a contact!

Grinning, Kyle forced himself to pay attention to the terrain and threats. The radio was Wade's gig. He flashed Nasima a smile as he turned, and she grinned back, eyes crinkling in real happiness and relief.

They could still get very dead, though, and Kyle pushed his awareness to the limit. It would be ironic and suck royally to get clipped now.

Far back and higher up, there was movement. It was just discernible as a man on a horse. The question was, should he take the shot now and risk blowing their temporary concealment, or push on and risk letting them get too close?

Stealth, he decided. The cavalry would literally be here soon.

Ahead, Wade said, "Roger, Bouncer Five, Roadkill acknowledges. And we owe you many beers if soon we meet. Roadkill out." He turned and said, "They had to relay through their battalion, to aviation, to Bossman, but the word is they're circling down this way and will have us in twenty minutes. They've got choppers warming now. They'll leave about the same time."

"Right, so how long?" Kyle asked. He was trying to estimate himself, but his brain was foggy from fatigue.

"About an hour after that."

"Eighty minutes," Kyle said, considering. That was a long time.

"We can do it," Wade said, sounding sure.

"Right, we keep walking," Kyle said.

It wasn't a hard walk, but they'd been doing it for days. The stress damage to his left foot, the blisters he could feel sheathing his toes, heel, and instep, and the increasing shin splints were not fun. They were hungry, thirsty, worn, and ragged. Still, they'd proven that two U.S. soldiers were better than al Qaeda's remaining best.

So had Nasima. He wondered what they thought of that.

She was looking out of it. Despite her earlier grin, she was a trifle unsteady, and her eyes had a thousand-yard stare that was obscene on a face so young and vibrant. They owed her a lot, and Kyle wished there was something beyond money they could do. Perhaps State Department could arrange for better school facilities? Or even just prod the Pakistani government into a bit of action.

Meanwhile, they were still slogging along. Afterward, Kyle would sit down with a map and figure out just how many miles they'd covered up, down, and over these mountains and plateaus.

"Down," Wade whispered.

Kyle dropped at once. Nasima was barely slower. He wasn't sure it was conscious reaction; it seemed as if he'd collapsed. "What?" he asked.

"We've got bad guys across the ravine, searching. Likely some above us, too."

"And some behind on horses, lower down," he said. "I would bet on some on foot on this ridge."

"So it's very prickly," Wade said. "Your call. Hide, find a position, or keep moving?"

Kyle made a quick scan. Up ahead, the valley widened. That would reduce the threat from across the way. They were also getting lower, the cliffs building above and to the northeast.

"We go a bit farther," he said. "Distance from any of them helps. Where it widens, we'll try to hole up with a solid front."

"Okay," Wade said, and crawled forward. He rose to a crouch and shuffled along.

The only good thing about being out of water, Kyle reflected, was that his gear was forty pounds lighter. Though given his raspy, parched throat and the throbbing headache that was coming on, he craved that weight. Food was one thing, and could be acquired most places. But water was the biggest logistical problem for covert operations. There was just no way to carry enough, and their pursuers likely knew that.

They knew about the lack of water, the lack of food, that a small civilian woman was along, and probably that they'd been calling for help and not finding any. Now that backup was coming, Kyle concluded, either this group didn't have a radio and didn't know, or didn't care and were determined to nail them before the choppers arrived.

So they should be expected to do something rash.

With that in mind, Kyle moved at the crouch, too. It was sheer hell on his lower back and knees, though it did take some load off his shoulders.

Up ahead, Wade whispered hoarsely, "This is Roadkill, Bossman. Go ahead, over."

Yes! Kyle thought. Just a few more minutes. Any good defensive position, or a hide, preferably, as he had no need to prove anything else and no desire to get into a pissing contest, and they could kiss this pimple on the asshole of the world goodbye.

"Roger that, Bossman. Our coordinates are—"

Not that it wouldn't be nice to see Quetta and that reservoir again, as a tourist. The art and culture was amazing. But these hills were worse than Nevada, and the natives worse than any Appalachian nightmare.

"Roadkill acknowledges, Bossman. Roadkill out," Wade said. He continued speaking back over his shoulder. "Sixty-two minutes until they get here, maybe sixty-five. We'll use flare and smoke to get their attention. And guess what? We're in Afghanistan. Friendly territory."

"And the bad guys are, too," Kyle observed. "And will see the smoke."

"We won't pop until they are right on top. At that point, we'll have fire support in seconds."

"Right. We've got a Blackhawk coming? Or an Air Force Fifty-three bird?"

"Well, my friend," Wade said softly, a chuckle hidden underneath, "it seems we rate the One Sixtieth Special Operations Aviation Regiment."

Kyle was silent for a moment, then said, "That's some serious fucking firepower. Sorry, Nasima."

"It's okay," she said. "Right now, I'd like to see this serious fucking firepower."

And Kyle tried not to laugh at the scene of this tiny, religious woman swearing like a soldier.

Wade spoke again, and his voice was soft but urgent. "Kyle, I estimate at least thirty hostiles. We've got ten down below that I can see, a dozen across the ravine, and I'm going to assume an equal number above. We've got to get somewhere safe."

"Yeah, I'm open to suggestions," Kyle said. Having bad guys above was very unappealing.

"Lower is all I can suggest," Wade said. "And close to one wall, so that squad, at least, can't get a clear field of fire."

"Well, twenty is less than thirty," Kyle agreed. "I can't think of anything better."

"We can angle down farther ahead," Wade said.

"Lead the way. How are you on ammo?"

"One twenty-three," Wade said.

" 'One shot, one kill' is the motto," Kyle said sarcastically.

"Right. You ever used only one shot?"

"I'm sure I have," Kyle said. "I just can't recall when right now."

"Here's a crevice. I can slide down."

"Go," Kyle said.

The cracked rock had a narrow chute that dropped perhaps twenty feet. It was a good start, and would cause the enemy to have to maneuver again. Wade squirmed and cursed, stuck in the tight confines. Finally, he looped his ruck's strap around his ankle and let it dangle.

"Please don't land on the radio," Kyle said, guts churning.

"I won't," Wade said, not joking for the time being.

There were scraping and slipping noises as he dropped out of view, and one slight bang of the carbine against the side. Kyle eased forward and looked over. Wade was scrabbling lower, the native garb hindering him somewhat.

Then he was down. "Nasima, you're next," he said.

She gulped and said, "Okay." She handed the pistol to Kyle. Shimmying around, she got over the split and paused, a scared look on her face. "What do I do now?" she asked.

"Hang your legs over, then press one forward and one back to hold yourself in place," Kyle said.

She nodded and twisted. An indication of her fear was that her skirt hiked well up her thighs, and she didn't seem bothered by the immodesty. She was too busy holding on. "What next?" she asked, voice tight but controlled.

"Move your rear foot forward and down below the other," he said. "Then just walk down with your back to the wall." Wade had been able to scissor across the gap, but Nasima had too little length for that.

He held her hand as she worked lower. It wasn't of any real use as support, but if it kept her morale up, it was a good thing. The friction pulled her robe up until it was past her head. It would be full of grit, too, though that seemed minor. Nor did Kyle have any time to bother with a great view of her body. He took one glance, pulled his eyes away, and focused on the descent.

She slipped past his grip with a look of panic but didn't fall. "Keep going," he said in encouragement. She nodded once and stepped down, down.

Wade called from below, "Almost here. I won't touch you, because that would make you fall."

"Okay," she said, and kept moving.

Then she was down, and leaning against the

side in relief. Kyle started to twist around for his own descent.

That's when the fire started.

He swore, spun, fell rather than dropped into the crack and shoved both hands out. He slipped at once, caught with one foot, tumbled sideways and cracked his skull and shoulder. Eyes tearing up, he shoved both hands out to keep from falling farther, and worked his feet down. Three healthy steps that strained the backs of his thighs got him down.

"Where the hell did that come from?" he asked as he shook off the pain and jitters.

"Across," Wade said. They were all bunched up together. The crack was wider at the bottom, but still very cramped. It was hard to maneuver.

"They've got us pegged. Where do we cover?" he asked.

"Right here for now," Wade said. "We can clear the front, then move into those rocks below."

Kyle looked down where Wade was pointing as he handed Nasima back the Beretta.

"Okay," he nodded. "Nasima, we'll tell you when to fire, but if someone is within thirty feet, give them two shots. Only two. If they don't flinch, give two more. Ammo is low."

"Two shots at a time. I understand," she said. She was still rearranging her dress, but didn't seem flustered anymore.

"Target," Wade whispered.

"Where?" Kyle replied, unslinging the Enfield and raising it.

"Large outcropping ahead, up twenty degrees. Left and below. Man with AK. Two hundred," Wade said.

Two hundred meters. Kyle found the place, found the man, leaned against the cliff for support and worked the bolt. He squeezed the long trigger, and felt the shot kick him. The noise was deafening in the tight confines, but he rode through it.

The shot was good, and the man jerked and crumpled.

"I suggest we get lower right now," Kyle said. He dropped prone and slithered out onto a shelf.

"Yeah," Wade said. "Go, Nasima."

It was none too soon. As soon as the target's buddies figured out what had happened, they cut loose with everything. Automatic fire scythed across the rock face, and Kyle jerked as a spent, flattened bullet dropped in front of him.

"What an exposed place we have here!" Wade said. "There's rocks below. Over the edge, quick!"

Kyle was glad of the information, and rolled over at once. He didn't look. There wasn't time, and he trusted Wade implicitly. Wade was his spotter. Just as Jeremy had been. But Wade was still alive, and Kyle intended to maintain that state of affairs.

They were all down and hunkered in a cluster of rock, with thick, desiccated dirt underfoot.

"How's the time?" Kyle asked. He and Nasima had their backs to boulders and the enemy. Wade was sprawled low and facing them.

"Forty minutes," Wade said.

"I say we stay here for a few," Kyle said. "If they get nasty, we'll move lower. But there's a limit on how far down we can go."

"Okay."

Another flurry of shots hit the area above them. Kyle wasn't sure if the enemy thought they were still there, or were unable to get a better angle.

Two minutes later, he had an answer, as a round cracked right over his rock. Someone had either seen them earlier and told the others, or was seeing them now. If the latter, it was time to move.

Another round snapped between Nasima and him, making her flinch and gasp. Yes, someone had spotted them. Time to move down another layer.

"Wade, out to your right and down more."

"Sure, it's my pleasure to act as decoy," he said. He pushed with his feet, crawled over the lowest part of the rock and crawled down. As his knees cleared the edge, he dropped suddenly.

Nasima went next, Kyle holding her feet while Wade took her hands and swung her down. Another shot cracked overhead as he released her, and he dove over himself, ruck catching on something. He was hung by his arm for just a second, then it snapped free.

"Not bad," Kyle said. They had solid, tall spires of rock on three sides. The valley notched to their right, spreading out into a broad arc. To their left, it ran alongside, but one convenient tower of granite would block incoming fire until the enemy moved around.

There was the risk of being infiltrated from below, of course. Kyle wasn't sure what to do about that.

Fire started coming from above and to the right.

Kyle swung, found a target, and shot without waiting for Wade. Someone was leaning over a shelf with an AK. It wasn't accurate fire, but there was a lot of it. He put a round through the man and cycled the bolt.

A torrent of rounds came in reply. The snipers and Nasima ducked, shifted, and tried to find better holes to shoot from.

"Warn us before you do that again, huh?" Wade said, humorously brave in face of disaster.

"Yeah," Kyle agreed. He hoped the 160th SOAR was fast. This was beyond terrifying. Nasima was crouched in back, a good place for her, and clutching the pistol. Hopefully, they wouldn't let the enemy get close enough for her to need to shoot.

The fire from the above right wasn't slacking off. It seemed they were going to shoot until the rock was chipped to nothing. Every few seconds, a round would find one of the gaps between the spires and crack past. But Wade had found a small trough that led under and shimmied into it. He fired several rounds. Incoming fire paused for just a second as the onslaught hit them, and Kyle rose rifle first, leaned, shot, and dropped back down. He'd only had a moment, but a man's head had been in his sights.

"Miss," Wade reported as he came back out. "Close, but a miss. They'll think twice about standing up, though."

"Yeah, let's watch that side. Or do we split?" Kyle asked. "And how long?"

"I'll cover up, you cover down. There'll be fewer targets, we hope, and not expecting it. Thirty-two minutes."

"Good."

They shifted, and Kyle flashed a smile to Nasima, who was crying but trying to smile as tears streaked her cheeks. She was doing better than most recruits, and far better than he'd have expected. "Soon," he said. She nodded quickly.

The squad from the far side was working its way down into the ravine, intermittently visible. "Wade, spot now," he said.

Wade fired five rounds rapid and shimmied back over. "What? Ah," he said, as Kyle indicated. "Start at top and back, I'll spot you down."

"Right," Kyle said. In a moment, he slumped over the rock, aimed, and squeezed. The man had been just stretching to place his foot for a step, and died with a bullet through the top of his chest.

"Outcropping below him, man to left hidden," Wade said.

"Waiting," Kyle said. Waiting. The enemy knew they were under fire now, and were being more cautious. Though the enemy now behind them were picking the fire back up. Kyle reminded himself he had solid cover, and steeled himself not to flinch.

Patience paid off. His target stood, and Kyle plugged one right through his skull.

Just as he did, Wade said, "Notch in rock below and right, one man," and Kyle swung and shot. Miss.

An explosion rocked them, shards of granite showering down. They stung and burned and cut the flesh.

"RPG!" Kyle shouted. His ears were ringing. "Move now!" he said, and reached back to clutch Nasima's hand.

Wade fired four short bursts on auto, then tossed a grenade down ahead of them. There was no need to risk a face-to-face encounter. On a count of three, it exploded, throwing debris back up. Kyle already had tossed a high-concentration white smoke grenade behind them, and amid the billowing, acrid cloud they jumped over.

It worked. They weren't shot. The smoke also seemed to confuse some of the al Qaeda, who fired furiously into it. Two of them were standing up as they did so. Wade got one, Kyle got the other.

"Where the hell is that RPG?" Kyle asked. What else was along? A mortar? Machine guns?

"Not sure," Wade replied.

Fire slacked off audibly. That set alarm bells ringing in Kyle's head. They might be leaving, but they also might be . . .

"To our left!" Wade shouted.

A handful of men were dodging through the rocks, and Kyle fired five times as fast as he could work the bolt. He hit at least one, who flinched and fell. He had no idea if it was a wound or a kill. Nasima fired two rounds, then two more. Wade was firing about once a second. He also nailed at least one.

"Close on them," Kyle said.

"Right," Wade agreed.

Kyle pulled Nasima forward. "Trust me," he said. There were no more than six or seven bad guys to their three, and their buddies were demonstrating that they wouldn't shoot into that crowd. Kyle just hoped that stayed true. He didn't like six to three odds, with an untrained civilian in the three, but it was better than the twenty to three or worse they'd been facing.

Nasima fired again at once. Good girl, Kyle thought. No one had told her not to. He fired twice more, then once again, while Wade tossed a grenade. "Fireinthehole!" he shouted and they all dropped.

The grenade banged like the devil on a trash

can, the sound assaulting them from all sides. Wade had made a quick, dangerous battlefield calculation, and there was a bare lip between them and the grenade blast, that deflected the shock wave and only left an overpressure pulse to snatch at their breath.

Wade stood, leaned over and fired an antipersonnel cartridge from the 40mm. There shouldn't be much left interested in screwing with them, but they came over the ledge with weapons out. Nasima shot twice at a twitching body, and hit it at least once.

"Good girl!" Kyle said. He was starting to think they'd get out of this yet. Someone else moved, and Kyle put a round through him. It was amazing, he thought, how the rocks reflected and dispersed shock waves and fire.

The incoming bullets picked up the pace again. Wade said, "May as well use the HE now. Agreed?"

"Do it," Kyle said. Wade nodded and grabbed his four remaining 40mm grenades. He ducked low, picked a target that seemed to be a source of trouble, and fired. He opened the action, reloaded, picked another.

Massive fire came in retaliation, from a machine gun. Kyle spotted the puffs of dust around its muzzle and started methodical fire at it. On his third round, it stopped. He shoved another clip of five rounds into the Enfield to keep the magazine topped off.

"Better drop lower again," Wade said. "And twenty-seven minutes."

"Lower," Kyle agreed. He wasn't sure they'd survive that long, however, but was damned if he'd give up. He might wind up using the Enfield as a club before this was over.

They crawled downward, weaving through jutting chunks of rock. If the estimate of thirty bad guys was correct, Kyle thought, then they should be down to about fifteen. Of course, there may have been more, or they may have called for backup. It occurred to him that they could listen in on the enemy's radio, too, but that would take personnel and time they didn't have.

There was a sloping curve of granite, its surface fairly smooth. There was nothing to do but slide feet first down it, and hope the drop at the end wasn't too high.

"Me first, then drop the radio," Kyle said.

"Got it," Wade agreed.

Trying not to think, Kyle slid up and over, and shoved to get moving. He got to vertical and fell about seven feet, landing hard. He fell backward, and would have cracked his tailbone but for his gear. It cushioned well enough, though the impact jarred his whole torso and neck. No additional damage was done, but his already injured foot flared in pain.

What he hadn't considered was how Wade would know when to drop his gear. Wade had figured that out. The ruck appeared, hooked on

Nasima's right foot. He nodded and held up his arms, she released it. It thumped him hard in the chest, knocking his breath out, but it was a good catch. He laid it down carefully, held his arms back up, and Nasima let go of Wade.

She dropped, dress tangling, and it was a good thing Kyle caught her. There was no way she would have made the landing with all that fabric caught on her legs.

Moments later, Wade dropped down, too, staggering but not falling. "Okay, they'll have to acquire us yet again."

"Don't bet on it," Kyle said. "Look." Wade looked.

They were now in the very bottom of the ravine, with stark walls on two sides and a steep climb on a third. The way forward was fairly level, and would leave them exposed.

"Let's hope the choppers are fast," Kyle said. "This is as far as we go."

"So let's stall for time and then shoot when we have to," Wade said.

"What else can we do?"

19

IT GOT QUIET. AL QAEDA HAD FIGURED OUT THEY were hiding, and were controlling their shooting until they had a target. The silence was eerie after all the shooting.

Wade wordlessly mouthed, "Twenty-two minutes." Kyle nodded.

Nothing happened for long seconds, perhaps minutes. Nasima started crying again, her lips trembling. "I'm sorry I'm so scared," she whispered.

"It's okay," Kyle whispered back. "We're scared, too. You're doing great, and we'll be out of here in minutes." Then he held a finger to his lips. She nodded.

The tension was thick. No doubt someone hoped the pause would make them break. All it would take was one hint, and fire would pour in on them. That RPG was still out there, and the machine gun was likely still functional, even if Kyle had bagged the shooter.

But the longer it went on, the closer they were to rescue from the helicopters. Kyle focused on that and took a deep breath.

The reprieve lasted another minute. When it broke, it was with another RPG round just outside their little hollow.

Nasima shrieked as the round crashed. Kyle and Wade both shouted in pain and fear as debris whistled overhead. But that was as far as it went.

Wade said, "Behind you, ledge, protruding shelf." Kyle turned, drew up the SMLE and fired at a figure who was hastily trying to get back. The shot took him in the shoulder, and he cried, dropping the launcher. It bounced off the edge and out of sight.

"Good enough," Kyle muttered, but he thumbed the bolt and took another shot. The man was still squatting there, hurt. The second shot went through his right eye and exploded out the back. That should stop the pain, asshole, Kyle thought as he dropped back down.

He turned to see movement on another ledge, and fired over that way. He wasn't sure if it was good, but they were on the offensive for the moment, and they should press that advantage against these clowns while they could.

Shots were coming from all around now. Most were wide, a few close, and a handful were obviously aimed with intent. Figures were leaping among the rocks, and some were getting lower and closer. Kyle caught one as he stepped between two protrusions, and the man dropped like a sack.

"Targets of opportunity," Kyle said, amazed at how calm his voice was. "Ask for backup if you need it. It's been a privilege serving with you."

"And you," Wade replied.

"Yes," Nasima said.

The odds of surviving more than two or three minutes were pretty damned slim. Flitting figures presented themselves, but Kyle held his fire. They'd be closer and clearer soon enough. He gripped the Ed Brown in its holster, just to remind himself it was still there.

"We might as well be moving targets. They know where this spot is. Over toward that face there," he pointed. They nodded, and he said, "Go!"

They were up, and none too soon. Five figures were creeping over the rocks. Wade swung, pointed, and shot. Kyle picked the rearmost, but paused as the man threw himself behind cover.

They were just getting to the cliff, a solid backing they could rely on. Kyle was first, as he had only paused once. Wade was right behind him, having taken a moment to heave another grenade far out at someone hiding on the ground. It detonated about five feet up, and if his aim had been good, that person was scorched goo.

Kyle turned, prepared to give cover fire, and Wade crashed in alongside him, as if tackling the wall. Then a shot came from their right.

Nasima's body was tossed like a rag doll. It wasn't bullet energy that did it; small arms aren't that powerful. It was muscle reaction as her nerves convulsed.

Her robe tore open in a gout of red, chunks of rib flying free. She tumbled off her feet and broke across a sharp rock face, her gurgling scream becoming audible in a break in the fire.

"Nasima!" Kyle shouted, clutching at his ruck to get the medical kit, knowing it was too late. She'd lost a lung or her heart or both on that shot, and was dead where she lay, even if her hands were still trying to hold her ruined body together and tears were running down her cheeks as her mouth worked soundlessly.

Seeing that, Kyle came back to his weapon. There was nothing he could do but kill as many of them as he could until he ran out of ammo, so that's what he'd do.

Bolt action rifles are fast in the hands of professionals, and Kyle Monroe was not only a professional, he had been shooting them since he was seven. There was no one better, as these assholes were about to find out. He swung the Enfield up and fired, shooting a man right under the chin. His hand and the bolt shot back, then forward and he fired. Another one down, right through the breastbone. Work the bolt and fire, and another lost the top of his head. That was the last round.

Heedless of incoming rounds, standing, he dropped the clip he held between the fingers of his left hand into the open receiver, thumbed the rounds down with his right, then flipped the empty clip away and closed the bolt. Incoming fire tore past him, but he didn't notice, and Wade was doing an outstanding job with that little carbine, 5.56 rounds cracking past him and ripping holes through their aggressors. Kyle had his rifle back up in less than three seconds and fired again, and again. Five rounds on the clip, reach for another, and reload.

"*Kyle!*" he heard behind him and ducked behind rock before turning to glance at Wade. Wade said, "Grab that AK and stay the hell behind cover!"

Nodding, he snatched the weapon in question from the outflung hand of a corpse he hadn't seen while it was alive, and slung it over his shoulder. He still had a dozen .303 rounds and he wasn't going to leave a loaded weapon for the enemy. Besides, he'd been through a lot with the Smelly. If he could, he would keep it. He had no other souvenir, and his only local friend was now dead.

The survivors had taken cover now. The fifteen or so corpses in front of the two Americans had either scared them or wised them up or both, because they were not visible. That brought its own dangers. The fire was still coming in, but from concealment.

"Get us out of here," Kyle rasped, unable to speak in a normal voice. It was due to the breath burning in his throat, and too much yelling, and the cold, and a little bit was a combination of fury and pain at Nasima's death.

"Cover me," Wade said. He tossed the M-4 at Kyle as he ducked low and got the radio handset. "Bossman, this is Roadkill, over."

It made sense. The M-4 was not only familiar, it had the grenade launcher. The acquired AK was an unknown quantity. Kyle nodded. Wade had adapted very well to combat: calm nerves, cool head.

Right then, something stung his leg. He'd been shot, he knew. It couldn't be bad, he told himself, as he was still standing, leaning over the rock. He panned the M-4, both eyes open, seeking the telltale dust tossed by shots. There. He swung the muzzle until the illuminated reticle of the Holosight covered his best guess, then fired three rounds; one on that spot, one two feet to either side. He took a deep breath and shook his head to clear the splotches in front of his eyes before seeking another target.

"Roger that, Bossman. Roadkill out." Wade changed frequencies and said, "Nightstalker Seven, this is Roadkill, over . . . Roger that, Nightstalker, we are glad to hear your voice! Kyle, we've got choppers!"

"Good," Kyle replied. He wasn't sure he meant it. She was dead. Like Jeremy. Why?

He needed to ask Wade if there was a load in the M-203, and if so, what type. He didn't dare take the time to inspect the chamber. But Wade was busy with the helos, and he didn't want to disturb that golden hope. No matter how he felt, Wade deserved to get out alive.

He was down to one spare magazine plus a few rounds in the weapon. He counted five of the al Qaeda gathered behind an outcropping, based on muzzle movement. Worse, they were higher than he was. However, they had a slight overhang above them, and they were about sixty meters away, so they were outside the minimum range, even if it was risky. Hell, letting them shoot at Wade and him was risky.

But Kyle had never tried to *snipe* with a grenade launcher. Still, it looked like a good time to start. He hoped to hell it was loaded—it certainly hefted like it—and hunched lower, easing it forward. He checked the tangential sights, checked the Holosight, made his best guess along the barrel . .

"Roger, Nightstalker, we will mark with flare and smoke. I'll be on air, but might be away from the mike a moment or two. Hope you understand. Roadkill, over."

. . . the fire was really picking up now, as he took another check of both sights, made his best, professional estimate—professionals don't guess—and drew the trigger.

Boonk! Slam! The HE shell impacted on the ledge right above the creeps. At that range, the explosion tore them to bloody mush. A piece of what he thought was a rock splinter whistled overhead, spinning like a boomerang, and Kyle realized it was a bent AK. Rocks were tumbling onto the ledge, crushing whatever was left, and a blood-soaked man ran screaming off into space.

He'd been climbing up to join his buddies and had just enough cover to be alive. Whether it was his blood or another's Kyle didn't know. He'd automatically taken the snap shot as the body appeared, however. Between the explosion, Kyle's round, and the impact on the rocks below, the man was way dead.

Kyle had to admire their persistence. And what was it the manual said? "Break contact. Do *Not* engage in a drawn out battle with a larger force." He laughed, the manic gesture relieving some stress. He fired again and felt the bolt lock back, magazine empty.

The M-4 would be needed badly here shortly, with its one lonely magazine and the single canister round Wade had left. Then they had pistols and grenades. They'd never had a chance to use the claymore. This fight wasn't over yet. Pistols weren't much of a threat, but a scared enemy seeing a rifle he didn't know was empty, and hearing a pistol, would think twice about sticking his head up to do a comparison. Kyle laid the M-4 down where Wade could get it, and raised the Enfield again.

Moments later, Wade was shooting again. "Just stand by, they're en route. Maybe five minutes. Get ready to pop a flare and pop smoke."

"Roger," Kyle agreed, swinging up to his right and dropping a man who'd thought to flank them from the right by crawling through spiky scrub. His leg was screaming at him now. He'd forgotten he'd been shot. Twisting and putting weight on it was excruciating. He hoped it was a quick five minutes. It could be a god-damned long time with rounds coming in every second. And they were coming in like a swarm of angry hornets.

But he had seven rounds left for the Enfield, and he cycled them through quickly, seeking movement. As he drove the last clip down into the magazine, he felt pressure against his hip. It was the AK he'd forgotten about. "Wade, stand by for cover fire," he said. "Pick your targets." The M-4 was a far more inherently accurate weapon, and had much more consistent ammunition compared to the AK. But he could rapid fire or auto fire at exposed targets and keep them down while Wade took them out.

He took his last shot with the Enfield, slung it over his left shoulder as he unlimbered the Kalashnikov. "Fire!" he commanded, then stood and commenced shooting.

His leg was on fire, numb at the bottom, burning and freezing all the way up and making his groin twinge, too. But it was still supporting his weight. He aimed through the smoke and dust, hoping visibility was good enough. There was movement to the right, under a ledge at their own level, and he said so to Wade. "Fire on my impact," he ordered, leaned in and fired five rounds rapid. They chewed chips from the rock and worked down into the hollow.

There was movement under the overhang, and Wade put three rounds down into that shadow.

There was no obvious response, but the incoming fire seemed to slow. Dropping back down by the simple expedient of taking the weight off his legs, Kyle grunted in pain. He rolled to the left, got low between two comforting knobs of rock and found another nest. "Fire on my impact," he ordered, and gave it five rounds. Wade cracked three sharp, barking 5.56 rounds between the crags in question, and seemed to score a hit; another rifle tumbled out.

But the Kalashnikov was empty, its firing pin dropping on an empty chamber.

"Flare now!" Wade yelled. Kyle dropped low behind the rock, discarded the AK, snatched the flare from his belt and let fly, pointing it generally upward and yanking the lanyard. It arced up into the air and lit, a bright red star even in daylight. "Sixty seconds, then the smoke!" Wade said.

Kyle nodded and couldn't tell if Wade had seen him. His voice was too ragged to speak, his throat dry and papery, tinny tasting from propellant and gilding metal. He pushed up painfully using his left foot, and leaned over to shoot at anything that moved. It was all he could do, as he was down to his Ed Brown, with two magazines plus three rounds. At least they were eight round mags.

But the bucking, kicking, roaring .45 was a comfort to him. He gripped it firmly but not too tightly, arm solid to support it and rocking slightly with every shot. It was an extension of his arm and he pointed at movement and shot, shot.

"Smoke now!" Wade reminded him. "I'm empty!" he added.

Kyle stuffed the .45 into his belt, grabbed the AN-M8 smoke, yanked the pin, and tossed it. The "Pop!" of the fuze firing was barely discernible, but billows of white gushed reassuringly from it. Ideally, one used a bright color smoke for extraction. White was what they had and would have to do. It also provided concealment.

It also provided concealment for the bad guys. "Oh, shit, this is not *good!*" he commented. He had eleven rounds left with the fresh magazine he'd just slid in. The slide dropped, clacked reassuringly into battery, and he raised it to provide cover fire as they retreated to the left and away from their backing. It wasn't the best choice for superiority of position, but they'd have to hope that chopper was here shortly anyway. If smoke was out, they should be here. So where were they?

Behind him, Wade said, "Roger, Roadkill confirms white smoke." Just in case some bright boy on the other side had a different color going. It had happened before.

Kyle thought at first something was wrong with the pistol. He couldn't believe the noise and the pressure slapping at his ears. Then he realized it was an incoming helicopter. The choppers had arrived.

"One casualty, civilian. All element members healthy under the circumstances . . . Roger, out!" Wade yelled. "Danger close!" he said to

Kyle, and they both ducked down close behind the boulders.

Then the world exploded.

Four choppers came in. Two AH6J Little Birds were hitting the area with their pods of 2.75" rockets. The craft came into view just after a huge multiple pressure front slapped the air. Kyle didn't know the danger close distance, but the pilots apparently did. Other than ringing, stinging ears and a thump to the chest, he thought he was okay. But rock was flying and the enemy suddenly was very disinterested in them. The little craft darted around like humming-birds, firing as they saw fit.

It was best not to take chances, and the 160th Special Operations Aviation Regiment were not the type to let an enemy off easily. The doorgun-ners on an MH-60K Blackhawk were hosing the landscape with 7.62mm miniguns. Another MH-60 with M-240 machine guns was punctuating with "normal" automatic fire. They knew ex-actly where the friendlies were, there was no risk of collateral damage, and there was no reason not to shoot anything that moved. It was also day-light. Those were choice working conditions, and the gunners' enthusiasm was clear as they swept their mechanical bullet hoses back and forth, bursts chewing anything suspicious into dust.

Overhead was an Apache. It likely wouldn't be needed, but too much firepower is always better than not enough.

The smoke from the canister joined dust that was whipped up and blown swirling by the blades. A farting explosion blew a stream of fire through the smoke; a 7.62 minigun firing a burst of perhaps 200 rounds. At 6,000 rounds a minute, that was two seconds.

The MH-60 rocked over the draw, buffeting winds bumping back against it. But the pilot knew exactly what he was doing; it held position, even if it wobbled. Then a figure on a cable started winching down.

"You first!" Kyle yelled over the roar. "Take whatever you can. We ain't leaving dick for these assholes to play with."

"Understood!" Wade shouted back through the din.

Wade met the rescuer when he touched down. In moments they were winching back up fast. That left Kyle alone, looking over at Nasima's corpse and knowing he couldn't do a damned thing. Nor could he go over and say goodbye. His pickup was right here. He kept his attention on the rocks, wondering if some last, dedicated al Qaeda soldier would fire a suicidal shot to kill one more American.

Then the penetrator on the end of the cable was dropping back down and it was his turn.

The ride up was brisk and wind tugged at him. He dragged himself aboard the chopper's deck and nodded thanks. Then he cleared his throat of a cubic yard of dust and spat.

"Check on the woman!" he shouted, voice ragged and losing control.

"Kyle, she's dead!" Wade replied, taking his arm.

"*Check on her!*" he screamed, throat stinging from the force.

The soldier nodded. He said to Wade, "We'll check anyway, sir. Stand by."

The crew were professionals. The chopper lifted, swayed over to Nasima's location and hovered as the two gunners rapped out short, steady bursts at movement. There likely wasn't much opposition left, but one always assumed movement was action and shot to keep it at bay. The medic was out the side and down the winch almost as fast as it could unspool, the flight engineer watching the mechanism.

After a few tense moments, the cable started rising again.

The look on his face said everything. "She's dead, sir," he said. Hands helped ease her battered and bloody body onto the deck, wounds gaping blood everywhere. Her eyes had a vacant look, her mouth open in an expression of sheer agony. She hadn't died painlessly. Almost no one does.

Then the deck tilted and the chopper surged, vacating the area in a hurry. A silent streak to starboard as they broke the ridgeline resolved itself as a U.S.-made Stinger. It had missed. The Apache unloaded a ton of ordnance on that location. Whoever had fired wasn't around anymore, because half the cliff face came loose and slid down, the dust looking like oil in motion and the large chunks dropping straight, not tumbling.

Kyle bid a farewell to the rocky crags of the Toba Kakar range and followed it with a one-finger salute. It really wasn't a chunk of real estate he could justify fighting over. The deck tilted, Gs pushed at him, and then they were in level flight.

Then he looked down at the broken corpse and the empty eyes. She'd been a hell of a young woman. And the bastards who'd killed her had been her own people. That's what made it so disgusting.

In a moment, he knew what to do. "Wade, map, please," he shouted over the din of the thumping rotors. Wade nodded and drew the creased, stained, and tattered sheet from inside his shirt. It was a bit of an icon of their mission to hell, and he planned to keep it as a souvenir.

Kyle took it, flipped it over and around, jabbed his finger down, and said, "We're going here, first. Berishtiya."

"Sir?" the flight engineer asked.

"That's her home. We're returning the body." It was all he could do, but he'd damned sure see it done.

"Yes, sir," the sergeant agreed. It wasn't on their route, but there wasn't any reason not to, and they seemed to realize Kyle wasn't in the mood to argue. The map was passed forward for the pilots to compare to their charts.

The medical sergeant spoke to him from the other side. "Sir, I need to treat your leg. Please lie back and relax the best you can."

Kyle nodded and reclined, loosening the straps of his ruck and letting them ease him out and up to a litter. He winced slightly as his pant leg was cut away, but said nothing. As his sleeve was rolled up, however, he said, "No IVs! Not until we're done with Nasima."

Sighing, the man said, "Very well, sir. But this is going to hurt like a son of a bitch." There was a half smile on his face as he said it, from exasperation or amazement or both.

"Fine, get on with iiiit!" Kyle said, gripping his harness and restraining a cry of pain. He snuck a quick peek, then decided he didn't want to watch. The medic was debriding the torn flesh and sterilizing the wound. It was close enough to the surface to be a rip rather than a hole, but it still hurt worse than anything he'd felt before. "Superficial" did not mean "Painless." As he recalled that statement, he scowled.

Twenty agonizing minutes later, his leg was bandaged and he had some candy—Motrin. It wasn't much, but it took the edge off and he was alert, mostly. He washed it down with what felt like a gallon of water. Then they were landing at the edge of Berishtiya. He vaguely knew that the variation on the flight was a hassle for the AWACS people, and had caused various other air assets to be standing by, just in case. He really didn't care. They owed him, and they owed Nasima.

A crowd started to form, only five or six people at first, but then more. Many of them were children. Wade and the flight engineer hopped out, Wade's weapon replenished with a fresh magazine, and more in his gear. The doorgunners stood ready. The crowd was only curious, not threatening, but there was no reason to let them get close.

Kyle stood on the deck, swaying a bit until his balance returned. He crouched and wiggled his arms under her corpse, which seemed so light now. She wasn't large as women went, and even as . . . dead weight . . . was negligible. He slid out, got his feet on the ground, stood and turned.

Several children cried out. They knew who she was even from there. He strode painfully toward them, every step aching and stinging, the dust swirling from the whipping rotors. In moments, four men came forward, jabbering away. He didn't know enough Pashto to handle this.

But one of them said, "She is dead," in English, and he nodded.

"Nasima. Yes, dead. She was our translator and . . ." he wasn't sure what he should tell them. "She was very faithful. Pray to Allah for her." Dammit, there was nothing else to say. He tried unsuccessfully to restrain tears.

The man nodded. He and the other three were apparently parents of her students. They wore simple knitted hats over their bright vests, not the turbans of the more conservative. He trusted they'd treat her properly. They took her gently and laid her on the ground. One of them shouted out and he caught the word for "cart." The children were gathering around and crying. They'd seen death before, but this one was important to them.

He couldn't kiss her goodbye. Not only would she not have wanted him to, it would grossly offend these people. Then he remembered. He reached into his pocket and drew out her matted, blood-encrusted scarf. Gently, he laid it over her face. "Go with Allah," he said in Pashto.

"We have to go," he said. "But I will send a letter explaining." He wasn't quite sure how, but he'd do it.

They nodded, he nodded, someone said, "Go with Allah," and he turned. He wanted to leave this country at once. He limped back to the waiting chopper, and heard the rotors and turbine whine as the pilot prepared to lift. Everyone backed in, climbed aboard, and then they were lifting.

Kyle had expected to be debriefed in theater. However, no one in Afghanistan cared about anything except helping them leave. Kratman didn't meet with them, and the staff in personnel simply signed them in and back out. Kyle did make a point of providing a map with the location of the Barrett marked. Even without a bolt, the Army would want it back, or would want to destroy it. A .50-barrel by itself was too useful to the fractured clans and factions in the area.

Everyone was polite and helpful, but no one knew what to do with them, and the easiest thing for all concerned was to shuffle them out quickly. They dumped the native garb. The Army considered it to be its property, and would likely just throw it out. They surrendered and receipted the remaining cash. Weapons and gear were crated for transport. They wound up on the same C-141, same crew, and headed back for Kuwait.

"Shave now, or after we land?" Wade shouted from three feet away. They were back in uniform, and looked like hell with beards and hair brushing their ears. Even after showering, they were a mess, deeply tanned and lined from the sun, obviously sore and tired, ragged and wired.

"I really don't care," Kyle replied. "We'll be swapping back to civvies as soon as we land, so whenever we damned well feel like it. After all, we're done and we don't need to pretend we weren't here as long as we don't brag about it."

"Good enough. I'm going to crash back and nap."

But Kyle was already asleep, even if his face indicated he wasn't getting much rest.

Epilogue

TWO DAYS LATER, AFTER TIME TO SHOWER, shave, sleep for a solid nine hours in a bed and get a good meal of pork chops, they were in a briefing room at Fort Benning again. This one was in garrison proper, and had more amenities, which they'd be using to debrief for the next few days. It wasn't an appealing concept, sitting and talking and typing, while everything was nitpicked by bureaucrats, but it was necessary. And they were Stateside. Kyle decided it was better conditions than he'd had two days ago.

Robash greeted them warmly when he arrived, and said, "Well, gentlemen, you done good. I'll sit on the complaints. It may not have been by the book, and there may have been a few liberties, but the job got done and nobody got hurt, as far as the Army is concerned. And as it never officially happened, it's hard to complain. You did a hell of a job, and a lot more than expected. Thank you." After a moment, he added, "I'm sorry you lost a friend, guys." He seemed to understand, without the weirded out or snide looks a lot of people had given them both, Kyle especially.

"Thank you, sir," Wade said first, Kyle echoing it just behind him.

"And, sir," Kyle continued. He waited a moment for Robash's attention. "I need to speak to Mr. Gober about getting something translated."

Robash nodded and said, "I'll email you his contact info. Congratulations again, gentlemen. And I told the debriefers you'd be starting tomorrow, not today."

They stood, saluted, he left, and that was it.

They continued standing. It had been only a couple of days, and they were both still wired from the mission, the trip home, and the pending debriefing. Hair-trigger nerves stuck out from them, and they were bristling even at each other. Finally, Wade said, "Come on, buddy, I'll buy the first round."

Kyle nodded. "Actually," he said, "I think I won't drink."

"Oh?" Wade asked.

"Later, I'm sure," Kyle said. "It's not that I'm turning Muslim on you . . ." and they both chuckled, though they each had a new respect for the good Muslims, as opposed to the nutcases who made the news . . . "but I don't think I should mix stress and booze. I did that for a year and regretted it."

"Good deal," Wade said. "So I'll buy you a

Coke and you can overdose on mild stimulants. When you're destressed, you can buy the beer. Better deal for me."

Laughing, Kyle asked, "Club, or off post?"

"Hell, you can't really cut loose unless you're in town. Let's see if my car still starts."

Acknowledgments

I am indebted to numerous people for this project. Ms. Noreen Khan, as a native of Pakistan, was most helpful with details. As to technical expertise, I was taxed to the limit of my knowledge and I am grateful to many other veterans for input. Especially, I would like to thank Ms. Elsie Jackson, CPT Jason Kostal and the cadre and students of the U.S. Army Sniper School for hosting me and my barrage of questions, not to mention a photographer, for a day of research. I have taken liberties, I'm afraid, for the purposes of an entertaining story, and the responsibility for such inaccuracies is solely mine. After all, accuracy is their primary product.